ESTMAR COLLEGE LIBRARY
W9-CCM-120

Education in Metropolitan Areas

THE ALLYN AND BACON SERIES
FOUNDATIONS OF EDUCATION

Education in Metropolitan Areas

SECOND EDITION

ROBERT J. HAVIGHURST
University of Chicago
DANIEL U. LEVINE
University of Missouri at Kansas City

Allyn and Bacon, Inc. Boston

800

~~370~~ LC
~~.H3 H8~~ 5115
~~H388~~ .H38
1971

Copyright © 1971 by Allyn and Bacon, Inc.
Copyright © 1966 by Allyn and Bacon, Inc.
470 Atlantic Avenue, Boston, Mass. 02210

All rights reserved.
No part of this book may be reproduced
in any form, or by any means,
without permission in writing
from the publisher.

Library of Congress Catalog Card Number: 70–117371
Printed in the United States of America

91689

Contents

PREFACE ix

ACKNOWLEDGMENTS xi

1 METROPOLITAN SCHOOLS AND SOCIAL STRUCTURE 1

Three Schools of the Metropolis 1
The Social Structure of a Metropolitan Area 9
Black Man in the Social Structure 13
Social Mobility 17

2 URBAN AND METROPOLITAN DEVELOPMENT 25

The City in an Essentially Rural Society 26
The City in an Industrial Society 27
Types of Urbanization 28
Metropolitan Development 31
The Emerging Metropolitan Era 44
New Definitions of Metropolis 48

3 SOCIO-ECONOMIC AND RACIAL STRATIFICATION IN METROPOLITAN AREAS 54

The Socio-economic Ratio 55
Racial Segregation in Northern Cities 57
Stratification Within the Central City—Effects on the Schools 60
Polarization Between Central City and Suburbs 65
Stratification of Suburbs 70
The Pathology of Socio-economic and Racial Segregation 75
Effects of Socio-economic and Racial Stratification and Segregation in the Schools 79
Response of the School System 86

4 SCHOOLS IN THE METROPOLITAN AREA 93

Socio-economic Characteristics of Schools in the Metropolitan Area 93
Atmosphere and Internal Working of the School 99
Types of Elementary Schools 100
Types of High Schools 112
Private School Systems 116
Functional Types of Schools 117
Diverse Functions of a Metropolitan School System 121
The Urban-Community School 126

5 SUBURBAN SCHOOLS IN THE EVOLVING METROPOLITAN AREA 134

Problems in Financing Suburban Education 138
Suburban Schools in the Metropolitan System of Education 151

6 URBAN RENEWAL, METROPOLITAN PLANNING, AND THE SCHOOLS 158

New Directions in Urban Renewal 164
Metropolitan Areas as Functional Regions for Development 166
Movement Toward Metropolitan Cooperation and Regionalization 174
Planning and Coordination for Metropolitan Development 176
Metropolitan Cooperation Among School Systems 181
Approaches to a Regional Metropolitan Education System 183
The Metropolitan Area of the Future 190
The Crucial Issue of Stratification and Segregation in Metropolitan Development 196
Education in Metropolitan Development 199

7 SCHOOLS AND THE BLACK REVOLUTION 204

Urbanization of Blacks 206
School Factor versus Family Factor 213
The Black Revolution 219
Integration in City Schools: 1954–70 221
Equality of Opportunity or Equality of Achievement? 239

8 TEACHERS IN METROPOLITAN SCHOOLS 253

Social Origins of Metropolitan Area Teachers 257
Social Origin as a Factor in Educational Performance 260

Attitudes of Big City Teachers 263
Training of Inner-City Teachers 267
An Activist Role for the Metropolitan Teacher 270
Teachers' Organizations 272
Black Teachers and Administrators in Metropolitan Schools 277
The Career Line of the Metropolitan Educator 284

9 SCHOOL SYSTEMS AND OTHER SOCIAL SYSTEMS IN THE METROPOLITAN AREA 290

Goals of Metropolitan Development 291
Social System Defined 292
Inter System Cooperation 293
Intra-system Functioning 301
Paths to Metropolitanism 310

APPENDIX 317

BIBLIOGRAPHY 333

INDEX 347

Preface

THIS BOOK is about metropolitanism—not about urbanism or suburbanism. It looks at education from the point of view of the metropolitan area as a whole.

Defined by the Census Bureau as a city of 50,000 or more plus the surrounding county and the contiguous counties functionally bound to the central city, the standard metropolitan statistical area (SMSA) has become the major geographic arena in which the inhabitants of our modern urban society live and interact. In 1790, only 5 percent of the population lived in urban "places" which had 2,500 or more inhabitants. In 1970, 65 percent of the people of the United States lived in metropolitan areas. By 1985, when the U.S. population exceeds one-quarter of a billion people, it is estimated that 178 million persons—approximately 71 percent of the population—will live in metropolitan areas.

The metropolitan area came into existence at first as a simple geographical area occupied by people who had some of their business in common. But the metropolitan area was more complex than the city in its governmental and economic and social structure, and problems were created by this complexity. Municipal boundaries had to be adjusted. Many people did not live in the municipalities where they worked. To what unit should they pay taxes? The metropolitan area was fragmented into cities, towns, and unincorporated areas; into a variety of school districts; into park districts, water districts, and sewage disposal districts. Something had to take the place of the city, something with unity, to bring order out of the chaos.

The metropolitan area is taking the place of the city. All kinds of people increasingly think of the metropolitan area as their community. Educators, government officials, and businessmen are developing a theory of the relations of the physical environment to human satisfactions in the metropolitan area. The attention of educators will be increasingly fixed on the development of the metropolitan area rather than the growth or decline of a city, or the proliferation of suburbs.

Metropolitanism is at once a set of events occurring in contemporary society and a set of *goals* or *tasks* which society should achieve if it is to become a better society.

These two aspects of metropolitanism will be treated in this book. They will be kept separate, as far as possible. The facts of metropolitan development will be presented with special reference to the schools. The ways of improving the schools through metropolitan area cooperation will be discussed as part of the general task of improving the conditions of life in the United States.

The first half of the book is a systematic description of metropolitan social structure and the evolution of the contemporary metropolitan area. Its aim is to help the student understand the society in which he lives and the way the school system functions in this society.

The second half of the book deals with the sharp changes that are taking place during the present decade, as men try to do something about the problems of metropolitan growth, complexity, and stratification.

The book closes with a general analysis of the social system of a metropolitan area, showing how the school system is related to other systems, such as the local government, the private school system, the cultural agencies, the welfare agencies. The school must cooperate both in planning and in doing its present job with these other social systems. As it adopts new functions, teachers and administrators must adapt their roles to the new demands.

We wish to express our special thasks to Edythe M. Havighurst and Marjorie Thoelke who have typewritten the manuscript and taken care of the many details that go into the preparation of a manuscript for publication.

ROBERT J. HAVIGHURST
DANIEL U. LEVINE

Acknowledgments

THE AUTHORS wish to acknowledge and thank the following publishers for permission to reprint substantial sections from copyright materials quoted in the text:

The American Political Science Association, *American Political Science Review*, vol. 61, no. 4, pp. 953–970, 1967.

Public Administration Service (Chicago), *Urban Renewal and the Future of the American City* by C. A. Doxiadis, 1966.

Doubleday and Company, Inc., *The Hidden Dimension* by Edward T. Hall, Copyright © 1959.

Random House Pantheon Books Division, *The Levittowners* by Herbert Gans, Copyright © 1967.

University of Toronto Press, *The Suburban Society* by S. D. Clark, 1966.

St. Louis Globe-Democrat, January 25–26, 1969.

Saturday Review, Inc., *Saturday Review*, vol. 52, no. 3, pp. 59–60, 70–72, January 18, 1969.

Loyola University Center for Research in Urban Government, *Perspectives on the Future of Government in Metropolitan Areas* by James M. Banovetz, 1968.

McGraw-Hill Book Company, *The American High School Today* by James B. Conant, 1959.

National Education Association, *American Public School Teacher*, Research Monograph 1963—M2; *Financial Status of the Public Schools, 1968*, NEA Committee on Educational Finance.

Board of Public Education, Philadelphia, *Educational Survey Report*, William Odell, Table 1, p. 35.

American Sociological Association, *American Sociological Review*, vol. 28, pp. 76–85, 1963; vol. 30, pp. 97–103, 909–922, 1965.

Committee on Economic Development, *The Changing Economic Function of the Central City* by Raymond Vernon, table from pp. 74–75.

CHAPTER

1

Metropolitan Schools and Social Structure

THREE SCHOOLS OF THE METROPOLIS

MRS. JAMES walked into the Whittier School at 8:15, smiled at the school clerk who had just opened the door of the principal's office, and went up to her second floor classroom, which had the number 212 and the name Fifth Grade stenciled in black paint above the door. She opened a window to let in the spring air, and looked out a moment at the children as they sauntered into the playground.

Whittier was a good place to work, in a good area to live. She was glad she could live within walking distance of school, and could go home for lunch; or bring a sandwich to eat when she wanted to be sociable with the other teachers, most of whom lived farther away. She had been teaching at Whittier for fifteen years; she had gone back to teaching after her children were grown.

By this time some of the children were entering the room, in couples or small groups. Sidney came in with his friend Jim, whose father was a bus driver. Sidney's father had a drug store in the neighborhood. He was a smart Jewish youngster who knew he was going to be a doctor when he grew up. Jim was new this year. His family had moved into a six-flat apartment on the edge of the district where rents were low, and not far from a public housing project that had some real "trash" living in it, Mrs. James thought. Jim was a kind of rough diamond, and would make good in school, she was sure. She was glad to see him chumming with Sidney, because she thought Sidney would stir up Jim's good mind, which didn't get much stimulation at home–though she liked Jim's mother whom she had met at the PTA meeting and who seemed a quiet, timid woman.

She was glad that she had nobody in her class from the housing project. They were mostly younger children, several of them Puerto Rican, who were not doing well in school. She was sure these newcomers would lower the standards of Whittier, but she thought Whittier could do something for them, if there were not too many of them. Perhaps the new school social worker would help these children get a good start in school. Whittier was lucky to have a social worker half-time on the staff, she thought. The pupils and their families were becoming so varied, with so many different kinds of people, that she was sure the school needed someone to help the families that were not accustomed to a good standard school, as Whittier had always been.

Elizabeth arrived with her friend, Alice. Both were dressed carefully, with neat cases for books, pencils and pens. Mrs. James knew their mothers in the Congregational Church. Elizabeth's father was a lawyer and Alice's father was a doctor. There was a little talk of the two families leaving the area to move to a suburb, but Mrs. James hoped this would not happen. Alice's father had his office in the downtown district, as did Elizabeth's father, and there was really nothing to keep them in the Whittier district except their friendships and their comfortable large homes.

It was now time to start the first lesson, but Mrs. James waited to see whether Bonnie would come dashing in at the last moment, making a big noise attracting everybody's attention. This is just what happened. Bonnie was an eleven-year-old, already showing the signs of puberty, and she had a provocative way that irritated Mrs. James and made her think of the attraction this girl would be to the bigger boys in the school pretty soon. Bonnie's family was new to the community. Nobody knew her parents, but it was said that her father was not living with the family. Mrs. James had to admit to herself that she was irritated by this girl's manner. She was so different from Alice and Elizabeth. Perhaps she would be influenced by those girls, but so far there was no sign that she was interested in their friendship. Instead, she chummed with a couple of sixth-grade girls who were already causing some trouble by their interest in boys.

As the class settled down to the arithmetic lesson, Mrs. James let her mind stray to the thoughts that came more and more frequently. Might it not be just as well to quit teaching? There was plenty of work to do at home, and in the church, and soon there would be some grandchildren to visit. She could quit now and draw a small pension as soon as she was sixty. And her husband's income was ample, anyway.

There was something about the school, and about the community, that upset her sometimes now. There were changes. New kinds of children in the school. New kinds of families in the neighborhood. It seemed as though she was having to work harder to teach the children, and she was paying more attention now than formerly to where her class stood on the city-wide achievement tests.

• • •

Miss Clarabelle Nelson stood at the girls' entrance to the big old red brick school making sure that the girls formed an orderly line ready to march inside when the buzzer sounded. A big eighth-grade girl said to her, "Miss Nelson, can I talk to you after school this noon?" "Of course, Eleanor," Miss Nelson said. "Just come to my room." She knew what it was about. Eleanor wanted to ask what she should do about the two boys who were asking her to go to the movies. How much necking should she permit them? Should she pick one of them to go steady, or should she keep them both? Eleanor needed help to make up her mind, but there weren't any easy answers. What would have been a good answer for her, Clarabelle Nelson, might not work for Eleanor, whose mother was receiving Aid for Dependent Children, and who did not know her father.

It was a noisy line, waiting for the buzzer to sound, but Miss Nelson was no longer bothered by the noise, as long as it was good natured. She had learned to control the fighting that at first had frightened her. She learned the names of the girls most likely to start fights, and gained some control over them just by telling them that she would not permit fighting within school grounds. Then she reported two of them to the principal, who gave them a good talking-to in her presence, and told them that he and Miss Nelson would not stand for this kind of behavior.

Miss Nelson followed the line into the school and then climbed the stairs to the third floor where her class was making a good deal of noise. She smiled as she walked into the room and said "Good morning, boys and girls."

"Good morning, Miss Nelson," several of them said, and smiled back at her.

A big boy in the back now went over and raised a window. She had taught him to do this, and to keep an eye on the thermometer, so as to keep the room close to 70 degrees. "At least he'll make a better janitor than most of them," she thought, "because he has a sense for comfortable temperatures."

Thirty-five boys and girls stood beside their desks in five rows and, placing their hands on their hearts, they repeated the pledge of allegiance to the flag. Miss Nelson had grown to enjoy this ceremony. It was not so much the idea of patriotism, because she thought there were better ways of teaching patriotism, but it was the idea of all being together and doing the same thing equally well that she liked. There were a great many differences among pupils in this class, and it was her business to understand the differences, but she liked the idea that they were all equal in this one thing.

They were all equal, also, in the fact that they were all Negroes, though some were dark and some were light, and she had long since given up the idea that their skin color made them equal to one another or to her. When she stopped to think of it, she would have preferred a mixed class, which was what she had been used to as a child. She had never been in an all-black class until she came to teach in the Carver elementary school.

Growing up in a northern city of fifty thousand where there were not many Negroes, she had been one of a few black pupils in elementary school and even fewer in high school. She knew something of segregation, because her father was the pastor of a Negro church, but she had never seen an all-black school until that September day, three years ago when she started her first teaching job at Carver Elementary School.

It was hard for her. She hated the idea of segregation. What made it harder was the fact that her pupils were all slum children—children of poorly educated and low-paid people. She could hardly understand their dialects, which were different from anything she had heard among her own friends. Only a half dozen of her 36 pupils spoke English with the kind of accent and grammar to which she was accustomed. Frequently she found herself using an hour a day to coach her pupils on how to speak English—getting them to read aloud, and correcting them again and again. If only half of them had spoken clearly, she would have had an easier time. But she and a handful of pupils were in the minority, and she wondered how the minority could correct the majority. Last year she had gotten a cheap tape recorder and taught the children to record their own speech and listen to it. Some of them would stay after school to play with the tape recorder and she encouraged this.

Clarabelle Nelson had a good fifth-grade class, and she and her class were proud of it. She let them know where they stood on the arithmetic and reading tests that were given to all schools in the city. While they never ranked very high, they led the other fifth-graders at Carver, and they always made more than a year's gain when they were in her class.

They were working now, on their arithmetic, and she looked them over. Several of them were really quite good in arithmetic, and she had several special books for them with some extra material about numbers—some of the "new math" that was being developed experimentally by mathematicians trying to teach children to "think like mathematicians." But the majority were not very good, and the average of the class was in the fourth-grade level. For one thing, they did not do homework, as a rule. Very few of the children had any place to study at home, and no teacher could count on a class doing homework. In fact, few teachers even permitted children to take school books home, because they lost so many of them. Miss Nelson had some special books that she let children take home, after she got to know them well. About a third of her class could be counted on to use books at home and to bring them back in good condition.

Miss Nelson thought about that first year of teaching—that horrible first year. She couldn't understand her pupils when they talked. She couldn't stand the language she heard on the playground and in the hall, what she could understand of it. She couldn't control the pupils in class. They talked and laughed and every now and then they fought. If it had not been for the principal she would have given up after a month of it. He was an elderly white man, patient, firm with pupils, and he reminded her in some ways of her own father. He came to her room sometimes and helped her quiet the children. He helped her to find out the ones she could trust to work quietly. He worked with her at disciplining the unruly ones. And he was always optimistic about the Carver School. "This is the best thing in the lives of many of them," he said, again and again. "Some of them have good homes and they make good use of the school. Others have very poor homes, and the school is the best thing there is for them. Just to watch some of the children grow up is a joy."

Then Clarabelle had registered for an evening course at the local university, during the second semester. The course was in sociology, a subject she had never studied in teachers' college. There she learned about "culture shock," the experience of a middle-class person who comes into close contact with another culture—the culture of the lower-class blacks, in this case. This course helped her to see herself and her job more clearly, and to see how important her job was, if she could do it well.

By the end of her first year, Miss Nelson could come to school in the morning without feeling uncomfortable in her stomach. She decided to stay with it a second year, if only out of loyalty to her principal. During the second year she began to have success with some of her pupils, and she learned to control her class. Then she began to measure the progress her class was making, compared with other classes in similar schools. She and her class became proud of each other.

By the end of her second year, Clarabelle Nelson had enough seniority to be able to apply for a transfer to another school—an all-white school, or one in a mixed neighborhood where more middle-class blacks lived. But by this time she decided to stay at Carver. She would not spend her life teaching at Carver. She was engaged to be married, and probably she would quit teaching to have a family. But she knew, now, that she liked to teach in a school like Carver, and if they still had such schools when she was middle-aged and might resume teaching, fifteen or twenty years from now, she would choose Carver again.

• • •

Miss Bond was seated at her desk in a corner of the room as her fifth-graders came in from the schoolgrounds. They went first to the coatroom to hang up their coats and then to their seats. A few gathered in little groups, talking to one another. School would not start for another two or three minutes. Looking out the window Miss Bond could see other children arriving, many of them in automobiles driven by their mothers, with a child occasionally coming in a long black Cadillac driven by a chauffeur wearing a dark cap. Other children walked from nearby houses.

She rose to pull the drapery across one window where the morning sun bore in too directly. Outside, she could see the sloping curve of the grounds landscaped with dark firs and spruces. The children played in the large field on the other side of the building. Now the last boy sauntered in, and the class was slowly getting to work, most of them at their desks grouped in one half of the room, while a few were sitting at worktables using reference books. It was a large, light, airy room, with green chalkboards and green-colored bulletin boards on which brightly colored posters were mounted. The flourescent lights were not needed this morning, but it was cool, and the floor was comfortably warmed by inlaid heating coils.

Forest Park School was a show place, and Miss Bond felt fortunate to be able to work in such a fine building, in the finest suburb of the metropolis. For five years now she had taught in this school, after ten years at Homeville. She was an excellent teacher, for the best of teachers were employed at Forest Park and then only after they had shown quality elsewhere. She had fewer pupils than she had had in Homeville, and the school had much better equipment with which to work.

The children were all engrossed in work now, most of them on arithmetic, though one small group worked at a table getting together a report about the first Thanksgiving. They were a clean good-looking lot, Miss Bond thought. There was Estelle Woodford, taking charge of the committee, acting just like her mother who was president of the Garden Club and who had been PTA president last year. Tommy Beauregard raised his hand to ask for help. He was a plodder, certainly not one of the stars in the class, but he kept at his work. She knew that he would work hard through high school and then through Princeton, and then probably work up into the management of the industrial machinery company of which his father was president and principal stockholder.

Helen Fischer sat in a corner, studying from a sixth-grade arithmetic book. She had finished the fifth-grade book and was going ahead on her own. The girl was too much on her own, thought Miss Bond, as she looked at Helen's slender back and black hair. Dr. Fischer was a psychiatrist who had just bought a big house and moved his family out from the city. Neither the girl nor her mother seemed to have made friends yet, as far as Miss Bond could tell from her observations of the children at play and the mothers at PTA meetings. She would like to help Helen get on more friendly terms with the other children but she hardly knew how to go about it. If this had been Homeville, she would have spoken to some of the mothers and suggested that they invite Helen to their daughters' parties. But in Forest Park she did not know how to do this. She supposed the little girls had parties, but she knew nothing about them. She had thought of speaking to Mrs. Fairbairn, her PTA room mother, but Mrs. Fairbairn seemed so occupied with her own plans for the year's activities and so sure of how Miss Bond should fit into them that the teacher felt there was no room for her to make suggestions about the welfare of Helen Fischer

There was only one pupil who reminded her even faintly of her own childhood. That was Anna Metzger, whose father had a bakery shop in the small shopping center of the town and who lived with his family in a flat above the store. Miss Bond's father had owned a small grocery store in a small town. Anna was indeed as much of a teacher's pet as Miss Bond would ever allow herself, and the teacher was pleased when the girl showed attachment to her by bringing little gifts and occasionally something good to eat from the bakery. Anna had friends among the children, for she was good-natured and friendly and quick at games. But Miss Bond wondered whether Anna would be accepted into the clubs and the social life of the younger set of Forest Park when she reached high-school age.

In any case, Anna would be an acceptable student and would certainly finish the Forest Park high school and go to college—the first one of her family to accomplish that much in the field of education. Nobody could attend school in Forest Park and make average or better grades without feeling the pressure of the expectation to go to college. Anna's family might not press her to go to college, but her schoolmates and her teachers would do so, and consequently Anna would do better school work and more of it than she would have done if she had lived in Homeville, where the average student finished high school and then went to work.

Miss Bond wondered whether Anna would be as happy in Forest Park as she would have been, growing up in an average town like Homeville. In fact, Miss Bond wondered whether she herself was as happy living and working in Forest Park as she had been in Homeville. While she knew that she was respected and liked as a teacher in Forest Park, she was not nearly as comfortable in the church as she had been in Homeville and she had fewer close friends—only a small group of teachers and a larger group from other suburbs and from the central city whom she saw at meetings of the State Teachers Association or at conferences at the University. Occasionally she went to the home of one of the parents as a representative of the PTA to help plan a school program. On these occasions she felt uncertain as to what kind of clothes to wear and whether to wear gloves. The women spoke of the eastern colleges they had attended and Miss Bond was afraid they would ask her where she had gone to college. Suddenly the state college which had meant so much to her was something to keep quiet about.

THE SOCIAL STRUCTURE OF A METROPOLITAN AREA

These three schools are all in one small piece of the United States, known as a metropolitan area. A metropolitan area is a natural unit of the national society. It is an area inhabited by a group of people who support each other by their work, and who are numerous enough to enjoy almost all of the complexities of American life. It contains industry, wholesale and retail trade, banking, a whole range of schools reaching generally up to the college level, a variety of churches, a number of local governments, social and fraternal clubs, and welfare organizations.

Metropolitan areas vary in size from New York, with 11,500,000 inhabitants, to Meriden, Connecticut, a town and its countryside with 52,000 population.

A metropolitan area has a social structure made up of groups. People fall into groups. They work in groups and play in groups. They worship in groups, and they tend to live in group neighborhoods. The community's physical structure reflects these groups. It is cut up by expressways, railroad tracks, and factory and business areas. The people living in one district may be different from those living in another district.

The various social groups have cultural differences. A culture is a common and standardized set of ways of behaving and believing. The different social groups in America have different sub-cultures, while they all share a common culture, which consists of such things as speaking English, using a decimal money system, a British system of weights and measures, a liking for ice cream, and a knowledge of the game of baseball.

One type of social group that is especially important for educators to understand is the *social class*. A social class is a group of people who have similar manners, feel "at home" when they are together socially, tend to belong to the same social organizations and tend to intermarry. They have rather similar amounts of education, types of homes, incomes and tastes in leisure activity.

The social classes are arranged in a hierarchy of power and prestige. The people living in a society determine by common consent who are in the higher and who are in the lower status positions, and the social scientist discovers the social classes by asking people in a community where they would place their neighbors and acquaintances on a scale of social status. When a social scientist studies a community in this way, he finds that the people in a community recognize and describe a number of social classes. There is no set number of such classes, since it is possible for people to define as many as nine or ten social classes in a large community, while this number can be reduced by making wider definitions of a social class. For the purposes of educational research, a set of five social classes is useful, as follows:

	Percent of Population
Upper	1–3
Upper middle	7–12
Lower middle	20–35
Upper-working class	25–40
Lower-working class	15–25

The percent of the population in a given social class varies from one kind of community to another. In metropolitan areas of 100,000 or more, the proportions in the various classes are much the same.

A method frequently used to measure social status and to identify social classes is to use an *index of socio-economic characteristics*. This method uses information on a person's occupation, education, housetype, residential area, source of income, club or association memberships as a basis for ratings on the various social characteristics. These ratings can then be combined into a single score that represents his social status. The most important single fact is occupation, but this is usually supplemented by at least one other fact, such as amount of education or type of house, because certain occupations have a broad range of social status. The occupation of salesman, or of business owner, or of lawyer, can be held by people within a wide range of social status.

Another objective way to define social status is to describe the "style of life" or the culture of a social group who are recognized in the community as having the same general social position. This *description of a sub-culture* contains information about the attitudes of the people toward education, religion, politics, family, property, etc.; about the ways they use their leisure time; about their choice of furniture and house styles; and other visible signs of a way of life.

The differences between classes are expressed in two ways. Sometimes a class is described as though all of its members were like a typical person right at the middle of that class. The upper-middle-class person is described as though he must be a college graduate with an income of fifteen thousand dollars, because many upper-middle-class people are like that. Yet there will be some who have barely graduated from high school, who make eight thousand dollars a year, but have other characteristics which are definitely those of the upper-middle class.

The lower-middle-class person is described as though he must be a high-school graduate who makes seven thousand dollars a year. Yet there will be some lower-middle-class people who are college graduates and make ten thousand dollars a year, but have other characteristics which are definitely those of the lower-middle class. Thus it is misleading to describe a social class as though all its members were alike in every respect.

Another way of describing the differences between social classes is to do it in statistical terms. The upper-middle and the lower-middle classes differ by a certain number of years of education, *on the average;* by a certain number of dollars of income, *on the average;* and by a certain number of points on a scale of occupational status, *on the average*. Yet, being contiguous classes, they overlap slightly on all three variables.

Thus the concept of social class is a statistical one. Most people have an extremely high probability of being in a certain class, while others have a 50–50 chance of being in one or the other of two contiguous classes.

This fuzziness of the boundaries between classes is essential in an open class system, the kind that is always found in a democratic society. A modern democratic society always has social classes, but people have opportunity to move from one class to another on the basis of their ability and effort.

The Usefulness of the Social Class Concept

Any concept of group membership is useful in education if it predicts with a fairly high degree of accuracy some important things about its members. Among the various social group concepts, social class probably has the greatest usefulness. It has more predictive value for educational purposes than religion, race, nationality background, region of the country, and every other common social group identification. Knowing the social class composition of a school or a class enables a teacher to plan with a better understanding of such important items as the following:

The general level of educational achievement of the group.

The educational aspirations and plans of the group. Will the majority be interested in job-training, or in college entrance, for example?

The values of the group in certain areas of life that are important for education—such as the drive for achievement, and the willingness to postpone gratification (to do things that are difficult or uncomfortable in the expectation that they will bring a gain in the future).

Above all, social class is the main group determiner for the *family factor* in children's mental development, which will be described in Chapter 6.

The three teachers in our illustration teach in very different kinds of schools though they all teach in one metropolitan area. Mrs. James teaches in a school that has a kind of cross-section of the child population of the city. There are children of professional men and children of bus drivers. Miss Bond in her exclusive suburb has, by comparison, a homogeneous group. Almost all her pupils come from "good" homes where great importance is placed upon the quality of education and preparation for college. Miss Nelson, teaching in what is often called a "slum" school, also has a fairly homogeneous group in terms of socio-economic characteristics, although it is at the other end of the social scale from Miss Bond's.

Culture Shock and the Teacher

In describing Miss Clarabelle Nelson and her school, reference was made to her experience of "culture shock." This referred to the fact that when she began to teach in the Carver School she came for the first time into direct contact with children of the lower working class. She had been raised in the middle class. She went to school as a child with middle-class children. Her family associated closely with the middle-class people, although there were some working-class people in her father's church. These people, however, were from the upper part of the working class, and they did not seem particularly different from others in the church, partly because they shared the church with her and other middle-class people, but did not share other aspects of life.

When Clarabelle Nelson first came into contact with lower working-class children she felt a kind of physical revulsion. They looked dirty. They smelled dirty. They talked dirty. They seemed to come from a different social world, and a lower world. She had not realized that people like that existed—or at least existed in such numbers that they could populate whole schools in the city.

To a more limited extent Miss Bond experienced culture shock when she went to teach in Forest Park. She was most at home with lower-middle-class people, and in Forest Park she met an upper-middle-class group with some upper-class members. Their ways of speaking and their social events frightened her a little. She was not sure that she could "hold her own" in their social circles. She felt more comfortable with her teacher friends from other suburbs, who were more like her. But in her class she had no experience of culture shock. The children were well-behaved by her standards. They talked the standard midwestern American-English that she knew and spoke, and their educational attitudes were like her own.

BLACK MAN IN THE SOCIAL STRUCTURE

In so far as blacks have a separate social existence as a group from other groups in the United States, it is possible to ask about the place of the black man in the social structure. Although there is very little evidence that blacks have a separate sub-culture, they have been considered a separate group for so long that it is necessary to consider them separately in order to understand the social structure of the United States and also to understand the place of blacks in the social structure of a metropolitan area.

Caste and Caste-like Groups

When one group of people is separated from other groups by a rigid barrier that prevents movement from one to the other, when the society prevents or punishes intermarriage, and when it passes this status from parent to child, the group may be called a caste.

The blacks and the whites of the United States are castes or at least caste-like groups. There is a barrier of both law and custom against movement from one group to another in many states of the United States, and a barrier of custom in all other states. However, the barrier is less effective now than it was earlier in the twentieth century, and consequently it is well to speak of blacks as being a caste-like group rather than a caste in the strict sense. In recent years the earlier practices of segregation of blacks in schools, colleges, churches, railroad cars, restaurants, hotels, and theaters have been reduced and even abolished in most states. Furthermore, the former bars against Negroes in certain professions and trades have been lowered. Still, largely by reason of the difference in skin color between blacks and whites, some of the elements of caste-like status are present.

While it is not necessarily inherent in a caste system that one caste has higher rank and social esteem than the other, generally there is a distinction in status between castes, as there has been in America where blacks occupy the lower position.

There are other caste-like groups in the United States such as the Mexican-Americans, the Filipino-, Hawaiian-, Japanese-, and Chinese-Americans, and the American Indians. However, these groups have less of a caste-like status than the Negroes, because there is less of a bar to intermarriage between these groups and others. The single best test of whether or not caste difference exists between two groups is the test of intermarriage. If intermarriage is strictly forbidden, and if the children of mixed unions are always relegated to the lower caste, then we can say that caste does exist.

Social Structure in the Black Group

Within a caste-like group there is likely to be a social class structure if the group is large enough, and if it has a degree of economic opportunity great enough to enable some members to secure property or occupations that confer leadership and prestige. This has happened in the black group.

There is a social class system among blacks similar to that existing among whites. The main difference is that relatively more blacks are in the lower classes. For example, in the "Georgia Town" study, the proportions of black people in the five social classes were 0.3, 2, 9, 26, and 63 percent respectively, as compared with corresponding proportions of 4, 21, 36, 29, and 10 among the whites. (Hill and McCall, 1950.)

In the metropolitan area of Kansas City, in the early 1950s, it was estimated that 2 percent of the black population was upper-middle; 8 percent, lower-middle; 40 percent, upper-lower; and 50 percent, lower-lower. (Coleman, 1959.) The smaller proportion at the lowest social level, as compared with Georgia Town, reflects both geographical and urban-rural differences. By and large, economic opportunities are greater for Negroes in large cities and in areas other than the Deep South.

The socio-economic distribution of nonwhites in the United States was compared with that of whites by Nam and Powers (1965) by using the 1960 Census data and computing for each head of a family a socio-economic status score based on occupation, education, and family income. These scores ranged from zero to 100. Figure 1.1 shows the percentage distribution of white and nonwhites in the central cities of the metropolitan areas of the country, in the urbanized areas around the central cities, and in the remainder of the country which lies outside of urbanized metropolitan territory. There are blacks at all socio-economic levels in this Table, but the proportions of blacks in the upper half of each graph are substantially smaller than the proportions of whites. This type of difference reflects an earlier, more rigid caste structure in which blacks were systematically subordinated. If present trends continue for another hundred years, it is probable that the social class distribution in the black part of the society will become similar to that of the white group. In the South, with a relatively strict caste line,

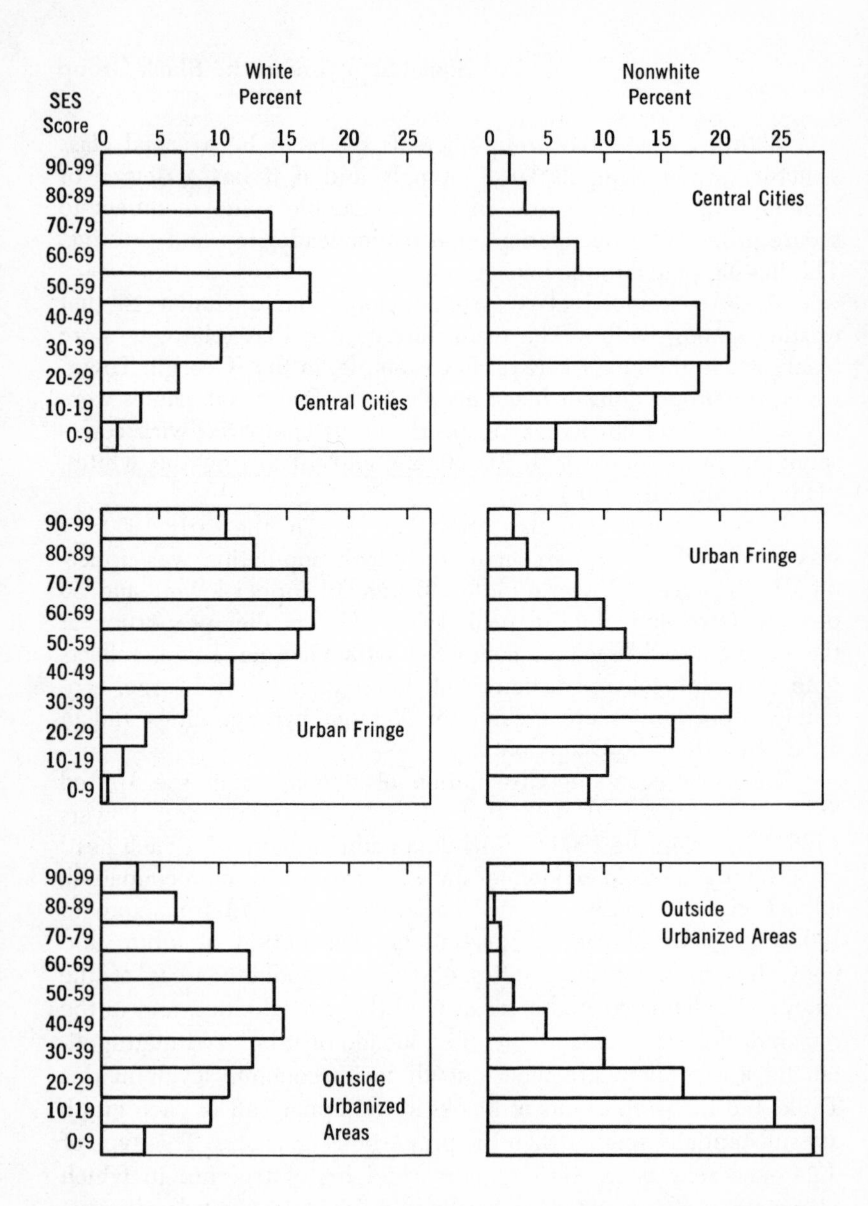

Figure 1.1 Socio-economic Status of Family Heads by Race and Residence in the U.S.A.: 1960. The higher the score, the higher the status. The sum of percentage distributions is 100 for the whites and for the nonwhites in each type of census unit. Source: Nam and Powers, 1965.

only small black upper and upper-middle classes have developed. In northern industrial cities, on the other hand, there recently has been a striking increase in the size of the black middle class.

The increasing size of the black middle class in the big cities has enormous importance for the system of public education in metropolitan areas. The time has already come in several cities—Washington, Manhattan (New York), Philadelphia, Chicago, Detroit—where there are large numbers of middle-class black students in the public high schools and in the public junior colleges, and teachers colleges.

SOCIAL MOBILITY

One essential characteristic of a complex democratic society is that a considerable degree of movement from one social class to another is permitted and encouraged; the ideal of equality of opportunity demands it. The term social mobility—as we shall use it—refers to the movement of an individual from one position to another in the social structure.

Mobility may occur in only one phase of life, such as in occupation (when a man moves from the position of factory worker to that of factory foreman) or in living arrangements (when a family moves from a small house in one part of town to a larger house in a "better" part of town). We shall, however, use the term social mobility to mean movement from one social class to another, involving the consolidation of the various elements of the new social position, including occupation, income, type of house, neighborhood, new friends, and new organizational memberships.

Mobility is an intrinsic element of the American social class system where social classes are open and where each class gains members and loses members. The principal distinction between class and caste is that individuals can move from one social class to another, but they cannot move from one caste to another. (Mobility is possible *within* a caste, however, if the caste contains a social class system.)

Upward Social Mobility

Since the several social classes have somewhat different cultures, mobility from one class to another requires the learning of a new culture. For example, to be born into the family of an unskilled laborer and to rise to a position in adulthood as a business executive or a lawyer requires at least the following kinds of learning:

1. Learning the techniques and the information necessary to be successful in the middle-class occupation.
2. Learning to speak English like a middle-class business or professional man, using the appropriate vocabulary, intonation, and inflections of speech.
3. Learning how to choose appropriate clothes.
4. Learning how to converse with and to agree and disagree with men of upper-class and upper-middle-class status.
5. Learning to talk about current books, theater, art, tennis, golf.
6. Learning the social skills of middle-class life—how to meet strangers and introduce them to one's friends, how to converse with women, how to take a room at a first-class hotel, how to check ones' coat and hat, order a meal, and tip the waiter at a first-class restaurant or club.
7. How to take part in professional or business associations.
8. How to take a leading part in charitable and civic associations.

Upward mobile people learn these things in a number of ways. The most important thing for most persons who move from lower to middle class is to get a high-school education, then a college or university education. The mobile person watches and imitates friends and acquaintances who belong to a higher social class. He reads, travels, and observes the ways other people act in new situations. The mobile person learns also from a wife or husband who has higher social status.

Upward mobile people usually have a strong desire to rise on the social scale, they are quick learners, and they work hard to learn what is necessary for mobility. Thus, intelligence as well as initiative is required of a mobile individual.

The importance of social mobility in a democratic society can hardly be overestimated. The essence of democracy is equality of opportunity, not equality of people. And the kind of opportunity that most people want in a modern society is opportunity to get a better job, to make more money, to live in a better house than one's father. There are other kinds of opportunities, valued by many people—opportunity to speak one's mind freely on political matters, opportunity to enjoy good music and art, opportunity to enjoy leisure time. These are not closely related to social mobility, but they are not inimical to it.

The school system of a big city *must* maintain educational opportunity as the avenue to upward social mobility.

Individual Mobility

Whether or not there is a net upward social mobility in a country or society, there is a great deal of balanced upward and downward individual mobility in a democratic country with an open class structure. In England it appears that there has been at least 30 percent upward mobility balanced by approximately the same amount of downward mobility. The causes of individual upward or downward mobility are the following:

I. *Talent, Especially Intellectual Talent.* A bright boy or girl of working-class or lower-middle-class origin is very likely to move up the social scale in the United States. What this person needs is educational opportunity. An example of individual upward mobility is seen in the case of *Lawrence.*

> *Lawrence.* His family is a typical lower-middle-class family. The father has a modest white-collar job, and has been able over the years to pay for a bungalow in a quiet neighborhood of unpretentious homes, and to keep it up quite well with a neat lawn and flower beds.
>
> Lawrence was always an outstanding student in elementary and senior high school. He was not an athlete or a social leader, though he was well thought of by his fellow students. He has always been slender and good-looking in a quiet way. As a young man he is now a tall, neatly dressed individual who would be acceptable but not noticeable in any social group.
>
> After graduating with high honors from the state university, where he had a scholarship that paid something like half of his living expenses. Lawrence went immediately to an Ivy League university on an all-expense fellowship for graduates who expect to enter college teaching. There he earned his Master's degree in comparative literature and is continuing toward a Doctor's degree. He says he wants to teach in a private university rather than a state university because he thinks it will give him more academic freedom.
>
> At the state university he commenced in commerce but shifted to literature after the first year, after talking with his English instructor, and then during the summer with his employer in the store where he worked. His boss told him, "Lawrence, you are too good a student to be a salesman."

The interviewer mentioned that Lawrence had been one of the top students in high school and asked whether he really had to work hard for his high marks. "You bet I had to work," said Lawrence. "It gets me when people say they got good grades without working. I knew maybe one or two people who could do that but I did not have that much ability."

Lawrence appreciated the friendships he made in college. "College gives you a different outlook on life; and it is amazing the things a person doesn't know before going, and not necessarily in your own subject field. I think I appreciate many things I did not appreciate before." He was not a member of a social fraternity but he did belong to a language club and for a while belonged to a political club.

He is an independent person. During his freshman year at the state university he worked on the school paper, but he quit after having a disagreement with the editor, "because I didn't want to make it my whole campus life."

"I like to walk and at the university I do some running just for exercise. I used to play tennis but I gave that up since I didn't feel too competent at it. I read as much as possible except in the summer." Lawrence is not married and has no plans for marriage in the immediate future. He may go overseas to do some research for his Doctor's degree.

As he has gone ahead into graduate work, he finds it more interesting than undergraduate work which was too often "just busy work. In graduate work you are able to get right at the material you want to study."

II. *Social Effectiveness.* A boy or girl with at least average intellectual ability is likely to move up the social scale if he or she is socially effective—gets along well with people and is something of a social leader. This kind of person is valuable in business or industry and is frequently found in such professions as social work. Also, this kind of person is likely to get administrative positions in the field of education. This kind of person is not so closely dependent on educational opportunity, but in the United States generally needs at least a high school education and frequently a college education simply to become eligible for promotions due to his social effectiveness. An example of this kind of mobility is Paul.

Paul. Paul was an average student in high school. He liked physical activities and played on the high school basketball team. He had many friends and his sociability gave him a high degree of social effectiveness. He is of stocky build, usually dresses in a sport shirt and slacks, and wears his hair cut short. He is a very talkative, outgoing individual, and is a happy person. He does not use precise English but his personality makes an impression. He is not a leader but when he is with people he is well liked; he is "one of the boys." The interviewer made several phone calls before contacting him because he was out with his friends, but the interviewer found this to be the most enjoyable interview he made. Paul's family is upper-working class.

The interviewer mentioned that Paul had made a good average record in high school. "I took mostly the courses I could get by on. I did have quite a bit of mathematics, three or four years, and I had biology. I took chemistry but I dropped that because I thought I would have to work too hard in it. I guess I had a pretty good time in high school."

While in high school Paul had a number of basketball scholarship offers. He attended a state university for his freshman year, but he failed to maintain an adequate grade average and dropped out at the end of the school year. The following year he worked on a state highway survey team. The next year he returned to a second college and has continued there on a board and tuition basketball scholarship. He will return to college this year as a senior.

The interviewer asked how hard he has studied in college. "Not very hard. I am not saying I am doing too well either. I guess that is because I don't apply myself. I didn't study hard in high school either. Of course everyone told me to; they told me to then and they have told me since but for some reason I don't have good study habits. I wouldn't say that I don't enjoy studying. It is just a matter of forming habits early. I might enjoy studying if I could just sit down and do it. It is not as bad as it used to be. I see people ahead of me now who graduated in my high school class. Some of them were teaching here this last year. That kinda hurts and makes me think a little more of the educational values. I am not swayed quite as easily as I used to be when the boys want to go out. It used to be 'Let's go get a coke,' and of course, now it's 'Let's go get a beer,' and I went often enough, and I still do but not as much. I think everybody is swayed to some extent."

When asked about his major study in college, Paul replied, "I am majoring in Business. I was going to get an accounting major, you know accounting is an open field, but football practice interfered with some of those accounting courses because it came at the same time. I guess I'll go into personnel management or, bad as it sounds, sales work."

Paul is not an impulsive sort of fellow; he likes to plan. He recently became engaged to a girl who will be a junior at his college this fall, but they have no definite plans for marriage at this time. He thought they would wait until he had at least finished his military service. He said that he would just as soon not have his wife work when they do get settled.

Paul will undoubtedly succeed in business, and will be mobile from upper-working class and upper-middle class. His social effectiveness is his strong point.

III. *Ambition and Drive.* Often a person with only average intellectual ability and social effectiveness succeeds in becoming upward mobile through industrious effort. This is likely to happen to working-class youth who move up into lower-middle-class positions. Education is not so important to this kind of person, though he generally completes high school. An example is Robert.

Robert. Robert came from a stable working-class family. He had average ability and made average grades in school. He was a mild and pleasant-mannered youth with a good number of friends. As a young adult he is still a rather quiet person, has a youthful appearance, and speaks with a soft voice. He has an initial adult status of lower-middle class.

Robert and his wife now have three young daughters and live in a small two-story bungalow that is situated right along the sidewalk in an old section of town. The building is well maintained. The rooms are small but they are reasonably well furnished even though things are a bit crowded because of the small size.

He was in a distributive education program in his senior year in high school. "I realize I should have studied harder and taken more subjects than I did. I just took average classes. I guess I should have taken more difficult classes like science and mathematics."

Since leaving high school he has worked only in supermarkets, where he was trained on the job. He worked for a local market and then his firm transferred him to a town in another state where he was an assistant manager. He quit that job to come back to his home city about a year ago. "The main reason I quit was that I was putting in an extra amount of hours for what I was getting paid. It got so I couldn't see my family at all. It was strictly voluntary work, but the work was there and it had to be done and somebody had to do it. When we came back here I got a job as a stock clerk in another store and I made as much at that as I did as assistant manager before. About a month ago I became assistant manager of this store. Actually, this is part of a training program. If I am good enough to stay in the program I will then go into a co-manager position, probably in another town and then from that into a store as manager. This will probably take about six or seven years, but I can wait. I don't want it before I really think I can handle it because it is a job I would want to stay with a long time when I get it."

Robert's wife worked for a while when they were first married but she does not work now. They are members of a church but they do not belong to any kind of social group. "We go to shows a lot and we go with my folks. They have a boat and we go up the river and ski and swim. I guess we don't do things separately much; most things we like to do together."

The interviewer asked Robert how he felt about early marriages. "Well, we were married the year after I got out of school. I guess it all depends upon the person. For myself I think it worked fine. I know if I had it to do over I would get married at the same time." Robert was asked if he was pretty well satisfied with the way things had gone since he left school. "Well, yes; but I am not really satisfied. We want more; we want to advance but so far I think it has worked out all right."

These cases illustrate the fact that educational opportunity is essential for much individual upward mobility in the United States, especially among boys. If the schools of the big cities which serve a growing proportion of working-class youth are inferior and do not effectively provide educational opportunity, then the society of today is in serious danger. For the quality of the young people who move up the social scale tends to determine the quality of our society, and this quality is increasingly dependent on the schools of the big cities.

SUGGESTED ACTIVITIES

1. On the basis of your experience, describe the social class composition of the elementary school that you attended for the longest period. Can you describe some children who deviated from the typical social class composition of that school?
2. Draw a simple map of the town or city in which you live, or obtain a map with the principal streets and the main features on it. On this map, mark out a set of residential areas that you know something about, and label them from 1 to 5, in order of their social status. Then locate a number of schools on the map, and comment on the nature of these schools.
3. Write a brief sketch of someone you know fairly well who has been upward mobile. Describe this persons' family background in socio-

economic terms and tell what part his or her schooling had in making him a mobile person.

4. What are the characteristics which differentiate the upper classes from the middle classes, and the working classes from the poor? How would you go about obtaining evidence to support your answer?

SUGGESTIONS FOR FURTHER READING*

1. For a more detailed treatment of social classes and social mobility and their relation to the school system, read Chapters 1 and 2 of *Society and Education* by Havighurst and Neugarten. A more technical treatment may be read in *Social Class in America,* by Warner, Meeker and Eells.
2. An interesting description of the various social classes in the Peninsula area, south of San Francisco is given by Harold Hodges in his book entitled *Peninsula People.*
3. For a description of the social structure of a small city, see the first chapter of *Growing Up in River City,* by Havighurst, Bowman, et al.
4. Consult the *Encyclopedia of the Social Sciences* for papers dealing with social class, social stratification, and other topics concerned with the sociological analysis of modern society.

* Complete authors' names and titles appear in Bibliography.

CHAPTER 2

Urban and Metropolitan Development

Great cities are relatively new as the habitation of large sections of the human race. Jerusalem was a city of 25,000 in the time of King Solomon, and this was a big city. Babylon at her height was somewhat larger, and Athens may have had 150,000 inhabitants in the fifth century B.C. Rome may have reached a million at her height, but her population declined to 20,000 in the Dark Ages. Constantinople was the largest city in the western world in 1500. Paris was the largest in 1600 when according to Lewis Mumford (1961) she had about 180,000 inhabitants. London was the largest city in the world in 1800. There were only twenty-one cities of 100,000 or over in Europe in 1800, and none with a million.

During the nineteenth and twentieth centuries the cities have grown. By 1950 there were 46 cities of a million or more and 700 with a population between 100 thousand and a million. Europe and North America each had fifteen cities with over a million, Asia had ten, South America had three, Australia had two, and Africa had one.

The first large cities grew up before the advent of modern technology, which brought large numbers of industrial workers together to create the modern urban center. Before that, the great cities were the centers of political and military power, great trading posts where landways and waterways came together, and brilliant collections of palaces and temples where the powerful people lived and worked.

Until 1800, the large cities were still close to the field and the pasture, and the people were spiritually close to land and sea. Even when Paris was the biggest city in the world, in the seventeenth century, its citizens when out for a walk could see the windmills of Montmartre and drink goat's milk on the Champs Elysées.

Table 2.1 shows the locations of the cities over 100,000 by continent in 1960. This table also shows the proportions of the total population living in metropolitan areas of 100,000 and over.

TABLE 2.1
Great Cities in 1960

Continent	*Areas with over 100,000 Population*	*% of Total Continental Population in Metropolitan Areas:*	
		1,000,000 & over	*100,000 & over*
North America	153	27.2	49.7
Latin America	68	14.7	27.4
Europe (inclusive of Russia)	435	12.5	29.6
Asia (exclusive of Russia)	435	6.2	12.3
Africa	64	2.6	8.1
Australia-Oceania	11	23.6	43.3
TOTAL	1,166	9.6	19.9

Sources: United Nations Statistical Office, Department of Economic and Social Affairs, *Demographic Yearbook, 1960*. New York: 1960.
Homer Hoyt, *World Urbanization*. Technical Bulletin No. 43. Washington, D.C. Urban Land Institute, 1962.

THE CITY IN AN ESSENTIALLY RURAL SOCIETY

Until 1800 the people of even the most powerful and up-to-date societies were mainly engaged in getting food and water from sea and land—some 80 percent of the population were tillers of the soil, or sheep and cattle tenders, or fishermen or foresters. Then the growing productivity of agriculture and extractive industry enabled fewer people to produce more food and mineral and forest products, and the excess population of the rural areas moved toward the cities. From 1800 to 1960 the proportion of people in the United States living in urban places (2,500 population and over) rose from 6 to 70 percent.

In the pre-industrial millennia there were empires which required military and political organization, and these produced large cities to serve as their administrative headquarters. Babylon, Rome, and Constantinople are examples.

As the rural population raised itself above a subsistence level and produced a surplus, trade became important and trading centers came into existence. The major trading centers were located at the intersections of busy land routes or at places where land and water routes met. Paris and Moscow represent the first type, and Hamburg, New York, and Buenos Aires the second. The great European colonial empires of the nineteenth and early twentieth centuries developed cities as trading centers. Examples are Calcutta and Bombay in India, Singapore, Hong Kong, Saigon, Rangoon, Manila, and Cape Town.

After 1800, as industry developed, some industrial cities grew to serve as the centers of industrial complexes. Melbourne served this purpose in Australia, São Paulo in Brazil, Pittsburgh in the United States and the Ruhr complex of Duisburg-Dortmund-Essen in Germany.

THE CITY IN AN INDUSTRIAL SOCIETY

Industrialization and urbanization have gone together. The urbanization of the United States (proceeding from 6 to 70 percent between 1800 and 1960) was paralleled by a reduction in the proportion of the labor force engaged in agriculture from 80 percent to 8 percent during the same period. It was not until 1820 that any American city reached 100,000.

For the world as a whole, Kingsley Davis (1955) estimates that in 1800, some 1.7 percent of the world's population were living in cities of 100,000 or over, and this figure had increased to 20 percent in 1960. Even basically rural countries such as Mexico and Brazil have their urban population increasing three times as fast as their rural population.

It sounds paradoxical, but it is true that poverty stricken people go to the big cities because they are better off there. The rural poor are not so visible, and perhaps they do not feel poverty as much as the city poor. But the big city has a magnetic attraction for poor people. Thus nearly every big city has slums which are eyesores. They are more picturesque in some cities than in others. When seen from a distance the slums are almost beautiful in Rio de Janeiro where they are perched on the steep hillsides. But they are ugly in São Paulo, and Buenos Aires and Santiago de Chile, and Lima, just as they are ugly in Johannesburg, London, Milan, and Chicago. Only a few medium-large cities in northern Europe seem to have conquered the problem of urban poverty.

TYPES OF URBANIZATION

In the modern world the big cities and the big urban agglomerations dominate practically all countries. But some of these countries are not really urbanized. To be urbanized a country needs more than a few large cities. It is useful to make a distinction between *sporadic* and *systematic urbanization.*

Sporadic Urbanization—Big Cities in Rural Countries

Countries which have the majority of their population engaged in agriculture need a few large cities to serve as trading and manufacturing centers. Australia is a striking example of sporadic urbanization. Though its economy is essentially rural, over 50 percent of its inhabitants live in a few provincial capitals, with Sydney and Melbourne each having over a million inhabitants.

Looking at Table 2.2, which reports the metropolitan areas with three million or more population, one sees examples of this type of urbanization in São Paulo and Rio de Janeiro in Brazil, Buenos Aires in Argentina, Mexico City in Mexico, Cairo in Egypt, Calcutta and Bombay in India, and Seoul in Korea. Also, the big Chinese centers, five of them, serve an enormous country whose population is 85 percent rural.

Other examples of sporadic urbanization are the cities that

TABLE 2.2
The World's Largest Metropolitan Areas: 1965–1970

Rank	City and Country	Approximate Population
1.	New York City, U.S.A.	15,000,000
2.	Tokyo-Yokohama, Japan	10,680,000
3.	London, England	7,900,000
4.	Paris, France	7,400,000
5.	Buenos Aires, Argentina	7,000,000
6.	Shanghai, China	6,900,000
7.	Chicago, U.S.A.	6,800,000
8.	Los Angeles-Long Beach, U.S.A.	6,800,000
9.	Moscow, Russia	6,500,000
10.	Peking, China	6,100,000
11.	Mexico City, Mexico	5,450,000
12.	Rio de Janeiro, Brazil	5,000,000
13.	São Paulo, Brazil	5,000,000
14.	Essen-Dortmund-Duisburg, Germany (West)	4,800,000
15.	Philadelphia, U.S.A.	4,700,000
16.	Osaka-Kobe, Japan	4,400,000
17.	Bombay, India	4,150,000
18.	Chungking, China	4,070,000
19.	Detroit, U.S.A.	4,060,000
20.	Leningrad, Russia	3,700,000
21.	Hong Kong	3,700,000
22.	Djakarta, Indonesia	3,500,000
23.	Seoul, Korea	3,470,000
24.	Cairo, Egypt	3,350,000
25.	Berlin, Germany (East and West)	3,300,000
26.	Tientsin, China	3,300,000
27.	Calcutta, India	3,000,000
28.	San Francisco-Oakland, U.S.A.	3,000,000

Source: Authors' estimates, based on census data since 1965.

grew up in the colonies of European powers of the nineteenth century to serve as centers of colonial trade and government. During the twentieth century there was rapid growth of important cities in the African colonies which continued after they became independent. Examples of cities over 200,000 which hardly existed in Africa in 1900 are: Elizabethville, Leopoldville, Abidjan, Accra, Lagos, and Nairobi.

Systematic Urbanization

An urbanized country is one with a relatively large urban population which is engaged in manufacturing and trade. Western Europe began to become urbanized in the sixteenth century. After 1600 a number of large European towns became substantial cities. Paris, London, Naples, and Milan had over 200,000 inhabitants; while Palermo, Rome, Seville, Lisbon, Antwerp, and Amsterdam exceeded 100,000. Subordinate to them grew a large number of medium-sized or small cities.

The United States went through this process of urbanization rapidly after 1850, as can be seen in Table 2.3. The systematic nature of this process is indicated by the fact that there are many towns and small and medium-sized cities that are distributed in a regular manner related functionally to the large cities. At the same time, the rural or farm population functions efficiently in the economy, producing a surplus of materials for sale and buying manufactured goods and a variety of services. A country which is

TABLE 2.3

Growth of Urban Population in the United States

	DISTRIBUTION OF URBAN POPULATION (BY PERCENT)		
Year	*Places of 2,500 and over*	*Places of 100,000 and over*	*Metropolitan Areas*
1790	5	—	—
1810	7	—	—
1830	9	2	—
1850	15	5	—
1870	26	11	—
1890	35	15	—
1910	46	22	46
1930	56	30	54
1950	64*	29	59
1960	70*	29	63

* Current U.S. Census definition of "urban" adds about 5 percent to number based on pre-1950 definition.

Source: *U.S. Census of Population: 1960, Selected Area Reports. Standard Metropolitan Statistical Areas.* Final Report PC (3) 10, p. 1.

systematically urbanized has very few "subsistence farmers," who try to produce all the food and other material they need for a bare subsistence, without selling much of their product or buying much from other parts of the economy.

Most countries of Western Europe are systematically urbanized. The Soviet Union is moving rapidly in that direction, and it is supposed that China is beginning this process.

METROPOLITAN DEVELOPMENT

Modern cities grew in sheer physical size by annexing land around their edges. Sometimes the land was open farmland which was laid out in city blocks with new streets and sidewalks. Other times the newly-annexed area was a town or village which had grown up separately and then was engulfed by the city as an amoeba spreads itself around a foreign object. Cities thus became larger in area as well as in population.

In another form of growth, cities extended their economic and social nets to take in people who did not live within the geographical city limits. Many people living outside of the city bought their furniture and clothing in the central city. People from a wide surrounding area came into the city for theater, concerts, and lectures. Thus the city was the intellectual and economic capital of an area that extended out some distance from its physical boundaries.

By the middle of the current century it had become clear that a new type of community was in existence. The U.S. Bureau of the Census recognized this fact by defining a "standard metropolitan statistical area," as a city of 50,000 or more with its county and any contiguous county that is economically and socially integrated with the central county. A number of SMSAs contain two or more cities, such as Minneapolis–St. Paul, Philadelphia–Camden, and San Francisco–Oakland–Berkeley–Richmond.

In 1968 there were 233 metropolitan areas in the United States with 127 million people or 64 percent of the population. Although the population of metropolitan units gained 36 percent between 1950 and 1968, central cities gained only 11 percent, while the suburban areas gained 62 percent. In fact, some of the central cities actually lost population. There were 225 central cities included in the SMSAs of 1950. Of these, 72 lost population between 1950 and 1960, while 153 gained. Of the five cities with populations of one million or more, only Los Angeles gained. Among cities that lost population were Boston, St. Louis, Detroit, Minneapolis, Washington, Philadelphia, Cleveland, Chicago, Cincinnati, Baltimore, and New York, with losses ranging from 15 to 3 percent. While 225 central cities as a group moved up from 51 million in 1950 to 56 million in 1960, their suburban areas expanded with almost explosive effect from 36 million to 53 million.

The land area of SMSAs in 1967 was about 10 percent of the country's total. There were 404 counties in the 227 SMSAs surveyed in the federal government's 1967 Census of Governments, or 13 percent of the number of counties in the country. There were 4,977 municipalities and 3,255 townships. There was a total of 20,703 government units, including five thousand school districts.

The most populous SMSA in 1960 was New York, with 10,694,000 inhabitants and the smallest was Meriden, Connecticut, with 52,000. The median size was 218,000. In 1967, the 218 metropolitan areas which had been designated as SMSAs in 1960 were distributed by size as follows:

More than 3,000,000	5
1,000,000 to 3,000,000	19
500,000 to 1,000,000	32
250,000 to 500,000	54
100,000 to 250,000	90
50,000 to 100,000	28

There are only two states without at least one SMSA—Wyoming and Vermont.

Many of the metropolitan areas, 118 of them, consist of only one county, but there are nine counties in the New York SMSA, six in Chicago SMSA, and six in the Kansas City SMSA. When a county without a central city of 50,000 is included in an SMSA, it must satisfy certain criteria of economic integration with the central county in the area. (See Bollens and Schmandt, 1965, pp. 7–8.)

This means that very few metropolitan areas contain much rural territory or open land. However, there are a few exceptions to this rule. For instance, San Bernardino County, the largest county in the United States, is the central county of a metropolitan area. This county stretches from Los Angeles County on the west almost 200 miles to the Nevada state line, and much of this area is desert.

The number of SMSAs was increased to 233 by the Bureau of the Census in 1968 on the basis of the latest census data. Probably another eight or ten will be added by the 1970 Census. The United States has become a metropolitan country. Two-thirds of its school children and school teachers are located in metropolitan area schools.

The Evolution of a Metropolitan Area

The growth of a metropolitan area has taken place in five stages as described in the following pages.

I. *The Beginning.* It all commences with a town which is a small trading center, such as Chicago was in 1840. This center grows over a period of years to be a medium-sized city of 25 to 50 thousand.

By this time the city has a fairly well-defined structure that is related to the incomes and social statuses of the people who live there. One area is where the well-to-do people live. Sometimes it is called the "country club area" because it is close to the country club to which the "upper crust" of society belong. Another part of the city becomes a slum area, with small, old, run-down houses. There is usually one side of town which is spoken of as "on the wrong side of the railroad tracks," where working people live. The houses are generally well-kept and the lawns are neat, but it just is the wrong place for people to live who want to move in "the best social circles."

The schools reflect the socio-economic stratification that is beginning to take place. Probably the oldest school in town will be in the slum area. People who can afford to live where they choose try to avoid living in the district of the "poorer" schools. There are one or two modern schools where most teachers like to work and where the parents most interested in the education of their children try to live.

During this period there is only one public high school, drawing a cross-section of youth in terms of ability, educational motivation, and socio-economic status.

II. *The Structured City.* Oscar Handlin in his book *The Newcomers* tells how New York City grew from the first into the second stage. If the city in stage I is located in a strategic place with respect to water and railway transportation, raw materials, or markets, it attracts large numbers of people who come there to work. Soon it develops industries, and grows to be a center of several hundred thousand. By this time the areas near the center of the city become industrialized, or their houses deteriorate and their owners move away from the center of the old town. Slum areas develop, and choice residential areas appear on the edges of the growing city. Sometimes these areas are annexed by the city.

During this period the schools separate out into types with qualities of the areas in which they are located. Some elementary schools become entirely working-class in character; others, middle-class. At the same time a number of high schools are built, generally to serve youth of geographical districts which contain eight or ten elementary schools. The single comprehensive high school that served all kinds of youth in the smaller city is replaced by a variety of schools with contrasting student bodies. Some schools get a reputation for college preparation; others begin to specialize in vocational education.

Even if a city developing out of stage I does not grow to a size of several hundred thousand, it may go through some of the same changes while growing to be a hundred thousand, like Canton, Ohio, or Decatur, Illinois. The city develops a geographical structure related to its social structure and the schools develop accordingly.

III. *Central City and the Suburbs.* By the end of World War I a number of American cities had gone through stage II and were moving into stage III, while other smaller cities followed them into stage II. The main characteristic of stage III is the appearance of choice residential suburbs at first strung out along the railway lines that lead into the city.

These suburbs are exclusive residential areas, expensive to live in, with gardens around the houses, parks and country clubs and tennis clubs, and with superior schools provided at no greater cost to the taxpayer than in the central city. These suburbs are heavily upper-middle class with a fringe of upper-class and of lower-middle-class residents. Their schools, elementary and secondary, are homogeneous along socio-economic, racial and ethnic lines.

When these suburbs first came into existence it was almost impossible for a Jewish family to buy or rent a house, and blacks were unknown except as servants.

The principal reason given by people for moving out from the central city to a suburb was and still is that it is better for their children. The schools are better, there is more play space for children, and the children can find congenial playmates. In addition, many people like the gardening, the golf and tennis, and the other leisure activities that are easily found in the suburbs.

During this phase, which, for cities already in stage II by 1920, lasted from World War I to World War II,* some of the suburbs developed well-known public schools along "progressive" lines. Known throughout the educational world were the school systems of Winnetka, Bronxville, Manhasset, Shaker Heights, Clayton, and Pasadena. This was an interesting development in view of the fact that the people in these suburbs were politically conservative. In educational matters they were progressive, and their schools have tended to retain many of their progressive features during the conservative reaction in education that followed World War II.

Since the suburb is a part of the metropolitan complex, the fact that it draws mainly middle- and upper-class people results in an increase in the proportion of lower-class population in the central city. As population in general expands, and as more persons move into metropolitan areas, the working-class areas of the central city expand, with obsolescence and reduced money values of former middle-class residential areas. Slum areas expand. The area of solid middle-class residences becomes smaller and is often cut up into small islands within lower-class areas.

Theories of Urban Evolution

As the growing American cities moved into stage III, the sociologists who were studying city growth thought they saw that all American cities were going through similar changes, and began to look for "laws" of city growth. One very popular theory was that developed by the "Chicago" school of sociology, which centered in the University of Chicago and used the City of Chicago as a kind of social observatory. Professors Park (1952) and Burgess pointed out that as the big city grows, it forms shells or rings growing out from the center.

* There are some metropolitan areas just now in stages II and III, and other small cities are becoming metropolitan areas. Thus, at present, all stages of metropolitan development are visible. The newer metropolitan areas are evolving more rapidly than the older ones, and some may combine stages III and IV, since the automobile has largely replaced the railroad as a means of transportation.

The first shell, around the business center, consists largely of warehouses and industry and run-down dwellings; yet this area in the early years of the city was generally a choice area for living. The fine dwellings are torn down to make way for warehouses, or they are converted into apartment and rooming houses or funeral parlors. This process can be seen today in many cities of 100 to 200 thousand.

The second shell consists of solid residential areas that housed middle-class people for a couple of generations. The houses became obsolete, and the middle-class people moved further out to a new shell, leaving their houses to be sold or rented to the growing number of workers, often immigrants, who were moving into the growing city. New shells were formed as the city grew. The outer shells tended to be the most desirable, from the point of view of social status.

Thus a shell stretching from five to seven miles from the center of the city would have certain characteristics of income level, occupation, types of churches and schools, no matter whether it was north or south or east or west of the city center. Of course this structure was modified by the physical geography of the city. Chicago had Lake Michigan to prevent eastward growth, Detroit had the Detroit River; New York City had various bodies of water; San Francisco had a bay on three sides which distorted its growth.

The general sequence of obsolescence of dwellings, conversion to other uses or to slum dwellings, and outward growth of the city with the working-class population closer to the center than the middle class was a familiar North American phenomenon.

Another theory of city growth sees cities as growing out from the center by sectors (Hoyt, 1939.) In one direction from the center are the houses of the wealthy people, while the houses of poor people extend out in another direction. These sectors tend to grow outward—the children of the wealthy people build their houses farther out along the same avenues. The middle income people fill up the sectors in between. A growing Negro population tends to move out from the center in one or two sectors.

This theory is linked to the development of suburbs, which grow outward from the central city along railways and later along major highways. Thus the suburbs extend out along what look like the spokes of an expanding wheel. Along these spokes of the wheel were located small towns 5, 10, 15, and 20 miles from the city when it was in stage II. People move out to these towns and turn them into suburbs. Some completely new suburbs come into existence. By 1940 the major cities all had this kind of structure. The spaces between the spokes of the wheel were open country, often used for market gardening. Then gradually industrial plants came into these areas, with branch railway lines built to connect them with the main lines.

The coming of the automobile, the motor truck, and the super-highway changed this picture after World War II. But the concentric shells and spokes of a wheel structure continue to control and condition the life of the contemporary city. Schools and residential areas reflect the structure. Much of modern city planning for urban renewal is an effort to break out of this pre-war structure.

Still another view of urban development sees it as taking place around a number of nuclei. (Harris and Ullman, 1945.) Business gets located in one place, and develops. Industry is located in certain areas where transportation is good, land is cheap, and there are no wealthy people living nearby. An immigrant group settles in a certain area and expands outward from this nucleus. An upper-class group build their homes around a small lake and golf course. The city consists of this collection of nuclei and their subsequent growths.

All three of these theories of urban development are useful in explaining the pattern of growth in the Los Angeles area, according to a set of recent studies. (Burns and Harman, 1968.) No one theory could account for the complex structure of Los Angeles. The University of Southern California and the University of California at Los Angeles have been nuclei around which parts of the city have been structured. The more recent state universities and colleges are now serving a similar function.

The American City Is Not Like Cities in Other Countries

The big cities in other parts of the world are generally quite different from the North American model. Most of them did not develop such a marked concentric shell structure, though the spokes-of-a-wheel structure was evident. Generally, the big cities retained areas of upper- and upper middle-class residence close to the city center on an arc of 90 to 180 degrees, while working-class sections stretched out in other directions. Thus Paris had the fashionable area west of the Arch of Triumph, Berlin had the Tiergarten and Kurfuerstendamm to the west and south of the city center. London had Hyde Park, Regents Park and the area north and west of the center. Buenos Aires had the area north of the city center, out from the Opera House. Mexico City had the Reforma area stretching northwest to Chapultepec.

One reason why the big cities of the United States had their own peculiar structure is that they were built at first largely of wood which does not last as well as the stone and brick of the European and South American cities. A wooden house deteriorated in 30 to 40 years unless it was repaired frequently, and its owner generally moved to another area rather than rebuild or recondition the old house. In contrast, Paris has fine stone houses two or three hundred years old. Furthermore, the very rapid growth of the American cities put a premium on selling an old house and buying or building a new one. With new people crowding in and renting or buying the older houses, an owner in one of the older districts would find himself living among people he did not know and did not want to know, while his former friends had moved farther out to new houses. Hence he sold and moved out.

IV. *Appearance of the Metropolitan Complex.* Up to the close of World War II, the big city appeared to be growing in a rational manner which served fairly well the interests of the diverse groups who lived and worked in the metropolitan area. However, in the fifteen years after World War II, a new stage of metropolitan development began to threaten the well-being of urban society. As the society became a metropolitan one, it discovered a set of problems which seriously threatened its democratic existence.

Rapid growth of suburbs was the obvious characteristic of this phase of development. Table 2.4 shows how the distribution of metropolitan area population changed from a 66–34 ratio of central city to suburban numbers in 1920 to a 46–54 ratio in 1968. The period of most rapid change was the 1950–60 decade. During this decade suburbs of the five largest SMSAs increased about 70 percent while four of the central cities actually lost population.

Two things combined to give the suburbs their rapid growth. First, the pre-war pattern of migration of middle-income people

TABLE 2.4
Division of Metropolitan Area Population between Central Cities and Outside Central Cities: 1900–1968

Year	*Total SMSA Population (000)*	*Percent of SMSA Population Within Central Cities*	*Percent of SMSA Population Outside Central Cities*
1900	31,895	62.2	37.8
1910	42,094	64.6	35.4
1920	52,631	66.0	34.0
1930	66,915	64.6	35.4
1940	72,834	62.7	37.3
1950	89,317	58.7	41.3
1960	112,895	51.4	48.6
1963	118,761	50.0	50.0
1968	127,477	45.8	54.2

Source: U.S. Bureau of the Census. *U.S. Census of Population: 1960. Selected Area Reports. Standard Metropolitan Statistical Areas.* Final Report (PC(3)–1D). Also Series P-20, No. 181, April, 1969.

from the central city to the suburbs intensified. The most frequent reason given by the people for moving out to the suburbs was that it was better for children. Thus, in one study of recent migrants to suburbia, 83 percent said they had moved to the suburbs, for such reasons as "better schools," "nicer children for playmates," and "more healthy for children." (Dobriner, 1958.)

The second cause of rapid suburban growth was the decentralization of industry. Formerly there had been a few small industrial cities around the fringe of the big cities, such as Chicago Heights, Harvey, Whiting, and Gary—south of Chicago; Passaic and Elizabeth—outside of New York; and Alameda and Richmond—outside of San Francisco. After the war, there were various economic factors, as described by Vernon (1959) that led to decentralization of industry. "Light industry" manufacturing electronic equipment, plastics, pharmaceuticals, airplanes and airplane parts became established in suburban areas. This in turn pulled workers out from the central city into new working-class suburbs. Here the people were mainly upper-lower and lower-middle class, with relatively high incomes and with automobiles that enabled them to travel to work independent of railways and electric lines. Examples of this type of development are seen in the new suburbs northwest of

Chicago, in North Kansas City, in Edwardsville and other suburbs across the Mississippi from St. Louis, in some of the new suburbs in central Long Island, and in the northern and southern suburbs of Los Angeles.

Express highways leading into the central city and going around the city from one suburb to another permit new suburbs to grow up in the open spaces between the older suburbs.

At the same time, if there is a substantial black population, as in Chicago and Detroit, a few black working-class suburbs come into existence. With a large black slum area developing in the central city, black middle-class people find their way into mixed black and white middle-class residential areas in the central city, and into middle-class suburbs.

Workers tended to follow industry as it decentralized, and therefore to move out of the central city, though in smaller numbers than the numbers of middle-class people. This was part of a long-term process which is illustrated in Table A–1 (page 317). This Table shows that the proportion of production workers in manufacturing plants who lived in the central cities and worked in the metropolitan area has been decreasing since 1899. For the 48 largest metropolitan areas, Vernon (1959) found that the proportion of manufacturing production workers living in the central cities decreased from 67 percent in 1929 to 38 percent in 1954.

The net effect of this differential growth of suburbs and central city was to impoverish the central city. The poorest people remained in the central city, or migrated from rural areas to the central city, while those with means moved out to the suburbs. Data from the Detroit area illustrate this generalization, which applies also to most, if not all, of the other great cities.

According to a study of incomes of families in Detroit and its suburbs, conducted as part of the Detroit Area Study of the University of Michigan (1960), the median income per family in the Detroit metropolitan area was related to the distance the family lived from the central business district. For families living within six miles of the central business district, the median income rose 3 percent between 1951 and 1959, to a total of $3,800; but the cost of living rose 12 percent. Thus in 1959 the median family in this area had less "real income" than the median family who had occupied this area eight years earlier. Families living further out, between the six-mile radius and the city limits, gained 18 percent in median income and reached $6,000, which gave them a small gain in real income. Meanwhile, families living in the Detroit suburban area gained 47 percent in median income, reaching $7,200.

Thus the central part of the city grew poorer during this decade, while the suburbs grew richer. Or, in other words, the central part of the city became more solidly working class in composition while the suburbs became more middle class. This was due to the movement of middle-class people out of the central city.

Some of the effects of this process on schools can be seen by looking at what happened in a particular elementary school in a northern industrial city between 1955 and 1960.

> Leibnitz School in 1955 was attended by 1,250 pupils coming mainly from lower-middle- and upper-middle-class families of German, Dutch, and Swedish origin. The district was situated about seven miles from the city center, and close to transportation lines. Parents of some of the pupils had attended the same school.
>
> Then came a period of rapid change. Some of the three-story apartment buildings were cut up into smaller units and rented to southern white and Negro families who were moving into the city in large numbers. By 1960 the school enrollment was 2,400. The school was running on a double-shift schedule, with one group of children coming in the morning to one shift of teachers, and another group coming in the afternoon to a new shift of teachers.
>
> The campus of Leibnitz School was at one time beautifully landscaped, but it has now been filled with gravel to accommodate the hundreds of pupils who arrive at noon and mill around while waiting for their shift to begin.
>
> Transiency at the Leibnitz School is calculated at 70 percent, which means that 1,900 pupils transferred in or out of the school during the year from September, 1960, to June, 1961. At times of heavy turnover the children waiting to transfer in or out are seated in the auditorium, in some cases with their parents; in some cases, without. One clerk sits at a desk on the stage and processes transfers and records from incoming children; another clerk sits on the opposite side of the stage and processes papers for the outgoing children.
>
> The records of transfers out during the past several years show that most of the children leaving the school have transferred to schools farther out from the city center, or to the suburbs.

Metropolitan Area Problems

The metropolitan complex which had come into existence by 1960 brought with it a host of problems for which the society was ill-prepared. As the suburban population increased, and the central city population became relatively impoverished, there was growing difficulty for the government and the school systems of the central city. The suburbs, in turn, found themselves facing unexpected difficulties during the mid-sixties.

The large suburban cities closest to the central city became increasingly like the central city during stage IV. Their growth slowed down as they reached their geographical limit, their houses aged and some became run-down or obsolescent. Slums grew up, and there was an interchange of black for white population. This happened in Mount Vernon, next to New York; in Oakland, across the Bay from San Francisco; in University City, next to St. Louis; in Highland Park, next to Detroit.

In the Chicago area, seven close-in suburbs suffered a net out-migration between 1950 and 1960, and continued to grow only because of the natural increase of their residents. Berwyn, Blue Island, Cicero, Evanston, Forest Park, Oak Park, and Maywood had a total net gain in population of 9,300 (three of them actually lost population) and an out-migration during the decade of 22,300.

It is likely that the volume of out-migration from such suburbs will grow larger, unless they develop urban renewal programs that hold people and attract new middle-class residents. Meanwhile, the suburbs further out exert a strong pull on the inner suburbs as well as the central city.

Thus, stage IV has produced a metropolitan complex in which the earlier simple distinctions between central city and suburbs are losing their validity. As the problems of the metropolitan area increased during this stage, the movement of urban renewal gathered momentum in preparation for the next stage, the one in which the major cities are now involved.

Metropolitan growth has currently produced a set of problems which are partly to be solved by improvement in local government, and partly by the efforts of school systems, welfare agencies, church groups, and business groups.

Central cities are faced with growing slums, overcrowded schools, increased juvenile delinquency, heavy unemployment and welfare burdens, and the breakdown of local transit systems. At the same time, the tax base threatens to decrease.

Suburbs are faced with chaotic intergovernmental relations, inadequate public services such as water supply, sewage disposal, police and fire protection.

These problems which have arisen out of metropolitan growth and complexity are the setting for a type of action called *urban renewal,* which is the fifth stage of metropolitan development.

V. *Urban Renewal.* Urban renewal had its official start with the Federal Housing Act of 1949, which authorized federal grants to cities to acquire and clear blight areas which could be used for subsidized public housing or for sale to private land developers. The clearance of obsolete buildings and redevelopment of the area was the main goal of urban renewal until about 1965, when the goals of *social urban renewal* came into some prominence.

Urban renewal has had two aims—to make living conditions for poor people better in the central cities, and to make the central city more attractive as a place to work and to live for all kinds of people. As we shall see in Chapter 5, the broader aim is coming more and more to dominate this stage of metropolitan development, and the concept of urban renewal is being applied to the entire metropolitan area—to the suburbs as well as the central city.

At its minimum, urban renewal consists of tearing down the worst of the slums and building large blocks of public housing for low-income families. Beyond that minimum, urban renewal consists of planning the growth of the metropolitan area from the center out to the suburbs, with parks, shopping centers, libraries, churches, and schools organized to serve people near where they live; and with industry, the central business district, and the centers of residence linked by fast, comfortable transportation, public and private. Billions of dollars are being spent on bold new physical structures of shopping plazas, garden villages, high-rise apartment housing, and expressways.

Since more than three-fifths of American children go to school in metropolitan areas, and three-fifths of all teachers work in these schools, the schools can hardly be insulated from these momentous events. In fact, organization of school systems and the programs of schools are likely to be determining factors in the forms which urban renewal will eventually take.

This stage of metropolitan development overlaps stage IV and even stage III of some of the smaller cities. Urban renewal funds are available to small and medium-sized cities which do not have much metropolitan complexity, but do have obsolescent housing.

THE EMERGING METROPOLITAN ERA

As late as 1900, the burgeoning cities of the United States seemed foreign both in spirit and in composition to the land of vast open spaces and expanding frontiers. The cities of those decades were fed by streams of European immigrants. Chicago in 1890 seemed as much foreign as American. There were only two German cities (Berlin and Hamburg) with greater German populations than Chicago; only Christiania and Bergen had more Norwegians than Chicago; and only Stockholm and Goteborg had more Swedes. New York City had half as many Italians as Naples; twice as many Irish as Dublin; as many Germans as Hamburg; and one half as many Jews as Warsaw. (Martindale and Neuwirth, 1958.)

The cities of the late nineteenth century had many problems. They had inadequate roads; the majority of streets were unpaved and became seas of mud in rainy weather. Horse cars and cabs were not adequate for urban traffic needs, and electric trolley lines were just coming into use in 1890. Josiah Strong, writing in a prophetic vein in 1898 about the "Twentieth Century City" said, "We must face the inevitable. The new civilization is certain to be urban; and the problem of the twentieth century will be the city." (Strong, 1898, p. 53.)

The city has supplied its share of social problems, but it has put its stamp upon the twentieth century. One of the great American sociologists, Robert Park, wrote a famous essay which commented on the city as follows:

> The city . . . is something more than a congeries of individual men and of social conveniences—streets, buildings, electric lights, tramways, and telephones, etc.; something more than a mere constellation of institutions and administrative devices—courts, hospitals, schools, police, and civil functionaries of various sorts. The city is, rather, a state of mind, a body of customs and traditions, and of organized attitudes and sentiments. . . . The city has, as Oswald Spengler has recently pointed out, its own culture: "What his house is to the peasant, the city is to civilized man. As the house has its household gods, so has the city its protecting

Deity, its local saint. The city also, like the peasant's hut, has its roots in the soil." (Martindale and Neuwirth, 1958, p. 34.)

Not only did the city produce an urban type of man. It produced urban fauna and flora: insects such as the bedbug, cockroach, carpet beetle, and silver-fish; animals such as rats and alley cats; birds—the English sparrow, pigeon, and starling; plants—ragweed and tree of heaven. The city blotted out the stars with its smoke and created a new atmospheric phenomenon—smog.

The city was always changing. Some of the characteristics referred to above were true fifty years ago, but they seem quaint and archaic to modern city dwellers. Cities are no longer full of newcomers from other parts of the world, though ethnic groups still are strong political and religious elements. Cities now recruit their newest members from rural America.

What the students of the city in 1900 did not foresee was the coming of the metropolitan area as the unit of human social living. The metropolitan area is taking the place of the city as the most useful geographical unit for thinking about the coordination and the organization of educational, governmental, and other social systems. Educators and government officials and businessmen are developing a theory and a practice of the relations of the physical environment to human satisfactions in the metropolitan area. The attention of educators will be increasingly fixed on the development of the metropolitan area rather than the growth or decline of a city, or the proliferation of suburbs.

The growth of population in the United States since 1900 has taken place largely in metropolitan areas, as is shown in Table 2.5, and the growth in metropolitan areas has taken place increasingly in the suburbs, as is shown in Table 2.4. In 1963 the central city was balanced in population by the suburbs. Between 1950 and 1960 the central cities in metropolitan areas increased only 1.5 percent when annexations are not counted, while the areas outside the central cities grew 62 percent.

It is possible that a balance between suburb and central city is now taking place. The economic and racial polarization between them probably has reached its maximum and may be starting to recede. From now on it is likely that the suburbs and central cities will become more like one another, rather than more different from one another.

From now on, suburbs and central cities will increasingly rec-

TABLE 2.5

Population Growth in Metropolitan and Nonmetropolitan Areas: 1900–1968

	UNITED STATES		SMSA		NON-SMSA		
Year	*Population U.S. (000)*	*Percent Increase by Decade*	*Population (000)*	*Percent Increase by Decade*	*Population (000)*	*Percent Increase by Decade*	*SMSA Population as Percent of Total Population*
1900	75,995	—	31,836	—	44,159	—	41.9
1910	91,972	21.0	42,012	32.0	49,960	13.1	45.7
1920	105,711	14.9	52,508	25.0	53,203	6.5	49.7
1930	122,775	16.1	66,712	27.1	56,063	5.4	54.3
1940	131,669	7.2	72,576	8.8	59,093	5.4	55.1
1950	150,697	14.5	88,964	22.6	61,733	4.5	59.0
1960	178,464	18.4	112,385	26.3	66,079	7.0	63.0
1968	198,234	11.1*	127,477	12.9*	70,754	7.9	64.3

* Increase for an 8-year period.

Source: U.S. Bureau of the Census. *U.S. Census of Population: 1960 Selected Area Reports. Standard Metropolitan Statistical Areas.* Final Report PC(3)–10, p. 1. Also Series P-20, No. 181, April, 1969

ognize their similarity, and their common interest in cooperation. This will come soon in the more technological aspects and processes of the human enterprise, such as water supply, sewage disposal, streets, and fire protection. It has already come in the area of communication, with newspapers, radio and television serving the entire area.

Cooperation between suburbs and central city will come slowly and with more difficulty in the areas of government and education. These complex social systems are so entrenched in law and custom that they will be hard to change. For instance, the six counties around and including Detroit have more than five million inhabitants. In this metropolitan "community" there are 214 local governmental units, with 17 special districts and 159 school districts. The Detroit area will soon become one continuous community in the physical urban sense. It is already a community to the newspapers and television stations. How rapidly will it become one community in the governmental sense and the educational sense?

Formation of the Megalopolis

In the more populous areas the metropolitan areas stretch out and touch each other, with almost no open farm or forest land between them. To the greatest of these urbanized complexes has been given the name "megalopolis" by Jean Gottmann, the French geographer. Stretching from northeastern Massachusetts through Rhode Island, Connecticut, and along the seaboard and the great bays of New York, New Jersey, Delaware, Pennsylvania, Maryland, and Northeast Virginia, this region is given the name "giant city" by Gottmann who says of it:

> In this area, then, we must abandon the idea of the city as a tightly settled and organized unit in which people, activities, and riches are crowded into a very small area clearly separated from its nonurban surroundings. Every city in this region spreads out far and wide around its original nucleus; it grows amidst an irregularly colloidal mixture of rural and suburban landscapes; it melts on broad fronts with other mixtures, of somewhat similar though different texture, belonging to the suburban neighborhoods of other cities. (Gottmann, 1961, p. 5.)

This area had 34 SMSAs with 42 million inhabitants in 1970, or one-fifth of the population of the United States. Airplanes shuttle back and forth, and buses and private automobiles traverse the distances between cities on expressways in half the time they needed 30 years ago. On a clear night, jetting in an airplane over this megalopolis, one is never out of sight of the red glow of one or another city.

Other megalopoleis, not yet so large, extend from San Jose through the San Francisco Bay Area to Richmond and Marin County; from San Diego through Los Angeles to Bakersfield; from Milwaukee through Chicago, Gary, South Bend, across southern Michigan to Detroit, Toledo, Cleveland, and over to Pittsburgh; and there is one in the making from Houston to Dallas—Fort Worth.

NEW DEFINITIONS OF METROPOLIS

As urban growth sprawls far beyond central city boundaries and metropolitan areas overlap each other to form megalopoleis, some critics have begun to question whether the concept of the Standard Metropolitan Statistical Area really provides the most useful and accurate means available for portraying and analyzing the ecological patterns of metropolitan society. Among the criticisms made are that the criteria currently used to define the metropolitan area fail to reveal the interdependence which exists between urbanized settlements in adjoining SMSAs, arbitrarily exclude urbanized areas which are metropolitan in character but have no central city of 50,000, and designate as "metropolitan," rural territory which is little different from land outside the SMSA. For example, because the definition of the SMSA is based primarily on the use of the county as the component unit, the large size of counties in California leads to anomalies such as the inclusion of large stretches of the Mohave Desert within the San Bernardino–Riverside–Ontario SMSA.

One new way to characterize emerging urban society in the United States is in terms of what John Friedmann and John Miller of the Massachusetts Institute of Technology have called the *urban field*. The basic problem, according to Friedmann and Miller, is that existing criteria for describing urban and metropolitan settlements draw attention away from the "inter-metropolitan" periphery from which metropolitan areas attract population. Population loss in these rural areas, in turn, is inextricably linked with decline in the rural economy and with magnification of social problems in the central cities, and this underlying linkage should be conceptually recognized in definitions used to describe urbanization. To do this, they propose to utilize the criterion of interdependence more fully by distinguishing an *urban field* which consists of

> metropolitan spaces and non-metropolitan spaces centered upon core areas of at least 300,000 people and extending outwards from these core areas for a distance equivalent to two hours driving over modern throughway systems. . . . This represents not only an approximate geographic limit for commuting to a job, but also the limit of intensive weekend and seasonal use (by ground transportation) of the present periphery for recreation. Between 85 and 90 percent of the total United States population falls within the boundaries of the system . . . These are facts of signal importance, for as the area of metropolitan influence is substantially enlarged, nearly all of us will soon be living within one or another of the 70-odd urban fields of the United States. (Friedmann and Miller, 1965.)

Professor Brian Berry of the University of Chicago also has been critical of existing criteria for defining the SMSA. Based on a study conducted for the Social Science Research Council under a contract with the U.S. Department of Commerce, Berry has concluded that

> The areas socially and economically integrated with given central cities are far more extensive than the 1960 SMSAs . . . Because the commuting patterns and attendant variations in degree of labor market participation are so closely related to many other socioeconomic gradients, the effect of the existing criteria is to . . . [obscure] real limits such as the transitional zones or break-points where one commuting field leaves off and socioeconomic characteristics begin to respond to the commuting pulls and employment opportunities of another city. (Berry, 1968.)

Utilizing journey-to-work data, employment data, and other sources of information, Berry has proposed that the concentration and growth of urban centers be described in terms of Consolidated Urban Regions and Functional Economic Areas based on specific definitions to designate the operation of actual *commuting fields* and labor markets in the United States. Application of the criteria he proposed would have resulted in the designation of 31 Consolidated Urban Regions to portray the nation's population patterns as of 1960.

A major reason for describing urban society in terms of concepts such as the *metropolitan area,* the *urban field,* or the *consolidated urban region* is to identify functional units within which interdependence of social and economic activities makes it necessary to coordinate planning and action throughout the unit. It is possible that at some time in the future new terms such as those described above will supplant the metropolitan area as the most useful concept to describe ecological patterns in modern, urban society. Even if this happens, however, the necessity for *metropolitanism*—that is, for responding with an areawide orientation to the problems of interdependent regions—will remain essentially unchanged.

Planning for Metropolitan Development

These changes and the problems they have created have caught the attention since 1950 of government—local, state, and national—of the business organizations of the country, of the church organizations, and of the educational systems. All of these groups through their national and regional organizations have commissions or "task forces" that are actively studying the metropolitan complexity.

This has caused the phrase "urban renewal" to take on a much wider meaning than its original sense of physical slum clearance. It is now a process of planning and developing a rationally-operating metropolitan area, as will be seen in Chapter 6.

Metropolitan areas have most of the people, most of the money, most of the jobs, most of the schools and colleges, theaters and museums. They also have most of the problems—debt, political corruption, racial tension, delinquency, unemployment.

It was inevitable that the national government would pay special attention to metropolitan areas through a cabinet department, and President Johnson made this clear in his 1965 message to the Congress in which he proposed the new Department of Housing and Urban Development. He redefined the city as "the entire urban area—the central city and its suburbs." He said:

> Numbers alone do not make this an urban nation. Finance and culture, commerce and government make their home in the city and draw their vitality from it. Within the borders of our urban centers can be found the most impressive achievements of man's skill and the highest expressions of man's spirit, as well as the worst examples of degradation and cruelty and misery to be found in modern America.

> The city is not an assembly of shops and buildings. It is not a collection of goods and services. It is a community for the enrichment of the life of man. It is a place for the satisfaction of man's most urgent needs and his highest aspirations. It is an instrument for the advance of civilization. Our task is to put the highest concerns of our people at the center of urban growth and activity. It is to create and preserve the sense of community with others which gives us significance and security, a sense of belonging and of sharing in the common life.
>
> Aristotle said: "Men come together in cities in order to live. They remain together in order to live the good life."
>
> The modern city can be the most ruthless enemy of the good life, or it can be its servant. The choice is up to this generation of Americans. For this is truly the time of decision for the American city. (Lyndon B. Johnson, 1965, I.)

For the remainder of this century, the greatest domestic social task of the United States is to develop a rationally-operating metropolitan area, with appropriate planning, urban-suburban cooperation, and political-social reorganization.

Metropolitan Development Around the World

The North American experience with urban and metropolitan development during the current century parallels that of most of the rest of the world. Metropolitan areas exist in every part of the world.

In order to make comparison possible, the International Urban Research group at the University of California at Berkeley has developed a set of criteria to define a metropolitan area as one with 100,000 or more inhabitants, containing at least one city of 50,000 or more. The territory adjacent to the central city must have at least 65 percent of its labor force working at non-agricultural occupations.

Table 2.1 shows the numbers of such urban centers in 1960. According to Gibbs (1961) there were 1,064 of them in 1959. The United Nations' Demographic Yearbook reported 858 in 1950 and 1,166 in 1960.

Among other characteristics, the metropolitan areas of industrialized countries show faster growth in their suburbs than in their central cities.

Growth of metropolitanization is world-wide, in underdeveloped countries as well as in the economically developed countries. Hoyt (1962) estimated that the proportion of the world's population living in metropolitan areas will increase from 20 percent in 1960 to 42 percent in the year 2000.

SUGGESTED ACTIVITIES

1. Study and report on the development of the metropolitan area in which you live. In what stage of development is it? What were the approximate dates for the preceding stages? What can you predict for the next 20 years?
2. If you live in a metropolitan area of 100,000 to 300,000 try to apply the "concentric ring" theory of urban growth to your area. Make a set of maps to show the structure of the city at various times in its history.
3. If you live in a large metropolitan area, try to apply the theory of "multiple nuclei" to its development. Draw a map showing these nuclei and show how they fit into the total pattern of development.
4. If you live in a city of less than 50,000, study it and its county as an example of conflict between urbanizing and rural styles of life. How do the schools fit in? Do they tend to work toward urbanization?
5. To what extent do people you know identify themselves with the local communities in which they live or grew up? Is this sense of local identity increasing or decreasing among people in the metropolitan area? What percent of the adults with whom you come in contact live in the same community where their grandparents lived?

SUGGESTIONS FOR FURTHER READING

1. For a good general description of the development of metropolitan areas in the United States, read Chapters 1–6 of *The Metropolis* by Bollens and Schmandt.
2. For studies of the structure of developing cities, read Robert E. Park, *Human Communities,* and Amos H. Hawley, *Human Ecology.*
3. *The City in History* and *The Urban Prospect* by Lewis Mumford provide historical perspective on the development of cities. *Redoing America* by Faltermayer and *The Living End* by Starr provide a broad picture of metropolitan and urban development in the United States.
4. Urbanization in the United States and other parts of the world is described in detail in *Urban Society* by Gist and Fava.
5. Excellent sets of readings on urban and metropolitan America are

found in *Perspectives on the American Community* edited by Warren and *Taming Megalopolis* edited by Eldredge.

6. Several chapters in *Environment for Man* edited by Ewald combine contemporary and historical perspectives on the evolution and meaning of urban development.
7. The evolution of the metropolitan area, the development of the megalopolis, and the possible emergence of the "ecumenopolis" are described in the writings of city planner C. A. Doxiadis and in the monthly journal *Ekistics*.
8. Max Lerner's "City Lights and Shadows" in *The Schools and the Urban Crisis* is a moving essay describing the promise and problems of urban and metropolitan development.

CHAPTER

3

Socio-economic and Racial Stratification in Metropolitan Areas

METROPOLITAN DEVELOPMENT is a name for a vast redistribution of people and jobs which has been going on during the present century and especially since 1920. From the open country and the small towns and cities people moved toward the larger cities, where the jobs in a rapidly industrializing society were located. Then, from the cities they streamed out into the suburbs, to live and often to follow the decentralization of industry and business which occured after World War II

During the process of metropolitan growth, the central cities gained in their proportion of working-class residents and of Negroes, while the suburbs gained in their proportion of middle-class white residents. Thus the metropolitan area became stratified along economic and racial lines. The inner shells of the city are populated largely by people with low incomes; and the outer shells of the city contain people with middle incomes; and the residents of the outer edges of the city and the suburbs have high incomes.

Since the total population of the metropolitan areas has increased, an area that had 500,000 people in 1940 might have

1,000,000 people in 1960. The number of working-class people was approximately doubled, and the number of middle-class people also doubled. They tended to live in separate and segregated residential areas, which thus grew in size. As a result of this process, children grew up with less contact with children from other types of families than their parents had experienced as children.

In effect, schools became more homogeneous with respect to socioeconomic status. From 1920 to 1965, the segregation of children by social class (and by race in northern cities) was increasing. This means that the percent of middle-class children attending schools in which 80 percent or more of the students are middle class has increased since 1920; and the percent of working-class children attending schools in which 80 percent or more of the students are working class also has increased. In the northern cities, the percent of black children attending schools in which 80 percent or more of the pupils are black has also increased.

The purpose of this chapter is to explore the phenomenon of increasing stratification in metropolitan areas and to explain its implications for education. To do this we need to use a method of measuring the socio-economic composition of an area, and we do this with the socio-economic ratio (SER).

THE SOCIO-ECONOMIC RATIO

The socio-economic ratio is essentially a ratio of white-collar to blue-collar workers. It has been slightly refined by the procedure described below, but it is easy to work out with ordinary census data, and can be determined for any city or metropolitan area with a few minutes' work.

The census data on occupations in the male labor force, aged fourteen and over, is the base of the SER. The occupations are placed in four categories, as follows:

A. Professional, technical and kindred occupations
   Proprietors, managers and officials
   Farm owners and managers (one-fifth of total)

B. Sales and clerical occupations
   Farm owners and managers (two-fifths of total)

C. Foremen, craftsmen and kindred occupations
   Operatives and kindred occupations
   Farm owners and managers (two-fifths of total)

D. Service workers, including private household workers
Laborers, including farm laborers

There are some obvious errors in these categories, if a true hierarchy of occupational prestige is wanted. For example, policemen and firemen are included in service workers, but they rank above factory operatives in occupational status. However, the errors tend to neutralize each other, since semi-skilled workers such as truck drivers are included in category C but probably should be in category D. In order to test the SERs, the ratio was computed more exactly for the male labor force of the USA aged 25 to 64 in 1960. Farm owners and managers were distributed between A, B, and C, according to their levels of education. Men with occupations unreported were distributed between the four categories according to their incomes. The resultant SER was .80, quite close to the value of .82 obtained with the cruder method.

The SER is computed by the formula $\frac{2A + B}{C + 2D}$

Categories A and D are given a double weighting because they represent more fully the upper-middle- and lower-working-class characteristics.

This form of the SER could be improved by taking account of the unemployed, which is a relatively large category in low-income areas of the city. The unemployed could be added to category D. There are other refinements which might be made, but the simple form of the SER is adequate for the purposes of this chapter.

The increasing degree of economic stratification in a metropolitan area is illustrated in the data of Table 3.1. A socio-economic

TABLE 3.1

Socio-economic Ratios of the Chicago Area (Based on male labor force, aged 14+)

Year	*USA*	*Chicago SMSA*	*Chicago City*	*Chicago Suburbs*	CHICAGO CITY *White*	CHICAGO CITY *Nonwhite*
1940	.66	.71	.69	.77	.75	.17
1950	.71	.77	.73	.86	.84	.18
1960	.82	.92	.69	1.28	.82	.25

ratio has been computed for the years 1940, 1950, and 1960 for the USA, and for the metropolitan area of Chicago as well as for the suburbs and the central city of Chicago.

Looking at the SER for the USA, we see that this ratio has been increasing since 1940, and especially since 1950. This expresses the fact that the proportion of white-collar jobs in the American economy is increasing while the proportion of blue-collar jobs is decreasing. The SER for the Chicago Metropolitan Area shows a similar increase, and is higher at all three dates than the SER for the USA as a whole.

In 1940 the city of Chicago was slightly below the average of the metropolitan area. In 1950, the Chicago city SER had increased from .69 to .73, while the total metropolitan area increased from .71 to .77. Clearly, the suburbs were carrying up the metropolitan area total, for they increased from .77 to .86. The city was lagging. The flight of middle-class people to the suburbs was in full course.

But the decade after 1950 saw changes much greater than those which had occurred previously. The city of Chicago decreased in SER from .73 to .69, while the total SMSA increased from .77 to .92, and the suburbs jumped from .86 to 1.28. The central city was decreasing its average socio-economic level in the face of a country-wide increase, as well as a sharp increase in the Chicago area suburbs.

The racial aspect of this phenomenon is also seen in Table 3.1 for the city of Chicago. While the SER of white male workers was going up from .75 to .84 and down to .82 between 1940 and 1960, the SER for nonwhites (almost all blacks) was increasing very slowly, from .17 to .18 to .25. Since the proportions of nonwhites in Chicago increased from 8.2 percent in 1940 to 22.9 percent in 1960, it was the in-migration of nonwhites with relatively low SER that caused a substantial part of the change in Chicago.

RACIAL SEGREGATION IN NORTHERN CITIES

As a part of the increase of socio-economic segregation, there was increased racial segregation in most northern cities. Large, black "ghettos" came into being, and the schools reflect this fact. For instance, the 1958 report of New York City's Superintendent of Schools (New York City, 1959) showed a net loss of 15,000 white pupils per year for the preceding five years, pupils who had moved out to the New York suburbs. Negroes formed 20 percent of the school enrollment, and Puerto Ricans, 15 percent. (Because of the heavy immigration of Puerto Ricans into New York City after World War II, data were kept on them as a separate group, though most of them have white skins.) In 1958, of 704 public schools, 455 had 90 percent or more of their pupils of one group, either black or white or Puerto Rican (Morrison, 1958). Only one in five schools could be said to be "integrated" in the sense that it had more than 10 percent of pupils who did not belong to the majority group for that particular school.

Racial segregation in the schools was a direct result of residential segregation in the cities. Residential segregation grew up after World War I in the northern cities as Negroes migrated to those cities. Home owners and real estate dealers in the northern cities used the device of the "restrictive covenant" to prevent blacks from buying homes in areas that were white in composition. The restrictive covenant was written into the deed of ownership of the house, binding the owner not to sell or rent to a black person. This tended to confine Negroes into areas where the former home owners and the real estate companies by mutual agreement quit enforcing restrictive covenants. But an individual home owner in an all-white area could be brought into court if he sold his house to a black person in violation of the restrictive covenant in the deed to his house.

Restrictive covenants were declared illegal by the courts toward the close of World War II, and thus it became possible, in theory, for a black to acquire a house anywhere in the city, if he could pay the price. Still, most black people including the new immigrants lived in segregated areas due to a general unwillingness of white people in these cities to live in an area that contained substantial numbers of blacks.

Because of the very rapid increase of Negro population in the northern cities after World War II (see Table 7.3 in Chapter 7) there was a severe pressure for housing, which caused whole city blocks and groups of blocks to "change" within a few months. First a few houses would be sold or rented to blacks. Then "For Sale" and "For Rent" signs would appear on the other houses. Under the pressure of black in-migration, there were always buyers or renters for houses available to blacks. White people who wished to remain in integrated residential areas were in such a small minority that they were generally powerless to influence enough of their white neighbors to maintain a stabilized inter-racial neighborhood.

A few areas of middle-class white people resisted the segregation movement by forming local community conservation groups that welcomed Negro neighbors who could afford to buy middle-class housing and would keep up the property, and by insisting on the enforcement of housing codes so as to prevent subdividing of houses and apartments with resultant overcrowding and deterioration.

Also a few housing projects were developed for middle-income apartment dwellers in favorable locations in the central city. An area which had become largely slum would be torn down and new middle-income apartment buildings built, to serve a racially mixed clientele. This proved fairly successful on a small scale in several cities. The people who rented the apartments were generally young married people without children or with small children, or older couples whose children were grown up. Thus these people were not especially concerned with the schools. These middle-class residential islands were too small to populate schools of their own, except occasionally an elementary school. For children of high school age, the nearest high school was often an all-black and largely working-class school.

The growth of the black population (and correlatively, of segregated schools) is illustrated by Table 3.2, which shows the population of whites and nonwhites in the central city and the suburbs of

TABLE 3.2

Population of Chicago and Suburban Area: 1940–1980

	CITY OF CHICAGO		SUBURBAN RING	
Year	*White*	*Nonwhite*	*White*	*Nonwhite*
1940	3,115,000	282,000	1,148,000	25,000
1950	3,112,000	509,000	1,512,000	45,000
1960	2,713,000	838,000	2,588,000	82,000
1965	2,579,000	980,000	2,980,000	113,000
1970 (est.)	2,125,000	1,200,000	3,525,000	175,000
1980 (est.)	2,234,000	1,540,000	4,499,000	347,000

Source: U.S. Census and *Population Projections for the Chicago Standard Metropolitan Statistial Area and City of Chicago*. Population Research and Training Center, University of Chicago, 1964.

Chicago. From 1940 to 1970 the numbers of white residents of Chicago decreased while the numbers of nonwhite residents increased sharply. Similar population changes took place in all the big northern industrial cities.

Projections of School-Age Population in Chicago SMSA

Unless something happens to alter the trends, there will be further stratification along racial and economic lines. Table A–2 shows the projections of school-age population by race for the City of Chicago and its suburban ring. This is based on careful analysis of census data by the Population Research Center of the University of Chicago. It assumes that present trends of birth rates and death rates will continue and that the rate of black migration from the South will be reduced while the rate of black migration to the suburbs will increase. Even with these assumptions, the school population of Chicago will increase substantially in its black population.

There is every reason to expect the same trends in other urban and industrial areas—Philadelphia, Cleveland, Detroit, Cincinnati, St. Louis, Kansas City, Los Angeles, Portland. On the other hand, projections are not facts. Trends can be changed if people work to change them. And the aim of the contemporary movement for social urban renewal is to change these trends, so as to produce a more balanced and mixed metropolitan area population, with all kinds of people in terms of income and color living all over the area.

STRATIFICATION WITHIN THE CENTRAL CITY —EFFECTS ON THE SCHOOLS

In addition to the blacks, several other visible minority groups have collected in the central cities of the metropolitan areas since 1940. These groups are somewhat similar to the European nationality groups who came as immigrants between 1840 and 1910, but they have certain characteristics that tend to make their assimilation into the main social system of the country a slower process.

The numbers of these "new" minority groups are not fully known at present, since the 1970 census has not been published. But rather well-founded estimates of those numbers can be made as follows:

Minority Groups in Central Cities of SMSAs (1970 estimates)

Negroes	16,000,000
Chinese-Americans	300,000
Japanese-Americans	500,000
Spanish-Americans	2,000,000
Puerto Ricans	1,000,000
American Indians	150,000
Appalachian-Ozarkan Whites	300,000
TOTAL	20,250,000

The children of these groups fare variously well in the schools, generally in accordance with the socio-economic status of the parents. Two groups do especially well in school—the Japanese and Chinese. Several research studies show that the children of these groups average just about at the national averages in school achievement. Furthermore, as noted in Table 7.1, Japanese and Chinese men have more education than Caucasian men in the United States, and a higher proportion of them have white-collar jobs.

The other minority groups mentioned here show below-average school achievement. Within each group, however, there is a fraction who have stable white-collar or blue-collar employment, stable family patterns, and whose children do average work in school. For the majority, however, it is necessary to speak of a "lower-working-class group" whose children do below-average work in school. This group consists not only of the minority groups noted above, but also of approximately twice that number of native-born Caucasians. That is, about 35 million people in the USA live in conditions of poverty and are not able to give their children a good start in school. About half of the people in this group live in the central cities of metropolitan areas.

The school achievement of pupils in schools of the central city and the suburbs reflect their socio-economic differences. Studies of school achievement in relation to socio-economic characteristics of the school neighborhood show a clear relationship within the central city. Havighurst (1964) reported this in the Chicago School Survey. Table 3.3 shows how the elementary schools in Chicago's 21 school districts reflect the socio-economic status of their neighborhoods. The median family income and the median level of education of adults in the various districts were combined into a single measure

TABLE 3.3
Socio-economic Status, School Achievement, and Race by School Districts in Chicago

Rank Order in SE Status District No.	*IQ*	*Grade 6, 1963 Achievement in Reading & Arith., Grade Level*	*Grade 1, 1963 Reading Readiness, % Average or Above*	*October 1963 % of Elementary Pupils Negro*
2	111	7.5	75	0
18	104	6.8	74	37
1	112	7.8	89	0
17	108	7.4	74	7
16	101	6.4	67	77
4	107	7.1	78	1
3	107	6.8	74	0
14*	95	5.8	48	85
7**	94	5.8	44	48
5	109	7.2	85	0
15	109	7.2	79	16
10	96	6.0	48	67
20	93	5.7	47	100
12	103	6.7	65	1
6	99	6.3	52	69
21	91	5.5	41	92
8	89	5.4	33	81
11	92	5.5	45	96
19	93	5.6	45	61
13	90	5.5	42	100
9	90	5.3	34	81
City wide	99	6.2	55	51

* District contains University of Chicago, with many children going to the University School (private).

** District includes North Side "Gold Coast," with many children in private schools.

Source: Robert J. Havighurst, *The Public Schools of Chicago,* Chicago: Board of Education, 1964 p. 39.

of socio-economic status, and the 21 districts are recorded in Table 3.3 according to this index. The IQ, achievement level at the sixth grade in reading and arithmetic on a standardized achievement test, and the performance of the beginners of Grade 1 on a reading readiness test are related quite closely to the socio-economic rank of the school district.

It will be noted in Table 3.3 that the seven school districts lowest in socio-economic status contain 61 percent to 100 percent black elementary school pupils; and that the reading readiness scores indicate that only one of the seven districts has as many as 50 percent of first graders "ready" to learn to read. According to the manual for the Metropolitan Reading Readiness test, a child who does not score average or above average on the readiness test has very little chance of learning to read in the first grade unless he receives a great deal of individual attention from the teacher. In classes with 50 to 65 percent of first graders needing individualized instruction, the ordinary first-grade teacher with 35 pupils can hardly be expected to supply this kind of help unless she has assistance. On the other hand, in the top third of the school districts according to socio-economic status, the number of pupils needing individual help varies from one-tenth to one-fourth, and the first-grade teacher may be able to work with that many.

A study made by Patricia Sexton (1961) in a big northern city shows how the socio-economic characteristics of pupils are related to other factors. She obtained the average incomes of families living in the various school districts, and then grouped the 243 schools by their income ranks. The schools in a given group tended to be located about the same distance from the central business district, with the highest income schools farthest out.

The schools in the lower income areas had poorer records of achievement, intelligence, behavior, and drop-outs; while the schools in the higher income areas had more pupils chosen in elementary and junior high school to participate in a program for "gifted" children, and more senior high school pupils going to college. Also, the schools closer to the center of the city had higher proportions of families with mothers working, and with mothers receiving Aid for Dependent Children, indicating that a father was not present in the home.

A more recent study made under the auspices of the National Association of Secondary School Principals (1970) reported on the relation between socioeconomic status and other student characteristics in the 640 public high schools of the country's 45 largest cities. As is seen in Table 3.4, the higher status schools have high proportions of students in college preparatory programs, more foreign languages offered at the 4th year level, and lower propor-

TABLE 3.4

Socioeconomic Status and Characteristics of Pupils in Big City High Schools
1968–9. $N = 640$ High Schools in 45 Largest Cities

SES of School	*% of Schools in Category*	*Average % of Enter. Students in Col. Entrance Curriculum*	*Average % of Enter. Students Who Are Disadvant. Economically*	*Average No. of For. Languages Offered at 4th Yr. Level*	*Average % of Enter. Students 2 Yr. or More Retarded in Reading*
A. Middle Class Predominates	21	80	0	3.0	5
B. Comprehensive, with Strong Middle Class Component	30	55	5	2.6	15
C. Lower Middle and Upper Working Class	28	35	15	2.0	25
D. Working Class Predominates	21	25	35	1.3	55

Source: *A Study of Large City High Schools* by Havighurst *et al.*, National Association of Secondary Principals, 1970.

tions of entering students who are 2 years or more retarded in reading.

Effects on an Elementary School

We have already seen (in Chapter 2) how the Leibnitz Elementary School changed during a five-year period from a school serving a stable working-class and lower-middle-class community into a slum school with an extremely high transiency rate. In 1955 this school had an SER of about 1. Then the process of subdividing apartments and renting them to working-class families with large numbers of children caused the socio-economic ratio to drop. In this case the crowding of the school, the introduction of a double-shift program, and the appearance of black children all combined to cause some people to move away. This resulted in a rapid lowering of the SER and by 1960 this was .06.

Such a school has the following characteristics: First, there is a wide spread of intellectual ability and achievement within a single grade. There are a few children of relatively high IQ, there are some average, and many below average. Their achievement, as measured by standard tests, shows a range of six or seven years in the intermediate grades. Some seventh-grade children will be reading at a tenth-grade level while others will be at the third-grade level. Second, there is a wide spread of educational motivation. A few children are extremely eager to achieve academically. They will work hard for the teacher, and their parents encourage them to work hard. Many other children are indifferent about school, or actively hostile to it.

Usually in such a school there is a system of ability grouping of the children. As long as the school maintains special classes for the brighter children, a few lower-middle class families will stay in the area and the stable lower-class families will be satisfied.

POLARIZATION BETWEEN CENTRAL CITY AND SUBURBS

The migration out from the central city to the suburbs has consisted largely of middle-income white-collar people. As was noted in Table 3.1, this migration produced a kind of polarization of the metropolitan area, with the lower status and low income people making up the majority of central city residents, while the higher status and higher income people placed their stamp on the suburbs.

By 1960 it was definitely established that the suburban areas had higher socio-economic status than the central cities, and the basic facts are shown in Table 3.5. This Table combines occupation, income and education into a single scale of economic status, and compares the residents of central cities with the residents of the urbanized portion of the suburban area. It omits the residents who lived on farms or in non-urbanized villages in metropolitan areas.

The urban fringe exceeded the central cities in the proportions of residents in the highest fifth on a scale of economic status, while the central cities had more than twice as high a proportion of residents in the lowest fifth.

Nevertheless, Table 3.5 indicates that the economic distinction between suburbs and central city is only one of degree. There are many low income people in suburbs and many high income people in central cities. Further study of metropolitan areas shows that the general pattern is set by the large northeastern and middle western metropolitan areas, while the smaller SMSAs and those in the South and the West do not fit the pattern.

The variation in degree of polarization of the larger areas is

TABLE 3.5

Proportion of Population, White and Nonwhite, by Economic Status Residing in Central Cities and in the Urban Fringe: 1960

	SOCIO-ECONOMIC STATUS SCORE			
Place	*80–99 (highest status)*	*50–79*	*20–49*	*0–19 (lowest status)*
Total Population				
Central Cities	13.7%	42.4%	35.2%	8.6%
Urban Fringe	22.8	50.1	23.4	3.7
White Population				
Central Cities	16.0	46.8	31.1	6.1
Urban Fringe	23.7	51.3	22.0	3.0
Nonwhite Population				
Central Cities	3.0	21.9	54.5	20.6
Urban Fringe	3.6	25.2	52.7	18.4

Source: U.S. Bureau of the Census. Current Population Reports, *Technical Studies,* Series P. 23, No. 12, July 31, 1964.

TABLE 3.6
Polarization in Metropolitan Areas in Terms of Education of Adults Within Central City and Outside Central City (Percent at ages 25 and over who are at least high school graduates)

SMSA	1960		1940	
	Outside CC	*Central City*	*Outside CC*	*Central City*
High Polarization				
Cleveland	55	30	45	21
Chicago	52	35	31	25
New York	52	37	33	22
Washington	65	48	43	41
Philadelphia	46	31	27	19
St. Louis	41	26	23	18
Newark	50	27	33	17
Milwaukee	53	40	29	22
Buffalo	44	30	23	20
Baltimore	41	28	21	19
Medium Polarization				
Detroit	47	34	27	26
Boston	57	45	39	32
Minneapolis–St. Paul	60	47	27	34
San Francisco–Oakland	58	49	41	37
Cincinnati	41	34	21	25
Atlanta	48	41	26	31
Kansas City	52	47	27	40
Pittsburgh	43	35	22	24
Low Polarization				
Los Angeles	54	54	42	42
Houston	46	45	27	36
Seattle	56	56	31	43
Dallas	48	49	31	40
San Diego	54	55	38	41

Source: 1940 Census of Population, v.2; 1960 Census of Population, Tables 73, 74, 76 of State Reports in Series PC (1) C and PC (3) 1D, Table 8.

seen in relation to regions of the country in Table 3.6. This Table presents data on the proportions of the adult population (over 25) who have graduated from high school, comparing the central cities with the area outside central cities for twenty-three of the larger SMSAs. Those with a high polarization, or a relatively large excess of high school graduates outside of the central city, are all in the Northeast and Middle West. Those with little or no difference between central city and suburbs are on the West Coast or in Texas.

The same regional difference is seen in Table A–3 (page 319) which reports that college graduates are more likely to live outside the central city than in the central city, unless they are in the western states.

Table 3.7 throws more light on the matter with its report on regional differences in population growth in central cities and outside central cities. In 1930 the central cities of the North and East had practically stopped growing, while the suburbs were growing rapidly. In the West and South, however, central cities were growing vigorously, though not as rapidly as suburban areas. This means that the central cities of the West and South have had room to grow, partly by annexation of suburban areas and partly by build-

TABLE 3.7

Population Growth in Central Cities and Outside Central Cities by Regions: 1900–1960

	North and East %	*South* %	*West* %
1900–10			
Central Cities	32.4	41.2	89.0
Outside Central Cities	21.7	18.3	64.7
1910–20			
Central Cities	24.6	37.8	37.7
Outside Central Cities	20.8	10.3	39.2
1920–30			
Central Cities	18.8	38.3	45.1
Outside Central Cities	31.7	19.6	63.8
1930–40			
Central Cities	2.4	14.4	11.9
Outside Central Cities	9.7	23.7	29.3
1940–50			
Central Cities	7.4	29.9	33.0
Outside Central Cities	24.9	43.5	79.3
1950–60			
Central Cities	0.3	28.5	31.9
Outside Central Cities	43.7	47.7	65.9

Source: U.S. Census Bureau: *U.S. Census of Population: 1960 Selected Area Reports. Standard Metropolitan Statistical Areas.* Final Report PC(3)–1D.

ing on vacant property. Thus they have maintained attractiveness for the more affluent residents.

The factor of size of the SMSA is brought out in Table 3.8, which shows the ratio of the number of families with incomes over $10,000 (in 1959) to the number with incomes under $3,000, and gives these ratios for central city and outside central city in SMSAs of various sizes. This table shows that the smaller SMSAs are quite different from the larger ones in this respect. The smaller SMSAs have smaller ratios of affluent to poor families. The smaller SMSAs (those below 250,000 in population) have more of their high-income residents in the central city than outside.

The polarization of central city and suburb was further accentuated by the migration of southern rural blacks into the central cities after World War II. Table A–4 (page 319) shows how the growing numbers of blacks were distributed between central city and suburbs. After 1940 the proportion of nonwhites in central cities increased rapidly, while the proportion of nonwhites outside of central cities decreased slightly. Moreover, as seen in Table 3.5, the nonwhite population did not reflect the economic polarization within itself that was true of the white population. Middle- and low-income blacks were distributed evenly between suburbs and central cities.

TABLE 3.8

Ratio of Number of Families with Incomes over $10,000 to Families under $3,000 by SMSA Size: 1959

Population of SMSA	*Entire SMSA*	*Central City (CC)*	*Outside Central City (OCC)*	*Difference in Ratio: (OCC-CC)*
United States	124.2	93.9	169.4	75.5
Over 3,000,000	183.0	126.7	311.5	184.8
1,000,000 to 3,000,000	160.5	97.3	238.9	141.6
500,000 to 1,000,000	95.6	73.8	129.3	55.5
250,000 to 500,000	82.8	78.6	87.4	8.8
100,000 to 250,000	70.3	73.1	66.6	− 6.5
Less than 100,000	67.0	76.3	44.0	−32.3

Source: U.S. Bureau of the Census. *U.S. Census of Population: 1960, Selected Area Reports, Standard Metropolitan Statistical Areas.* True ratio is multiplied by 100.

As we shall see in the next section, there are forces tending to bring about a new balance between suburbs and central cities, and to reduce the economic polarization which probably reached a maximum during the 1960s. Leo Schnore (1963) studied central cities and their suburban fringes in 200 SMSAs, and he noted that in the newer metropolitan areas, central cities generally outrank the suburbs in occupation, education, and income. Table A–5 (page 320) shows how the age of the SMSA is related to polarization. He sees no basis for a prediction that the higher status groups in the new metropolitan areas will repeat the process of shifting to the suburbs.

STRATIFICATION OF SUBURBS

While the process of socio-economic stratification has gone on in the central city, the suburban area has not been an unmixed upper and upper-middle-class preserve, as might be supposed from the over-simple generalizations that sometimes are stated about polarization of suburb and central city. The area around the central city has independent villages and smaller cities which retain some of their character while the metropolitan area surrounds them and takes them over. There are favored directions of growth for high-status residential areas. The high-status suburbs may develop along a lake shore, or along the high banks of a river, or on the side of the city that itself has been a high-status section, or around a country club.

For example, the following account of the development of upper-class suburbs of Milwaukee shows the influence of a lake shore and a favored section of the central city. Richard Dewey (1948) described the experience of Milwaukee before 1950 as follows: "The clear-cut directional movement of the upper-class migration started with the move to the upper east side of Milwaukee proper, thence to Shorewood, Whitefish Bay, Fox Point, and River Hills. One climbs the social ladder by following this route, as is evidenced by the fact that the persons whose names are listed on the *Social Register* live almost exclusively in the areas named. Fox Point and River Hills have the greatest proportions of population listed in the *Social Register.*"

In other directions from the central city there may be heavy industry, or a swampy region, or city dumps, which make these directions unsatisfactory for middle-class suburbs. Thus the suburban area takes on a social structure, and the suburbs become differentiated into communities which are predominantly upper-middle, or lower-middle, or upper-working class. The city dweller who aspires to a house in the suburbs will find that the amount of money he can pay for a house determines the type of suburb he will live in. If he is employed as a manual worker in an auto assembly plant or an electronics factory located fifteen miles out of the city, he is likely to make a payment on a two-bedroom bungalow in a real estate development in which there are hundreds of similar houses, all variants of one basic design, all on small lots with a plot of grass in front, a garage and clothes-line in the rear. He will live in a working-class suburb. If he is a lawyer with an office in the city he will buy a ranch-type house on a large lot in an area where all other houses are of similar size and cost, in a new section of a well-established upper-middle-class suburb that has a reputation for good schools and a good country club.

The New York metropolitan complex shows this decentralized stratification more clearly than other centers, partly because of its size, and partly because it contains several large and mature industrial cities, such as Jersey City, Bayonne, Newark, Paterson, Passaic, and Elizabeth, none of which is part of the central city of New York. Members of the lower-working class live in Manhattan, Brooklyn, the Bronx, and in the Jersey industrial cities. Craftsmen and foremen live out beyond the lower-working class and also in some of the residential suburbs such as Mineola on Long Island, Tuckahoe in Westchester County, and Roselle Park in Union County. The upper-middle and upper classes live in Manhattan (on the upper East Side), in Westchester County to the north, Nassau County on Long Island, and Essex and Bergen counties in New Jersey.

The suburban stratification is partly due to decentralization of industry after World War II. After the war, there were various economic factors, as described in Chapter 2, that led to further decentralization of industry. In the 48 largest metropolitan areas, the proportion of manufacturing production workers living in the central cities declined from 67 percent in 1929 to 58 percent in 1954.

By the 1960s, the older, larger, and closer-in suburbs were developing their own structure, like that of the central city. An example of this kind of situation and its influence on the high school is seen in the Madison Township High School.

Madison is a small, semi-industrial city which has been surrounded by residential suburbs since World War II. Several of these small suburbs have elementary schools of their own, but send their teen-agers to Madison High School. Until recently the high school had a SER of approximately 1, with a cross-sectional student body including about 10 percent Negroes.

About five years ago a middle-class suburb five miles from Madison which had been sending its pupils to Madison High joined with a new suburb farther out to set up its own high school. This was somewhat disturbing to people in Madison, but just then a new middle-class residential area on the outskirts of Madison was being built, and it supplied a number of middle-class students who replaced the earlier group. This new suburb, Elmwood, continued to grow, and just last year established its own high school, which took away about one-fourth of the students of Madison High, and reduced the SER of Madison to .40. There is a black working-class suburb which sends its students to Madison, and appears to be content with this arrangement. But the faculty and the dwindling group of middle-class parents in Madison High are now fearful that their school will become a slum-type school, and they argue that the behavior of the Elmwood group in forming its own high school was undemocratic.

Types of Suburbs

In a contemporary complex metropolitan area there are suburbs of three major types. They are distinguished principally by differences in the ratio of the numbers of people who live in them to the numbers who work in them. More technically, this ratio consists of the number of members of the labor force who *live* in the suburb divided by the number of members of the labor force who *work* in the suburb. This ratio varies from 0.1, for a suburb in which nearly all the adult males commute to work in the central city, to 2.0, where most of the local adults plus a considerable number of people from outside the suburb come to work in the suburb.

A Dormitory Suburb. One in which at least half of the local residents work outside of the suburb, generally in the central city, though they may work in other parts of the metropolitan area is a dormitory suburb. There is nothing but small local business in this suburb. There are middle-class and working-class dormitory suburbs. For instance,

Glencoe and Park Forest of Chicago, Bronxville and Scarsdale of New York, Shaker Heights of Cleveland, Clayton of St. Louis, the Shawnee Mission district of Kansas City, San Mateo of San Francisco, Pasadena of Los Angeles, are middle-class suburbs of the metropolitan areas named. Working-class dormitory suburbs are more difficult to find. They generally are quite young, having been formed since World War II. There are black working-class dormitory suburbs, as well as those occupied by whites. For example, the town of Robbins, southwest of Chicago, has 10,000 residents, all black and nearly all working-class. They work in the industries of the southern suburbs of Chicago. There are about a dozen dormitory suburbs populated largely by white working-class people in the Chicago area.

An Employing Suburb. An employing suburb is one in which more than half of the local residents work in the suburb, while relatively few non-residents work there. It tends to be economically self-sufficient, and a kind of cross-section of the area in terms of socio-economic status. Those who work in this suburb are employed in local business, sometimes in a local college, in the area's airport, often in a light industry such as electronics or plastics, or in a business estabishment such as the regional office of an insurance company. Examples in the Chicago area are Evanston, Blue Island, and Des Plaines. Owing to the post-war decentralization of industry, employing suburbs have grown rapidly since World War II.

A Manufacturing Suburb. One which imports workers for its industry is a manufacturing suburb. Most of the people living in this suburb work in local business and industry, which is likely to be one or more large manufacturing plants—steel products, electric products, airplanes, automobiles, chemicals, etc. Examples in the Chicago area are Chicago Heights, Cicero, and Melrose Park. In terms of socio-economic ranking, this type of suburb generally falls somewhat below average, having a higher proportion of manual workers than the average of the metropolitan area.

All three types of suburbs have grown rapidly since World War II. In the North and East the dormitory suburbs have grown more rapidly than the other types, in the large metropolitan areas. But this is probably not true of smaller SMSAs and of those in the West.

The New Balance

It appears that a new balance between suburb and central city is becoming established. The economic and racial polarization between them has probably reached its maximum and may be receding. From now on it is likely that the suburbs and central cities will become more like one another, rather than more different from one another.

The forces which were to bring about the new balance were already dimly visible by 1960. For instance, one of the new postwar suburbs of New York City, Levittown on Long Island, became less middle class and more working class in composition between 1950 and 1960. Whereas 62 percent of the adult males were in white-collar occupations in 1950–51, the proportion dropped to 50 percent in 1961. (Dobriner, 1958, p. 98.)

The suburbs tend to decrease in average socio-economic status for two reasons. One is the decentralization of metropolitan industry and business. Light industry; big shopping centers; and the central and regional offices of certain kinds of business, such as insurance companies, are being located in suburbs. Many lower-middle- and working-class employees of these concerns seek to live nearby and thus build up new "common man" residential areas. The other reason is that the older suburbs are becoming obsolescent, following the patterns of the central cities, and higher-status families move from there out to newer suburbs, or back into the central city.

There is also a "reverse migration" that takes place from suburbs to the central city. As urban renewal clears old buildings from attractive sites, new middle- and high-income homes and apartments are built, which offer space to people who prefer to live in the central city. There has been a good deal of such rebuilding since 1950, and probably more since 1960 than during the previous decade. However, the volume of reverse migration is low, according to the information now available. Karl M. Taeuber and Alma F. Taeuber (1964) studied migration between central city and suburban areas in the 12 largest metropolitan areas for the years 1955–1960. They found that migration from suburbs to central city within a given SMSA was one-sixth as great as migration from the central city to the suburban area. The in- and out-migrants were better educated than the non-migrants.

Census bureau estimates suggest that the movement of people from the central cities to the suburbs has continued at a high rate throughout the 1960s. White population gains in the suburbs averaged about 1.7 million per year between 1960 and 1966, and 1.3 million per year between 1966 and 1968. Black population gains in suburbs increased to 221,000 per year in the latter period, compared to 19,000 per year in the former. However, we may speculate that the volume of migration from suburbs to central city is increasing during the current decade. But, the people who migrate into the central city are probably largely older people without children of school age or young people who are just starting their families.

Another evidence of the growing similarity of suburbs and central city is the growth of Roman Catholic schools in the suburbs. Since 1950 the Catholic school enrollments in central cities have just about stayed constant, while their enrollments in suburban areas have increased sharply. This means that Roman Catholic city dwellers have been migrating to the suburbs, which earlier were largely Protestant.

Speaking of the *new balance* between suburbs and central city does not signify that the balance has arrived in 1970. The next ten years may see a substantial movement toward this balance, and it would be registered in the educational field as early as anywhere else.

THE PATHOLOGY OF SOCIO-ECONOMIC AND RACIAL SEGREGATION

It may be argued that people are exercising a democratic freedom of choice when they form neighborhoods or residential areas of people like themselves. People tend to feel comfortable when their neighbors have the same style of life that they have. They like to have their children grow up with children from families like their own. Consequently, it may be argued, it is not only natural but also desirable that there should be homogeneous areas of the city, and that suburbs should be socially homogeneous communities.

On the other hand, one of the foundations of democracy is the cooperation of its members in government and other forms of social activity. Such cooperation is likely to be increased and improved if people of various social, economic, and racial backgrounds mingle freely and get to know and understand one another. This argues for heterogeneous residential communities, in which the children and the adults of various social groups associate freely in schools, churches, libraries, parks and political and social activities.

Furthermore, a democratic society establishes and maintains as much opportunity as possible for social and economic betterment of the individual. This requires that the individual have opportunity to study with, work with, and grow up with people who have the characteristics he wants to acquire—the attitudes toward work, the language habits, the social manners—which he needs in order to achieve his socially valuable aims in life.

Arrangements for living and working in a metropolitan area are affected by these arguments. Since men can influence the social structure of the metropolitan area by adopting and applying social policies, there are efforts to direct and control the impersonal forces of society so as to improve the conditions under which they and their children live and work.

One aspect of society which nearly everybody agrees is pathological stems from poverty and its correlates. Along with poverty go unemployment, crime, juvenile delinquency, bad housing, broken families, and residential segregation. The social measures so far adopted to combat poverty are not fully satisfactory. Public welfare payments to poor people, aid to mothers of dependent children who do not have husbands to support them, subsidized public housing in large segregated settlements, are well-intentioned, but they do not get at the causes of poverty.

Meanwhile, poor people tend to be segregated, and the segregation of the poor does not contribute to the cure of poverty.

One way by which poverty has been segregated in the United States is through subsidized housing. On the one hand the federal government has subsidized the construction of predominantly middle-income areas, primarily through income tax reductions for middle-class home owners. In 1962, for example, the federal government subsidy for housing middle-income Americans (mostly in stratified middle-income communities) was nearly three billion dollars. On the other hand, the government has made grants to local government agencies for the clearing of slums and the building of public housing projects which are then rented to low-income families at below-cost rents, depending on family income and size. The local housing authority, which receives the government funds, constructs the new houses and administers the project, generally locating the new project in an area that has been cleared of slum buildings. It generally builds high-rise apartment buildings, though sometimes it builds blocks of two- or three-story buildings spread over an area of one or two city blocks. The typical housing project contains two to three hundred apartments with a thousand or more residents. For example, in 1965 Washington, D.C. had 37 projects housing 8,400 families with 41,500 people. To qualify for public housing, a family's annual income in the Washington projects could not exceed $3,200 to $5,100, depending on the size of the family. Once a family was admitted, the income could rise to $4,000 to $6,400, again depending on size; and a family which succeeded in getting above these income levels was forced to leave the project.

After some initial attempts to maintain a policy of integrated residence in public housing projects, most housing authorities practiced segregation, operating some projects for whites and some for blacks. In many cities, there was a predominance of black residents. For instance, the *Washington Post* of December 18, 1965, reported that 98 percent of Washington's public housing residents were blacks. At the same time, 92 percent of Chicago's public housing citizens were blacks.

Recently the public housing authorities have been trying to avoid segregation based on economic status and race through small four- or six- family houses which can be built on vacant lots in any part of the city. Although most all-white and middle-class communities have objected to having even small public housing units in their midst, a few such communities have requested the local housing authority build this type of project.

There is also some discussion of allowing residents of public housing projects to stay as long as they please, no matter what their income, and using a sliding scale of rents which rises to a level the same as that for private housing when the family's income rises above the poverty level. This would have the effect of building local leadership from the more successful families in housing projects. Under current policies such families are expelled because they are economically successful. This plan would also result in making public housing projects more nearly self-supporting, and by giving people a choice between renting from a public housing project and renting from a private corporation or landlord at the same rates, would bring public housing into competition with the real estate business.

Is Segregation Always Bad?

Any form of segregation that is forced upon a person against his will is likely to be opposed and resisted by him. Therefore a democratic society tries to maintain as much freedom as possible for its members to go where they wish, to live where they wish, and to work where they wish. Segregation may be imposed as punishment, as in the case of sending a person who has committed a crime to prison or sending a child who has misbehaved to his room.

If, under freedom of choice, people of a similar economic status, nationality background, or skin color get together in their own social organizations and residential communities, this is acceptable in a democratic society as long as they do not monopolize some scarce good, such as a lake shore, a park, choice schools, and the like. Thus a certain amount of freely-chosen segregation is to be expected in a democracy.

However, a democracy depends for its welfare on the welfare of all of its citizens, and therefore must provide opportunity for all of them to share in the things that are important to the good life for them—education, business activity, employment, use of public facilities such as hotels, restaurants, transit lines. A democracy cannot systematically deny full opportunity in these areas to any of its members and still be a democracy in fact as well as in name.

This is the reason that *de facto* segregation in schools, whether along racial lines or along socio-economic lines, is bad for a democracy. Since it has been proven to the satisfaction of the United States Supreme Court that segregation by race in the public schools is a denial of opportunity to the minority racial group, racial segregation is now officially believed to be undesirable, whether it be expressed through law or through custom.

But socio-economic segregation is also undesirable, in the eyes of people who believe in democracy and who have studied the effects of such segregation or stratification in the schools. From social scientists who have studied the relation of schools to society, from judges who have studied the significance of the American Constitution for the educational system, and from social philosophers and religious leaders, has come a common agreement on the importance of the school as a place where boys and girls from all social groups can learn together. It has been affirmed by the courts that schools that are limited by law or by residential segregation to blacks are not good for black youth, and should be changed. It has been found by social scientists that schools attended predominantly by children of lower socio-economic status do not succeed in teaching these children as well as do schools of mixed socio-economic composition.

EFFECTS OF SOCIO-ECONOMIC AND RACIAL STRATIFICATION AND SEGREGATION IN THE SCHOOLS

Every school has its own special characteristics: special folkways, customs, and legends. Not only do schools have different insignia, songs, and symbols, but they differ in less tangible ways. In one school the relationships between teachers and pupils are unusually intimate and friendly; in another, unusually formal. One school has an atmosphere of regimentation; another emphasizes individual differences among pupils. In one school, competition is played up; in another, it is played down. There is often a special history and tradition that develops. In one case, students may feel fierce pride in their school and its accomplishments. In another, there may be a feeling of resignation among both children and adults, as if mediocrity is all that can be expected in any school endeavor.

The culture of the school has a profound effect upon what children and adolescents learn and the ways in which they learn. There is a saying that children learn not what is taught, but what is "caught." Much of what is caught (attitudes toward learning, toward authority, values of right and wrong, and so on) comes not from the formal curriculum but from the pervading culture of the school.

In a school there is usually a dominant group of students which defines and establishes the *ethos* of the school. When the dominant group of students is in accord with the values and expectations of the teachers and the parents, the resulting ethos or set of values has a strong effect upon nearly all students. When the parents and teachers expect a school to prepare most of its students for college, the school program reflects this expectation, and the students share the expectation. But when the parents have no educational goal for the children beyond high school, and if teachers get the notion that the students in this school cannot learn well, the ethos of the school reflects this set of expectations, and it affects the performance of most of the students.

In this same connection, a study (Wilson, 1959) of eight different high schools in the San Francisco–Oakland Bay area provided good evidence that the ethos of a given school affects the academic achievement and occupational aspirations of its students in measurable degree. The eight schools varied considerably with regard to the proportion of students who came from families of different occupational levels, and thus showed differences in regard to the climate of values that prevailed. It was found that in schools that were predominantly lower status (the majority of fathers were manual workers), the *proportion of middle-class boys* who planned to go to college was significantly lower than in schools of predominantly middle-class students. Congruently, a lower-status boy attending a school in which the majority of his classmates were middle class (their fathers were upper-level white-collar or professional workers) was more likely to plan to go to college than if he attended a school in which the majority of his classmates were working class. The investigator interpreted these findings as evidence that the school milieu and peer-group norms can significantly modify the effects of social class in influencing the adolescent's values.

Furthermore, Wilson found that the school environment affected the grades obtained by a boy. A working-class boy attending a school with a predominance of middle-class pupils was more likely to get good grades than a working-class boy *of the same IQ* who attended a school with a predominance of working-class pupils.

Wilson (1963) also studied the elementary schools of Berkeley, California, and found that a child of a particular social class and ethnic group would achieve differently in a school of one socio-economic composition than he would in a school of another socio-economic composition.

A similar finding is reported by Havighurst and his associates in their study of school dropouts in River City. Boys and girls who dropped out without graduating from high school were paired with others of the same IQ and socio-economic status who did graduate from high school. The stay-ins lived in areas and went to elementary schools of higher socio-economic status than the dropouts, on the average. (Havighurst, Bowman et al., 1962, p. 184.)

More evidence on the influence of *type of school* upon the educational aspiration and educational achievement of students is given in the next chapter, and comes from the study of types of high schools in the Kansas City metropolitan area.

The following two cases illustrate the influence of the ethos of a school upon educational achievement. In both cases the boy was above average in learning ability, but not superior.

Case of Sidney, 17 years old. Sidney started school in 1952, attending Kelly school, and transferred to Holmes, Roosevelt, and Douglas elementary schools in that order. As far as he remembers there was not much difference among them except for Roosevelt. The class at Roosevelt was behind the comparable class at Holmes, and Sidney just loafed through that year. Douglas was harder, and he worked harder.

Sidney started ninth grade at Washington High School in 1960.This school had an SER of .22 and had 35 percent of its ninth-grade class in Basic English, which meant that they were reading below the sixth-grade level. After four semesters, Sidney's family moved to the south side and he transferred to Jefferson High School, which had an SER of 2.50. He continued in the College Preparatory Course of Study. At Washington, Sidney had been an average student, with grades of C and B. His weakest subject was math. In his first semester at Jefferson school he almost failed, receiving grades of D and E. There were four courses he continued at Jefferson school which were started at Washington:

English: At Jefferson there was more required reading and thus a faster reading speed was important. They were more thorough in testing what was read. At Washington he could "bluff" his way through with little effort. He had developed bad study habits due to a lack of demand on the part of the teachers and his own "goofing off." His reading was slow although in grammar school he had had a high reading rate. The same series of books were used and others in addition were of the same caliber in both high schools. However, at Jefferson they were further advanced.

French: At Washington, Sidney had six different teachers in his first semester. They started the first chapter six times. There was little work required. At Jefferson he found himself very far far behind, and passed with a C after receiving a D at midterm. At Jefferson the books were newer and much more was required.

History: He had taken a history course in his first semester at Washington and was considered an outstanding student, although he exerted little effort. His first semester at Jefferson, he took another history course and found it much more difficult.

Music: Both schools were just about equally good. Washington has an outstanding band and is noted for this. Sidney has a special interest in music and received top grades at both schools.

In Sidney's experience the teachers at Jefferson were older, better and more stable. Washington had many more subs, especially in history and language. Subs are very rarely used at Jefferson. Washington places a great deal more stress on sports, especially basketball, than Jefferson. In fact it stresses sports more than scholastic standing. Jefferson has more of a variety of sports and they are not stressed above scholastic standing.

Sidney has buckled down to work and is now making above average grades at Jefferson High. This will get him into a selective college. More important, since he is up against stiff competition at Jefferson, he will not find college work much more demanding than his high school work now is.

Case of Donald, 21 years old. Donald graduated 10th in a class of 110 in an all-black high school with an SER of .28. With an IQ of 112, and scoring at the 83rd percentile of the college aptitude test, he had done constantly superior work in science and mathematics. It seemed a good choice when he entered the school of engineering at the state university. His father and mother were both high school graduates, and his father had a stable job as maintenance man.

Donald wrote, as a high school senior:

"For as long as I can remember, I have always wanted to go to college and become a mechanical engineer.

"I attend the AME Church where I help teach a young boys' class in Sunday School. The children are very nice and usually want to learn, so I get a joy from being able to share my knowledge with them. I enjoy reading and working difficult mathematical problems. My hobby is tinkering with motors of all kinds.

"My family is behind me one hundred percent."

His teachers recommended him highly, though one of them commented, "With a little more aggressiveness, Donald could develop into an outstanding college prospect."

Donald got all C's and D's in his first year and was placed on scholastic probation. The next year he repeated a mathematics course but did not get a good start and withdrew from school until the second semester, when he started again. This time he withdrew after six weeks, and gave up on his college career. He took a civil service examination and got a job in an office in the city government.

Donald had the misfortune to go through a high school with relatively low standards, and he never learned what was expected of a student who could do acceptable work in a good engineering school. It seems probable that if he had attended Jefferson school, the one Sidney is now attending, he would have learned the study habits and skills that he so badly needed when he entered college.

Both of these boys were affected by the school environment, which in turn was affected by the stratification of the metropolitan area.

Consequences of Metropolitan Stratification for School Finances

Social stratification tends also to produce a growing disparity in ability to support education between the central city school district on the one hand and suburban school districts on the other. Until the 1950s average per pupil expenditure in the central cities was higher than in the suburbs. However, with the movement of low-income families to the cities and the exodus of middle-income families to the suburbs, the central cities began to lose much of their ability to raise funds for education. With the central cities' populations consisting increasingly of elderly citizens on fixed incomes and disadvantaged adults lacking opportunities and skills to earn high incomes, with taxes for sanitation, police, and other public services rising very rapidly, and with much of their land given over to tax-free institutions such as museums, colleges, and sports facilities that serve the entire metropolitan area, many central cities began to find it nearly impossible to raise substantial tax levies and pass bond issues for public education. Despite the greater difficulties involved in educating disadvantaged students as compared to middle-class students and despite the wide variations which exist in capacity to support education in suburban school districts, by 1969 it was estimated that the average central city per pupil expenditure on education was only two-thirds that of the average suburban expenditure.

Information concerning the relative difficulties encountered in supporting education in central city and suburban school districts is given in Tables 3.9 and 3.10. Table 3.9 presents data on per capita income and expenditure in the 37 largest metropolitan areas for the 1964–1965 school year. These data show that central city families

TABLE 3.9
Fiscal Disparities Between Central City and Outside Central City Governments in the 37 Largest Standard Metropolitan Statistical Areas, 1964

	Median Family Income	*Per Capita Income*	*Per Capita Taxes*	*Taxes as Percent of Income*	*Per Pupil School Exp.*	*Per Capita School Exp.*	*School Expenditures as Percent of Gen. Exp.*
Central Cities	$5,940	$2,607	$199.53	7.63	$449	$ 82	27.9
Outside Central Cities	6,707	2,732	152.10	5.55	573	113	52.5

Source: Advisory Commission on Intergovernmental Relations, *Fiscal Balance in the American Federal System.* Volume 2. Metropolitan Fiscal Disparities, Washington, D.C.: U.S. Government Printing Office, 1967.

were poorer, on the average, than families outside the central city, and although per capita taxes were nearly one-third higher inside than outside the central cities, per pupil expenditures on education in the central cities were considerably below per pupil expenditures elsewhere in the metropolitan area.

Table 3.10 presents information on relative tax effort in the twenty-two largest metropolitan areas in 1962. Data in this table show that per capita tax effort in the central cities of these SMSAs was considerably higher than in the suburbs, but that the gap would have been much less had not taxpayers in the central city had a heavier burden financing welfare services, health services, and educational programs for disadvantaged students.

In a special report in the magazine *Nation's Cities*, the National League of Cities has taken note of such figures and has pointed out that problems associated with welfare and health and with education and other services for the poor are not

> . . . local problems or local responsibilities in the same sense, or to anything like the same degree, that police and fire protection, water supply, garbage collection, sewage disposal, parks and playgrounds, local streets, off-street parking, suburban com-

TABLE 3.10

Measures of Tax Effort in Central Cities and Suburbs in 22 Largest Standard Metropolitan Statistical Areas, 1962

	Adjusted Tax Revenue					
	Actual Tax Revenue		*Total Tax Revenue Minus Estimated Local Expenditures for Public Welfare, Health and Hospitals*		*Total Tax Revenue Minus Estimated Local Expenditures for Public Welfare, Health, Hospitals and Education of Children in Families with Incomes Less Than $3,000*	
	Cities	*Suburbs*	*Cities*	*Suburbs*	*Cities*	*Suburbs*
Mean per capita tax revenue as percent of per capita income	7.6	5.7	6.3	5.1	5.8	4.8

Source: National Education Association, *Financial Status of the Public Schools,* Washington, D.C.: NEA Committee on Educational Finance, 1968, p. 51.

mutation and urban mass transportation are local responsibilities. Half the people on relief in about every city and half the ward patients in the city hospitals came there from somewhere else; half the children in the city schools came from somewhere else and will grow up to work somewhere else. ("What Kind of City Do We Want?," *Nation's Cities,* April, 1967, p. 29.)

Not only are the problems of poverty and inadequate education metropolitan and national in their origins and effects, the League argues, but central governments in other industrial nations take account of this situation by paying all or nearly all of the costs of free public education for all citizens. The report concludes that since much of this burden falls on big city governments in the United States, the cities are forced to "cripple themselves financially" in order to subsidize the federal government.

RESPONSE OF THE SCHOOL SYSTEM

There are two alternative approaches to the solution of the problems of socio-economic and racial stratification in the metropolitan area. One is a process of adaptation to the trends of metropolitan evolution; the other is a bold and fundamental effort at reversing some of these trends, and at designing and building the metropolitan area of the future with appropriate physical and institutional features. Both approaches require cooperation by the schools, and both approaches involve considerable changes in school programs and school organization.

Adapting to Existing Trends

The policy of adaptation to existing metropolitan trends assumes that the future structure of metropolitan areas will follow present trends. The belt of lower-class residential areas around the center of the city will expand and grow wider. The flight of middle-class families to the suburbs will continue. Suburbs will increase in number and size and variety. Low cost public housing will gradually make a physical improvement in the "grey areas" and will result in physical renewal of slums. Expressways will give automobile owners quicker and more comfortable access to all parts of the area. The present trend toward residential segregation by socio-economic status will continue, together with at least as much racial segregation as now exists. Only a few small counter-trends will be seen, such as the construction of expensive apartment houses near the center of the city for well-to-do people who have few school-age children, and the growth of working-class suburbs.

Educational Adaptations

The major educational adaptations will consist of attempts to provide educational stimulation and opportunity to the children of the slum areas, combined with identifying the abler children and separating them in special classes in the school. This approach will involve:

I. *A Multi-track System* which separates children into several different groups according to learning ability and social status. This has the effect of maintaining at least one sub-group with fairly strong academic motivation in a school that is located in a slum area or is threatened by encroaching slums. The children of higher social status tend to be placed in the superior group, which makes the school more tolerable for their parents. Whatever may be the value of homogeneous grouping in helping children to achieve according to the level of their intelligence (and this is repeatedly questioned by research studies), there is no doubt that teachers and parents alike favor a multi-track system in a school where the SER has fallen below the critical point. This is because the multi-track organization gives some assurance to middle-class parents and to working-class parents who seriously want their children to get the most out of education that their particular children will be given special help and special consideration.

II. *Enrichment Programs* for working-class children who achieve fairly well. This is a supplement to the multi-track program, and involves placing the more promising children in smaller classes, giving them special counseling and guidance, encouraging their parents to take more interest in their education, and giving them access to museums, libraries, theaters, and concerts. A widely-known example is the Higher Horizons program of Junior High School No. 43, Manhattan, and the George Washington High School of New York City (Hillson, 1963). This program stimulated a considerable group of boys and girls to graduate from high school and to enter college who would not have done so if they had not received special attention. Financial assistance for college attendance is a necessary part of such a program.

Since the New York City project, scores of similar projects have been developed for high school youth who are doing fairly well in school but give evidence of being able to do really superior work if they are stimulated and given higher standards to work for. A number of private schools and colleges offer special summer schools for such youth, with frequently a preference for black youth, on the ground that there is more unrealized potential in this group than in white working-class youth, who have not suffered so much from discrimination. Also, several public school systems have experimental scholarship-fund programs which recruit potentially able youth in the early high school years and guide them toward college, with a promise of a college scholarship if they do well in high school.

III. *Enrichment Programs* for culturally disadvantaged children at the pre-school and kindergarten-primary level. A number of large cities are trying out a type of program that gives special assistance to the primary grades in the slum schools, on the theory that many of these children lack parental examples and stimulation from parents to read and to achieve well in school. They fail to master the task of reading, and stumble along for the first few years in school, after which they become confirmed non-learners, and tend to be social misfits in the school during their adolescence. By putting specially-trained teachers into relatively small classes, by using a social worker or visiting teacher to bring the home and school into contact, and by giving the children a variety of enriching experiences which middle-class children are more likely to get in their homes, these children will get a better start in school and thus a better start in life.

Assisted with funds under the Economic Opportunity Act of 1964, and the Elementary and Secondary Education Act of 1965, a vast program of "compensatory education" is now under way at the pre-school and kindergarten-primary levels.

IV. *Work-Study Programs for Alienated Youth.* Under present conditions some 15 percent of boys and girls fail to grow up successfully through the avenue provided by the schools. They become non-learners, and react to the school either with hostility and aggression or with apathy after about the sixth grade. In slum areas this proportion is likely to reach 25 or 30 percent. These children are alienated from the values and ways of behaving of the school and other middle-class institutions. It is these boys and girls who make teaching so difficult at the seventh, eighth, and ninth grades, and who make the junior high school and the early years of senior high school so difficult for academically-motivated youth in schools where the SER is low. For alienated youth, especially for the boys, there is a good deal of experimentation with work-study programs which aim to give these youth a chance to grow up satisfactorily through the avenue of work.

V. *Suburban Developments.* If present trends continue, it appears that educational programs in the central city will be increasingly aimed at providing opportunities for working-class youth in relation to their abilities and needs, while the suburbs are likely to be the scene of experimentation with ideas and materials aimed at higher standards of educational performance for middle-class youth. The suburbs will have more money to work with than will the central city, and their predominantly middle-class character will make them responsive to proposals for the use of new methods, new kinds of school buildings, and new types of school programs.

Educational Programs for a Transition Period

It now appears that a number of metropolitan areas are ready for a fundamental program of urban renewal that will have the cooperation of suburbs with central city. The evidence for this proposition will be developed in the next three chapters. Such a program would need to provide for a transitional period of perhaps twenty years, during which time the planned-for metropolitan organism would emerge from the present metropolitan chaos.

Certain educational policies would need to be adopted for the transitional period, aimed at: (1) stopping the flight of middle-class people from the central city, and (2) building self-contained communities of 50,000 to 200,000 people, which are cross-sections of the social composition of the entire area. Some policies would be temporary, while others would become permanent parts of educational policy for the metropolitan area of the future.

The call is for the *mixed school*—the school with a mixture of socio-economic groups and a mixture of racial groups where there are such groups in the community. The mixture need not necessarily reflect the exact composition of the city, but it should not be more than perhaps 50 percent black, or 60 percent working-class, according to the judgment of practical people who have been working with the problem of social integration.

The mixed secondary school is practically a necessity for the success of what is being called *social urban renewal.* In distinction to *physical urban renewal,* social urban renewal consists of the redevelopment of the central city so that all kinds of people—rich and poor, black and white—will want to live there and raise their children there. This means that there will be large areas of the central city in which middle-class and working-class people will live, and blacks and whites will live, within a few blocks of each other if not in the same block. But those who can afford to move to another area or to a suburb will not stay in a local community if they do not like the schools, and middle-class people will not live in an area where they must send their children to a school that is dominated by working-class children. White people will not live in an area where they must send their children to a school dominated by black children. On the other hand, working-class parents and black parents will send their children to schools dominated by middle-class or by white children, because they think the standards of such schools are better.

Therefore, to serve the process of social urban renewal, the schools must be organized *as far as possible* as mixed schools. The phrase *as far as possible* is important here, because it may be impossible to organize all elementary schools as mixed schools, since they serve such small geographic areas and are likely to continue to serve a neighborhood. It may be impossible, also, to organize all secondary schools as mixed schools, in an area which is predominantly working class or black. In such a case, the concept of the regional high school district is useful. This is a district containing several high schools, where students have considerable degree of choice among the schools. There may have to be one school that is predominantly black in such a district, or one school that is predominantly working-class through its location; but there should be at least one and preferably more mixed schools in a high school regional district, thus making that region acceptable to all families in the region who insist on their children's attending a school with a substantial white middle-class college preparatory group.

This chapter can be summarized by saying that metropolitan development as it has taken place in America during the present century has made it more difficult for boys and girls to get a good education, both in and out of school. The schools have been handicapped by the growing economic and racial stratification of the metropolitan area. Urban renewal of a fundamental kind will restore and create educational values in the city. But urban renewal cannot take place without substantial changes in educational organization and policy.

SUGGESTED ACTIVITIES

1. Study the suburbs of your metropolitan area. What was the pattern of growth? Where did the high-status suburbs develop, and why? Are there any working-class suburbs? How did they develop? Are

there any black suburbs or suburban neighborhoods? How did they develop?

2. Select a particular suburb and study its development. How did it get started? Was it an independent community before it became a suburb? What was its social structure in earlier periods and what is it now?
3. Make a socio-economic classification of the suburbs or suburban districts in your metropolitan area, using the typology suggested in this chapter.
4. If you are acquainted with a school in an area that has changed its character rapidly, describe these changes and how the school was related to them.
5. Write a report on public housing in your area and discuss its contribution in making the area a better place to live.
6. Interview several inner-city parents to find out what they consider to be the major problems in raising children in a low-income area.

SUGGESTIONS FOR FURTHER READING

1. An interesting set of readings about suburban life will be found in *The Suburban Community* edited by William Dobriner. Compare this book with *The Exurbanites* by Auguste C. Spectorsky.
2. Several of the large metropolitan areas have been subjects for extensive research and writing about their past, present, and future. A general discussion may be found in *The Exploding Metropolis* by the editors of *Fortune,* published as a paperback. Of special interest is the New York Metropolitan Region Study, made under the auspices of the Graduate School of Public Administration of Harvard University. The Harvard University Press is publishing a series of books on this research; the last volume to appear is entitled *Metropolis, 1985,* by Raymond Vernon. Jean Gottmann's *Megalopolis* gives a striking account of metropolitan development in the chain of urban areas stretching from Boston to Washington, D.C.
3. A provocative book by Jane Jacobs is *The Death and Life of Great American Cities.* Mrs. Jacobs believes that much of modern physical city planning destroys the values of neighborhood life. She argues for more attention to *social* rather than *physical* factors in urban renewal.
4. For graphic descriptions of the extreme difficulties youngsters experience growing up in a big city slum read *Manchild in the Promised Land* by Claude Brown and *Down These Mean Streets* by Piri Thomas. Contrast these books with the experiences of earlier inner-city groups such as the Jews, the Irish, or the Italians.

5. *The Social Order of the Slums* by Suttles, *The Airtight Cage* by Lyford, and *Tally's Corner* by Liebow provide excellent case study material from observers who lived in the inner city.
6. A national survey of educational achievement in relation to socio-economic status and racial segregation was directed by James S. Coleman on behalf of the United States Office of Education. Entitled *Equality of Educational Opportunity*, this big book will be a landmark of educational research. Data are given on educational achievement by children of various minority groups as well as by children of various socio-ecomomic status.
7. Philip Hauser's 1968 presidential address titled "The Social Morphological Revolution," given to the American Sociological Association (printed in the *American Sociological Review*) summarizes much of the evidence dealing with the effects of stratification and segregation in metropolitan society.

CHAPTER 4

Schools in the Metropolitan Area

AMONG THE 20,173 operating public school districts that existed in 1967, 706 of them accounted for 20.4 million pupils, or 46 percent of the total number. These districts all had more than 10,000 pupils, and nearly all of them were in metropolitan areas. In addition, there were another 4,500 smaller districts located in metropolitan areas. Table 4.1 shows how school districts are distributed according to enrollment size in metropolitan areas. In 1967, 97 percent of public school enrollment in metropolitan areas was in school systems with more than 1200 pupils.

Public school enrollments in 1968 were distributed as follows between central cities, outside central cities in metropolitan areas, and outside metropolitan areas: 26, 39, 35 percent, respectively.

SOCIO-ECONOMIC CHARACTERISTICS OF SCHOOLS IN THE METROPOLITAN AREA

With such a large number of schools, and with such diversity as exists in a complex metropolitan area, it is useful to think about these schools in terms of socio-economic characteristics.

TABLE 4.1

Public School Systems Inside and Outside of SMSAs; 1967

A. *Enrollment Size of School Systems*

No. of Pupils Per System	*Total No. of Pupils in SMSAs (000)*	*Number of School Systems*	
		In SMSAs	*Outside of SMSAs*
1200 or more	27,503	3,112	3,468
300–1,199	855	1,218	4,344
150–299	72	333	1,758
50–149	35	358	1,872
15–49	6	201	2,472
1–14	1	57	2,329
Nonoperating		250	1,618
	28,472	5,529	17,861

B. *Number of Public Schools*

IN SYSTEMS WITH:	*In SMSAs*	*Outside of SMSAs*
20 or more schools	22,101	6,085
10–19	7,682	9,801
3–9	11,266	18,761
2	1,162	4,154
1	1,542	9,373
	43,753	48,174

Source: U.S. Bureau of the Census, *Census of Governments:* 1967, Vol. 1. Governmental Organization Tables 2, 17, pp. 24, 25, 89.

SERs in Various Schools

In Figure 4.1 the social class compositions of three quite different high schools are shown, together with their respective SERs. School B is a typical comprehensive high school in an employing suburb, or in a town or small city which has only one high school that serves all the students or a cross-section of the population. The total high-school population will not be distributed in the same way as the elementary school population, or the ninth grade alone, because some of the high-school students drop out of school without graduating. Hence the actual SER is not .6, as it would be in a cross-sectional elementary school, but instead is approximately 1.0.

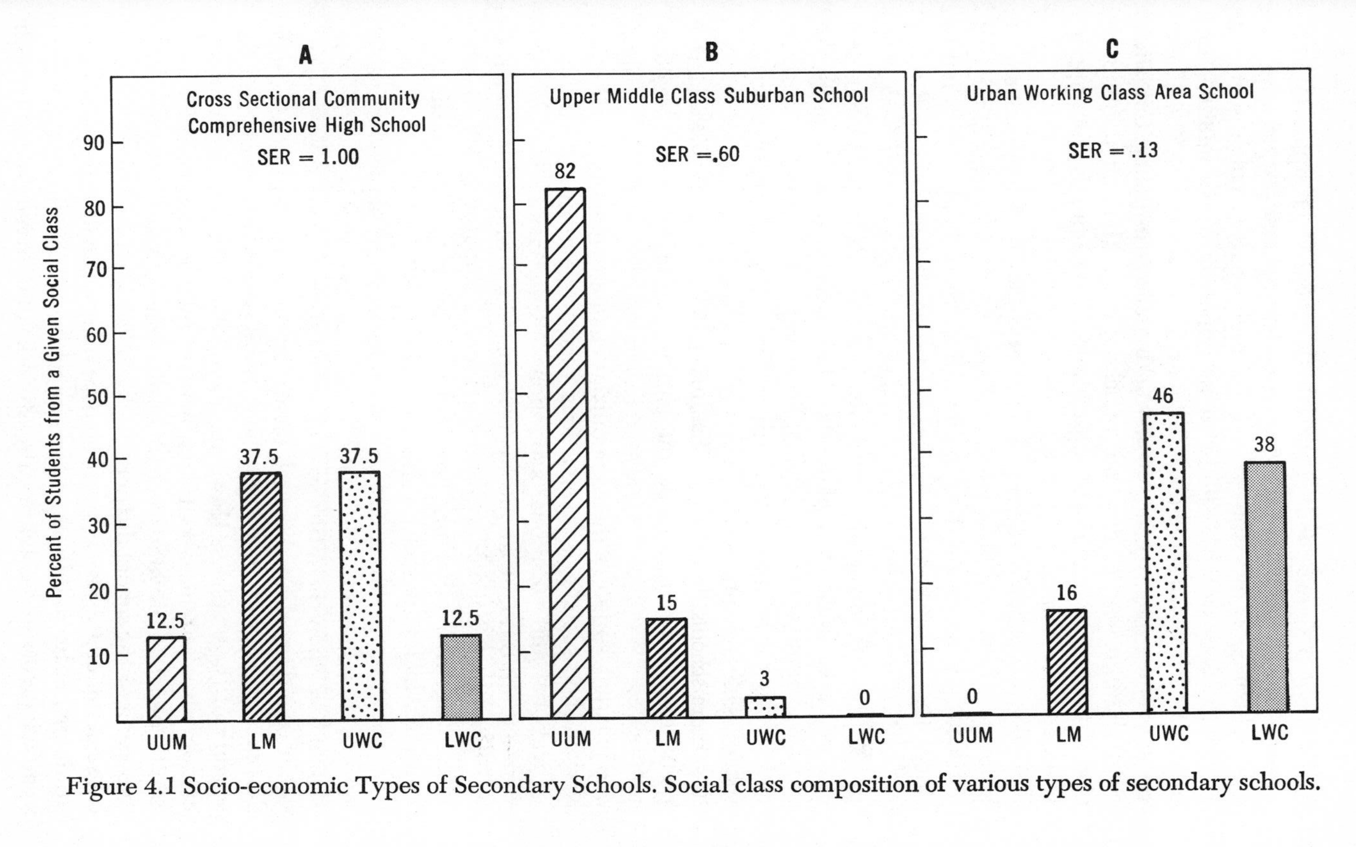

Figure 4.1 Socio-economic Types of Secondary Schools. Social class composition of various types of secondary schools.

School B shows the SER of a high school in an upper-middle-class suburb, where there are very few working-class people.

School C shows the SER of a high school which serves a working-class area where there are no upper- or upper-middle-, and only a few lower-middle-class families. In such an area there may be an actual majority of lower-working-class residents, but since their children tend to drop out of school early, the actual composition of the high school shows a preponderance of pupils from upper-working-class homes.

There is probably a critical point in the SER of most schools, a point at which middle-class parents are likely to become anxious and consider removing their children from the school. This is not to imply that parents tend to think in terms of the SER itself; but rather that middle-class parents, as they become aware of increasing proportions of lower-class students in a school, begin to fear the effects upon their own children. They may fear a drop in the academic standards of the school, or changes in curricular offerings, or unwelcome influences upon their own children's motivations for school achievement.

Parenthetically, it might be noted, with regard to the latter point, that such attitudes on the part of parents are not altogether unfounded. We have already referred to the study by Wilson (1959) that supports the generalization that when student bodies vary in their social class proportions, their students develop different educational and vocational aspirations. Wilson says, "The *de facto* segregation brought about by concentrations of social classes in cities results in schools with unequal moral climates which likewise affect the motivation of the child . . . by providing a different ethos in which to perceive values." (Wilson, 1959, p. 845.)

The point at which a school becomes undesirable in the eyes of middle-class parents (the critical point in the SER) is subjective, depending upon the attitudes and experience of a particular parent, and depending also upon such factors as the tradition of the school, the racial composition of the school, the type of curriculum, and the quality of the teachers. However, there is enough consensus among middle-class parents about such matters so that they tend to agree on the question of when a school has become a "poor" school, and to move out of the school district.

Secondary schools, more than primary schools, are vulnerable to desertion by middle-class parents when the socio-economic ratio reaches the critical point. As already indicated, in a community with a cross-section of the American population in terms of socio-economic status, the high school tends to have a SER of about 1.0. Thus, the SER is higher than that of an elementary school in the same community, because a number of lower-class boys and girls drop out of high school, leaving a disproportionate number of middle class. In an upper-middle-class suburb the SER is very high. In the central city, the slums continually encroach upon high schools in formerly middle-class areas, and reduce the SER in such schools toward the critical point. At that point there tends to be a rapid flight to the suburbs by middle-class families who have children of high-school age.

A High School in a Rapidly Changing Area

An example of what happens when the SER reaches the critical point may be seen in the case of Benjamin Franklin High School, located in a large city which is now in stage IV of metropolitan development. Franklin High School is situated in what was a middle- and upper-class area about 1910, some six miles from the center of the city. In 1910 this was the school with the best academic record in the city, sending a high proportion of its graduates to college, and winning most of the prizes for academic excellence on the part of its students. The school's SER in 1910 was probably about 1.5.

Between the two world wars many of the upper-class people moved out to suburbs, and some of the upper-middle-class residents took over the old upper-class mansions, while other upper-middles moved out to a high school district farther out from the center of the city. Several areas of middle-class houses deteriorated, and some of the old, large apartment buildings were "converted" into small, low-rent apartments. A considerable number of working-class people moved in. On one edge of the high school district an area of old apartment buildings was turned over to Negro occupancy after the apartments had been "converted." By the beginning of World War II the SER of Franklin High was about .80.

Immediately after World War II, there was a further influx of working-class blacks into a formerly middle-class area. However, there was also some new building of apartments, and some well-to-do blacks began to buy the old upper-class mansions. The SER of Franklin High gradually dropped to .60 by 1955. With a large rate of dropouts of working-class pupils in the ninth and tenth grades, this meant that the SER of the ninth grade was .35, while that of the twelfth grade was 1.5. The SER for the ninth grade was well below the critical point for middle-class parents, and they began to move away from the area when their children were ready to enter high school.

At about this time the community sensed that a crisis had occurred. An organization was formed by the middle-class people in the district whose goals were "community conservation" and urban renewal. With the aid of government funds, deteriorated houses were torn down and replaced by middle-class houses. The high school was reorganized on the basis of a multi-track program, with the upper track consisting of college-going (and largely middle-class) pupils, thus achieving a high SER for this sub-group. These measures partially stemmed the outflow of middle-class families, and brought some new middle-class families with small children into the area.

However, in the same high-school district another area where there was no community conservation movement (the area served by the Leibnitz elementary school, already described) also "changed" sharply after 1955. Its graduates tended to force down the SER at Franklin High. At this writing there seems to be a close balance between the forces that tend to make Franklin High into a slum school, and those forces that will preserve it as a school with an academic ethos serving a community with a substantial proportion of middle-class families.

Socio-educational Motivation

What parents desire in the education of their children is a kind of school that stimulates children to do well academically; encourages them to finish high school and go to college; and offers something useful and interesting for children from all kinds of families. Looking for these things, they try to sense the spirit or *ethos* of the school. The SER can be improved upon as a measure of school ethos by replacing the percentages of children from various social classes with the percentages of children with certain kinds of socio-educational motivation.

If the latter data are available, the substitution would allow for the fact that children of any one social class have a range of educational motivations.

It is possible to describe four levels of educational motivation, each level indicating the kind of occupational aspiration held by the individual as well as the probable educational level he will attain.

Table 4.2 gives data of this kind for the ninth grade of a high school which represents a cross-section of the American society. In this school the SER is 50 ÷ 80 or .6. The SER can be replaced by a *motivation ratio* which is computed as follows: 2A + B ÷ C + 2D, where the letters refer to the motivational levels shown in Table 4.2. In this case the motivation ratio is 90 ÷ 60 or 1.5. While this ratio is a better measure of the academic ethos of a high school than is the SER, it requires so much more knowledge about the students that it is likely to be used less frequently than the SER.

TABLE 4.2

Socio-educational Motivation of Male Students in a Cross-Sectional High School (Percentages of Male High-School Students at 9th Grade Level)

Probable Educational Level	*Characteristic Motivation*	*Social Class*				*Total Percent*
		U + UM	*LM*	*UWC*	*LWC*	
College	A. Academically motivated—major white-collar job	10	16	8	1	35
High School Grad	B. Minor white-collar career	—	9	7	4	20
H.S. Grad & Dropout	C. Skilled blue-collar career	—	5	20	5	30
Dropout	D. Alienated	—	—	5	10	15
TOTAL		10	30	40	20	100

Motivation Ratio $\frac{2A + B}{C + 2D}$

ATMOSPHERE AND INTERNAL WORKING OF THE SCHOOL

The nature of a school depends on the teachers and on the educational program in the school as well as on the characteristics of the

91689

parents and of the pupils in the school. While these are all interrelated, they are not so tightly bound that one can predict accurately the school atmosphere on the basis of knowledge of the socio-economic status of parents.

To a considerable extent the atmosphere and the internal working of a school depends on the principal, the teachers, the supervisors and specialists, the parent-teacher organization, the librarian, the supply of books and teaching materials, and the curriculum. Therefore an attempt has been made to discover types or categories of schools by looking into the school itself rather than by looking at the socio-economic situation of the school.

TYPES OF ELEMENTARY SCHOOLS

This attempt has been carried out successfully by Russell Doll (1969) in his study of elementary schools in Chicago, and his study serves as the basis for the categories to be presented here. Doll studied intensively 40 elementary schools. He interviewed 185 teachers of grades four to eight, and made systematic observations of each school.

The visit to a school consumed a full day and often an extra day was added. In general, the research worker conducted the following: (1) interviews averaging 45 minutes with each teacher; (2) interviews and discussions throughout the day with the principal; (3) short observations of the children in the classroom; (4) observations of the children at recess, moving in and out of the building at lunch time and after school; (5) observations of teachers at their lunch time, at sign-out time, and at their break times; (6) observations of principals handling cases sent to the office or of parents coming to the school; (7) observation of the inside and the outside of the school building. (Havighurst, 1964, Ch. 8.)

Four types or categories of schools were identified, and given names as follows:

A. *High-status* schools—generally found toward the edges of the city, in high income areas, and in upper-middle-class dormitory suburbs.

B. *Conventional* schools—generally found in areas of lower-middle class dominance and in cross-sectional employing or industrial suburbs. May be found in upper-middle and upper-working-class areas.

C. *Common-man* schools—generally found in areas of stable working-class residence, in the central city and in working-class residential suburbs.

D. *Inner-city* schools—generally found in slum areas of low income, high transiency, high delinquency, both black and white.

Although these names come from geographical and social characteristics, the categories are really based on internal characteristics of the schools, as is seen in Table A-6 (p. 320). Doll found that teachers can identify the category of school in which they work by using the chart of Table A-6 as a check list. They agree fairly well among themselves and with a skilled observer in classifying their schools.

High-Status Schools

A teacher in a high-status school said "We're so conscious of the gifted here. We've based our whole course of study on the gifted. It is the same with the curriculum guides. As for discipline problems, well, they are practically nonexistent."

These are schools with a high degree of most desirable characteristics. The children are extremely well prepared for what the school demands, and parents are willing and able to supply equipment needs over and above what is needed, and are taking an active part in school life. The children have high academic scores and provide only a small number of discipline problems and, in the majority of cases, no active discipline problems at all. The disturbed children are few and for the most part can be handled in the school setting.

One teacher's description of a high-status school area is as follows: "The school community is an old established residential area made up of middle-class families who are economically comfortable. They are proud of their community. The parents are well-educated and interested in the educational opportunities provided for their children and often compare these to neighboring schools in suburban areas. The majority of students are academically motivated. The PTA is a cooperative active group. On the whole the parents are eager to work with the school to ensure the success of their children in the educational program."

Teaching is most rewarding in this type of setting and once a teacher enters such a situation, it is very seldom that he leaves. In one such school the length of total teaching experience was as follows: a range of from one year to 32 years with the teacher of one year's experience having had a total of ten years of teaching experience in other situations. The total faculty median was fifteen years. As one principal stated, "My teachers only leave to retire, or if they are married, when they become pregnant." There are also few sick days used by the teachers. "It's always a pleasant place here. We really do not have many teachers who take too many days off. In fact, they only take a day off when they are very sick."

Because of the high ability level of the children, the curriculum guides and supplements not only may be used to their fullest, but must even be supplemented. One teacher said, "The guides and supplements suit our students well. I think they're constructed in an excellent fashion. They are realistically attuned to my class, but nevertheless, I have to provide some degree of variety, no matter how good the supplement and guide are. This is because the majority of my children do reference work in the library."

The backgrounds of the students aid the teacher in the presentation of the curriculum and undoubtedly offer the necessary information and skills for success in school—which success again provides the teachers with a rewarding experience. As one teacher stated, "Given a good curriculum, you can really teach in this type of situation. Culturally, these kids have an advantage. I would say about 99 percent of my kids have an encyclopaedia at home, 75 percent have traveled to interesting places, and at least 60 percent have been to the city and have visited all the museums—the Museum of Science and Industry, the Museum of Natural History—and these children take advantage of the school library and the public library. Culturally, they rate high."

Conventional Schools

A teacher in a conventional school said, "This is just a nice typical school situation with nice typical kids." Conventional schools are those which have a majority of academically oriented children, but they also have a greater number of discipline problems and parental problems than have the high-status schools. However, these are not enough to interfere with the academic program. This type of school has a majority of children with a strong background of family experience preparing them for school work. However, such a school will have a visible minority of children with poor reading and below-average school achievement. While there are discipline problems, the majority of them can be handled between the teacher, the parent, and the principal. This is a school which is psychologically *in the city,* whereas the high-status school is more suburban in nature. The children and parents of the conventional school exhibit behavior and achievement patterns associated with the mainstream of American culture and society.

The areas in which conventional schools are found show a great diversity in socio-economic status and social composition. Since conditions within the school are the ranking criteria rather than only socio-economic factors, one may find conventional schools in a cluster of common-man and inner-city schools. In general, though, clusters of conventional schools are found in stable areas geographically removed from the inner-city, in areas with young families, in areas of new housing developments, or in other areas in which parents are experiencing upward mobility.

In the newly settled areas, the parents are not quite sure what their role is in relation to the school, and some either withdraw or become somewhat critical, more so than in the stable conventional schools. One teacher said, in a newly settled black middle-class area, "Oh, I get some parents up here who don't understand what we are attempting to do. They want to know what the school is doing for their child, and they think the school can do a better job. I tell them that we have to concentrate on the academics, and if they want their children to be taken to museums, to be taken to these extra events, it is up to them to take them. Eventually, they see our point and realize that they cannot expect us to turn out a good academic product and yet spend all our time in these acculturating activities." And as one principal in a similar area stated, "We attempt to explain the program to the parents, and many become involved on their own; but as concerns community outreach, I think at some point we reach a point of diminishing returns because a lot of these parents just won't be drawn into the framework of the school, and consequently one expends one's energy in areas that are not fruitful."

In general, in this type of school, the majority of parents and the community support the schools and the teachers. In one newly settled area, the principal reported, "I gathered together many of the important people of the community and told them the importance of our preparing the children to go to college. I outlined for them what the school was attempting to do and I told them what they could do to help the school. They loved it. I realize that this can't be done in all places and communities, but here, the parents respect the principal's word."

With respect to curriculum guides, a teacher in a stable area said, "I think they fit our children well, at least those with good backgrounds; but I wouldn't try to exceed the guides as they do in the schools north of us. We're just right now because our children are very eager to learn and we don't have to pull it out of them."

Conventional schools' discipline problems are not very severe. Those problems which they have may be handled in the school situation. As in the high-status schools, there is seldom if ever any overt hostility on the part of the student and very little verbal hostility directed towards the teacher. In very rare instances is there any physical hostility. The discipline problems consist of cases of the classroom being upset by behavioral antics or inattentiveness on the part of the children. A stable conventional principal says, "The crisis in this school is: 'Johnny pushed me going home' or else, 'Mary stuck her tongue out at me.' Our discipline problems are not really discipline problems, but they are more or less just little misunderstandings among children. I am usually able to handle them if the teachers send them down to me. But in most cases, the teachers are able to handle them themselves."

Teachers in conventional schools feel the pressure of lack of time, as preventing *them* from teaching effectively. A teacher with eight years of experience, who had a relatively slow group in a new area, said,

> Most of the children in my slow group have trouble using the text. This means I have to do most of my presentation orally or with worksheets, and these I have to mimeograph myself. I simply do not have enough time for this preparation. There are always forms and reports to be made out for the district office or for downtown. This takes up the time for grading papers and other time I could be using in preparation. Since my children can't use the text so much, I have to find time somewhere for this mimeographing. As well as the fact that I have a husband to look after. If I could only have some time each week, or a free period, to get this stuff in order! My biggest problem is time.

Common-Man Schools

A teacher in a common-man school said, "They sure play rough, and they get rough in fights, but they're not bad kids when you really get to know them." As in conventional schools, common-man schools show a great diversity in student body, parental cooperation, home background, and ability to use the curriculum. The student population tends to be less academically oriented, more independent when dealing with the school and the teachers, and less inclined to identify with the school and its personnel than in the conventional schools. The mass media set the behavioral patterns for many of the students. Parents, for the most part, desire an education for their children and push verbally in this direction, but are not quite certain what educational goals should be achieved, nor how one goes about achieving them. Being good in school behaviorally is equated with doing "good" in school academically.

The schools may or may not be close to the center of the city geographically but they are definitely city oriented. They are attended by a large percentage of second generation foreign-born and/or Spanish-speaking and black children.

A school with a long history as a common-man type is the John Paul Jones, which has always been in a working-class area. This school now has an SER of .26, which has probably been the same for 50 years. Originally settled by Irish, Germans, and Swedes who built their frame houses near a foundry and steel fabricating plant where they worked, the community was gradually populated by Poles, Lithuanians, and Czechs, who worked in the foundries and the car barns, and some of whom have recently become truck drivers and factory operatives.

A teacher who has taught at John Paul Jones for a long time describes the neighborhood as follows:

> The neighborhood is an old one, but the buildings are kept in excellent repair. The great majority of the people are laborers, many truck drivers and factory workers. Many are third generation in the neighborhood. Lately there are a few transient families. Most of the families had little education and because of fairly comfortable living, they desire little education for their children. The only drawback to teaching in this school is the parents' lack of interest in education. They want their children

> to be clean, well-behaved, and healthy; but they really (for the most part) don't care if they're educated.

An observer of this community reports:

> During the past 20 years there has been a good deal of moving out toward the suburbs by young adults, and there is some defensiveness in the attitudes of those who have stayed. Although there is a tendency to apologize for their having lived in the neighborhood so long when they feel they have "bettered themselves" economically, they are quick to point out that those who have moved "might be sorry." Although they will claim that someone who moves out is not really missed, one finds that they do keep in touch with one another and visit occasionally. Actually, the people are missed, but for a much deeper reason. Egress is a threat to their personal security, to the group as a whole, and to the stability of the neighborhood. Consequently, it is with great reluctance that they admit to each other that someone is "really going to move."

The John Paul Jones school and its community may go on as a kind of working-class backwater where non-mobile people can live and raise their children, but its residents are apprehensive of the threat of the expanding black working-class group who live only a quarter-mile away. These people have strong prejudices against living in the same neighborhood as blacks, and will probably move farther out from the city center rather than stay in an integrated community. Industrial and employing suburbs are likely to have some common-man elementary schools.

One principal, with many years of experience in a stable common-man school, remarked, "The parents could keep closer watch on their children and on their activities. They shouldn't let them roam the streets as they do. There's also too much TV. Some parents seem rather messy, and surprisingly enough, come up to the school in slacks and the like. Many do not wear the proper street attire."

One stable common-man school teacher notices differences between his own students and the nearby conventional students. He commented, "Those from the conventional school are better academically and better in behavior. The kids in our school, although they're not problems, nevertheless are slower and don't reach as high a level of achievement, but they're good kids. We are very heavy with foreign-born and foreign-speaking homes, and this may be one reason for the low achievement."

Despite the problems, the teachers in the common-man schools see themselves in a better situation than in an inner-city school, and seem to be, in the main, as positively oriented to the majority of these schools as those in the conventional schools. A teacher who had been in an inner-city school stated:

> I feel like a different person here. I really do. I'm enjoying my teaching now and I feel like I'm getting some kind of a reward. A problem that is considered a great problem here just didn't count at the ———. Oh, we have problems at recess. We do have some pretty bad problem kids, but at the ——— we really had our problems. When I was going to transfer, the principal of this school visited me and told me that this school wouldn't be any different than the ———. But it is as different as night and day. And the strange thing is, these kids don't come from any worse backgrounds than the kids at the ——— do. At the ———, discipline was terrible. In the morning there would be kids left over from the previous day, lined up outside the office. One day I just went down and put my name on the transfer list and I came to this school. And it is different.

Probably the greatest difference which teachers perceive between the problems of the inner-city schools and other schools is in the degree, consistency, and direction of hostility which the teacher experiences. This hostility seems to be more direct, more frequent, and more overt in the inner-city schools.

The ability to handle the curriculum varies drastically from one type of common-man school to the other. In the main, the curriculum must be altered downward in all schools of this type, but more so in the rough common-man schools. Again, this adds more to the teacher's burden, for the teacher does not only have to teach, but also must construct a curriculum. One principal said, "When you have reading problems, you have problems in curriculum, I don't care how good the curriculum is. We can't find things to use in the eighth grade. What are you going to do with a kid that is reading at the fifth-grade level and is in eighth grade? To a great extent, it is vocabulary that is a problem. But the difficulty, and I say it again, is mainly in reading. The teachers have to prepare most of the work outside of the textbook, and this is killing."

For teachers in common-man schools the problem of time is a problem of getting enough of the child's time to accomplish something with and within him. The school time is especially valuable for learning because neither the child nor his family can be counted on to see that he studies at home or uses his out-of-school time in ways that improve his school work. The teacher must adapt curriculum material and prepare work sheets in any time she can find, outside of class. She must do an active job of teaching, in class. One teacher said, "There is one consolation. We know that the school does all. Anything positive that happens to these kids, we know we did it."

Inner-City Schools

A teacher in an inner-city school said, "Each day I'd enter the school, each day the problems would begin, and each day I'd say, 'Dear God, what can I do?' "

Inner-city schools face the gravest problems of any schools in the system. They also face the greatest challenge in any attempt to remedy the problems. For these schools, the problems are rooted mainly in the subculture and subsociety beyond easy reach of the schools and, indeed, beyond the effective reach of many agencies designed especially to deal with these subsocieties.

What we are calling the *inner-city school* is not necessarily a school located in the inner-city in a physical sense. There are actually a number of common-man schools and even some conventional schools located in areas where inner-city schools predominate. The inner-city school is a psychological as well as a sociological phenomenon. Whether a given school will have inner-city or common-man characteristics depends partly on the principal and his faculty and their relations with the parents and children.

For example, a teacher in an inner-city school in New York's Harlem says,

> A few blocks from here there is a good school. It's eighty years old, with multiple wings and stairs like ours; there are hundreds of places for children to hide—and they never do. Every child in the school is in his room all day. Low truancy, zero lateness. Notes go home with aides at nine-thirty if a child isn't there. The school reads on grade level. The principal is a Negro woman, but that's not the point. She has the same cross section of teachers as anywhere else. They come from the same school board, same distribution of assignments. But this level is what she demands. Her being a Negro may play a part, though, because she *intends* her school to produce children who can read. From nine to ten

> o'clock the whole school is reading; ten to ten-thirty, phonics and nothing else.
>
> So it runs that way because she runs it. A school can't be left to what emanates from the Board—which isn't putting real thought into teaching these children. . . .

The inner-city school suffers from a syndrome of problems. Covert and overt hostility to the teacher; lack of self control on the part of pupils; lack of experience and background needed for success in school; an outer society which hardens, alienates, and produces a negative type of maturation; and intellectual apathy in the student all combine to produce in many instances an unrewarding and impossible teaching climate. It is a situation in which the teacher's hardiness and physical stamina count as much as teaching ability. It is a situation in which the young experienced teacher survives better than the young inexperienced or older experienced teacher. It is a difficult situation.

The inner-city respondents feel to an overwhelming degree that they are cut off and abandoned. In most cases, the curriculum guides cannot be used, and it is felt that the curriculum planners are drifting even further away from an understanding of what is needed. With a feeling that their problems are not understood by the downtown office; that those who are to offer assistance, such as psychologists and consultants, are either too few in number or out of contact with their problems; that these problems are covered up by those in authority or that no one in authority or in the public really cares—buffeted by all those forces they feel are out of their control, the inner-city school teachers often give up in frustration after entering with dedication. As one assistant principal contemplating transferring said, "If I was a teacher instead of the assistant principal, I would have been out of here long ago. In fact, I never would have come if I had known what the school situation was. There are dangers that I face all the time that I shouldn't have to. Why do I have to pin boys to the floor? This has happened. Why do I have to take away knives? Why do I have to break up fights? I always thought that I was a teacher, but I'm no teacher. I'm a bouncer and a policeman with the assignment of dangerous duty."

A sixth-grade teacher with four years' experience in an inner-city school remarked, "My biggest problem is not teaching. My biggest problem is keeping some semblance of an academic environment in my room. Some of these children are so nervous that they just can't handle the school materials. I have five or six in my group that just cannot be reached. These poor kids are just starving for individual attention. But what can I do? These are the same ones that go through school with their problems; these are the same ones that will end up with problems when they reach the upper grades."

A newly assigned teacher who is having some degree of success in an inner-city school commented, "My class is not too bad. In fact, without bragging, I would say it's one of the better ones in the school. I'm very authoritarian and I have a booming voice, and this may be why I've got my class under control. But I don't see why this should be necessary in a school system. I don't know why I should be a warden. I don't know why I should have to spend most of my time just keeping the kids under control. Why, oh why can't I be a teacher?"

A mature woman had this to say:

> Academics take second place. I wasn't aware of this, I just was not aware. I heard stories from other teachers, but you just never know. You never realize until you're exposed to it. I've worked since I was thirteen years old and I've never worked so hard in my life as I have in teaching. I never heard worse cuss words come from people than I have from these children. I don't know, I simply don't know how the others stand it. I try to use the theories that I was taught in school; I try to use the methods, but I just can't. And I have an advantage on a lot of these young teachers because I entered teaching late. I see a lot of those young teachers just out of college. Many of them are genteel and soft spoken. My heart just bleeds for them because I know what's going to happen. And again I ask, why does it have to be like this?

In most instances, the teachers are at a loss to explain the motivation behind the hostility. Even teachers with many years' experience in these situations feel at a loss at times. One teacher with 12 years' experience, and described by her principal as a superior teacher, stated,

> They are hard to handle. They think little of talking back, even to me. They know me. To some extent, this hurts. They can be extremely rude without any type of provocation whatsoever. I realize what causes this. They bring a lot of problems to the school. You know, I'm no stranger here. They know me and I know them. But I had to fill in with a fifth-grade class and because of the fact that I wasn't their regular teacher, I had a hard

> time. Now, this is hard to take, this is hard to understand. You know, I come to the school lots of times prepared for a good day. I have things planned. I know I'm going to teach and I can get slapped down in just five minutes, and I wonder why, why this happened. All you have to do is just make such a simple statement as "Please hang up your coat." Then you get snapped back to you, "I won't," or "I don't have to," or "Nobody's going to make me hang up my coat and *you* can't make me hang up my coat." Then, with this greeting you in the morning, how *can* you really teach? It just seems to be that the whole class picks it up, like some type of a signal. Then *you* try to control it.

Tardiness and a slow start in September also hinder the teaching situation. Out of 2,000 enrollment in a particular school, there may be as many as 200 children tardy in a single day, some arriving as late as 15 to 20 minutes after the bell. In the fall, children are still entering the school at the end of September and as late as October. The principal said, "When they come in in September, they trickle in. We really don't start school until October. The truant officer this year had 300 names he had to round up to get to school."

A man who had taught for four years at a large inner-city school commented:

> I'm not saying that the case is hopeless. I am saying that something is going to have to be done on the home level before you can do anything in the school. Look, you get kids coming in with no paper. They can't even get up a dime to buy a pad of paper. So, what do you do? You make it up to them, you supply the paper. What do you do in the situation in which there's five, six, or seven kids sleeping in one room, and even more than one kid in one bed? Many of these people don't have any medical aid, as well as the fact that there's no challenge in their society for school. I had a kid in my room who was walking around with an excruciating toothache for three days. The parents had to wait a long time to get him into the County Hospital to the dentist. So what do you do? It's not that I'm making a fortune. I hate to see the kid in pain, so I took him to the dentist. The tooth had to be pulled. Here's a poor kid walking around suffering. Can you study with a toothache?

As the sixth-grade teacher said, the major problem in the inner-city school is to keep order, so that the children can study and the teacher can teach. This is never a problem in the high-status school, and seldom in the conventional school.

TYPES OF HIGH SCHOOLS

High schools may be classified in much the same way as elementary schools. The high schools of a metropolitan area have been studied in the Kansas City area by Levine, Mitchell, and Havighurst (1970), and they were able to describe five types as follows:

1. *Middle-class schools*—generally found toward the edges of the city, in high-income areas, and in upper-middle-class dormitory suburbs. More than 75 percent of the graduates go on to college.
2. *Comprehensive high schools*—between 40 and 75 percent of the graduates go on to college. This kind of school is the most common one. It serves a cross-section of the population in socio-economic terms.
3. *Working-class schools*—serve a predominantly working-class area of a big city. Only about 40 percent of the graduates of white working-class schools enter college. Also, there is a high drop-out rate in the ninth and tenth grades, which makes the twelfth grade less representative of working-class families than the ninth or tenth grades.
4. *Small schools*—have an enrollment of less than 500 and less than 100 in the twelfth grade. These schools generally draw from rural areas and small outlying districts of a metropolitan area. They fall between the comprehensive and working-class types in terms of socio-economic status and are similar to white working class schools in proportions of graduates entering college.
5. *Private schools*—are mostly Catholic schools, though there are a few high status non-church-related high schools that are like the middle-class schools in social composition. The church-related high schools are generally like the comprehensive schools in socio-economic character.

Table 4.3 shows the relative numbers of students and the 12th grade socio-economic composition of the high schools in the Kansas City metropolitan area in 1967. Table A-7 shows the percentages of youth in the various types of school who said in May, 1967, that they expected to enter college the next autumn. Several studies have shown that these are fairly good estimates of the numbers who actually do enter college.

In Table A-7 we see the same phenomenon noted by Wilson in his Oakland Study. Students of a given socio-economic group are more likely to expect to enter college if they are in a high-status school than if they are in a low-status school. Also Table A-7 shows that black students in the predominantly black high schools were

Table 4.3

The Socio-economic Composition of High Schools in a Metropolitan Area
(Percentage Composition within High School Types—12th Grade Students)

	Socioeconomic Status											
Type of	*I*		*II*		*III*		*IV*		*V*			
High School	*No.*	%	*No.*	%	*No.*	%	*No.*	%	*No.*	%	*Total*	*12th Grade*
Middle-class	464	33	479	34	410	30	69	5	—	—	1,422	16
Comprehensive	543	13	764	19	1,537	37	1,121	27	145	14	4,110	47
Working-class	53	3	165	11	422	28	677	45	204	13	1,521	18
Small	23	3	88	11	273	33	345	42	99	12	828	10
Catholic	66	8	138	17	254	32	300	37	46	6	804	9
TOTAL	1,149	13	1,634	19	2,896	33	2,512	29	494	6	8,685	100
All American Youth (est.)		10		15		27		38		11		

Sources: Levine, Mitchell, and Havighurst, *Opportunities for Higher Education in a Metropolitan Area,* Bloomington, Indiana: Phi Delta Kappa, 1970.

more likely to say they expected to enter college than white students of the same SES level.

To examine the differences between the middle-class and the working-class school further, we may look at Table 4.4 which shows data from two contrasting schools in a big city. School C is a working-class high school and School B is a middle-class type. They have SERs of .22 and 2.50 respectively.

School B is in a section of the city with the highest socioeconomic ratings on occupation, income, and education of adults. School C is in the lowest section of the city. Table 4.4 shows the ages of the students in each of the four high-school grades. The

TABLE 4.4

Comparison of Two Contrasting High Schools (Schools C and B)

	Grade 9		*Grade 10*		*Grade 11*		*Grade 12*	
	C	*B*	*C*	*B*	*C*	*B*	*C*	*B*
	Percentage Distribution of Ages							
11-9 to 12-8	2	0						
12-9 to 13-8	6	16	0	0				
13-9 to 14-8	31	53	2	10	0	0		
14-9 to 15-8	39	23	25	58	4	14	0	0
15-9 to 16-8	18	7	43	23	35	56	10	14
16-9 to 17-8	3	1	24	7	38	28	35	69
17-9 to 18-8	1	0	5	2	18	2	38	16
18-9 to 19-8			1	0	4	0	15	1
19-9 & over								
Number	2,039	668	1,246	549	676	524	503	443
	Percentage Enrollments in Basic, Essential, and Honors Courses							
Basic course								
English	35	0	23	0	–	–	–	–
Mathematics	19	0	0	0	–	–	–	–
Essential course								
English	30	12	36	0	42	0	31	0
Mathematics	56	14	44	0	–	–	–	–
Honors course								
English	1	12	2	5	4	5	7	6
Mathematics	2	12	0	23	0	10	0	18

underlined figures indicate the age groups which are normal. For instance, a child who entered school at the age of six would be between 13 years, 9 months and 14 years, 8 months at the beginning of the ninth grade if he had made average progress, never failing a grade and never "skipping" a grade. School B has more than half of its students just at the "normal" age, and about 25 percent over-age. But School C has 61 percent of its ninth graders over-age, and 55 percent of its twelfth graders. School C has only a fourth as many twelfth graders as it has ninth graders. At least half of its entering ninth graders drop out of school within the first two years. School B has very few drop-outs. (The ninth grade is larger than it was two or three years earlier, and thus the apparent drop-out figures are exaggerated.)

The two schools show a great contrast in the proportion of pupils in the various "tracks" of the program. School C has four tracks or ability groupings, called Basic, Essential, Regular, and Honors. School B does not have the lowest, or Basic, track.

The two schools contrast sharply in their offerings of Basic, Essential, and Honors courses. Students with reading or arithmetic scores below a grade level of 5.9 are placed in "basic" courses. These pupils are three years retarded or more, since they are in the ninth grade or above. Furthermore, many of them are over-age, and therefore even further retarded. Those with a reading or arithmetic score between grade level 5.9 and 7.9 are placed in "essential" courses. They are from one to two years retarded if they are in the ninth grade.

School C has 65 percent of its ninth graders in Basic or Essential English, and 75 percent in Basic or Essential Mathematics. By the sophomore year there have been many drop-outs, but Basic and Essential English still enroll 59 percent of the students. An Essential Mathematics course continues with 44 percent of second-year students. Essential English is continued throughout the four years, with 31 percent of the seniors in it.

In contrast, School B has nobody in Basic English or Mathematics, but has 12 and 14 percent of ninth graders in Essential English and Mathematics, respectively. After the ninth grade there are no Essential or Basic courses.

Honors courses enroll 12 percent of ninth graders in School B, in English and in mathematics, and they continue through all four years. But School C has only 1 percent of ninth graders in English Honors, and 2 percent in Mathematics Honors. Mathematics Honors does not continue, but English Honors continues, getting up to 7 percent of the senior class.

School C has 15 classes in foreign language, while School B (with a lower enrollment) has 41. School C has a one-semester course in trigonometry for 11th-grade students, and nothing beyond that, while School B has honors courses in advanced mathematics, analytical geometry, and calculus for 11th and 12th graders.

There are, in School C, about 4 percent of eleventh and twelfth graders who are in the top quarter of all students in the city in ability and achievement test scores. In School B, 63 percent are in the top quarter. Such a vast difference in the abilities and achievement of pupils means that the program of School B is probably better and richer for bright students. One might argue that the program of School C can be expected to be better for slow students. At least, it offers that possibility.

Both of these schools have unusually good faculties in terms of experience and interest in their work. The principal of School C has energy and insight and determination. Though this is his first year at this school, he has developed a plan for intensified teaching of Basic English which appears to be working well. He has also established biweekly meetings with new teachers to help them learn to teach in this kind of school.

PRIVATE SCHOOL SYSTEMS

Approximately 13 percent of elementary and secondary school pupils attend private schools, and the great majority of these schools are in metropolitan areas. For example, in the state of Illinois in 1960, 89 percent of the private elementary school enrollment was concentrated in the six SMSAs, compared with 71 percent of the public elementary school enrollment. And 79 percent of the private elementary school pupils were in the Chicago SMSA, compared with 55 percent of the public elementary school pupils. Approximately one-third of the elementary and secondary school students in the Chicago area attended nonpublic schools, and over 90 percent of this group were in a single school system conducted by the Roman Catholic Church.

The concentration of private school pupils in metropolitan areas is due to the fact that Roman Catholics tend to live in metropolitan areas, and 90 percent of private school enrollment is in Catholic schools. The remainder is about equally divided between other church-related schools and independent private schools.

As would be expected from the facts of out-migration of residents of the central city to the suburbs, the Catholic school enrollment has increased sharply in the suburbs in recent years, while barely holding its own or even diminishing in the central city. This is due to the increase of the largely non-Catholic black population in the central city.

Most parochial schools are of the conventional or the common-man types. A parochial school located in a slum area is likely to be a common-man type of school. This is due to the fact that the parochial schools draw children from the more stable working-class families in this kind of area, that the parents support the teachers in establishing an ethos for the school, and that the Catholic parochial schools tend to maintain a very orderly routine.

In the suburbs and also in many areas of the central city the Catholic schools are likely to be of a conventional type. There are a few high-status type Catholic schools, generally associated with a Catholic college which is interested in the training of teachers.

Since about 1960 there has been a growing pressure on the private nonchurch schools in the central cities. These schools have traditionally served upper-class families and a few upper-middles. Now the upper-middle-class pressure is increasing in the central cities where the public schools are believed to be less satisfactory than they once were. For example, in 1964 *The New York Times* made a survey of 50 private non-church affiliated schools in New York City with a tuition range of $400 to $3,000. The *Times* writer found a large increase of applications with little or no desire on the part of private school directors to enlarge their schools.

FUNCTIONAL TYPES OF SCHOOLS

Another way of categorizing metropolitan area schools is by their functions—the particular educational purposes they serve. The comprehensive elementary or secondary school, serving all kinds of pupils, is still the most common type, but there are others which have grown in number in recent years.

Schools for Maladjusted or Handicapped Children

Many of the large cities have one or more schools for socially maladjusted children. In New York City the so-called "600 schools" have this function. In Chicago there are two schools for boys and one for girls. Most cities have a residential school for children who are sent there by the courts because they have no families or their families have been judged unfit to look after them.

Although these schools are crowded, they have not been enlarged, as a rule. They are not adequately staffed for treatment purposes, and therefore they serve primarily as custodial institutions. Consequently the principals and counsellors and psychologists try to send pupils there only as a last resort, feeling that the best thing for the pupil is to be kept in a regular classroom as long as he shows any ability to adjust himself and as long as the teacher will tolerate him. These special schools are also limited to children of 12 or 13 years or older. Younger children who appear to be disturbed or disturbing are kept as long as possible in a regular classroom. There is now a tendency to set up special classes for maladjusted children in elementary schools, classes with small enrollment and specially-selected teachers to work with them.

As far as possible, the public school system is committed to helping children compensate for handicaps of various kinds—crippling conditions, deafness, blindness and innate mental retardation. Consequently there are special schools in the big cities for children with certain of these handicaps, and special classes in regular schools for children with handicaps that do not require special school equipment.

Middle Schools

The "middle school" is a school serving grades five through eight or six through eight. It is taking the place of junior high schools in some communities, and being introduced in other communities that have had a K–8 elementary school. The middle school is most popular in the larger cities, where it serves two purposes. First, it permits the use of a departmentalized faculty of teachers specially trained in the modern mathematics, or science, or the new methods in English, or the new materials in social studies. The school building may be specially equipped for team teaching with groups of various sizes. Second, the middle school offers a chance to get greater social or racial integration in areas where there is residential segregation in small areas, but black and white and other families live in an area that can be served by a middle school, an area perhaps of a one-mile radius.

The Comprehensive High School

The typical American high school has educational programs or curricula aimed to meet the needs of all the youth of the community. It is the "natural" type of school for a community up to 50 or 100 thousand, which needs only one high school. Beyond this size, the community's socio-economic structure affects the SER of the high schools. It is unlikely that a high school can be truly comprehensive if its SER is below .50 or above 2.0. A school drawing largely middle-class students will stress college preparatory work and may neglect the students who want to go to work immediately on leaving high school. On the other hand, a school drawing on a working-class area may stress vocational-type courses, and fail to provide the quality and variety of courses that are needed for college preparatory work in foreign languages, mathematics, and science.

Mr. James B. Conant (1959, p. 17) formerly President of Harvard University, and Ambassador to West Germany, in his study of the American high school, defined the objectives of the comprehensive high school as:

> . . . *first,* to provide a general education for all the future citizens; *second,* to provide good elective programs for those who wish to use their acquired skills immediately on graduation; *third,* to provide satisfactory programs for those whose vocations will depend on their subsequent education in a college or university. If one could find a single comprehensive high school in the United States in which all three objectives were reached in a highly satisfactory manner, such a school might be taken as a model or pattern. Furthermore, unless there were some especially favorable local features which enabled such a school to attain these three objectives, the characteristics found might be developed in all the other schools of sufficient size in the United States.
>
> Since state and regional differences do play some role in this vast country, I decided that I should attempt to locate satisfactory comprehensive high schools in different sections of the nation. To this end, I inquired through various sources as to the comprehensive high schools outside the metropolitan areas which had the reputation of doing a good job in providing education for students with a wide range of vocational interests and abilities. I specified that these schools should be of such a nature that less than half the boys and girls were going on to college and the distribution

of academic ability roughly corresponded to the national norm (median I.Q. 100–105).

Upon examining 22 high schools that were nominated, Mr. Conant found eight which met his criteria for effective comprehensive high schools. These were all outside of SMSAs.

The high-status suburban high school may not be a very good school for the minority of its students who do not have college-going abilities or interests. Still, the high school of an employing suburb and the high schools of certain sections of the central city which have a mixed population in terms of socio-economic status are comprehensive in their student composition. Such schools could become highly effective in terms of criteria set forth by Mr. Conant for a good comprehensive school.

The Specialized High School

In the central cities, now, there is open question whether it would be better to develop more specialized high schools, or whether it would be better to work toward making most high schools comprehensive as far as the characteristics of the student body permit the maintenance of a balanced comprehensive program.

Large cities, especially in the northeast, tend to set up selective college preparatory high schools which draw from the entire city or from a sector of the city those students who have superior scholastic aptitude and who want to take the trouble to attend a specialized school. Along with this policy may go one of developing a number of specialized high schools for pupils with artistic and other talents. New York City's High School of the Performing Arts is an example. Many large cities have one or more vocational high schools which train students specifically for skilled trades. Still, the common practice is to include courses leading to vocational skills in trades, industry and business in the general high school.

In the past ten years, there has been some experimentation with a kind of *pre-vocational high school,* for pupils who have not done well in academic work and are likely to quit school before high school graduation. This school, operating at grade levels eight to ten, attempts to teach simple vocational skills such as those involved in restaurant work, janitorial service, automobile service station work, and other simple service jobs. With the present high proportion of pupils of inner-city and common-man schools who are two or more years retarded in reading and arithmetic level when they reach age 13 or 14, it seems likely that such schools will multiply, either as separate schools or as separate divisions of comprehensive schools.

DIVERSE FUNCTIONS OF A METROPOLITAN SCHOOL SYSTEM

From the foregoing overview of types of schools in a metropolitan area it can be seen that the school system as a whole has a wide diversity of functions. These functions tend to be assigned to schools depending on their location in the metropolitan area, though some functions are more widely distributed than others.

High Status of General Education in American Society

The prevailing function of the schools in America is to provide as much general education as possible for as many students as possible. The American one-track school system holds out the opportunity (unrealistically, for many pupils) of graduating from high school and going to college for all boys and girls. Hence any school program that implies a termination of formal education without a high-school diploma which can lead to college entrance is open to a kind of ideological objection on the part of many parents and some educators. However, it appears likely that some high-school programs are now developing which will not lead to a regular high-school diploma but which are aimed instead at getting a boy or girl into a stable job.

The Function of Social Integration

A major function of American public school education is to promote social integration—that is, to give young people of all socio-economic levels and all racial and ethnic groups a common school experience in which they learn to work and to live together, and to accept one another as equal members of a democratic society. This function argues for the mixed school, and will be discussed at length in Chapter 7.

Adult Education

The most rapidly growing part of education in metropolitan areas is adult education. A program of adult education influences positively and immediately the economic and the cultural life of the area. The illiterate adult who learns to read and to calculate increases his own capacity to earn, and his city's economic capital. The adult who learns more about drama, literature, music, or painting becomes one of the participating audience needed to create a great cultural center. The adult who studies the social and civic affairs of a metropolitan area becomes one of a body of citizens capable of guiding the process of metropolitan development.

The American mass culture has the highest financial base in the world, and probably the lowest cultural level of the modern urban countries. This has been said in a variety of disturbing and stimulating ways by critics of culture in America and outside of it. They point out the great and growing amount of leisure "enjoyed" by American adults, and they find that wonderful opportunities for fuller living are missed through the indifference and insensitivity of many people.

In 1965 the Congress created the National Arts and Humanities Foundation with the objective of building up the cultural agencies of the country with federal government support. The Foundation is working through the larger metropolitan areas as regional centers for the development of theaters, symphony orchestras, ballet and opera companies. Schools and colleges are being encouraged to develop courses in the performing arts, to start the process of recruiting and training young people before they reach the more advanced stages of training to begin in the regional centers.

Adult education stands a good chance of being planned and supported on a metropolitan area basis, partly because it does not have a long history of small-district and neighborhood organization to shackle it to the past.

Compensatory Education

Since about 1960 as evidence has accumulated showing that a disproportionately large percentage of children of poor families do not reach average achievement levels in existing school programs, the concept of "the socially disadvantaged child" has come into use. This concept is defined and discussed in Chapter 7, but here we may simply say that children whose parents are poorly educated and do not set them an example of much reading and complex conversation—such children are socially disadvantaged.

It is generally supposed that these children are born as bright as children of families with higher socio-economic status. It is generally thought that these children, if raised from infancy in middle-class homes, would show middle-class levels of school achievement. Consequently, why should not society give them a special kind of remedial education just as it does to other children who are physically or mentally handicapped? The answer to this question has been a resounding affirmative—society should provide a kind of school that will compensate, to some extent at least, for the disadvantage suffered by these children at home. Thus came into existence the term "compensatory education."

After some path-breaking experiments in New York City and other big cities, the federal government in 1965 passed the Elementary and Secondary Education Act which provided more than a billion dollars to supplement and improve the education of children of poor families, in urban and rural areas. This amounted to something like $110 per disadvantaged pupil per year in 1967–68. The program started in 1965–66 and during 1969–70 is in its fourth full year of operation. It is being continued in substantially this form until 1971, when the Nixon administration promises to evaluate it carefully and to come forth with a program that will result from this evaluation and will presumably cost at least as much money, if not more.

The many approaches to compensatory education in cities can be placed into three broad categories, as follows:

Programs for high-school age students, aged 16–20
Programs for school-age pupils, aged 6–16
Programs for pre-school children aged 3–5

While only the program for school-age pupils comes entirely from the ESEA, the other two programs are partially funded with money from other federal sources and are intended as compensatory education.

Although these programs were hailed with widespread enthusiasm when they were started in the first year of the Johnson administration, the evaluations which were made of them after they had been going a year or more have tended to be discouraging. They have not accomplished as much as was expected.

The programs for high-school age students have mainly been funded as part of the War on Poverty, under the Office of Economic Opportunity. They include the Job Corps, Upward Bound, and the Neighborhood Youth Corps. Their purposes have been partly to keep disadvantaged students in school and to help them do better school work, and partly to help dropouts learn work skills and attitudes that will gain them stable employment.

The programs for school-age pupils have been funded under Title I of ESEA. Generally the money has been used for such things as: reducing class size in inner-city schools; bringing teacher aides in to assist the classroom teacher; providing an extra period of remedial training after school, on Saturdays, and during the summer. This program under ESEA has been watched carefully by the President's National Advisory Council on the Education of Disadvantaged Children. Annual Reports have been made by the Advisory Council. The 1969 report gives a limited positive evaluation as follows:

> It has long been clear that the mere addition of people, equipment, and special services does not by itself constitute compensatory education; success in making up for the educational deprivation which stems from poverty requires a strategy for blending these resources in an integrated program that strikes at both roots and consequences of disadvantage.
>
> The details of this strategy, however, have by no means been clear. For one thing, we still have not had sufficient experience with Title I, or compensatory education programs generally, to be able to fully and fairly evaluate their potential. . . .
>
> What is clear is that among the thousands of different programs and approaches labeled as compensatory education, some efforts are paying off and others are not. Some of these programs can be evaluated in terms of positive, easily identifiable changes such as improvement in reading scores; in this report the Council identifies a number of such programs which have proven successful by such measurements.

This report describes twenty-one outstanding Title I programs which have been reasonably effective. But this report also recognizes the widespread criticisms of many programs that they were simply giving children "more of the same" kind of schooling they had been failing in. That is, they gave the pupils an extra hour a day of schooling, or an hour a week of individual remedial instruction.

But the disadvantages of these children are such that they are not likely to profit much from more hours spent on the present curriculum. The consensus of critical opinion is that the learning experiences of the pupils must be changed. The successful programs appear to be affecting the motivations of the pupils.

The programs for pre-school children have generally been financed by the Office of Economic Opportunity under its Head Start program. This has been politically very popular. Starting mainly as a six- or eight-week summer school for children of five or six just before they entered kindergarten or the first grade, it has been shifted more and more toward a year-round program for four- or five-year olds, which gives them in effect a year's headstart in school over children who commence at the normal age.

Although the Head Start program was funded by the Office of Economic Opportunity, the most careful evaluations and experimentation with pre-school classes for the disadvantaged children have been done under Title I of ESEA or with research funds provided by the U.S. Office of Education. In addition, the OEO employed the Westinghouse Learning Corporation and Ohio University to answer the question—"Have Head Start classes made an intellectual and psychological difference to poor children who are now in the first, second, or third grades?" When Head Start graduates were compared with other children of poor families who did not have Head Start, there was very little practical advantage for the Head Start group—not enough to justify the expenditure of something like $1000 per year per Head Start pupil.

However, there were a few programs that appeared to have given the children a real advantage, and a number of the experimental programs supported by other agencies also produced substantial gains in IQ and in reading achievement over control groups of children.

Thus after its first four years, the very costly program of compensatory education has shown a few bright spots but a great deal of barely passable performance. The educators who are most interested are pushing for a vigorous but rigorously controlled program, based on the lessons learned in this preliminary period. The Nixon administration appears to hold this view and it has transferred Head Start to the new Office of Child Development in the Department of Health, Education and Welfare, a sign that the program may become a permanent part of the federal government's operation.

One basic question remains to be answered—at what age level

can compensatory education be used most effectively? How should government support be distributed over the three age levels which are now receiving support? Educators generally favor the preschool years as the period when added compensatory education will be most effective, but they also want to continue with programs at the school-age level and the 16–20 age period.

THE URBAN-COMMUNITY SCHOOL

The quality of the public schools is the greatest single factor in the decision of middle-income people to live in the central city or to live in the suburbs, and to live in one section or another of the central city or the suburbs. Knowing this as a fact, educators tend to divide into two groups with respect to their views on the proper ways to operate a school system in the contemporary metropolitan area.

One school of thought may be called the "four-walls" school. The basic principle is to do the best possible job of educating every boy or girl who comes into the school, whoever he is, whatever his color, nationality, IQ or handicap. This means building good school buildings, equipping them well, and staffing them with well-trained teachers. At its best, it means being courteous and friendly to parents and to citizens who are interested in the schools, but making it quite clear to them that the schools are run by professionals who know their business and do not need advice from other people. It means making use of the cultural resources of the city—museums, theaters, orchestras, TV programs—under a system which guarantees the safety of the children and meets the convenience of the teachers.

It means keeping the schools "out of local politics." Staff appointments are to be made on the basis of merit alone, and promotion of staff on the basis of performance. It means a limited cooperation with other social institutions, public and private. The welfare and public aid and public health agencies are asked for help when the schools need it, but they cannot initiate school programs. Youth welfare and delinquency control agencies have their jobs to do, which meet and overlap the work of the schools. On this common ground the schools' administration must have full control of the use of school personnel and school facilities. In the area of training youth for employment, the school system will use the facilities of local business and industry for on-the-job training according to agreements worked out. Over-all policy for vocational education is the responsibility of the school administration under the Board of Education, and local business and industry are not closely related to policy determination in this area.

The four-walls type of school system works for efficiency and economy, and attempts to free the creative teacher to do the best possible job of teaching under good conditions. The community outside of the school is regarded as a source of complexity and of tension-arousal if the boundary between community and school is not clearly defined and respected.

The other school of thought may be called the "urban-community" school. The educators who advocate this believe that the big city is in a crisis which has been in force for some years and will last for at least ten years and requires the active participation of schools in the making and practicing of policy for social urban renewal. This big-city crisis is reflected in feelings of uncertainty and anxiety on the part of parents and citizens. There is danger of a collective failure of nerve which saps the vitality and flexibility of the city's efforts at urban renewal. Parents and citizens of middle income are tempted in this situation to escape to the suburbs, where life seems simpler and safer, especially for children.

The urban-community school attempts to act constructively in this crisis by involving the parents and citizens in the decisions about school policy and practice. The educator accepts the frustration of working with people who themselves are confused and uncertain about the schools, believing that the only way to solve the problems of the city is to work on a give-and-take basis with citizens and community organizations.

The urban-community school includes the intraschool program of the four-walls school, but differs at important points on the relation of the school to the community.

Those who take the urban-community-school point of view believe there is no viable alternative. They believe that the four-walls school actually causes some of the problems of the community through its rigid rules about attendance districts and about keeping the public away from the classroom. They believe that the schools by their policies and practices either attract or repel people in the local community. Under present conditions, the typical school system repels people whom the central city cannot afford to lose as citizens. Proponents of the urban-community school believe that the present trend toward economic and racial segregation in the metropolitan area will continue, and the central city will lose quality, unless the schools take a more active part in social urban renewal.

The Urban-Community School Program in Flint

The community school is made to serve the needs of its particular local community, and to serve people of all ages. For example, the Flint, Michigan, public schools have developed a program that might serve any medium-sized central city. Although the community school program in Flint, an automobile manufacturing city, began during the Depression of the 1930s, it has gained momentum since then and is now a regular part of the program of the Flint Public Schools. The program started as one of using the schools in the evenings and on weekends for recreation and diversion to men out of work and to their families. When full employment returned, the program became even more popular. Most of the elementary schools are open evenings and Saturdays. All of the twenty or more new elementary schools built since 1950 have a "community wing" consisting of a community room, a kitchen, a gymnasium, and an auditorium.

A visitor may observe the following:

> Neighborhood elementary schools that are busier on almost any evening than during the day; 500 youngsters attending junior high school on Saturday mornings of their own accord to acquire skills they haven't found time for during the regular school week; an elderly woman going back to high school (one of 3000 persons enrolled each year in adult high-school education); a family reupholstering dad's easy chair in the school's arts and crafts room (part of 35,000 enrolled annually in 776 adult education courses); community players rehearsing their next production in the auditorium of an elementary school; a school person making neighborhood calls.
>
> The Flint community school also provides the facilities for regular sessions of the neighborhood Teen Club (one of 43 such groups with a card carrying membership of 13,000); for 7000 children on tot lots during the summer; for meetings in the community room of men's clubs, P.T.A.'s and various other organizations; for square dances for parents, teen-agers and the younger ones, and other recreational activities held in the large

gymnasium; for a Christmas party attended by 700 adults in a school with an enrollment of only 500. (Buehring, 1958.)

The community school program in Flint has continued to grow so steadily that the number of adults who participate in it now surpasses the number of students enrolled in the public schools. Courses are offered in any subject requested by five or more persons. Nearly 100,000 persons of many differing backgrounds participate in after-school activities in more than fifty schools. Widespread interaction among citizens resulting from the community school program may not be unrelated to the fact that Flint became the first U.S. city of any size to pass an open housing law by vote of the people in 1968.

The Urban-Community School and Social Urban Renewal

A more controversial quality of the urban-community school than the one just illustrated applies to the school system rather than to one or another particular neighborhood school. The urban-community school in this sense takes active part in the reshaping and renewing of the urban community. It adopts attendance or districting policies which are aimed at serving the purposes of urban renewal. If one of these purposes is racial balance in the schools, the urban-community school system adopts practices that work for racial balance. If another of the purposes is to reduce dropouts from high school and to reduce youth unemployment, the urban-community school develops a program of work experience, or remedial teaching or other devices to reduce dropouts and to prepare marginal youth better for employment. The urban-community school cooperates with nonschool agencies of urban renewal.

If it appears that parents and citizens of middle income are becoming concerned about standards in the city schools and are thinking of moving to the suburbs, the urban-community school attempts to act constructively by involving those parents and citizens in discussions and decisions about school policy and practice.

If the education of handicapped children is of low quality in the smaller suburbs, the urban-community school system gets together with other systems to form a cooperative program of special education for the handicapped. The urban-community school system in a metropolitan area also cooperates with other systems to maintain an area-wide program of educational television.

The Neighborhood School versus the Urban Community School

Traditionally an elementary school in a city has served a local community small enough so that pupils have only a few minutes' walk between home and school. American parents have grown accustomed to the "neighborhood school." As children grow older their range of movement increases, and consequently they can go longer distances to junior and senior high schools. Thus the neighborhood school expands as pupils grow older.

Serious questions and a great deal of controversy have arisen over the neighborhood school in recent years. Due to the progressive segregation of the population by income and race in the big cities, the neighborhood school has become an instrument of segregation. Therefore parents and educators who favor integration make efforts to modify the neighborhood school policy so as to get greater social mixture of pupils in spite of the surrounding residential segregation. On the other hand, parents, educators, and school board members who favor segregation tend to use the "neighborhood school policy" as a defense that allows them to give lip service to integration and at the same time to practice segregation.

Since the recent rise of black separatism (discussed in Chapter 7), there has been a small but vocal group in the Negro community arguing for the neighborhood school, with black teachers for black students. Thus the neighborhood school is being supported by white segregationists and by black segregationists.

As the school boards in large cities have adopted policies meant to lead toward integration, and as the Civil Rights Law has been invoked by the federal government to force school systems to move toward integration, there has been a movement toward greater local community control of the schools. This movement is supported by a variety of groups who have only one thing in common—dissatisfaction with the present situation.

Local Community Control. Local community control should be distinguished from "decentralization" of power and authority in big city school systems. Decentralization generally means breaking a big school system into a number of medium-sized school systems, each under a regional or district superintendent who has a great deal of authority delegated to him by the central school administration and by the Board of Education. For example, one proposal for decentralization of the New York City system would distribute the one million students into about 30 more or less autonomous districts each with about 35,000 students. But such a district would have a population of about 200,000 or a medium-sized big city. This is much larger than a "local community."

Probably a truly local community would have to be as small as 20,000 in population, with no more than 4,000 school pupils, in order to have a school board and parent advisory groups whose members are known personally to most of the parents and who can have face-to-face communication with parents.

Local community control in this sense is favored by three groups of people: white segregationists who wish to preserve the segregated residential and school character of their local community; minority group separatists who wish to maintain a segregated minority group community to build up minority group power; and a number of educators and parents who feel that the school is not now serving minority groups effectively, but can be made to do so by putting minority groups in charge of the school through boards and committees of their own choosing.

A number of experiments along this line are being tried in New York, Chicago, Detroit, and other big cities. They are controversial, and it is too soon to tell how they will turn out.

Educational Parks or Plazas

Almost the complete opposite of the neighborhood school and of the concept of local community control is the concept of an educational park. A relatively large acreage that contains a variety of educational institutions, the educational park has received a great deal of attention during the 1960s. It may contain schools ranging from kindergarten to junior college, in appropriate buildings. It draws students from a relatively large area, several square miles at least, and thus provides for greater social integration along socioeconomic and racial lines than can be achieved in local neighborhood schools.

The educational park may have a theater and an auditorium, a swimming pool, gymnasium and playing field, a library, several specialized learning resource centers, and other physical facilities that a neighborhood school cannot afford.

The idea of an educational park has been promoted in two kinds of metropolitan settings. It might work well in a suburb of as many as 100,000 population, which has a mixed racial and socio-economic composition. Such a small city generally has an area not much greater than a mile and a half in radius, which means that most of the older pupils could walk to school. A busing program for younger pupils and for those living far away from the educational plaza would not be very expensive. For example, there is serious talk of establishing an educational park in Berkeley, California. The other setting in a metropolitan area that might be suitable for an educational park is a sector of a big city that has up to 100,000 population which includes a variety of ethnic and income groups.

In either case, an educational park might serve to produce an efficient use of school facilities, or to provide integrated school experiences, or it might serve both purposes at the same time.

Plans for educational parks have been advanced in a number of cities, including Pittsburgh, Baltimore, Chicago, Syracuse, and New York City. The only one of these that had got past the discussion and planning stage by 1970, was the one in Co-op City, in northeast Bronx of New York. Co-op City is a housing development on vacant land, with a projected population of 60,000. Since there were no schools there in the beginning, it was easy to plan a single site for an expected 10,000 students, including a high school, two intermediate and two primary schools. The cost is estimated at $38 million. Two of the schools will be opened in 1970.

One big difficulty in the way of the educational park is that it generally is designed to take the place of existing schools, some old and obsolescent, but some new. Thus a system of educational parks, requiring an enormous capital outlay, might run into opposition because it would make useless a number of existing school buildings that are no more than ten or twenty years old.

For the urban community school idea, the educational park seems well suited. But the objections by the proponents of the neighborhood school or of local community control of schools, and the difficulty of financing an ambitious park plan, make a favorable prediction questionable.

SUGGESTED ACTIVITIES

1. In the inner city of your metropolitan area, how would you change and develop the school program so as to promote urban renewal in one or more specific neighborhoods? What cooperative relationships between school system and other agencies would be required?
2. Looking at the high schools that you know in your metropolitan area, which ones can be called truly "comprehensive"? What criteria do you use to define a comprehensive high school?
3. Study the activities of the War on Poverty in your metropolitan area. To what extent are these activities planned and administered through the schools? Is there any evidence that these activities will have a continuing influence on school programs if federal support for them is ended?
4. Analyze the opportunities in your area for a person to participate actively as an amateur and passively as a spectator of the spectrum of arts. To what extent is the school system acting to extend the quality and scope of such participation? How is your metropolitan area related to a State Council on the Arts, and to the National Arts and Humanities Foundation? Have federal funds been used to provide learning experiences in the fine arts and the performing arts?
5. Use Doll's checklist (see page 320) in gathering data from teachers in several elementary schools. Categorize each school according to the type it most nearly resembles.
6. Write to the Board of Education in Flint, Michigan for more information on the community school program and for information about borrowing the film "To Touch a Child."

SUGGESTIONS FOR FURTHER READING

1. A variety of publications describe programs for socially disadvantaged children and youth. Among the best sources are *Compensatory Education for the Disadvantaged* by Gordon and Wilkerson and the series on Successful Compensatory Education Programs published for the U.S. Office of Education by the government printing office in 1969.
2. *The School and Urban Renewal,* a pamphlet published by the Educational Facilities Laboratory, describes the role of the schools in renewal efforts in New Haven.
3. *Schoolhouse in the City* edited by Toffler includes a number of papers related to education and metropolitan evolution and to the role of the schools in urban renewal.

CHAPTER 5

Suburban Schools in the Evolving Metropolis

THE YEAR 1964 was a landmark in the history of the United States. In that year, following a long-range trend operating throughout the twentieth century, the percentage of metropolitan population living outside the central cities first surpassed the percentage living within them. Although some metropolitan residents outside the central city reside in unincorporated areas or in the urban-rural fringe, the great majority live in the suburban rings surrounding the central cities. This process of metropolitan decentralization, moreover, will continue for the foreseeable future: by 1985, it is estimated that 63.2 percent of the population of metropolitan areas in the United States will live outside the central cities. (Hodge and Hauser, 1968.)

Suburban Diversity

Because many of the early suburbs in the older and larger metropolitan areas were dormitory- or residential-type settlements, stereotypes arose which portrayed the suburbs as nearly uniform in middle- and upper-status socio-economic composition and their schools as correspondingly homogeneous institutions whose students nearly all graduate and go to college. Metropolitan growth, however, has destroyed whatever applicability these stereotypes once had.

In the larger and older metropolitan areas many of the families which had moved to the suburbs have been working-class families attracted by various economic opportunities and amenities available there, and industry has been moving to suburban locations to take advantage of proximity to the labor force and of lower costs for land and transportation. In addition, metropolitan growth in large SMSAs has meant that satellite cities and outlying industrial settlements originally located at a considerable distance in terms of travel time from the central city have been incorporated within the "urban orbit" of the metropolitan area. In newer and smaller metropolitan areas of the West and Southwest, central city boundaries were drawn large enough to accommodate considerable growth before the city spilled over into the suburbs. In either case, suburban areas often consist as much or more of "pockets" of poverty (frequently semi-rural in character) as of middle-class residential developments.

While differences between the central cities and their suburban rings are striking, differences between suburbs can be almost equally striking, particularly when employing and manufacturing suburbs are contrasted with dormitory or residential suburbs. Schnore's study of 300 suburbs in the 25 largest urbanized areas, for example, showed that in 1960 the percentage of white-collar workers among employed persons living in residential suburbs was 31 percent higher than the comparable figure for residents of employing suburbs. These two types of suburbs also differed considerably in other social and demographic characteristics as well. (Schnore, 1965.)

The great range in socio-economic and related characteristics which generally can be found among suburban communities in the same metropolitan area is shown in the information presented in Table 5.1 on some suburbs in the Boston SMSA. This information underlines the fact that suburbs are far from homogeneous in their social composition and character.

One reason why suburbs are sometimes thought of as homogeneous middle-class developments is because they have tended to be racially homogeneous. In 1960, only 5.2 percent of the metropolitan population outside the central cities was classified as nonwhite.

TABLE 5.1

Classification and Characteristics of Selected Communities Outside the Central City in the Boston SMSA

Community	*1959 Median Family Income*	*1966 Taxable Property at Market Value Per Capita*	*1962 General Expenditure Per Capita*	*Degree to Which Workers Are Employed Outside Town of Residence*	*Local Economic Base*	*Growth Rate*	*Special Characteristics*
Cambridge	5,923	5,170	270	Some	Balanced	Low	Education; industry
Salem	5,970	5,000	335	Some	Balanced	Low	
Lynn	6,021	4,700	238	Some	Balanced	Low	Manufacturing
Duxbury	6,452	9,890	260	Limited	None		Semi-rural; some resort
Manchester	6,664	11,000	203	Complete	None		Semi-rural
Peabody	6,749	5,030	193	Some	Balanced		Much retailing
Quincy	6,785	6,370	199	Some	Balanced	Low	Much industry
Medford	6,693	3,970	205	Much	Modest	Low	Education; industry
Weymouth	7,003	7,530	265	Some	Modest		Government installation
Bedford	7,893	8,040	271	Some	Modest	Low	Much service industry; military installation
Sudbury	8,538	7,800	203	Complete	None	Very High	
Wayland	9,363	7,800	217	Most	Little	High	
Lynnfield	9,413	7,540	262	Complete	None	High	
Dover	12,256	8,380	251	Complete	None		
Weston	13,703	9,510	215	Complete	None		

Source: Adapted from Alexander Gamy, "Fiscal Disparities in the Boston, Massachusetts Metropolitan Area," *Fiscal Balance in the American Federal System.* Vol. 2 Metropolitan Fiscal Disparities. Washington, D.C.: Advisory Commission on Intergovernmental Relations, 1967.

Even racial homogeneity, however, is beginning to be reduced. Particularly on the two coasts and in the larger metropolitan areas of two million or more population, substantial numbers of black families have been moving to the suburbs; as a result, some suburbs have become well integrated.

Marked changes also have begun to occur in the residential character of many suburbs. Inexpensive subdivisions built since the Second World War sometimes show obvious signs of disrepair, and the "second generation" of homeowners in these subdivisions often is unmistakably lower in social class background than the original residents.

In retrospect, it can be seen that the evolutionary process has begun to take on noticeable momentum as suburban settlements have grown diversified and more mature. What we are really seeing, as S. D. Clark noted in concluding a study of suburban growth in Toronto, is that nuclei of the city have been moving out into the suburbs and recreating on a smaller scale the patterns of stratification amid diversity which are characteristic of the metropolitan area as a whole.

> In truth, what suburban development meant was the reproduction of the city in the country. The reproduction came about fitfully. Some parts of the urban complex were more easily transferred than others. . . . In the end, however, there was not much of the urban society that was not reproduced in the suburban. The balance for long may have favoured the middle classes—it was people of the middle classes who could most easily afford the kind of houses being built—but the suburbs were not without their poor . . . and, as the type of development shifted from the building of single-family dwellings to the building of apartment houses, row houses, duplexes, and the like, a point was eventually reached where few elements of the urban population could not be accommodated in the suburbs. (Clark, 1968.)

Evolving stratification patterns in the suburbs combined with urban renewal in the central city mean that both parts of the metropolitan area are likely to have low-income as well as middle- and upper-income neighborhoods; in this they are not as dissimilar as popular imagery often suggests. What by definition does differentiate the central city from the suburbs is that while the central city is one large municipality, the suburbs encompass many governments, most of them relatively small in geographic size and population.

The consequences of these demographic and geographic patterns are of great importance to the educator.

In the central city, for one thing, large numbers of children are served by a single school district. Even in a metropolitan area such as Kansas City, where parts of eighteen different school districts are included within the municipal boundaries of Kansas City, Missouri, 80,000 students—more than half the public school enrollment in the city—are in the Kansas City Public School District. Suburban school districts, on the other hand, generally are much smaller than central city districts, and since the suburban population of the nation's metropolitan areas exceeds that of the central cities, naturally there are many more suburban than city districts. In some SMSAs suburban school district boundaries tend to coincide with town and village units; in others there is much overlap between the two sets of governmental districts. In either case, however, few suburban school districts enroll more than 15 or 20 thousand pupils, and fewer still approach the average size of central city districts.

One corollary of the relatively small size of suburban school districts is that there is a great deal of diversity in the characteristics of these districts and the problems which are most salient for the teachers and administrators who work in them. Despite this diversity, however, there are three types of problems which tend to be characteristic of a great number and perhaps even a large majority of suburban school districts.

PROBLEMS IN FINANCING SUBURBAN EDUCATION

The same myth which perceives suburbia as almost entirely upper-middle-class in socio-economic composition sometimes leads to the assumption that financing education at an adequate level is not a serious problem in the average suburban school district. Not only does such a view fail to recognize that suburban areas already contain a mixture of social classes and will become still more socially diversified in the future, it also ignores the facts that (1) the capital costs of organizing an educational system in a rapidly growing suburban area are very high—so high, in fact, as to seem unsupportable to local taxpayers simultaneously required to finance the construction of streets, sewers, and other public facilities; and (2) effective ability to finance education in a given school district depends on a variety of factors which include the size of the industrial and commercial tax base, the ratio of school-age children to employed adults, the percent of parochial- and private-school clients, and perceptions of equity in property assessment practices. Since many suburban areas, particularly the fastest growing ones, are primarily dormitory or bedroom communities with little or no industry and have a relatively high ratio of children to be educated, a sizable percentage of them face severe limitations in funding education.

Variations in the population composition and financial capacity of suburban school districts create extreme disparities and inequalities in the educational opportunities available to suburban students in the same metropolitan area. It is true that a few unusually wealthy suburban districts seemingly can raise almost unlimited sums of money to spend on public education: per pupil expenditure in such districts sometimes is three or four times as high as the metropolitan average. Immediately adjacent to these very wealthy districts, however, one is apt to find districts which are not able to finance education adequately even after receiving substantial amounts of state aid. In the Chicago SMSA, for example, Central Stickney District 110 spent $1,169 per pupil in 1964 with an education levy of $.40; next door, South Stickney District 111 spent $479 with an education levy three times as high. In the Detroit SMSA, similarly, the taxable wealth per pupil in two adjoining suburban school districts (Brownstone and Maplegrove) amounted to $383,940 and $8,416, respectively, in 1968. As indicated by a study conducted by Hickrod and Sabulao, moreover, between 1950 and 1960 suburban school districts as a group became increasingly stratified and unequal in ability to support education, thus leading to the formation of "sectors" or "clusters" of disadvantaged suburban districts (Hickrod and Sabulao, 1969).

Table 5.2 which shows the 1967 tax rates and expenditures per pupil for non-central city school districts in the Missouri portion of the St. Louis SMSA, illustrates the range of disparities in ability to finance education which exists among suburban districts in the United States.

By definition, an average suburban school district is neither as financially trouble-free as a few extremely wealthy neighboring districts nor as hard-pressed as some others which may be particularly impoverished. It is not at all uncommon, however, to find suburban school districts which either are unable to afford a kindergarten program or which must conduct such programs in churches and

TABLE 5.2

Expenditure Per Pupil and School Tax Levy, St. Louis County Public School Districts, 1966–67

School District	*Expenditure Per Pupil in ADA*	*1966 Tax Levy*	*School District*	*Expenditure Per Pupil in ADA*	*1966 Tax Levy*
Clayton	$1,176	$2.82	Riverview Gardens	$544	$3.71
Ladue	863	3.25	Lindbergh	538	3.50
University City	795	3.72	Mehlville	527	3.58
Jennings	785	2.87	Bayless	505	3.36
Brentwood	782	3.13	Rockwood	505	3.85
Maplewood	660	3.10	Parkway	504	4.35
Affton	660	3.41	Ferguson	495	3.98
Normandy	630	3.39	Hazelwood	491	4.15
Wellston	629	4.24	Ritenour	484	3.35
Webster Groves	621	4.07	Hancock Place	482	3.58
Kirkwood	607	4.20	Valley Park	431	3.89
Pattonville	601	3.62	Kinloch	425	4.23
Berkeley	551	3.20			

Source: *School District Organizaton for Missouri.* Report of the Missouri School District Reorganization Commission, November, 1968.

other non-school facilities that may not be suitable for the purpose. In many suburban school districts, similarly, class size may be considerably above the metropolitan average, and double shifts are frequent in rapidly growing districts in which enrollment increases sometimes far outstrip a district's building program.

Perhaps the most obvious examples of suburban school districts which metropolitan evolution has left all but incapable of supporting minimally adequate educational programs are those serving predominantly disadvantaged student populations. Until recently, such districts very rarely were found in metropolitan areas of the North or West; today, most of the larger metropolitan areas have at least one or two of them. They tend to be of two types, both of which are found in the St. Louis area for which statistics are given in Table 5.2.

The more common type is exemplified by the Wellston School District which is located just west of the city of St. Louis and which has been receiving a continuing influx of relatively low-income families from the black ghetto in the city. As newcomers have moved in, the out-migration of established middle-class families has tended to accelerate, thus duplicating the pattern of racial and social class transition which previously had been a central city but not a suburban phenomenon. The resulting financial crisis—along with the appearance of the full range of "inner city" problems in an evolving suburban area—is graphically described in the following excerpts from an article in the *St. Louis Globe Democrat:*

> The sudden influx of large numbers of poor people into the small community has had a drastic effect upon its school system. To put it bluntly, the quality of education has fallen off sharply, and nobody—not the teachers, the parents, the administrators nor the school—really knows what to do about it.
>
> Wellston teachers complain classes are too large and room space is too scarce for them to teach effectively. Classes of over 40 students are not unusual in the lower elementary grades. At Central Elementary School every closet and storeroom has been cleared to provide extra class space. There still isn't nearly enough, according to school principal James Reames.
>
> Not only are classes overcrowded; there are fewer of them. Several special classes for college-bound students and the entire athletic program were dropped this year. . . . "We *may* be approaching the point," said [Superintendent of Schools] Jackson, "when the students who come out of our schools won't be prepared for much of anything—neither to go on with their education nor to get jobs."
>
> What has happened, said Jackson, is that Wellston homes have been filling up with more and more school children at the same time that their taxable value has been declining. A home worth $15,000 ten years ago is only worth $7,000 today, he said. . . . Wellston has almost exhausted its bonding capacity, and now pays $.71 out of its $4.49 tax rate per $100 of assessed valuation for back debts on its present buildings.
>
> . . . Four times last spring, despite teacher strikes, Wellston voters failed to give a $.62 tax hike the necessary two-thirds majority. . . . Residents are understandably disgruntled at paying high taxes for poor education.
>
> Moreover, according to St. Louis County Superintendent George W. Vossbrink, there is nothing unique about the problems of Wellston Schools.
>
> "What has happened to Wellston can be expected to happen to several other mature school districts on the edge of the city. It is simply a matter of time before the poor spill over," says Vossbrink. (Andrew Wilson, 1969.)

The second type of low-income school district to be found in the suburbs is exemplified in the Kinloch Public Schools. Originally, Kinloch was a small semirural community inhabited by low-income black families which managed to eke out a subsistence living in domestic work, agricultural labor, and other low-paying pursuits. Eventually, the metropolitan population expanded and the area around and beyond Kinloch became suburbanized. Today, Kinloch is surrounded by modern residential- and employment-type suburbs with substantial middle-income populations. Effects on the Kinloch schools can be seen in the figures in Table 5.2 which show that Kinloch has the lowest per pupil expenditure rate in the St. Louis suburban area, even though its tax rate for education is among the highest in the area and its already disadvantaged young people must now compete in an advanced metropolitan economy. Although semirural, low-income communities of this type generally are absorbed into much larger suburban districts during the process of metropolitan evolution, it is possible that similar districts will be created in metropolitan areas where substantial rural poverty exists just beyond newly suburbanized outlying communities.

Diseconomies of Size

Closely related to the problem of financing education in suburban areas is the fact that most suburban school districts enroll fewer than 20,000 students. Because many educational programs and services such as vocational education and special education require a larger pupil population if they are to be provided at a reasonable per pupil cost, small school districts operating in isolation either must forego such programs entirely or must cut down other expenditures in order to obtain the funds to support them. Data processing equipment, for example, can be used to manage school district affairs more effectively and to individualize instruction or otherwise improve the quality of educational programs, but such equipment is inordinately expensive for school districts which are too small to utilize it more than a fraction of the school day. Learning resource centers, similarly, tend to require exorbitant expenditures unless the numbers of pupils who use them are large enough to justify full-time operation, thus reducing the per pupil operating cost to a feasible level. Economists refer to the special problems which relatively small organizations such as the suburban school district encounter in financing or purchasing services requiring a large population base as *diseconomies of scale*. The conclusion that most suburban school districts are too small to provide many desirable educational services economically can be inferred from Table 5.3. This Table shows estimates of the minimum population base needed to conduct selected services effectively without wasting some of the limited tax resources available for education within a particular school district or the metropolitan area as a whole. These estimates were obtained from specialists in many areas of education who participated in the Great Plains School District Organization Project as part of a study conducted by the state departments of education in Iowa, Missouri, Nebraska, and South Dakota and financed by the U.S. Office of Education. The figures in Table 5.3 clearly indicate that only a few extremely wealthy or unusually large suburban school districts are in a position to provide a full range of modern educational services for their students.

TABLE 5.3

Estimates of Pupil Population Base Required for Selected Educational Services

Service	*Population Base Needed for Efficiency of Organization and Economy of Operation*
Comprehensive vocational education	20,000–50,000
Special education	20,000–100,000
Business management	35,000 or more
Curriculum development and research centers	35,000 or more
Electronic data processing	60,000–100,000 or more
Coordinated teams of educational specialists	35,000 or more

Source: Great Plains School District Organization Project: *Guidelines for School District Organization,* Lincoln, Nebraska: State Department of Education. July, 1968.

Conflicts Over Educational Issues in the Suburbs

Although there are a number of small, homogeneous suburban school districts which experience little trace of controversy concerning the nature and quality of instructional programs, the diversity which exists in most suburban school districts generates considerable conflict on educational matters. Not only do disagreements over education become a major community issue in many suburbs, but conflict probably will increase as metropolitan evolution continues to create more diversity in the suburban environment. A number of typical situations involving the presence of differing social groups with divergent goals and needs that often cause conflict or related problems for suburban educators are described on the following pages.

Conflict Over Taxes for Education. One of the problems encountered most frequently in relatively new and rapidly-growing suburbs is conflict over financing between citizens who feel they are overburdened by taxes for a variety of public services and other citizens who believe that more funds should be raised to support the public schools. Every citizen wants good schools in his community, but not all citizens accept—or are able to accept—definitions of quality education that may be put forth by the professional educator or by civic groups organized specifically to support the schools. Clark has described a common source of such disagreement in reporting on the situation and attitudes of the many suburbanites who were interviewed in his study.

> The "good society" for most suburban residents was the society that made no demands upon them. Associations like the Home and School could hold out the promise of building a "better" community: a community boasting not only sewers, paved streets, and street lights, but also well-staffed schools, recreational centres, libraries, and a population informed about and alive to the affairs of the world at large. But building such a community could not be done without expenditure of time and money, and intent upon the main purpose which had led him to make the move to the suburbs—the establishment of a home for his family—the new suburban resident was in no mood to undertake such an expenditure. (Clark, 1968, p. 170.)

If most suburbs were homogeneous collections of upper- and middle-class families with no serious financial problems, public officials would find their constituents more willing to vote higher taxes for transportation, sanitation, education, and all the other public services which are part of suburban development. But since many suburbs do include a range of income groups including working-class families and lower-middle-class families with working class backgrounds, the costs of improving these services often seem too high to families struggling to meet other obligations and to acquire the personal possessions symbolic of middle-class status. Thus it is no surprise that an intensive study Bloomberg and Sunshine conducted of attitudes toward education held by voters in four different types of suburbs in upstate New York showed that ". . . opposition to increased taxes for the schools is part of a general opposition to allocating more local resources to local government." (Bloomberg and Sunshine, 1963.) The authors pointed out that the linkage between resistance to taxation and attitudes concerning local schools makes it necessary for educators to develop definite strategies for obtaining adequate funds to finance education in the suburbs.

Conflict Associated with Rural Urban Transition. Building a new suburban development in a previously rural area often generates a good deal of disagreement concerning the purposes and operation of the public school system. Many of the incoming parents hold educational expectations much higher than seemed adequate for an agricultural way of life, particularly if they are parents who may have left the central city primarily because they believed that the quality of education had been deteriorating there. Many of the original rural residents, for their part, own large amounts of agricultural property which would bear a significant portion of any increase in tax assessments for the schools. School board members in such districts may have been elected before the completion of the new development and may have several years to serve before incoming urbanites have an opportunity to elect their own representatives to the board. Situations of this type frequently lead to highly explosive battles over education in suburban school districts.

Conflict Over Curriculum and Instruction. Suburban school districts whose clients include a variety of social and cultural groups often undergo intense conflict concerning the purposes of the curriculum and how it should be taught. Upper-middle-class families and younger, well-educated parents often support innovative school programs which they think would provide up-to-date and challenging educational experiences for their children. Parents with lower-middle and working-class backgrounds, on the other hand, frequently oppose nontraditional practices which they believe violate values and approaches that made for successful education in the past, particularly if these innovative programs are likely to cost a good deal of money. In addition to questioning "radical" and "unproven" innovations such as modular scheduling, nongraded school organization, and independent learning projects, such parents may join with conservative political groups to oppose sex education, free inquiry methods in the social studies, use of controversial current literature in the language arts, or other approaches typically supported by well-educated parents in the community. Many suburban school districts now are in the throes of bitter community conflict over these issues. To some extent the outcome of these disagreements will depend on the orientation and leadership of the superintendent of schools and the board of education. In relatively diversified districts, the tendency frequently is to stick to traditional and "safe" policies and practices and thus avoid the possibility of making changes to which one or another group in the community might object. Such a stance also heads off trouble from constituents who may aggressively oppose higher taxes for education. This is essentially what happened in Levittown, New Jersey, where sociologist Herbert J. Gans lived as a participant-observer for two years and reported that:

> . . . in February 1961, more than 600, the largest crowd of Levittowners ever to meet together, jammed the auditorium in an angry mood to protest the proposed budget. . . . [Some] in attendance attacked the classroom size policy, pointing out that the parochial school was providing adequate education with 60 children per class; and a few people even objected to teachers' salaries, the highest of which . . . were then approaching the community's median income of $7,500. The opposition to teachers' salaries came largely from a handful of working class Levittowners who had never before encountered teachers earning more than they. . . .
>
> The meeting was extremely bitter, with angry charges and exaggerated claims freely traded. The conflict was clearly between the haves and the have-nots, for when one lone budget supporter ended his speech, he was asked how much he was earning. There was also conflict, as in the voluntary associations, between the (few) advocates of rapid growth who wanted a fully staffed school system *now*, and the (many) proponents of gradual maturation. . . .
>
> After public concern over the budget had died down. . . . [the] main course of conflict now was the superintendent's unwillingness to plan for the future. . . . Old differences with

C.A.P.S. [Citizens' Association for Public Schools] about what made for a good school . . . also contributed to the superintendent's downfall. . . . Yet these factors were only symptomatic of a more basic problem—his inability to adapt his previous rural experience to the wishes of the suburbanites. He could, perhaps, not have avoided antagonizing the minority who wanted an upper-middle-class school system or the less affluent Levittowners who demanded economy above all. . . .

. . . By September 1965, more than 8,000 students were attending five elementary schools, two junior (or middle) ones, and a high school. . . . the education they provided would prepare the students for about the same white collar, technical, and subprofessional jobs held by their parents and for the lower-middle-class culture that dominated the community. Perhaps the schools favored the restrictive subculture more than the expansive; the course offerings were quite traditional, and there was none of the "life adjustment" and "learning to get along with the group" approach that Whyte had found in Park Forest. The teachers gave their students individual attention and demanded neither superior intellectual achievement nor oppressive memorizing. As a result, the dropout rate was infinitesimal, and about 50 per cent of the graduates enrolled in college, although in 1963 a third of them chose junior colleges and teachers' colleges, and only 5 per cent went to "name" schools. It was, as one unhappy C.A.P.S. member put it, "the school system the community deserved." (Gans, 1967, pp. 97–101.)

Conflict Between Established and New Sections in Suburban School Districts. It often happens that the various residential neighborhoods which make up a suburban school district of any substantial size were built many years apart. In many cases the original suburban community consisted of large and expensive older homes built in the first two decades of the twentieth century. Neighborhoods of this type frequently include luxury apartment buildings and spacious estates; at the time they were built, these suburbs represented the outlying ring of metropolitan area in which only the wealthiest and highest status families could afford to live.

When movement to the suburbs greatly accelerated in the years following the Second World War, new housing tracts often were built adjacent to these residential neighborhoods and became part either of the original or an expanded school district that served the established suburban population. Many tract developments were quite large in scale and were sold mostly to younger families; this brought in hundreds and even thousands of children for whom existing school facilities were inadequate. The problems and conflicts produced in this type of situation typically are of three major types: (1) problems arise in connection with the difficulty many incoming students with working-class backgrounds experience in handling the high academic standards and competitive pressures characteristic of high-prestige schools; (2) the task of paying for a rapid expansion in educational facilities urgently needed to accommodate youngsters in newly-settled sections of the district is greatly resented by old-time residents whose children have grown up and left the community and who feel they bore a sufficient burden in financing existing facilities; and (3) rapid expansion in enrollment results in serious overcrowding in a prestige high school and forces the building of one or more additional high schools. Fearing that a new high school will be inferior and in any case will not have as high a reputation as the established school, parents of students assigned to the new school complain bitterly about discrimination and unfair treatment. This latter conflict is basically the type which Masotti has described at length in his case study of conflict in New Trier, Illinois. New Trier, according to Masotti, was a high-status suburb which had never lost a school bond election or had a contested school board election in the first half of the twentieth century. After the Second World War, however, changes associated with metropolitan evolution made the schools a focus of contention and disagreement within the community.

> . . . postwar social and demographic changes in the structure of the Chicago metropolitan area created disintegrative forces and a potential for social conflict within the New Trier community. The township population, which had grown only 3 per cent between 1940 and 1950, increased 42.3 per cent in the following decade. Population growth brought concomitant changes in the social structure, resulting in a less homogeneous community. Thus, at the same time that population growth made necessary new or expanded school facilities, growing socio-economic differentiation within the electorate made it increasingly difficult to gain public support for the Board of Education's expansion policies. (Masotti, 1967.)

Problems in High-Prestige Suburban School Districts. Although James B. Conant's 1961 book on *Slums and Suburbs* did much to alert educators and the general public to the explosive build-up of "social dynamite" in inner-city schools, hardly any attention was paid to the second half of the book in which he enumerated the special problems of prestigious schools in the suburbs. Basically, Conant was concerned with what he termed the "heavily college-oriented suburb" in which the dilemmas faced by the educator result from the many "cases where the parental ambitions outrun the offspring's ability; that is, where the boy or girl has difficulty mastering academic work in a school with high standards and yet is expected by his parents to attend a prestige college. If the student with limited ability fails to gain admission to a prestige college, the parents are likely to blame the public school. . . ."

While this problem exists to some extent in a wide range of suburbs, its impact is most obvious, Conant points out, in high-prestige schools located in predominantly middle-class residential suburbs in which there are

> relatively few . . . students with less-than-average ability and little interest in academic work. . . . Yet few as they are, they may present a problem and a different kind of problem from that presented by the existence of the same group in another type of community. . . .
>
> Aside from required academic courses, there is considerable question about the value of additional academic elective courses for below-average students. Art and music flourish in many suburban schools, and one finds less able pupils in academic areas often taking numerous courses in art and music—partially, I suspect, to fill out their schedules. It is as difficult to find a suitable elective program for these students in suburban schools as elsewhere. (Conant, 1961.)

Since many small, high-prestige suburban school districts do not have a large enough population base to sustain programs in vocational education and other specialized subjects, and since parental pressure often pushes insistently in the direction of narrower rather than broader curricula in these districts, it is difficult to provide a diverse and challenging range of educational programs and experiences in many predominantly middle-class suburban school districts. By cooperating with other school districts to develop and conduct special programs and services, school officials can overcome some of these difficulties and provide a richer and more diverse set of educational opportunities for all students in such highly academically oriented districts.

Another problem which is particularly salient in many high-prestige suburban high schools is student alienation and unrest. For a variety of reasons, upper-middle class students tend to be more critical of existing social conditions and institutions, including the schools, than are lower-middle class students. Particularly since 1966 or 1967 when aspects of the so-called "drug" culture or "youth" culture were spreading rapidly from a few large urban centers to the suburbs, alienation from public schools has become an important force among many youth in relatively affluent suburban homes (Gitchoff, 1969). In part, at least, alienation among youth in these communities reflects a feeling of being isolated from reality of life in other parts of the metropolitan area. Here again, educators may be able to moderate this problem by cooperating with other school districts to bring about more contact between students of different backgrounds and to give students more opportunity to become acquainted with communities and groups in other parts of the metropolitan area.

Racial Change and Desegregation. The material in an earlier section of this chapter describing changes in the Wellston, Missouri, School District illustrates a situation that may be a significant portent for the future of metropolitan education in the suburbs. As black families move out of overcrowded inner-city neighborhoods to seek better employment opportunities and more pleasant living conditions in the suburbs, many suburban school districts experience the beginnings of racial desegregation.

In many metropolitan areas substantial desegregation in suburban schools is still little more than a cloud on the horizon. In a few others, however, it is an accomplished fact which creates the same problems of student confrontation and similar needs for teacher retraining, curriculum revision, and provision of more specialized and diversified instructional programs as have arisen at many integrated schools in the big cities. A prototypical situation of this sort in the New York suburb of White Plains in 1968 has been fully described and analyzed in a study directed by Dan Dodson of the New York University Center for Human Relations and Community Studies. (Joint Study Commission, February 4, 1969.) The report concluded that lack of action to ensure successful integration in a school such as White Plains High School would encourage "the Negro minority . . . to withdraw into apartheid education. If this happens, then each of us withdraws into a kind of tribalism and concentrates on the lore of his tribe—rather than upon a common set of values." School officials in the suburb of White Plains, in other words, are facing much the same challenge to work for solution of the urban crisis as are their counterparts in the big cities. In more ways than one, the so-called urban crisis turns out to be a metropolitan crisis, and metropolitan evolution can be expected to make this fact more visible and inescapable in many more suburban school districts during the next few years.

Unless vigorous efforts are launched to achieve effective integration throughout the suburbs, black families will tend to concentrate in a few suburban school districts. Some of these districts probably will become entirely or largely resegregated, just as has happened in big city neighborhoods which have been nearly the sole targets for racial transition at a given point in time. Wellston, for example, already is 77 percent black, and soon may swell the ranks of the small number of all-black suburban school districts which already exist in the United States. Such districts will not necessarily be predominantly low-income in social class composition, as is the Kinloch School District described above. In any case, however, the problems associated with social disadvantage and minority status in a stratified society will have been transferred from the city to the suburbs, and educational as well as other institutions in the suburbs will be forced to deal more explicitly with the fundamental problems of the metropolitan area if metropolitan society is to thrive and prosper.

SUBURBAN SCHOOLS IN THE METROPOLITAN SYSTEM OF EDUCATION

This chapter has provided a brief description of problems which are characteristic of differing types of suburban school districts. The problems cited are not unique to the suburbs but are all related to the on-going pattern of metropolitan evolution which affects the suburban parts of the metropolitan area and their schools.

Certain implications are evident when suburban school districts are viewed as part of a metropolitan society which is evolving toward greater decentralization and at the same time is challenged to solve problems associated with complexity and stratification in the metropolitan area as a whole. The most important of these implications are described in the following pages.

1. Cooperative programs can improve educational opportunities in suburban school districts.

Several of the problems noted on the preceding pages require cooperative action to provide educational opportunities which many or most suburban school districts are in no position to make available on their own. Examples of such problems are the plight of the relatively low tax-base district which cannot raise adequate funds for education even with a very high tax rate, the impossibility of providing adequate special services such as vocational education in the great majority of districts which are too small to conduct them economically, and the limited range of offerings and programs available in many small, highly academic-oriented districts. In each case cooperation with other suburban districts and with central city districts is indicated to make adequate financial resources and educational opportunities available for all students. Thus suburban schools will benefit directly by taking the initiative to achieve the kinds of cooperative planning and action within the metropolitan education system which are described elsewhere in this book.

2. Suburban schools can take action to solve emerging problems while these problems are still relatively amenable to solution.

It is certain that in future years larger numbers of economically disadvantaged students will be appearing in suburban classrooms. Between 1960 and 1966, decline in the white population of central cities averaged about 150,000 per year. Between 1966 and 1968, the average annual loss of white population in the central cities was close to 500,000. (U.S. Department of Commerce, April 21, 1969.) A significant though indeterminate percentage of this decrease consisted of moderate- and low-income white families who moved out of central cities to the suburbs. Although the rate of movement of lower-income white families to the suburbs may rise or fall somewhat in the future, this migration doubtless will continue to be substantial, with economically disadvantaged white families swelling the pockets of poverty that already exist in the suburbs.

Soon after an influx of economically disadvantaged students occurs in a suburban school or school district, teachers may be heard to make such statements as, "I am at my wit's end trying to maintain control of my class," "I just can't seem to get many of my students to do their homework or hand in assignments anymore," and "If only I could be rid of three or four troublemakers, I would be able to really teach these kids something." In short, they begin to sound like frustrated teachers in schools in the inner core of the big city.

Another evolutionary change noted above is that significant numbers of black families have been moving into suburban neighborhoods in many metropolitan areas, particularly larger SMSAs in the Middle West and on the East Coast. Between 1960 and 1966, the Negro population of communities outside the central cities in the 212 areas designated as SMSAs in 1960 increased by only 19,000 per year. Between 1966 and 1968, by way of contrast, the increase in the black population in these communities was 221,000 per year. (U.S. Department of Commerce, April 21, 1969.) Some of this increase undoubtedly consisted of low-status black families following the movement of major industries to the suburbs, but more of it probably represented upward-mobile and middle-class black families seeking better living environments than could be found in the central city ghettos. In some cases the expansion of black population in the suburbs signals the creation or expansion of small racial ghettoes there; in other cases it involves the desegregation of previously white neighborhoods and schools. Depending on which pattern is predominant, the challenges to eliminate patterns of segregation within a biracial school district or to make integration function constructively within the desegregated school or classroom have been transferred from the central city to the suburbs.

A major difference between the central city and the suburbs is that suburban schools generally have more adequate time and resources to implement wise and effective solutions to problems associated with poverty or race. In addition, the opportunity to study the successes and failures of central city schools places suburban educators in an advantageous position to take preventive action to solve educational problems related to metropolitan evolution.

For example, central city educators are beginning to recognize that retraining teachers to work with disadvantaged students requires intensive in-service education programs lasting several years rather than traditional in-service education conducted for only a few weeks or months. Many suburban school districts can initiate such training programs before teachers of disadvantaged students begin to feel frustrated and defeated.

With respect to desegregation, similarly, suburban schools can provide intensive in-service training for teachers and administrators in the early stages of desegregation and can set up mechanisms such as biracial student committees to identify and deal with grievances and misunderstandings before serious racial incidents and polarization occur in a desegregating school. The alternative is to ignore the process of metropolitan evolution and in so doing repeat the mistakes made in other school districts in which "it can't happen here" attitudes eventually have frustrated and immobilized teachers and administrators.

3. Suburban schools can make a major contribution to the development of metropolitan society by demonstrating that educational problems related to stratification and diversity in the metropolitan area are not insoluble.

Because metropolitan evolution tends to proceed later and more slowly in the suburbs than in the central city, suburban school districts generally do not have extremely large concentrations of disadvantaged students. Since research indicates that teaching and learning conditions are much less conducive to improving the performance of disadvantaged students in predominantly low-income than in mixed social-class schools, suburban school districts have a great advantage in working to bring about maximum gains in the academic performance of these students. By demonstrating how this can best be accomplished, suburban schools have an important part to play in the resolution of fundamental problems in metropolitan society.

The situation with regard to desegregation is similar. Most desegregated suburban school districts do not yet have so high a proportion of black students as to make it difficult or impossible to place every child in desegregated classrooms, as is true in some of the big cities. Black families in the suburbs tend to be less frequently economically disadvantaged than is the case in central city ghettoes; thus the problem of overcoming extreme academic deficits tends to be a less severe by-product of desegregation in the suburbs than it has been in some central city schools. For these reasons, suburban school officials can concentrate more confidently and single mindedly on making integration plans work more successfully than has proved possible in many central city school districts. They can demonstrate that stable, high quality integrated education can be provided on a widespread basis.

Two highly respected suburban school districts already appear to be moving reasonably well toward this goal. Berkeley, California and Evanston, Illinois are suburban cities with populations of about 120,000 and 85,000, respectively, whose schools have a national reputation for academic excellence. In both districts, comprehensive plans have been put into operation following several years of intensive effort to prepare teachers and community opinion for district-wide integration. Initial reports from both districts indicate that appreciable progress is being made toward the goals of improving educational opportunities and providing positive interracial contacts for all students. If committed to proper planning and implementation, suburban school districts elsewhere can contribute equally instructive examples of action to reduce patterns of racial segregation in the schools and society of the metropolitan area.

4. Suburban schools can take the initiative in bringing about the contacts and accommodations among racial and social groups which are required to achieve and maintain a truly pluralistic and democratic society in the metropolitan area.

A suburban school district need not contain a significant percentage of disadvantaged students or minority students in order to play an active part in counteracting the negative effects of social and racial stratification in metropolitan society. For example, any suburban school district can examine and modify its curriculum in order to teach for improved intergroup and interracial understanding. Steps which should be taken include the replacement of all instructional materials which ignore the contributions racial minorities have made to American life or communicate negative stereotypes about them, and systematic development of instructional units which help students acquire scientific knowledge about race and an understanding of contemporary race relations problems in the United States.

The findings of modern social science, however, indicate that positive intergroup attitudes are very difficult to develop in the absence of sustained personal contact between students of different racial groups. Affirming that white suburban students who have little or no personal contact with black students in the central city are not being adequately prepared to live in the multi-racial society which exists in the metropolitan area, some suburban districts are cooperating with central city districts to bring middle class white students from the suburbs and low-income black and white students from the city together for common educational experiences.

As part of the 1969 Project Unique program, for example, 440 students from the inner city in Rochester, New York, were enrolled in schools in nearby suburban districts.* In Hartford, Connecticut, the number of inner-city students bused to school districts in the suburbs reached 800 during the 1968–69 school year; this figure represented nearly 10 percent of the population of disadvantaged students in the Hartford schools.

Another alternative for bringing central city and suburban students together for integrated educational experiences is being developed and demonstrated in the Chicago SMSA, where in 1968 Operation Wingspread brought more than 250 white students from suburban schools and 250 black students from central city schools together for summer courses. The project was considered successful by most participants, and it has been expanded to include an academic year program as well as a larger summer enrollment.

The popularity of the Broadway musical *Hair* among the young and the integrated composition of many "rock" bands indicate that many young people with different racial and social backgrounds are reaching out to make contact and learn to live in harmony with one another. This is very difficult to accomplish, however, in the face of broad patterns of socio-economic stratification and racial segregation which are characteristic of the current stage of evolution of the metropolitan area. Most white students are socialized in racially homogeneous settings which contribute to the perpetuation of racial stereotypes, and many black youngsters are growing up in large central city ghettoes which offer little or no possibility for constructive contact with whites. One goal for suburban school districts in the 1970s should be to take vigorous action to help reduce and overcome the effects of racial and social stratification in the schools and society of the metropolitan area.

SUGGESTED ACTIVITIES

1. Contrast the major types of problems to be found in several differing kinds of suburban school districts in a metropolitan area with which you are familiar. Individuals whom you might interview to carry out this project include school board members and school administrators or faculty at your college whose work brings them into contact with suburban districts.

* Added to Rochester's own program for moving students out of inner-city schools to schools elsewhere in the city, this meant that nearly 2,000 black students (approximately one-seventh of the district's black enrollment) were being removed from the difficult educational environment of the inner-city school.

2. Did you or someone else in your class attend high school in an academically-oriented, middle-class suburban school district? How adequate were the courses and alternatives for average and below-average students, and how much attention was given to their problems? Perhaps you can find information indicating what happened to the graduating seniors in a recent class and how well students were prepared for a variety of careers and occupations.
3. Identify and analyze the suburban locations in your metropolitan area where population is growing most rapidly. Is information available to portray the status and background of the people who are moving there? Are there any special problems appearing in the schools? If yes, what steps are being taken to solve them? Metropolitan planning commissions, power and light companies, or other organizations concerned with population growth may have information which will be useful to you in this project.
4. To what extent do people you know have an image of suburbs and suburban schools as being predominantly middle-class in socio-economic character? Conduct a small survey of people of different ages and experience to find out what they identify as the most important problems of several nearby suburbs.

SUGGESTIONS FOR FURTHER READING

1. In addition to a chapter dealing specifically with the public schools, Herbert Gans' study of *The Levittowners* contains a good deal of discussion on the problems and situation of children and young people in the suburbs. Much of this material has direct and indirect implications for education.
2. *The Educational Decision-Makers* by Cicourel and Kitsuse is a study of the problems and treatment of different types of students in a large suburban high school. It raises issues which are of great concern to counselors, teachers, and administrators in many suburban schools.
3. *Big School, Small School* by Barker and Gump compares the environment in a large, comprehensive suburban high school with that in a small rural high school and explores the implications of the differences between them.

CHAPTER 6

Urban Renewal, Metropolitan Planning, and the Schools

THERE HAS BEEN renewal of cities over a long period of time. Jerusalem was rebuilt by Nehemiah, Athens by Pericles, Rome by Augustus, Paris by Napoleon III, and Chicago by Mayor Daley. Sometimes a destructive catastrophe, such as an earthquake, a fire, or a bombing raid, sets the stage for creative renewal of a city. Thus sections of Rotterdam, Milan, and London have been imaginatively rebuilt after bomb damage in World War II.

The Development of Urban Renewal

More generally, in the twentieth century, urban renewal is a planned replacement of old and wornout parts of the city. The need for urban renewal made itself felt in the 1930s, just at the time that a number of eastern and north central cities had reached a stage of growth where large tracts of houses became obsolescent and substandard. This was also a time when the federal government was being called upon to provide jobs and materials for public works in order to rescue the country from the Great Depression. To stimulate the home building industry and at the same time clear out the worst slums, the Federal Housing Act of 1937 offered subsidies and loans to local agencies for the construction of subsidized public housing.

After the war, Congress passed the Housing Act of 1949 which provided grants to local governments to acquire and clear the land in blighted areas, and then to sell the cleared land to private developers, or to local housing authorities for public housing. By this time the goal was slum clearance and urban redevelopment rather than housing of slum-dwellers. In other words, the goal was *urban renewal,* a term which came into popular usage in the 1950s.

By 1965 many of the worst slums had been cut out of the major American cities. A slum section of over 400 acres in St. Louis was cleared. Much of Boston's oldest but least picturesque housing was torn out to make room for expressways. Hundreds of acres of tenement houses were torn down on Chicago's South Side. New York's Lower East Side, and the area in Washington south of the Capitol felt the iron ball of the building wrecker. Los Angeles cleared the area on which the new Civic Center was built. The Golden Triangle of Pittsburgh was modernized with smoke abatement, new office buildings and hotels, and expressways.

Not only are slums cleared; a major aspect of urban renewal is the attempt to arrest and reverse the process of decay of the city center. This means the building of a second generation of new and ultra-modern skyscrapers to take the place of those erected in the early 1900s. It also means the building of expressways to provide easy automobile transportation for commuters who do not use the old-fashioned rapid transit service. Furthermore, there must be new and attractive apartment housing within walking or taxi distance of the downtown offices and stores, for people who have the money and the inclination to live in upper- or middle-class style without going out to the suburbs or the city fringes.

Meanwhile the federal government has continued to award large sums of money to what is now called "Housing and Urban Development." The Act of 1965 provided a variety of aids for housing including substantial numbers of new low-rent public housing units, subsidized low interest rates for housing for people of moderate income, and rent supplements to aid low-income families to secure better private housing. At the same time there is substantial money for the improvement of metropolitan areas through the purchase of land for recreational, conservation and other public uses, and for the construction of community centers, health stations, and water and sewer facilities.

The modern city must be an organ of the Great Society and also an organ of a democratic society. It must be a good place to conduct business—to interchange goods and services. It must be a good place to raise children. It must be a good place to enjoy at least a part of one's spare time.

Urban renewal has the goal of restoring physical areas of comfortable middle-class living in the central city and also of establishing comfortable slum-free housing for working-class people. Beyond this, urban renewal has a social goal of making the whole metropolitan area a good place for all kinds of people to live. The leaders of urban renewal often speak of their goal as that of increasing the range and amount of choice people have among good ways to live. This is more than physical urban renewal. It may be called *social urban renewal.*

By the middle 1960s it was becoming clear that physical urban renewal was not enough to accomplish the task of urban redevelopment. Cities were becoming better physically without improving socially or morally. In particular, housing was no longer as large a problem. In 1940, the U.S. Census declared about half of the housing in the country was substandard. This proportion decreased steadily until it was 19 percent in 1960. In the large cities, only 11 percent of housing was classified as substandard in 1960, and only 3 percent was labeled "dilapidated."

By this time there was wide and growing disillusionment with simple physical urban renewal. It appeared that many families who were dispossessed of their living quarters by demolition of slums were relocated in only slightly better homes at higher rents. The British sociologist Peter Marris (1962), after a study of American urban renewal in 1961, concluded that, "On the whole then, it seems fair to say that relocation has provided only marginally better housing, in very similar neighborhoods, at higher rents, and has done as much to worsen as to solve the social problems of the families displaced. The dispossessed enjoy as their reward a distant view of luxury apartments rising over their old homes."

One of the first persuasive opponents of sheer physical urban renewal was Jane Jacobs (1961) who in *Death and Life of Great American Cities* argued that the close-knit neighborhoods of the central city were being destroyed and replaced by impersonal and alienating housing projects which lacked the human touch of the neighborhood delicatessen shop, drugstore, and the sociability of the sidewalk and front stoop of a tenement house. When a great public housing project was erected in East Harlem, with a wide rectangular lawn, the tenants said in no uncertain terms that they hated the lawn. When a social worker tried to find out why the tenants disliked the lawn, she concluded that it was for two reasons: the tenants had not been asked whether they wanted a lawn, and the bare lawn reminded them of things they no longer could have. One tenant said, "Nobody cared what we wanted when they built this place. They threw our houses down and pushed us here and pushed our friends somewhere else. We didn't have a place around here to get a cup of coffee or a newspaper even, or borrow fifty cents. Nobody cared what we need. But the big men come and look at the grass and say, 'Isn't it wonderful! Now the poor have everything.'" (Jacobs, 1961, p. 15.)

Charles Abrams, writing in 1965, in *The City Is the Frontier,* calls the city a frontier not only because it is an asphalt jungle, a lawless place, but also because it is "our last unconquered environment." He believes that central cities can be made into areas where all kinds of people can work and live and enjoy life, but this will not be done by the real estate business and the construction industry. The real problem is people, not just buildings or slums. Urban renewal has to influence people, and the physical improvement of their homes is not enough. A political scientist, Professor James Q. Wilson of Harvard University (1965), puts it this way:

> . . . it seems to me that, except in special cases where great national or community purposes are to be served, it is a mistake to continue a program, much less accelerate it, which has as its principal effect a reduction in the supply of low-cost housing. It seems to me that what we need today is to strengthen neighborhood ties and family ties and to encourage neighborhoods to become sufficiently stable so that a kind of neighborhood culture can develop, in which social controls are automatically exercised and do not have to be exercised by a police force which, in all too many of our large American cities, operates as a kind of army of occupation facing hostile natives.

Urban Renewal and the Schools

The inner-city schools are affected in several ways by urban renewal, some favorable and some unfavorable.

On the favorable side, urban renewal provides space in which to build schools and space for playgrounds in areas where there were no parks or playgrounds before renewal. For example, in Chicago as of the close of 1964, urban renewal land had been sold or was in the process of being sold to public and private schools for four new buildings as well as for the new site of the University of Illinois and an expansion of the Illinois Institute of Technology. At the same time, seven schools had secured land for playgrounds, and there were ten requests for playground space pending.

Also, a desirable element in urban renewal is the greater stability of families who secure apartments in public housing projects. School principals note that there is a great reduction of transiency in their schools when a large public housing project goes up nearby. Tenants do not move frequently. Many tenants are supported by public welfare funds, which give them a steady source of income and tend to keep them stationary.

On the undesirable side, urban renewal as it has been generally practiced has reinforced and magnified the pattern of economic and racial stratification which existed before. The subsidized public housing which took the place of slums has generally been concentrated into high-rise apartment buildings or two or three-story row houses covering several city blocks. The average housing project has over a thousand residents, with three or four hundred school-age children. Some housing projects are so large that their children fill up an elementary school. One especially large public housing project in Chicago has a small high school and three elementary schools serving it, alone. In this project, in 1965, were 2,070 children (not all of school age) who received Aid for Dependent Children; 661 families with annual income of less than $2,000; 612 school pupils severely retarded in reading, and 53 percent of the children in the first grade who tested on a test of reading readiness as not ready to learn to read.

Social anthropologist Edward T. Hall has studied these and other characteristics and effects of high-rise public housing projects, which he calls "vertical filing boxes." He concluded that:

> If one looks at human beings in the same way that the early slave traders did, conceiving of their space requirements simply in terms of the limits of the body, one pays very little attention to the effects of crowding. . . . [People] find themselves forced into behavior, relationships, or emotional outlets that are overly stressful. . . . When stress increases, sensitivity to crowding

> rises—people get more on edge—so that more and more space is required as less and less is available.
>
> Consider the public housing constructed for low income groups in Chicago which has tended to dress up and hide the basic problem. . . . Row after row of high-rise apartments is less distressing to look at than slums but more disturbing to live in than much of what it replaced. The Negroes have been particularly outspoken in their condemnation of high-rise housing. All they see in it is white domination, a monument to a failure in ethnic relations. They joke about how the white man is now piling Negro on top of Negro, stacking them up in high rises. The high rise fails to solve many basic human problems. As one tenant described his building to me: "It's no place to raise a family. A mother can't look out for her kids if they are fifteen floors down in the playground. They get beaten up by the rough ones, the elevators are unsafe and full of filth . . . are slow and break down. When I want to go home I think twice because it may take me half an hour to get the elevator. Did you ever have to walk up fifteen floors when the elevator was broken?" (Hall, 1966, pp. 121, 158–159.)

One of the newer subsidized housing projects in Chicago, the Robert Taylor Homes, is a series of high-rise apartment buildings stretching for almost two miles along South State Street. Not only do the children living in these homes make up most of the enrollment of several elementary schools; at the close of 1964 there were 56 elementary school classes meeting in apartments in the Housing Project, due to lack of space in the neighborhood schools. The Robert Taylor Homes has practically all black occupancy. When it was proposed to build these high-rise homes, there was objection from some people on the ground that it would tend to segregate low-income blacks, but the City Council voted to approve the project. Professor Roald Campbell (1965) later commented on this situation as follows:

> In many cases, housing patterns do more to determine the nature of the school than any action of the board of education. One might cite the decision to erect the Robert Taylor Homes, twenty-eight high-rise public housing apartments, down State Street in Chicago as one of the most dramatic examples. Apparently city council members were pleased not to have public housing dispersed over the entire city as had been advocated by Elizabeth Wood, then Director of the Chicago Housing Authority. In any case the two-mile strip of public housing on State

> Street did more to perpetuate *de facto* segregation in schools than any policy decision by the school board or any other body. But why was there not more collaboration between the board of education, the housing authority, and the city council? This lack of collaboration among agencies at both program and policy level is a notable problem in our cities. . . .

What has happened in urban renewal in Chicago has happened in practically all of the big cities. The same mistakes have been made, from the point of view of those who are interested in social integration. Yet it was not necessary to make most mistakes. Subsidized housing in other countries is not generally built to entrench economic stratification. (Garvey, 1969.) It is possible to build small public housing units spread widely over the metropolitan area, so that families living in public housing have neighbors with average incomes and send their children to schools of mixed socio-economic status.

NEW DIRECTIONS IN URBAN RENEWAL

Thus urban renewal as it was practiced from 1950 to 1965 was at best an uncertain force for the social health of the city. Knowing that the problem of the city was the major domestic problem of the time and that this problem was getting worse rather than better, the 89th Congress established a new cabinet post, and a new executive department—the Department of Housing and Urban Development (HUD). Meanwhile, little additional public housing was being built. By 1969, 400,000 housing units had been demolished under urban renewal, but only 200,000 had been planned to replace them, and only 20,000 of these were public housing units in urban renewal areas.

Since the establishment of HUD, federal as well as state and regional attention has been divided between the renewal problems of the central city and the planning needs of the metropolitan area as a whole, thus recognizing that these two aspects of metropolitan development are inextricably linked to one another.

A major new direction in attacking the problems of poverty and deterioration in the central city was taken with the Demonstration Cities Metropolitan Development Act of 1966, which established the Model Cities Program as the principal federal thrust for central city urban renewal. The purposes of the Program are to "rebuild or revitalize large slum and blighted areas; expand housing, job, and income welfare payments; improve educational facilities and programs; combat disease and ill health; reduce the incidence of crime and delinquency; enhance recreational and cultural opportunities; establish better access between homes and jobs; and, generally, to improve living conditions for the people who live in such areas."

Prior to the Model Cities Program, urban renewal efforts in the central city suffered from several clear deficiencies. Not only was physical renewal carried out with little attention to its effects on the lives of people in renewal areas, but the improvement and renewal projects conducted by many autonomous agencies and institutions were poorly if at all coordinated and sometimes even contradicted one another. The effect of this situation was to

> make the job of putting together a comprehensive urban development program somewhat . . . [similar to] that of assembling an automobile if only about half the components are available, if they could be obtained only by going to a hundred departments of a dozen stores (where some of the parts would be found to be too expensive), and if the job were to be done by a team of mechanics none of whom had ever seen an automobile and were working more-or-less independently with no set of plans. (Fitch, 1967, p. 348.)

The Model Cities legislation, which has remained the preferred urban renewal instrument of the Nixon administration, authorized HUD grants to enable cities to develop and execute comprehensive planning programs which would pull together all federal aids, plus local resources, in a concerted attack on the most difficult social problems in entire neighborhoods. One requirement in model cities planning is participation by elected representatives of people in the neighborhoods. By proposing innovative solutions to the problems which residents of a model city neighborhood have identified as most important to them, a city can pyramid the amount of money it is eligible to receive for urban renewal and improvement. Methods and approaches to involve people in model cities planning vary from city to city, but in any case it is anticipated that this requirement will make public institutions such as clinics, social welfare agencies, and schools more responsive to their clients and will force coordination among the efforts of local residents, community institutions, and city hall.

The broad goal of the Model Cities Program, then, is to provide a more effective system for delivering urban services and carrying out urban renewal in the central city. It is hoped that this will be achieved by combining social and physical planning into comprehensive planning for the redevelopment and strengthening of what in effect are partially decentralized sub-units within the central city.

One other central city thrust for urban renewal which should be briefly mentioned is the experimentation with neighborhood corporations to undertake development tasks within the central city. Neighborhood corporations are being formed with funds and encouragement from HUD or other federal agencies, private foundations, business or civic associations, local community groups, and even colleges and universities. Whether private or public and whether organized on a profit or non-profit basis, neighborhood development corporations may well become a principal instrument of urban renewal in the 1970s.

Emphasis on inner-city renewal did not blind the federal government to the need for areawide planning and action embracing both the central city and the suburbs. As noted in a later section of this chapter, the Demonstration Cities Metropolitan Development Act also appreciably strengthened regional agencies engaged in metropolitan planning. This legislation was foreshadowed in statements in which President Johnson and Robert C. Weaver, the first Secretary of Housing and Urban Development, had made it clear that the entire metropolitan area was the province of the department. Before joining the Cabinet, Weaver had written that

> The city today is, or should be in my opinion, the heart, and in a sense the soul, of a metropolitan area. The suburbs around it, to a large degree, draw their life and their spirit from the city's economy and culture. The city should be revitalized as the anchor holding together our metropolitan areas. It does not perform this function effectively today.
>
> I am not impressed by those who prophesy the demise of cities. I am convinced that the recent decline in the population of central cities has been due, in large part, to the concentration of new construction in the suburbs and the scarcity of competing living facilities in the central cities.

METROPOLITAN AREAS AS FUNCTIONAL REGIONS FOR DEVELOPMENT

By definition, the metropolitan area is a region which includes the people of a large urban center plus people from surrounding areas whose prosperity and well-being are closely tied to the urban center. It is a region because it constitutes a natural grouping of people and resources which developed and was molded in accordance with a definite geographic, economic, and social environment.

Some metropolitan areas are so large and diverse that it is useful to think of them as consisting of discernible sub-regions which have a definite economic and geographic character of their own. In many cases it is also useful to think of the metropolitan area as part of a larger region in which it is linked with other urban and rural areas that share similar characteristics.

Regardless of whether it is or is not part of a larger region or has regions within it, the metropolitan area is the appropriate region to serve as the locus of many functions and services in a modern, industrial society. What this means is that many functions and services cannot be carried out effectively and efficiently in the absence of metropolitan planning and coordination.

Advantages of an Area-Wide Approach

Reasons why many functions and services need to be planned, coordinated, and, in some cases, provided at the metropolitan level can be classified under five main headings having to do with the well-being of the people of the metropolitan area.

Allowing for Effective and Efficient Provision of Services. Many urban services require metropolitan planning and coordination if they are to be carried out without a good deal of waste and duplication. One obvious example is air pollution control. Since polluted air from one community spreads to many other communities with no regard to governmental boundaries, action designed to control it in one community may have little or no effect unless action is taken in other communities as well. Air pollution is a regional problem which requires a regional solution.

A mundane but instructive example of how lack of area-wide coordination can make it difficult or impossible to provide a service efficiently was given by a metropolitan planning official who told a conference of educators that:

> Lack of coordination even in something as simple as naming streets can create very troublesome situations. Consider, for ex-

ample, that in a single metropolitan area you may have five Elm Streets or five Oak Streets.

If a fire engine goes down the wrong one, as sometimes happens, the house can burn down before help arrives. I remember one city in which a ready-mix cement truck went down the wrong Sunset Drive and wound up clear across town; by the time it meandered to the right destination, the cement had hardened in the truck and they had to chip it out. (Levine, 1967.)

Some urban services require too large a population base to be supported by the private or public organizations of most local communities. Ambulance service is considered by one expert in the field to require a population base of 82,000 if it is to be provided efficiently and economically (Eisenhardt, 1967); below this size, not enough trips will be generated to keep personnel and equipment from sitting unproductively or uneconomically idle. One advantage of living in a city rather than a small town or rural area is that an urban area has enough people so that necessities and amenities within a society's technological capacity can be provided at a feasible cost. This advantage is not realized, however, unless cooperative arrangements are made for providing a given service to a suitably large population within the metropolitan area.

Increasing Freedom of Choice. In one sense planning and coordination of urban development and urban services require that limits are set on the freedom individuals and groups have to act as they might wish. For example, a community which cooperates with other communities in financing and laying out a highway no longer can designate routes and methods of construction on its own. An individual who is taxed to pay for a highway has less money to spend in any way he might see fit.

In a more important sense, however, planning and coordination increase rather than decrease freedom of choice. As one example, immense amounts of land and other resources are wasted when urban sprawl (unguided growth and development) is allowed to take precedence over planning and coordination:

The lack of planning which accompanies urban sprawl is reflected in the high cost and poor quality of public facilities. . . . Utilities such as water supply and sewage removal must be extended over great distances, resulting in higher costs for these services. . . . Unplanned traffic needs are created as the new scattered populations make their way to the increasingly distant city. The existing roads are inadequate to handle these problems and become clogged with traffic.

The land that is bypassed by urban sprawl is suitable neither for any economically productive use nor for public recreation. The small farmers, many of them tenants, who formerly lived on the land, often migrate to the central cities, creating further social problems. (Bosselman, 1968.)

Whenever land or other resources are wasted and the quality of the urban environment is diminished, citizens have less effective choice than otherwise would be available to them. Since unplanned and uncoordinated urban development produces these results, citizens of the metropolitan area are placed in the position of having to make unnecessary choices among desirable urban functions and services. For example, choosing to live either near a recreation area with good boating facilities or a cultural center offering diversity in the performing arts may necessitate living far from an individual's place of employment or in housing more expensive than one can afford. Of course, "trade-offs" of this nature never can be entirely avoided and to some extent must be viewed as a fact of life. Through planning and coordination, on the other hand, regional resources can be utilized in such a manner as to make a maximum range of high-quality goods and services accessible to a maximum number of urban residents.

The way in which lack of planning and coordination restricts freedom of action in a metropolitan society has been illustrated by one U.S. Senator as follows:

The prospect of a social order of massive complexity confronts us with a proportionately bigger dilemma: in order to assure every man of mobility in this mass society, we may, ironically, have to erect more organizational barriers and impose more discipline—or widen the corridors of movement at great public cost. Certainly the occupants of the 217,783 automobiles that choked the New Jersey Turnpike the Sunday after Thanksgiving 1965 causing ten-mile traffic jams and two-hour delays in getting over the Delaware River bridge—must have pondered their less-than-perfect mobility. (Pell, 1966.)

Achieving Equality of Opportunity. Much of the history of the past century could be written in terms of movement toward a broadening of our definition of equality of opportunity. At some point before the middle of the present century, for example, Americans began to look at access to modern medical services and decent housing more as rights than privileges. Reflecting the increasing importance of educational credentials as "passports" to social status and economic well-being, equality of educational opportunity is being redefined in terms of the adequacy of school inputs and outputs rather than mere availability of some sort of schooling. Before long, income guarantees high enough to assure a decent standard of physical comfort probably will be widely accepted as a fundamental component in equal opportunity.

Whenever large disparities exist in the quality of public services available to groups of people in different parts of the metropolitan area, opportunity to fully participate in or enjoy the benefits of metropolitan society is less than equal. By reducing inequities in the level of public services, areawide planning and action become an indispensable prerequisite for attaining the goal of equality of opportunity for all the area's citizens.

Facilitating Social Integration. The metropolitan area should be so structured as to bring diverse people together in schools, churches, and business and recreation centers. Although people should not be required to associate *in private* with people of another color or economic level, this principle should not be allowed to reduce any group's *access to the opportunities and resources* of metropolitan society or to limit *association* through residential or other forms of physical segregation. Entrenched patterns of physical segregation and stratification are unlikely to be reduced or eliminated in the absence of explicit areawide planning and coordination to achieve this goal.

Simplicity. Regional planning and action can reduce the complexity of governmental activity in the metropolitan area. Proliferating and overlapping jurisdictions are governed by a large number of public officials who tend to be relatively anonymous and invisible. When several services are provided by a single agency serving at least a fairly large section of the metropolitan area, citizens pay taxes and elect representatives to fewer overlapping jurisdictions. Simplicity in the government structure makes it easier for the citizen to know what government officials are doing and to assess their performance as trustees of the public welfare.

Advantages of Localized Decision-making

In contrast to these reasons for metropolitan planning and action to improve the quality of the physical and social environments in the metropolis, there are other reasons for administering urban functions and services as close to the local community level as possible.

Information for Effective Implementation. Decisions concerning the administration of a service should be made in the light of conditions existing at the level where the service is consumed. Moving away from the local level in planning or administering a service increases the likelihood that information will be distorted as it flows up or down an organizational hierarchy and decreases the probability that decisions will be made realistically.

Encouragement of Local Participation and Support. Providing people with an opportunity to participate in decisions concerning local services gives them a chance to understand how to use these services. Participation also decreases feelings of being excluded from political and social processes while increasing commitment to work or pay taxes to support public services.

Enhancing Accountability. Administering public services close to the local level provides citizens with maximum opportunity to determine whether public employees are responding intelligently and effectively to local needs and also gives the citizen access to personnel with authority to take action to improve the quality of a public service.

Balancing the reasons favoring areawide planning and action on the one hand and those favoring local administration and decision-making on the other, it is evident that the governmental system of the metropolitan area should be a sophisticated structure that combines, insofar as possible, the advantages of regionalism and the benefits of localism. At one extreme, the metropolitan area might be governed by a single elected body responsible for all its public functions and services. At the other extreme, all government functions and decisions might be determined and carried out independently by a variety of local agencies in small neighborhoods or communities. Somewhere in between these extremes, political arrangements should provide for regional or sub-regional planning and action on matters which most require joint coordination and determination and for local administration and autonomy on matters in which cooperation is relatively unnecessary or even undesirable. As indicated in the next section of this chapter, the present government structure in the nation's metropolitan areas is characterized by excessive fragmentation. New structural arrangements and mechanisms to accommodate regional planning and take action are badly needed to maintain and enhance the quality of life in the metropolis.

The Facts of Fragmentation

Although the ideal of metropolitan development is one of cooperation, coherence and integration, the facts as of the 1970s are quite different. Metropolitan areas are highly fragmented, the suburbs most of all.

There are many government units in the average metropolitan area. According to the 1967 Census of Governments, there were 20,703 local governments in the 227 SMSAs, or an average of 92 for each metropolis. These are all independent, with separate taxing powers, officials, and functions. They may be cities, villages, towns, boroughs, counties, school districts, and special purpose districts.

Table 6.1 shows how the local governments are distributed

TABLE 6.1
Local Governments in Metropolitan Areas, 1967

SMSA Size Group (1960 Population)	*Number of SMSAs*	*Number of Local Governments (1967)*	*Average Number of Local Governments*
All SMSAs	227	20,703	91
1,000,000 or more	24	7,367	30.7
500,000–1,000,000	32	3,878	121
300,000–500,000	30	2,734	91
200,000–300,000	40	2,919	73
100,000–200,000	74	3,123	42
50,000–100,000	27	682	25

Source: U.S. Bureau of the Census; *Census of Governments:* 1967, Vol. 1, *Governmental Organization* (Washington: 1968), p. 11.

among SMSAs by size. The Chicago SMSA had the most in 1967, with 1,113. Philadelphia had 876; Pittsburgh 705; New York 551; and St. Louis 474. But Baltimore had only 27 local governments while Madison, Wisconsin, with about 225,000 residents, had 88.

Table 6.2 shows the various types of local governments, and their numerical changes, between 1962 and 1967. Local school districts dropped by 29 percent in these five years, while special districts increased. The nonschool special districts have grown with the metropolitan areas. Established to perform one or two services for an area larger than a municipality, special districts provide such services as water supply, fire protection, sewage disposal, flood control, airports, and transportation.

Although the number of local school districts has been reduced by consolidation of small districts, there still were in 1966 an average of twenty-two school districts per SMSA. As Table 4.1 shows, there were 949 school districts with fewer than 300 pupils operating in SMSAs in 1967.

The Committee for Economic Development is one among many civic organizations which has recognized that "the bewildering multiplicity of small, piecemeal, duplicative, overlapping local jurisdictions cannot cope with the staggering difficulties encountered in managing modern urban affairs." Pointing out that, "Efforts to 'tidy up' a chaotic situation will not cure the chief illness," the Committee called in 1966 for a reduction of 80 percent in the number of

TABLE 6.2

Types of Local Governments in SMSAs, 1962 and 1967

Class of Local Governments	*Number in SMSAs 1967*	*Percentage of SMSA Total*	*Increase or Decrease in Number 1962–67*	*Percentage Change in Number 1962–1967*
All local governments	20,703	100.0	1,114	– 5.1
School districts	5,018	24.2	2,054	–29.0
Special districts	7,049	34.0	896	14.6
Municipalities	4,977	24.0	74	1.5
Townships	3,255	15.7	–27	– 0.8
Counties	404	2.0	– 3	– 0.7

Sources: U.S. Bureau of the Census, *Census of Governments:* 1967, Vol. 1, *Governmental Organization* (Washington: 1968), p. 11

governments in the United States and for a variety of actions including city-county consolidation, formation of multi-county federations, and elimination of many special districts in order to modernize government in the nation's metropolitan areas. (Committee For Economic Development, 1966, pp. 15, 40–48.)

MOVEMENT TOWARD METROPOLITAN COOPERATION AND REGIONALIZATION

In order to overcome this fragmentation of local government, metropolitan areas have tried a number of forms of cooperation among their local units. These range from the governing of the area by a single metropolitan government to a combination of area-wide governments with local governments and on to systematic cooperation among existing governments.

The one-government or metro-government approach has been adopted in only one large SMSA—Nashville. Nashville and Davidson County, Tennessee, combined the city and county governments into one government, and combined the school districts into a single county-wide district. This was done in 1962, after the voters defeated a similar proposal in 1958.

In Dade County, Florida, the effort was made in 1953 to abolish the city government of Miami and to make the county government the sole government of the area. When this was defeated by a close vote, a plan for a metropolitan charter was drawn up and approved by the voters in 1957. This was a "two-level" plan with a powerful county government combined with the limited action of local municipal governments, nineteen out of 26 having less than 10,000 population.

Following state legislation passed in 1969, Indianapolis and Marion County, Indiana, were merged into a new City of Indianapolis on January 1, 1970. The new government has six executive departments to replace the much larger number formerly responsible for government in the city and county: administration, metropolitan development, public works, transportation, public health, and parks and recreation. However, authority of the new city government does not extend to three predominantly white suburban towns, even though these towns elect representatives and pay taxes to the city. This arrangement raises grave questions concerning the motivations and potential effectiveness of the merger. Many think it was intended to perpetuate rather than reduce segregation of low-income and minority citizens in the inner core of the city.

Jacksonville, Florida, is another metropolitan area where recently-enacted city-county merger is being studied by political scientists and government officials to determine its potential for alleviating urban and metropolitan problems. The city of Jacksonville was merged with Duval County in 1967, but it is too early to say how much of an influence the merger will have in facilitating regional answers to regional problems. Nevertheless, at the present time city-county merger must be judged a particularly logical method for achieving metropolitan cooperation in the more than 100 SMSAs which lie entirely within the present boundaries of a single county.

A "federation" plan was adopted in Toronto, Canada, in 1954. This came about because the communities in the metropolitan area were suffering severely from lack of facilities such as water supply, sewage disposal, good schools, arterial highways, rapid transit, and low-cost housing. There is an areawide government which includes thirteen municipalities. The metro government has much power, but the thirteen municipal governments retain some powers. There is a metropolitan school board, which provides school sites and buildings and makes equitable per-pupil payments to the six locally elected school boards which operate the elementary and secondary schools.

Other proposals for metropolitan cooperation have failed, such as the one proposed for St. Louis and defeated at the polls in 1959 and 1962. Cleveland voters failed to approve a county-wide charter plan in 1959. The movement toward regional approaches to metropolitan government in many SMSAs is very much alive, however, even though it meets much opposition.

Meanwhile, there has been a growth of voluntary cooperation among governmental units in the larger metropolitan areas. Specially notable have been the formation of a metropolitan council to coordinate the activities of special districts in the Minneapolis–St. Paul area and the success of a voluntary, areawide effort called Forward Thrust in helping to obtain voter approval for bond issues totaling hundreds of millions of dollars for areawide development in the Seattle SMSA. But the major thrust toward voluntary metropolitan cooperation has been in the rapidly increasing number and influence of cooperative, multijurisdictional planning and coordinating agencies in metropolitan areas throughout the country.

PLANNING AND COORDINATING FOR METROPOLITAN DEVELOPMENT

The physical planning of a new city is an old practice, as old as the history of cities. The City of Washington was planned by Major L'Enfant. Salt Lake City was laid out by plan. But the nineteenth century saw relatively little city planning in the United States, less than in Europe, where Sweden adopted a city planning code in the 1870s. Probably the first conference on city planning in the USA was held in Washington in 1903. Most cities now have planning commissions, often only semiofficial and often composed of nonexperts.

Planning is a process by which responsible members of a community look ahead to future developments and prepare to guide them into desirable patterns of growth. The planning group may be official or unofficial, trained or untrained for the task. Sears, Roebuck and Company (1962) puts out a booklet on community planning and answers the question "Why do we plan?" as follows: (1) to meet events we expect to happen; (2) to accomplish things we want to happen; and (3) to avoid or prevent things we do not want to happen.

City planning now finds its strongest supporters among businessmen and newspapers. They have come to the conclusion that land use in urban communities cannot be left to the ingenuity and the capability of individuals without government control. The question today is not whether there should be government participation in community development, but rather what forms of planning are best.

The metropolitan area is a *product* of social changes. At the same time it is being recognized by more and more people and by more and more organizations as the best *agent* for directing and controlling social change in the interests of the people. Directing and controlling social change in the metropolitan area requires comprehensive planning, which includes the following seven aspects:

Arrangements for Convenient Movement of People and Materials. The increased use of automobiles and trucks has shifted the load of transportation to streets and highways from electric trains, subways, street cars, and buses which used streets and highways less. Between 1950 and 1958 the use of public transit facilities decreased from 17.2 billion to 9.7 billion rides per year. (Committee for Economic Development, 1960.) To meet this problem new forms of rapid transit are being tried, and subways are being expanded. Also the cities have bought up expensive land and removed it from the tax rolls in order to build networks of automobile expressways.

2. *Rules for Orderly and Esthetic Land Use. Zoning* is the term applied to community control over the use of private and public land. Zoning is generally done by ordinance, and is enforced by law. Different districts are zoned for different functions, such as: retail or wholesale business, heavy manufacturing, light manufacturing, office buildings, single family residences, multiple family residences. If this is not done, people cannot plan to use property with confidence in the future. A man building a fine house may find himself living next to a factory some years later.

3. *Location and Design of Public Buildings and Facilities.* Another planning function is the designing and locating of public cultural, educational, and recreational facilities. The quality of life in a city is enhanced by conveniently located and well-designed museums, convention halls, public libraries, art galleries and local community centers. The location and development of parks, playgrounds, botanical gardens, and zoos also have a major influence on the satisfaction people get from living in a city. The park system established in Kansas City at the beginning of this century has kept that city attractive; and the establishment in 1893 of a permanent Metropolitan Parks Commission covering 38 cities and towns did a great deal to protect recreational resources in the Boston area. (Cherington, 1958.) The city of Dunedin, New Zealand, has a belt of parks surrounding the central city, due to the wisdom of early planners who secured a "green belt" around the city's edges when it was smaller. The location of school buildings is especially important in city planning, since the presence of a well-built school attracts and holds families with children.

4. *Promotion of Health and Prevention of Health Hazards.* City planning must anticipate needs for pure water and pure air. Hospital location is important. Measures for sewage disposal and smoke and fume abatement are parts of this function. This becomes crucial as a city gets to be very large.

5. *Planning Neighborhood Services and Facilities.* These new and sanitary developments sometimes lack the homely touch of the old and deteriorating neighborhoods, where people knew their neighbors, had friendly relations with small tradesmen, and felt at home. To avoid this, new planned communities should be organized around neighborhoods, each with an array of facilities including a health center, child care center, swimming pool, playground, social center, and branch library. (Orland, 1952.)

6. *Urban Renewal.* A program of urban renewal generally has a master plan behind it, drawn by a planning commission. The master plan does not have the status of law, but is simply advisory, meant to guide public officials and private builders and investors. The planning commission generally publishes the master plan, with maps showing the areas of the city for which certain developments are suggested, and with a statement of the policies for transportation, land use and community facilities.

7. *Metropolitan Area Planning.* With the population of metropolitan areas outside of the central city as large as the central city population, the need for area-wide planning has become clear. Transportation must be planned for the area as a whole. Sewage disposal, police protection, and industry decentralization present problems which many small suburban governments cannot cope with independently. Small separate school districts need to cooperate to provide educational services that they cannot give singly. The function of a metropolitan planning agency is to coordinate the planning of the many local units, though it traditionally has had no power to enforce its recommendations. It must persuade and advise. For example, the Northeastern Illinois Metropolitan Area Planning Commission works over an area of 3,700 square miles, containing 250 municipalities and 700 other government units. The Commission has nineteen members, five named by the mayor of Chicago, one each by the six county Boards of Supervisors, and eight by the state governor.

Metropolitan planning agencies now take two principal forms: planning commissions and councils of governments (COGS). The typical planning commission brings together experts and administrators who can formulate and coordinate plans for metropolitan development. One of the major lessons learned from the history of city and metropolitan planning agencies in the United States, however, was that expensive plans for urban development were too seldom put into practice, in part because elected government officials who make final decisions were not closely involved in the work of these agencies. (Cox, 1967). Partly for this reason, there was an important movement in the 1960s to create councils of governments representing county, municipal, and special district governments as well as lay leaders and influential institutions in the metropolitan area. In some metropolitan areas, planning commissions have become a unit under a council of governments; in others, both have retained their identities but function in close collaboration with one another. In either case it is hoped that this cooperation will lead to more realistic planning and more effective implementation of regional and subregional plans. (Finlayson, 1967; Hanson, 1966.)

By February 1969, there were 242 multijurisdictional planning agencies in the United States, the large majority of them probably operating in at least part of one or more SMSAs. In 1962, by way of contrast, the federal Housing and Home Finance Agency was able to identify only 126 such agencies. One hundred and thirty-five councils of governments were in operation in 1969; only eight such councils were known to exist in 1965 (1969 Directory of Regional Councils). Multijurisdictional agencies of both types are becoming an increasingly important element in metropolitan development, and a National Service to Regional Councils has been formed to keep track of their growth and help them learn of new opportunities as well as the progress of others.

The formation of planning commissions and councils of governments during the 1960s was greatly spurred by federal legislation such as the Federal Highway Act of 1962 which limited eligibility for grants for highways built after 1965 to governments in regions with areawide mechanisms for comprehensive transportation planning, The Housing Act of 1965 which authorized HUD to pay two-thirds of the cost of many COGS activities, and Section 204 of the Demonstration Cities Metropolitan Development Act of 1966 which requires that all requests for federal aid in more than 30 different loan and grant programs be reviewed for compatibility with other areawide developments by officially designated agencies in the nation's metropolitan areas.

Reviewing progress toward metropolitan planning and coordination achieved in the first year of Section 204, the National Service to Regional Councils cited such examples as the following:

Seventeen separate sewage treatment facilities in five cities and three counties in the Portland area were under condemnation and applications for Federal assistance to upgrade these facilities to meet state standards were received by the Columbia Region Association of Governments (Portland, Oregon). After receiving the applications, CRAG recommended that the jurisdictions involved consider the construction of one larger, more advanced facility to replace the others instead of upgrading them. This recommendation was accepted unanimously by the jurisdictions and, in addition to operating savings, resulted in savings of $1.5 million over the cost of upgrading.

Cooperative metropolitan planning as represented by the establishment and growing activism of planning commissions and COGS is evolving toward action more systematic and more adequate to solve the problems of the metropolitan area than was possible under the strictly voluntary arrangements of a decade or two ago. Based on an analysis of existing COGS and a study of the success of efforts to initiate metropolitan cooperation in the Seattle and Minneapolis–St. Paul SMSAs, James M. Banovetz (1968) has concluded that areawide planning and action is beginning to be achieved in many metropolitan areas through an incremental process that includes the following stages:

Proliferation. . . . [In this stage] a number of independent special districts have been established . . . to service either the entire area or substantial portions of it.

District Coordination. This stage is characterized by the establishment of some degree of coordination between the plans and programs of the special districts, but such coordination is essentially negative in nature. In other words, the coordinating agency is empowered to veto or hamper those proposed plans or programs . . . deemed inconsistent with area development plans, but not to require positive action or the execution of particular programs.

Metropolitan Coordinating Authority. At some point, the authority of the metropolitan coordinating district will also be extending in certain carefully limited particulars over units of local governments other than special districts, such as school districts, municipalities, counties, and townships.

A Metropolitan Taxing District. At some point during this evolutionary cycle . . . metropolitan areas will probably establish some form of central taxing authority which will levy

> uniform, area-wide taxes . . . and redistribute the tax proceeds . . . among all area governments according to a formula based on population, need, or some similar criteria. (Benovetz, 1968.)

The development of metropolitan planning so far seems to be following Banovetz's script, and planning agencies are developing at a fairly rapid pace in accordance with objectives the American Institute of Planners identified in 1962 as follows:

> The function of metropolitan planning is to contribute to the formulation and implementation of optimal public policy for the metropolitan area . . . [and to serve] as a framework and a vehicle for the municipal, county and other local units of government and for relating these plans to the desirable development of the metropolitan area as a whole.

METROPOLITAN COOPERATION AMONG SCHOOL SYSTEMS

School districts in the metropolitan area are moving toward closer cooperation in two ways—by consolidation and by voluntary cooperation.

The consolidation of small suburban districts has already been noted, and Table 6.2 shows that this has been going on rapidly. Small districts with less than 300 pupils soon may very nearly disappear from most metropolitan areas.

Voluntary cooperation among school districts has generally taken the form of a Study Council or Superintendents' Study Group, in which a local university works with the school superintendents of the area. More than 65 such councils now exist in the United States. In some SMSAs more formal organizations have been created to facilitate voluntary cooperation on a systematic basis, as has happened with the establishment of the Educational Research and Development Council of the Twin Cities Metropolitan Area, Inc. The superintendents of the Minneapolis–St. Paul Area, together with members of the School of Education at the University of Minnesota, formed the Council in 1963. It consists of 39 public school districts in three counties within the metropolitan area, and these schools serve more than 40 percent of the pupils of the state of Minnesota. (Hooker, Mueller, and Davis, 1968.)

Another example of an organization formally set up to facilitate cooperation and provide cooperative services to school districts in a metropolitan area is the Board of Cooperative Educational Services (BOCES) of the First Supervisory District of Erie County, New York. The Cooperative Board, which serves a 900 square mile suburban area partially surrounding Buffalo, New York, employs more than 250 instructional and technical personnel and has an operating budget in excess of three million dollars. (Prentice, 1967.) Nineteen school districts with a combined enrollment of more than 80,000 students are included in the service area.

As of 1967, 1,400 students were taking academic courses at their home schools and were attending area centers at which the Cooperative Board provided vocational offerings in auto shop, cosmetology, practical nursing, electronics, machine shop, data processing, building maintenance, agriculture, heating and air conditioning, microbiology, welding, and other subjects. Sixty-eight classes for retarded or emotionally disturbed students were maintained.

The First District BOCES is a legally constituted regional organization which is a part of a statewide network of similar regional boards organized and financially aided by the state government of New York. The purpose of these boards is to enable school districts to combine resources in order to provide services they could not finance on their own. Since they are created and operate under state authority, regional agencies of this type are intermediate school units; that is, they are intermediate between the state government and the local operating districts which in effect choose to purchase services from them. They differ from the traditional intermediate unit in education in that they serve a region which often includes parts of several counties and they provide a variety of services; the traditional intermediate unit in most states is a county school district which has a county superintendent whose duties are primarily supervisory and regulatory in nature.

Although their powers and functions vary a good deal from state to state and region to region, statewide networks of regional agencies such as BOCES also have been established in Iowa, Michigan, Nebraska, California, Washington, Wisconsin, and Texas, among other states. (Wurster, 1968.) The term "Area Educational Service Agency" (AESA) or its equivalent is being widely used to describe this newer type of intermediate school unit. Area Educational Service Agencies can do much to coordinate and improve educational opportunities within a metropolitan area.

One further development that should be noted in connection

with metropolitan cooperation among school systems is the influence of Title III of the Elementary and Secondary Education Act of 1965. Title III has two major parts. The first provided funding for "innovative" and "exemplary" projects to improve the quality of education in local school districts. All but a few of the many hundreds of projects carried out under Title III have been cooperative efforts involving two or more school systems, a large percentage of which are located in metropolitan areas. As a rule these projects have been funded for three years, and educators are beginning to express great displeasure as funding runs out for projects which many believe have proven of great benefit to their students. It is too early to say how many districts will be able or willing to continue these projects with their own or state finances after federal funds no longer are available.

The second part of Title III provided for the creation of "supplementary" educational centers throughout the United States. In effect, this would have established a nationwide network of area service agencies. Funds for this part of Title III have been authorized but not yet released by Congress; in the meantime, primary responsibility for organization and administration of the centers has been transferred from the U.S. Office of Education to the state governments. This part of Title III obviously has great potential for bringing about constructive cooperation among school districts in the nation's SMSAs, particularly in states where state department of education officials may be more sensitive to and informed about problems in metropolitan society and metropolitan education than generally has been the case in these traditionally rural-oriented units of state government.

APPROACHES TO A REGIONAL METROPOLITAN EDUCATION SYSTEM

Whether cooperation is achieved through informal working relationships among a few school districts, through participation in a metropolitan study council, or through membership in a state- or federally-supported area educational service agency, it is a useful step toward coordinated planning and action in metropolitan education. For the following reasons, however, cooperation is not an adequate response to the problems of fragmentation, complexity, and stratification in the metropolitan area and its schools:

1. Districts most in need of assistance may be least able to purchase services from a cooperative area service agency.
2. Economies of scale may not be realized if many districts are unable or unwilling to participate.
3. The establishment of a cooperative service agency offers only a partial solution to the problems of school districts which are too small to operate economical programs and does very little or nothing to alleviate problems in districts which are too large for effective administration.
4. Cooperation does not reduce the number of school governments in metropolitan areas in which there are too many school districts to allow for joint planning with nonschool governments such as planning commissions and transportation authorities. Research on this matter suggests that the multiplicity of school districts which exists in many metropolitan areas is a major impediment to cooperative planning action between schools and areawide nonschool agencies. (Levine and Clavner, 1967.)
5. Voluntary cooperation among governments in a metropolitan area is likely to be more or less limited to matters which involve physical aspects (e.g., transportation facilities) of governmental programs. (Marando, 1968; Williams, 1967.) Despite the importance of joint planning and action on value-laden problems such as social stratification and its effects on metropolitan area schools, it is unlikely that enough voluntary cooperation will take place to resolve these serious underlying problems in the educational system of metropolitan society.
6. Cooperation does not produce the systematic change required to realize the goal of equal educational opportunity. Primarily for this reason, national organizations specially concerned with the crisis in our cities and metropolitan areas have begun to call for the establishment of metropolitan education agencies with legal responsibility for functions such as the financing of public education which are most appropriately carried out at the regional level. Perhaps the most respected and knowledgeable of these organizations have been:

   The American Association of School Administrators. A resolution passed by the AASA in February of 1967 states that, "The Association urges reorganization of metropolitan districts to create in each great metropolitan area comprehensive taxing, administrative, and educational units. We believe such arrangements to be necessary if equal educational opportunity is to be provided for the ever-increasing numbers of children enrolled in urban schools."

   The Advisory Commission on Intergovernmental Relations. Created by Congress, the membershp of the ACIR includes prominent state and municipal leaders as well as U.S. Senators and Representatives. In 1968 the ACIR called on state legislatures to enact model legislation, "establishing or authorizing an appropriate State agency to mandate the establishment of county or regional school property taxing districts . . . and authorizing the establishment by the State educational agency of educational facilities designed to make available on a multi-district basis a specialized educational capability, including special personnel to the children of the districts involved."

The National Commission on Urban Problems. One of the major recommendations of the Commission's 1969 report titled *Building the American City* called for collection of school taxes on a county or multicounty basis. The Commission report also was particularly unequivocal in calling attention to problems associated with fragmentation among governmental units in the metropolitan area: "Unless widespread, vigorous, and effective steps are taken to civilize the existing jungle of local governmental jurisdictions, the nation faces the prospect of a further and drastic centralization of governmental power and a possible smothering of the grass roots of American democracy."

Earlier in this chapter it was noted that the metropolitan area is the appropriate level at which to plan and coordinate urban functions which are regional in their effects and interactions and which cannot be carried out satisfactorily without metropolitan planning and action. Education has become such a function. No more than in the case of air pollution can the undesirable social and economic consequences of inadequate education in one part of the metropolitan area be confined to that single community. No more than in the case of highways can an adequate network of educational facilities be built entirely on the resources and discretion of each local area. Cooperation among school districts falls far short of achieving the five metropolitan goals of effective and efficient provision of services, increased freedom of choice, equality of opportunity, social integration, and simplicity in government structure. The next sections of this chapter describe three approaches which move beyond cooperation to a regional educational system in the metropolitan area.

Formal Division of Labor Between a Metropolitan Education Authority and Reorganized Operating School Districts

Some educational problems in the metropolis reflect primarily regional needs and require regional solutions; others require decision-making at a more local level. Just as political scientists have worked out an appropriate division of labor between regional and local municipal units of government (Advisory Commission on Intergovernment Relations, 1963; 1966, pp. 30–32), educational functions can be analyzed to determine the appropriate level at which principal legal authority should be located for carrying each one out. A logical way to organize the metropolitan system of education in accordance with the nature of metropolitan society is to assign legal responsibility for functions best handled on an areawide basis to a regional education authority and responsibility for functions best implemented locally to optimally-sized operating school districts.

The functions assumed wholly or partly by a metropolitan education authority probably should include the following:

1. Setting the tax rate and distributing funds for education.
2. Administering a basic state aid fund so as to help equalize educational opportunity.
3. Research and evaluation functions.
4. Special education, vocational education, and other highly specialized programs.
5. Recruiting, selecting, and certifying teachers.
6. In-service training for teachers and administrators.
7. Coordination with nonschool agencies such as metropolitan or city planning commissions.
8. Junior college education and, possibly, maintenance of a public university with a teacher training institution as part of it.

The creation and development of a Metropolitan Area Authority would not weaken the initiative and responsibility of local school boards. On the contrary, it would aid them to work more effectively for the educational development of their own local schools. These local school boards would have authority over the local schools, and might request the voters in their community areas to vote supplemental funds in addition to the support they receive from the state and metropolitan unit. School districts which were not financially viable would be eliminated. The central city might be divided into community areas of 50,000 to 100,000, each with its own local school board and district superintendent. It would be the responsibility of the Metropolitan Education Authority Board of Education to work with other branches of government to define the local communities in accordance with the goals of urban renewal and in cooperation with citizens' groups in the local communities. Some over-all strategy governing the socio-economic composition of the local school districts would have to be worked out, so that each local district had in it a variety of kinds of people.

An obvious issue to be addressed in organizing a Metropolitan Education Authority would be to determine the number and size of the operating school districts which would retain most of the powers and authorities presently possessed by public school districts. As suggested in Table 5.3, operating districts probably should enroll about 25,000–30,000 students; thus they would be large enough to carry on appropriate local functions such as curriculum development and instructional improvement and innovation with a good deal of efficiency yet still have some room to grow without becoming too large for effective administration. Such districts would be well inside the 20,000–50,000 range within which researchers suggest that "school districts do not suffer from negative effects of size." (Swanson, 1966, p. 41.)

One point which needs to be stressed is that the establishment of a metropolitan education district with legally-constituted, moderately large operating units and local boards of education is compatible with other reforms being explored to help the big cities and their schools. A trend toward decentralization of school and other civic functions is manifest in a number of big cities. In 1969 the New York Legislature reorganized the New York City schools so that some of the powers formerly discharged by the central city school board will be delegated to 30–33 local boards elected to help operate elementary schools within the city. Detroit has worked out a district organization which facilitates a degree of "home rule" by communities of approximately 300,000 population. One major purpose of such decentralization is to encourage a given community within the big city to tackle its own problem in a particular way—a way which might not be satisfactory to other communities either because they have a different situation which gives them different problems, or because their local leadership is not yet ready for the actions that another community wishes to take. The stress and strains of the urban renewal programs of the coming two decades may be such that they are best met by decentralized action of smaller communities than by the big city itself. The big city may have to solve its problems part by part, section by section, with strategies adapted to the social goals and social attitudes of the various sections; but with financial support and a degress of coordination provided by the central city government and by the central city school board.

A state school reorganization plan which proposed the establishment of regional metropolitan educational agencies along the general pattern described above was prepared by the Missouri School District Reorganization Commission in 1968. The proposal called for the reorganization of the state's 786 school districts into 20 regional districts made up of a total of 133 operating districts. The Missouri portion of the St. Louis and Kansas City SMSAs were to constitute two of the regional districts. The East-West Gateway (St. Louis) Regional District, for example was to consist of fourteen operating districts ranging in size from approximately 12,500 to 23,500 students. The boundaries of the regional and operating districts were drawn up in accordance with criteria which included those shown in Table A-17 (page 329), and responsibilities were to be distributed between the regional and the local units as shown in Table A-18 (page 330). The proposal was not enacted by the state legislature.

A somewhat similar proposal for a metropolitan education district with operating responsibilities legally assigned to "semi-independent" districts was proposed for the Louisville–Jefferson County area in August, 1966. (Cunningham, 1968.) The five primary functions to be performed by the metropolitan education district were to (1) provide general support, special-needs support, and capital-outlay financing; (2) assume responsibility for school construction; (3) do areawide research and planning; (4) offer some special education programs; and (5) operate centralized services such as data processing, transportation, and educational television. Although both the Louisville and Jefferson County Boards of Education supported the proposal, it narrowly missed being enacted by the state legislature.

Single Metropolitan School District

In one sense the simplest approach to regionalizing the metropolitan educational system is to have a single areawide school district responsible for public education throughout the region. This approach differs from the metropolitan education authority approach in that it does not provide for legally established subdistricts to perform most educational functions, but it should not be interpreted as excluding the possibility of establishing informal or advisory local school boards with a key role in decision-making.

Among the large SMSAs in the United States, there are three which have a single school district serving all or most of a metropolitan region: Dade County (Miami), Florida; Clark County (Las Vegas), Nevada; and Nashville–Davidson County, Tennessee. The Nashville–Davidson County School District was formed as part of the merger of the city and county governments in 1962. One of the boards established as part of the Metropolitan Government of Nashville–Davidson County was the Metropolitan Board of Education. An interesting account of how the transition to a single district was carried out and of the advantages for cooperation of having both school and nonschool governments under a single metropolitan agency is given in Harris, Hemberger, and Goodnight, 1968.

Limited Purpose Metropolitan Education Authority

A third approach to metropolitanism in education is to establish a metropolitan education authority to carry out certain designated functions with very little or no additional change taking place in the organization of existing school districts in the metropolitan area.

As recommended by the AASA, the ACIR, and the National Commission on Urban Problems, probably the most important single function which a metropolitan education authority of this type should be organized to perform is that of reducing financial inequities among school districts in a SMSA. Proposals for an areawide education authority to set the school tax rate and distribute funds in accordance with the needs of local school districts certainly would have many opponents but probably not so much opposition as would proposals for more comprehensive change and reform in the present structure of education in the metropolitan area. After a taxing authority was established and had functioned for several years, it might begin to provide additional services as the population of an area became more accustomed and knowledgeable concerning the concept and advantages of metropolitanism in education.

The best examples of limited purpose areawide education authorities in the United States are those responsible for junior colleges or, less frequently, vocational schools in SMSAs in several states.

The major disadvantage of this approach is that it does little to overcome the problems of districts which are too small or too large to operate effectively and efficiently and leaves untouched many other problems related to complexity, fragmentation, and stratification in the metropolitan area. Perhaps its major advantage is that it might serve as a natural beginning step to initiate an evolutionary process leading toward more adequate and comprehensive metropolitan planning and action in education. A logical transition plan to achieve this purpose has been outlined by Swanson and deserves to be tested in at least a few SMSAs. (Swanson, 1969, pp. 192–194.) In this regard, a limited purpose authority that could take on additional responsibilities and functions as it became well established is in line with Banovetz's prediction (see above) that government structure in the metropolitan area will evolve incrementally in just this manner.

Another likely possibility, at least in some states, is that cooperative area educational service agencies will evolve first into more formal limited purpose metropolitan authorities and then into more comprehensive areawide units. Perhaps the Title III supplementary centers which will be established on a regional basis in many SMSAs will serve as a catalyst for action to reform the underlying educational structure in many of these areas.

Choice of the best strategy to initiate more areawide planning and action in education will depend to a considerable extent on the conditions which exist in a given SMSA. With several promising approaches available, it is possible that the decade of the 1970s will see a good deal of movement toward achieving the goals of metropolitanism in education in many of the nation's SMSAs.

THE METROPOLITAN AREA OF THE FUTURE

New cities are being laid out all over the world. Some are capitals of developing countries such as Chandigarh, the capital of the Indian part of the Punjab, on the plain of northwestern India. Another is Brasilia, the new capital of Brazil, located several hundred miles inland from Rio de Janeiro, the traditional capital city. Others are the famous new communities of Scandinavia such as the city of Tapiola in Finland; the planned communities of Columbia, Maryland, and Reston, Virginia, in the United States; and the "new towns" of Great Britain. After World War II the British government authorized the development of fifteen new towns in the suburbs of the largest cities, eight near London and the others near Leicester, Newcastle, Glasgow, Edinburgh, and Cardiff. All were built around pre-existing small towns, and by 1963, their total population was about a half million, with none larger than 60,000. Though located near large cities, the new towns are intended to be partially autonomous through the development of local industry. The residential neighborhoods are each planned for a cross-section of people with various styles of life and incomes. All the dwellings are within walking or cycling distance of work, recreation, church, shopping centers, and schools. (Madge, 1962.)

An earlier section of this chapter noted that urban renewal of the central city increasingly is being carried out by concentrating resources in relatively self-sufficient subunits within the city. Through participation in model cities planning and in neighborhood development corporations, residents of these renewing communities can feel a greater sense of control over the decisions and conditions which affect their lives.

The concept of self-sufficient subunits within the city, the metropolitan area, or the urban field is also a defining characteristic of plans to build new communities as a means to accommodate population growth and accomplish urban renewal in an industrial society. Varying in population from 50,000 to 400,000, these areas are small enough to be thought about by their citizens as a single unified community.

Thus the directions being taken in urban renewal and urban development are toward the working out of new governmental arrangements which on the one hand would result in regional action large enough to guide and coordinate regional growth and on the other hand would provide for local identification with *decentralized* residential areas. In general, this concept calls for consolidation of suburban governments and school districts into larger units, and for division of the large central cities into subunits no larger than 400,000 or 500,000 people.

Specialists in urban planning and community development agree that the residential subunits of metropolitan society should be self-contained with respect to the ordinary needs of social living-shopping facilities, schools, libraries, and churches. Most believe that each residential subunit should contain cross-sections of the social structure with people of the upper, middle, and working classes living in the same area; otherwise the problems of the metropolis will be concentrated in low-income areas which will create insoluble problems for the rest of the society, and citizens with differing backgrounds will have too little contact with one another to maintain the constructive social relationships necessary for a democratic political system.

Many of the local residential subunits in the future metropolis will consist of smaller planned residential sectors such as the ones Constantine Doxiadis and other urban planners are designing in the new cities and new towns being constructed in many parts of the world. Doxiadis has described the advantages and characteristics of such sectors as follows:

> . . . we must gradually move toward the design of sectors that combine residential with employment possibilities, so as to create better balanced communities and eliminate much commuting on the part of residents.
>
> Also, in every residential sector, we need a shopping center and a number of services: barbers, hairdressers, cleaners, laundromats, and so on, as well as special handicraft and hobby centers. These do not spoil the character of a residential area: on the contrary, they strengthen it by providing employment, services, and activities that are needed close to home. . . .
>
> The most important principle to be established for the implementation of the sector pattern is to conceive of sectors on a human scale: as human communities. The proper size, according to our present experience, can be half a mile to one mile long and rather less in width. Within such sectors people can move by foot, in all directions, to satisfy their daily needs. . . . (Doxiadis, 1966, pp. 107, 147.)

One major goal of this pattern of decentralized development within regional planning units will be to counteract those aspects of urban growth which have resulted in what appears to be a growing sense of political and social alienation among the people of the metropolis. The rationale for such development has been described by Robert Dahl in the presidential address he delivered in 1967 to the Political Science Association:

> We may be approaching a crisis in the socialization of citizens into the political life of the democratic nation-state, a crisis that the challenges of nation-building, democratization, and overcoming the most blatant evils of industrialism have delayed or obscured. There are signs of malaise among young people, among the very citizens who shortly before the dawn of the 21st Cen-

> tury will have become—to use the word that has now become a mindless cliche—the establishment. If the malaise were only American, one could put it down to television, over-permissive child-rearing, the persistence of an unpopular and ugly war, or other causes more or less specific to the United States; but there are signs of this malaise among youth in almost all the democratic countries.
>
> I am not going to try to explain here a phenomenon too complex for brief analysis. But a part of the phenomenon . . . is a belief that the government of the nation-state is remote, inaccessible, and unresponsive, a government of professionals in which only a few can ever hope to participate actively and a still smaller number can ever gain great influence after years of dedication to political life.
>
> What we need, what they need, and what some of them are trying to create (often with incredible ignorance of elementary political wisdom) is a political unit of more truly human proportions in which a citizen can acquire confidence and mastery of the arts of politics—that is, of the arts required for shaping a good life in common with fellow citizens. What Pericles said of Athens, that the city is in general a school of the Grecians, may be said of every city of moderate size: it is a marvelous school. . . .
>
> . . . If there is an optimum size in the broad range from about 50,000 to about 200,000, as I have suggested further inquiry might show, then how can cities be maintained within this range—to say nothing of breaking up the giant metropolis? (Dahl, 1967, pp. 967–969.)

Guiding metropolitan growth to achieve decentralization within larger structures for regional planning and action will not be easily accomplished, but urban planners have devised a number of spatial patterns which are compatible with this concept. One such arrangement is the *galaxy* in which constituent cities and towns are spaced more or less evenly over the territory, with a network of highways and transportation lines leading to areas of specialized activity such as large industrial parks, airports, and financial centers. Another possible type is the *many-pointed star* or wagon wheel, with residential areas radiating out from a central business district, industry located in certain sectors of the star, and transportation routes leading out from the center and criss-crossing with other transportation routes which form concentric circles at various distances from the center. (Bollens and Schmandt, 1965, pp. 50–52.) Either pattern will accommodate the growth of many moderate-sized communities large enough to have colleges, medical centers, theatre, and diversified commercial centers, yet small enough to be intelligible and controllable through local political processes. Great urban centers can be spotted here and there to provide large stadiums for professional sports, specialized libraries for research and scholarship, internationally renowned zoos and botanical gardens, teaching and research hospitals, or other special urban facilities which require a very large population base to support and sustain them.

The outlines of a national program for achieving this type of metropolitan development began to take shape in the late 1960s. Mechanisms for cooperative metropolitan planning and action, such as planning commissions, councils of governments, school district study councils, and area educational service agencies, became much more widespread and vigorous than they had been before. Urban affairs analysts and scholars began to devise and publish comprehensive proposals for dealing with the urgent problems—particularly the racial crisis—of the central cities and for metropolitan and national responses to these problems. (Faltermayer, 1968; Schuchter, 1968.) Most important of all, specific federal government policies potentially capable of constituting a coherent long-range solution to the problems posed by complexity, fragmentation, and stratification were being put forward by influential advocates and even were finding their way into legislation. Conceptually, the thrust of these policies, as articulated by an Under Secretary of HUD, was simple:

> Federal government programs are designed to respond to the cities' differing patterns of evolution. They are directed at increasing the alternatives—the options—available to the 145 million Americans living in urban America. They seek to increase alternatives in three ways:
>
> —first, by reclaiming the central cities for residential living;
>
> —second, by finding alternatives to metropolitan sprawl;
>
> —and third, by helping to develop whole new communities where new urban patterns can be tried. (Wood, 1968, p. 2.)

Two of the most important of the government programs directed at these goals were the Demonstration Cities and Metropolitan Development Act of 1966 and the Housing and Urban Development Act of 1968. As noted elsewhere in this chapter, the Demonstration Cities Act created the model cities approach to urban renewal and also provided funds to encourage and facilitate areawide planning, among other things. The principal sections of the Housing Act included provisions authorizing: a substantial increase in the rent supplement program for low-income families; a reduction in interest rates for low-income families purchasing or renting new or existing housing; federal requirements that a majority of dwelling units in community residential renewal projects be designed for low- and moderate-income families; greater HUD assistance to sponsors of non-profit housing developments; federal guarantees for land acquisition and site development costs assumed by developers in new communities; and increased appropriations for model cities projects. (Adapted from Keith, 1968, pp. 35–37.)

Among the government commissions and organizations which helped develop detailed specifications for urban and metropolitan development in the 1970s were the President's Committee on Urban Housing which issued a report (1969) calling for the production of 26 million housing units—at least six million of them for low-income families—in the next ten years; the National Commission on Urban Problems' report (December, 1968) which contained more than 150 recommendations centering on the goal of building two and a quarter million new housing units a year until 1980, with 500,000 each year reserved for low-income citizens; an Advisory Commission on Intergovernmental Relations' report (April, 1968) detailing the need for a comprehensive national policy on urban growth; the 1969 report of the President's Task Force on Suburban Problems calling attention to and suggesting ways to meet the "quiet, slowly-building crisis" in the suburbs; and the May 1969 report of the National Committee on Urban Growth Policy calling for the building of 100 new communities of 100,000 population each and ten new communities of one million population each. Also noteworthy regarding the development of new towns were: (1) a 1968 background paper of the American Institute of Planners which presented "action priorities and recommendations" that included the creation of a National Urban Communities Commission by Congress, and "the award of no less than 300 franchises during the decade 1970–1980 for new communities with minimum ultimate target populations of 25,000 each" (AIP Task Force on New Communities, 1968); and (2) the publication by two experienced and respected urban planners of a paper describing how a ten-year program to build new towns providing 350,000 subsidized housing units per year could result in "elimination of the ghetto and the creation of a desegregated society." (Weissbourd and Channick, 1968.)

Other notable but less publicized developments which occurred at the federal level late in the 1960s included (1) the establishment in the Bureau of Public Roads of an Environmental Development Division staffed by a balanced team of urban planners, architects, landscape experts, sociologists, economists and engineers and the implementation of this interdisciplinary team approach in planning federally-supported highways in Baltimore, Chicago, and other cities; and (2) an award by the Office of Economic Opportunity of a $262,000 grant to the University of Louisville to plan a new town 20 or 30 miles from that city which will include high quality housing and good-paying jobs for 10,000 low-income families from rural areas and the inner city.

THE CRUCIAL ISSUE OF STRATIFICATION AND SEGREGATION IN METROPOLITAN DEVELOPMENT

It is too early to say how well the programs and proposals cited above will succeed in shaping metropolitan growth to ensure the well-being of people in our industrial society. Many new communities will be built in the outlying parts of the metropolitan areas and in the interstices between them. Through the Model Cities Program and other public and private efforts, new towns "intown" will be built in an attempt to reinvigorate the central cities and some of the older suburban areas. But much will depend, obviously, on the level at which Congress and the state governments fund sufficiently comprehensive and coordinated plans for metropolitan development.

Regardless of the adequacy of funding, the quality of the metropolitan environment of the future will depend in large measure on what and how much is done to deal explicitly and vigorously with the crucial problems posed by the overall pattern of social class stratification and racial segregation which exists in many metropolitan areas.

At least on paper, new communities will be open to low-income families and to families with racial and ethnic minority backgrounds. The open housing law of 1968, the rent supplement program for low-income families seeking housing in middle-income areas, mortgage-support provisions to help nonprofit sponsors of moderate- and low-income housing—these and other programs will offer opportunities to families trying to move out of big city poverty and racial ghettoes because they are experiencing extraordinary difficulties in trying to raise and educate children there. There can be no question, however, but that efforts to overcome the ill effects of stratification and segregation cannot succeed unless they are much more affirmative and far reaching than those which have been made in the past.

Understanding of the individually destructive and socially divisive effects of stratification and segregation in the metropolitan area appears to be growing, but no one knows whether comprehensive action commensurate with the problem will be taken before it is too late. One encouraging sign was a February 10, 1969, U.S. District Court decision that the Chicago Housing Authority was violating the fourteenth amendment by building public housing in low-income areas where its projects were certain to increase rather than decrease segregation. In the 1940s, Chicago public housing authorities had sought approval for plans to construct housing in suitable locations throughout the city, but aldermen from middle-income communities whose residents did not want low-income or minority families living among them vetoed these plans. This decision determined the development of Chicago for the next twenty years: by 1970 nearly one million black citizens were squeezed into predominantly segregated and deteriorating older parts of the city. Pointing out that "No criterion, other than race, can plausibly explain the veto of over 99.5 percent of the housing units located on the white sites . . . and at the same time the rejection of only 10 percent or so of the units on the Negro sites," the Court ruled that this "deliberate policy to separate the races cannot be justified by the good intentions with which other laudable goals are pursued." (Myers, 1969, pp. 2–3.) On July 1, 1969, accordingly, the Court ordered the Chicago Housing Authority to concentrate 75 percent of all subsequent public housing efforts in predominantly white areas in outlying parts of the city and the suburbs or not provide additional units at all.

Despite a few encouraging developments, and despite the arsenal of alternatives (such as the rent supplement program) which federal, state, and local governments now could mobilize to eliminate the poverty and racial ghettoes in the central cities, it is still questionable whether actual destratification and desegregation efforts will prove to be more than token and superficial. As yet, for example, there has been little to indicate that city and metropolitan planning commissions and COGS are ready to mount a real attack on stratification and segregation by (1) requiring radical change in suburban zoning practices which exclude low-income families; and (2) providing the incentives necessary to encourage low-income and minority families to move out of the ghettoes more rapidly.

The 1966 Comprehensive Plan for the City of Chicago, as one case in point, constituted a landmark in the field of city planning. For the first time, a long-range plan for the development of a major U.S. city not only gave as much attention to the social as to the physical aspects of urban renewal but included as one of its major objectives the statement that:

> All families must be free to seek an environment which they believe will satisfy their needs. To assure equal opportunity for all people throughout the metropolitan area, Chicago will press for adoption of state and areawide policies that will guarantee freedom of access to housing, education, and recreational facilities.

Despite the plan's probable good intentions, however, it did not spell out in any precise or step-by-step fashion exactly how the objective was going to be realized. As two informed commentators summarized the situation:

> . . . most white communities are not willing to initiate policies that will change their lot sizes, zoning or subdivision regulations to allow low-income houses to be built for Negroes. Consensus among communities on the abstract objectives of the Comprehensive Plan have no real significance. The interests of communities which do not wish to integrate will not be changed . . . the Comprehensive Plan poses more questions on racial problems than solutions. The solution posed will have very little positive effect upon the conditions of the ghetto. (Berry and Stafford, 1968, pp. 29–31.)

Similarly, in regard to metropolitan planning, otherwise comprehensive plans for metropolitan development still fall far short of providing specific guidance for dealing with the problem of stratification and segregation in the metropolitan area. During 1969, for example, the Bi-State Metropolitan Planning Commission of Kansas City, Missouri, completed its preliminary plan for the growth of the area in the next generation. Although this plan cost many thousands of dollars to prepare and embodied the contributions of many experts and skilled technicians in urban planning, it failed to spell out even one concrete plan designed to reduce the growing racial and poverty ghettoes in Kansas City, Kansas, and Kansas City,

Missouri. It was almost as if the metropolitan area's number one long-range problem did not even exist! The situation appears to be basically similar with respect to the metropolitan plans now being produced in most other SMSAs.

The obvious reason why government officials and planners generally fail to face up to the problem of stratification and segregation is that nobody knows exactly how to require each part of the metropolitan area to accept some real responsibility for the welfare of the larger community. As long as citizens in any significantly large part of the metropolitan area can effectively insulate themselves through zoning laws and other means from the problems of the inner city, the socially and educationally damaging consequences of stratification and segregation are concentrated and intensified among the people in the latter area. The National Commission on Urban Problems has recommended that federal grants for sewers, highways, and other expensive improvements required in suburban areas should be contingent on the inclusion of low-income housing within a "Workable Program" prepared by each recipient community. Until effective action based on this or equivalent recommendations is taken by federal, state, regional, and local governments, whether the nation is truly committed to solving the most critical problem of metropolitan society must remain in doubt.

EDUCATION IN METROPOLITAN DEVELOPMENT

This chapter has reviewed the development of regional planning and action to cope with the problems associated with complexity, fragmentation, and stratification in the metropolitan area. The material presented in the chapter indicates that education must be a major component in efforts to achieve social and physical urban renewal and ensure the well-being of people in the metropolitan area.

For one thing, there is a definite parallel between the problem of improving metropolitan governmental structure in general and that of improving the structure of the metropolitan educational system. In both cases what is required is movement beyond voluntary cooperation to a regionalization of appropriate functions combined with a decentralization of other functions among viable subregional units within the regional structure. Also evident is a degree of convergence in the thinking of those political scientists who believe that the optimal population base for local municipal governments is in the range of 50,000–200,000 people and the estimates of educators who believe that local operating school districts should enroll between 20,000 and 35,000 pupils. This convergence suggests that it might be desirable to aim for areawide governmental reorganization which makes operating school districts coterminous with municipal governments serving about 50,000–100,000 people, thus facilitating cooperation and coordination between the two types of governments.

Second, the single most critical problem in the metropolitan area as a whole—namely that of social class stratification and racial segregation—is also the most serious problem in metropolitan education. Just as patterns of stratification and segregation have resulted in deleterious physical and social conditions in the inner core of the central city, so, too, these patterns have created what till now have proven to be insoluble problems in the inner-city schools. Large amounts of resources are beginning to be expended to cope with the situation in the inner city and its schools, but there is no assurance that these resources will do much good as long as the poor and the minorities are confined to identifiable parts of the central cities. And even if there were vast improvements in economic, social, and educational conditions in the inner city, it is questionable whether a democratic political system could be maintained in a metropolitan area permanently divided along racial lines.

Third, the success of efforts to reduce stratification and segregation in the metropolitan area will depend to a significant degree upon leadership given by the schools. Social attitudes are formed early in life; unless schools take the lead in helping students of differing backgrounds get to know one another, stratification and segregation will tend to be perpetuated and reinforced.

Districts in all parts of the metropolitan area can help provide this leadership. Suburban districts with few poor or black pupils can enroll pupils from central city schools, as are Rochester and Hartford, and can work to achieve economic and racial heterogeneity in suburban communities. Suburban districts with economically or socially disadvantaged students can work for district-wide destratification and desegregation, as Berkeley and Evanston have done. Central city districts can enlarge school boundaries to increase integration, as in Syracuse; refuse to locate new school facilities in all-white middle-class areas, as the Columbus Board of Education has resolved to do; place high schools at the city outskirts where they will serve all types of students, as Flint, Michigan plans to do; and take other steps to reduce educationally and socially harmful patterns of segregation and stratification. Actions of this nature will play an important part in determining whether the metropolitan area of the future will be politically and socially viable.

Fourth, as an increasingly central function in urban society, public education is an indispensable element in action to achieve social and physical urban renewal. The leading role of education derives in part from the obvious facts that education is now the keystone for individual mobility and social progress in urban society and that the multiplicity of school districts is a prime source of governmental fragmentation and complexity in the metropolitan area. Beyond these truisms, it is also clear that the success of urban renewal often depends on how well education is tied into community redevelopment projects.

In Baltimore, for example, educators are working closely with governmental officials to develop a plan which will simultaneously provide new school facilities and solve that city's dilemma concerning the location of an interstate highway. High rise buildings in New York, Chicago, and other cities are being designed to combine residential and early childhood education facilities in a way that will make these buildings more attractive and functional. In most such cases, the inclusion of educational facilities makes it possible to obtain more adequate federal funds for an urban renewal project.

Plans being developed for the Fort Lincoln renewal area in Washington, D.C. illustrate how important education can be in the building of attractive "new towns intown" to strengthen the social and economic fabric of the central city. One informed architect has summarized plans for this renewal area as follows:

> Although most of the proposals followed the traditional new town planning program, there were two significant innovations. First, there was emphasis on the school system as a series of related specialized learning centers. The plan emphasized the school system for the success of the project. Altogether, 10,000 students would be accommodated on the site in a system whose parts would be related to work together. The District had agreed to support the construction of all facilities within the school system.
>
> The second significant innovation was a minirail spine. It applied transportation technology directly to the method in which development was handled. The related learning centers of the

> school system were related by the transportation system, and dependent on it. It was also intended to minimize internal vehicular circulation requirements in order to reduce the asphalt acreage and contribute a more attractive environment. (Paul, 1969.)

Emphasis in this chapter has been placed on the development of and future prospects for cooperative planning and regionalization in the metropolitan system of education. Without such evolution in the present structure and arrangements for education, metropolitan area schools will be unable either to deliver adequate educational services to their clients or to provide the leadership needed to help shape the metropolitan area of the future in desirable directions.

The future of the suburbs depends on the central city, and the city depends on its suburbs. The suburbs are here to stay, and no amount of urban renewal in the central city can stop their growth. However, the isolation and autonomy of the independent suburban community has to be reduced. As the suburbs grow, they will get into trouble with each other if they do not learn to cooperate among themselves and with the central city. No metropolitan area will survive as a middle-class suburban doughnut surrounding a central city slum ghetto.

The goals of a metropolitan society should include development of the personal and social resources of the people of the metropolitan area and maximization of choice in deciding how one wants to live. But this cannot happen so long as the metropolitan educational system is so fragmented and uncoordinated that it cannot deliver on its obligation to provide equal and adequate educational opportunities for all groups of pupils.

SUGGESTED ACTIVITIES

1. On the basis of your knowledge of your own metropolitan area, how would you subdivide it into "core areas" of relatively self-sufficient character? What would be the socio-economic and racial characteristics of these units?
2. If you know two metropolitan areas of approximately the same size, write a paper on their sense of community. Is one of the two much more conscious of itself as a metropolitan area than the other? What is the evidence?
3. Most metropolitan areas have a planning council or commission. Study the work of this council or commission in your area, and find out how the schools are related to their work.

4. How many school districts in the metropolitan area nearest to you are below 20,000 in pupil enrollment? How many of these districts appear to be severely handicapped in financing adequate education? One likely source of information to help you answer these questions is the division of school administration in your college or university.
5. If school districts in your region are carrying out projects cooperatively, prepare a brief description of these projects and explain how and why they were started. If there is an area educational service agency, find out what services it provides and the basis on which school districts participate in it.
6. Is there a metropolitan plan already prepared to guide the growth of your metropolitan area? If yes, analyze the plan with particular reference to its implications for stratification and segregation and its treatment of public education.

SUGGESTIONS FOR FURTHER READING

1. For a substantial discussion of forms of metropolitan growth and cooperation see Chapters 13–16 of *The Metropolis* by Bollens and Schmandt.
2. State governments are moving to assist metropolitan areas to reorganize their local government systems. The principal agency promoting this activity is the Advisory Commission on Intergovernmental Relations, made up of state and city officials, with an office in Washington, D.C. The Commission has issued a *State Legislative Program* which contains suggested state legislation that would improve government in metropolitan areas.
3. A stimulating description of the spatial patterns of the future metropolitan areas is given by Kevin Lynch, city planner at the Massachusetts Institute of Technology, in a special edition of "Daedalus" titled "The Future Metropolis."
4. Additional information on issues involving the organization of metropolitan schools on a regional basis can be found in several reports issued by the Great Plains School District Organization Project and published by the Nebraska State Department of Education.
5. Much of the material in the publications of the project on Designing Education for the future (New York: Citation Press) is relevant to the question of organizing school districts in the metropolitan area, particularly the chapter by William Wheaton in Volume 1.
6. Robert Bendiner's *The Politics of Schools* provides an excellent analysis of the reasons for a metropolitan education authority.

CHAPTER

7

Schools and the Black Revolution

THE HISTORY of the United States is one of progress toward a democratic cultural pluralism. People from a variety of nations came to this country as poor people or as people who disagreed with the dominant political or religious power in their native countries. They were free in this country to practice their way of life. As a rule, they prospered. As a rule, they merged their way of life with the developing American way, contributing some of their own cultural traits and taking on others that were new to them. This was cultural pluralism.

One European immigrant group after another became assimilated in this way. Commencing before the middle of the nineteenth century, the Irish, the Germans, the Scandinavians, Italians, Poles, Hungarians, Czechs, Greeks, and Russians, came to this country, one group after another, and prospered. Generally they settled in communities or in sections of cities where they could maintain their own language and religions and family cultures for the first one or two generations. Eventually they moved out into the wider stream of American life, choosing freely their occupations and the places where they would live. With the passage of time these ethnic groups tended to lose many of their nationality traits.

The process of assimilation of European immigrant groups was at its height from about 1840 to 1930. After World War I, restrictive immigration policies cut down the flow of new immigrants from foreign lands, but the development of industry in the United States required an even greater supply of new and unskilled labor. The new supply came largely from the rural areas of the United States, where the farm population was excessive. Large farms were becoming mechanized, and the small subsistence farms of the southern hills were being abandoned or combined into large commercial farms which required less manpower.

After World War I, the need of American industry for unskilled and semiskilled labor was met largely by rural Americans. They moved from their rural homes to nearby industrial centers and cities. From here they moved to the rapidly developing industrial centers in the Great Lakes area and the West Coast. They settled in the areas of the cities that had formerly been occupied by European immigrants who had moved up the social scale and out to more desirable residential areas. This great internal migration was interrupted by the Depression of 1930, and was stimulated again by the developing war industries of World War II, and by the economic boom of the post-war period.

The migration of southern rural whites and blacks to the cities and industrial areas was accompanied by a migration of Puerto Rican workers to the New York City area and then to other industrial cities in the northeast and north central areas. Mexican workers came to the cities of the Mountain States and the Southwest.

It was these groups that filled the places in the central cities left behind by middle-income people, old Americans and ethnic Americans, who moved out to the edges of the cities and to the suburbs, producing the socio-economic and racial stratification described in Chapter 3.

What is appropriately termed an "urban crisis" came upon the great cities shortly after World War II, as the central cities grew old and obsolete, physically, while the suburbs grew larger and more prosperous.

The new central city population appeared to be having trouble in taking full advantage of the economic and cultural opportunities of the United States. The educational level and the economic level of the central city resident did not rise as rapidly as did these indices for the country as a whole. And there was some evidence that the blacks were having special difficulty, as a group.

For example, Table 7.1 shows how the blacks and the Orientals (Chinese and Japanese) have fared in socio-economic status in recent decades. While the Orientals have gained greatly in these areas relative to the whites, the Negroes have not done so.

TABLE 7.1
Socio-economic Status of Nonwhite and White
Male Population: 1940–1960

	1940	1950	1960
Percent of Employed Nonfarm Male Population in White-Collar Jobs			
Japanese	45	36	56
White	39	39	42
Chinese	35	42	51
Black	9	11	14
Percent of Male Population, Aged 25+, with Four Years of High School and Over			
Japanese	34	57	69
White	24	34	42
Chinese	11	27	40
Black	7	12	18

Source: Calvin F. Schmid and Charles E. Nobbe (1965).

URBANIZATION OF BLACKS

During the past half-century the black has become urbanized. That is, while in 1910, 73 percent of blacks were living in rural or semi-rural conditions, 73 percent in 1960 were living in towns and cities of 2,500 or more. Fifty-four percent of the Negroes in 1968 were living in cities of 50 thousand or more.

Urbanization of blacks has taken place with about equal speed in all parts of the country except the South, where there is still a considerable number of rural blacks. Table 7.2 shows that about 95 percent of blacks outside of the South were living in urban places in

TABLE 7.2

Whites and Blacks in the Urban Population, 1960, by Region

Region	*Percentage of the Population Living in Urban Places*	
	White	*Black*
Northeast	79.1	95.7
North Central	66.8	95.7
West	77.6	92.6
South	58.6	58.4
United States	69.5	73.2

Source: *U.S. Census of Population, 1960. U.S. Summary,* Tables 155 and 233; PC(2)–1C, Nonwhite Population by Race, Table 1.

1960. Table 7.3 shows how the proportions of blacks have changed in populations of major cities. The northern cities had slow increases between 1900 and 1940, and very rapid increases between 1950 and 1960. The southern cities generally saw some percentage decrease after 1900, with fluctuation after 1940. The southern rural population lost both blacks and whites during this period.

The urbanization of blacks and their migration to the industrial centers of the country posed the problem of cultural pluralism in a new and most difficult form. As long as most blacks lived on a subsistence level in the rural South, they tended to be ignored by the rest of the country. But as soon as they moved into the cities, they would either become integrated socially into the cities or they would become a highly visible social group, suffering from discrimination and lack of cultural development and becoming a burden on the conscience of a democratic society.

A minority of blacks became integrated into the social and economic life of the cities. They followed the familiar pattern of other immigrant ethnic groups. They worked hard and saved their money. They secured as good an education as possible for their children. These children moved up the socio-economic ladder into professional and business occupations. Thus a black middle class developed.

But the majority of newly-urbanized blacks did not have this experience. They and their children are still set aside from the mainstream of American life, even though they live in the midst of the great cities. They are segregated residentially, with only a few exceptions. They are in segregated schools, with relatively few exceptions.

In metropolitan areas in 1965, 75 percent of black elementary school pupils attended schools in which more than 90 percent of their fellow pupils were blacks. In these same areas, 83 percent of the white pupils attended schools with more than 90 percent white enrollment.

The working-class urban Negro presents a social problem. The causes of this problem are certainly multiple. One cause is economic discrimination, which makes it difficult for the black to get into certain skilled trades, and limits the number of places where he can find work. Another cause is inferior education in the past and to some extent in the present. Still another cause is weakness of the black working-class family. The question of the black working-class family is a disputed one, during the past decade, and deserves careful study.

The Black Working-Class Family

The Negro in the United States has been studied by sociologists throughout this century, and they have agreed that the black family differs in general from the white American family as well as from the families of various European ethnic groups. To a considerable extent these differences are due to the fact that, under slavery, the Negro family barely existed. Black slaves could not legally marry in the United States, black men and women who were living together and had children could be separated and sold separately, as could their children. Black slaves had no legal protection. Other slave-holding societies recognized and protected the slave family, but not the American.

After the emancipation of the slaves, most of them continued to live in the rural South, where they developed a simple folk culture and a simple family structure to go with it. Women continued to have the dominant role in the black family, as they had before emancipation. The black male was greatly restricted in his access to jobs, to rights as a citizen, and to the initiatives which are expected of a man and the head of a family in American society.

After World War I there was a substantial migration of blacks to the northern cities, which continued through the 1920s, and it soon became evident that the working-class black family would not stand up as a stable structure for child-rearing and marital relationships under these conditions. Professor Franklin Frazier, the Negro sociologist, wrote the following in his book, *The Negro Family,* published in 1939.

> First, it appears that the family which evolved within the isolated world of the Negro folk will become increasingly disorganized. Modern means of communication will break down the isolation of the world of the black folk, and, as long as the bankrupt system of southern agriculture exists, Negro families will continue to seek a living in the towns and cities of the country. They will crowd the slum areas of southern cities or make their way to northern cities where their family life will become disrupted and their poverty will force them to depend upon charity.
>
> The impact of hundreds of thousands of rural southern Negroes upon northern metropolitan communities presents a bewildering spectacle. Striking contrasts in levels among these newcomers to modern civilization seem to baffle any attempt to discover order and direction in their mode of life. (Frazier, 1939, pp. 298, 487.)

Frazier's prophecy is supported by a mass of facts about blacks in urban areas. Negroes live under great economic disadvantages, and the children of working-class blacks grow up in families that are less stable and have less masculine influence than working-class white families.

For example, blacks have consistently suffered more unemployment than whites, as can be seen in Table 7.4. The unemployment rate has been about twice as high for nonwhites as for whites. The black family is much more likely to be headed by a woman than is the white family, as is seen in Table A-8. In 1968, 29 percent of black families living in metropolitan areas were headed by a woman. This condition is more pronounced in lower-income families and in urban areas, as can be seen in Tables A-9 and A-10. Among other characteristics, the working-class black male is less likely to be visible to the census taker than the corresponding white male. This is seen in Table A-11 which reports the ratio of males to females, by color and age. In the 25 to 44 age group, the black males are undercounted by about 10 percent, according to census experts. In this age range a considerable number of black males are just "unattached" to any family or institution, and therefore are not reported to the census enumerator. This is an example of the fact that a substantial group of Negro men do not fill the usual male role

TABLE 7.3

White and Nonwhite Population Trends in the Big Cities 1900–1970
(Population in Thousands)

	1900		*1940*		*1950*		*1960*		*1970**	
	Pop.	*Non-W.* %	*Pop.*	*Non-W.* %	*Pop.*	*Non-W.* %	*Pop.*	*Non-W.* %	*Pop.*	*Non-W.* %
New York	3,437	1.8	7,455	6.1	7,892	9.5	7,782	14.0	8,100	19
Chicago	1,699	1.8	3,397	8.2	3,621	13.6	3,550	22.9	3,325	32
Philadelphia–Camden	1,294	4.8	1,931	13.0	2,072	18.2	2,003	26.4	2,200	32
Los Angeles–Long Beach	105	2.1	1,669	3.9	2,221	7.9	2,823	12.2	3,410	21
San Francisco–Oakland	410	0.7	937	1.4	1,160	7.9	1,107	14.3	1,110	24
Detroit	286	1.4	1,623	9.2	1,850	16.2	1,670	28.9	1,700	47
Boston	561	2.1	771	3.1	801	5.0	697	9.1	675	13
Pittsburgh	452	3.8	672	9.3	677	12.2	604	16.7	610	21
Buffalo	352	0.5	576	3.1	580	6.3	533	13.3	510	22
Washington, D.C.	279	31.1	663	28.0	802	35.0	764	53.9	840	68
Baltimore	509	15.6	859	19.3	950	23.7	939	34.7	920	47
Kansas City, Mo.	164	10.7	399	10.4	457	12.2	476	17.5	500	24
Atlanta	90	39.8	302	34.6	331	36.6	487	38.3	540	39
Birmingham	38	43.1	268	40.7	326	39.9	341	39.6	354	40
Montgomery	30	56.8	78	44.2	107	39.9	134	35.1	160	32

* 1970 figures are projections from 1950–60 trends. These may be far from the 1970 reality.

Note: Nonwhites includes Orientals, who are present in noticeable numbers in San Francisco and Los Angeles, but not elsewhere in this list.

Source: U.S. Census.

TABLE 7.4
White and Black Unemployment Rates in Central Cities
Percentage Unemployed

Age Group	White 1968	White 1960	Black 1968	Black 1960
Both sexes 16–19 yrs.	12.3	9.8	30.4	22.7
Male, 20 yrs. and over	2.5	4.8	6.0	9.9
Married, wife present	1.8	3.4	4.5	7.5
Female, 20 yrs. and over	3.5	4.3	5.9	10.1

Source: Bureau of the Census. Series P-23, No. 27, Feb. 1969.

in family life. Most difficult for young black men is their high unemployment rates, as seen in Table 7.4. Between 16 and 19 years of age the black unemployment rate was two and one-half times that of the whites in 1968.

The facts which have been cited apply to the black working-class family and not to the black family in general. But the proportion of blacks in the working class is so high that data for blacks in general tend to reflect the black working class. There is evidence that the Negro population is becoming divided into a stable middle-class group of families that is growing stronger and more successful, a stable upper working-class group that is holding its own, and an increasingly unstable and disorganized lower working-class group. For example, middle-class blacks have fewer children than middle-class whites. This is seen in Table A-12. Nonwhite women who married middle-class men at the age when middle-class women are most likely to marry (22 or over) had 20 percent *fewer* children than white women of similar social circumstances. On the other hand, nonwhite women who were married at ages 14 to 21 to men of the lower working class had 20 percent *more* children than white women of similar social class.

The pernicious influence of the ghetto works hardship especially on the stable upper working-class group. Since they cannot get away from the ghetto they must live in an environment strongly influenced by the unstable and disorganized lower working class—and often in the same blocks and slum buildings. Victimized by enforced residence in the ghetto, they become angry and hostile against the system and the social structure which condemn them to this life.

The spotty character of economic progress made by blacks can be illustrated by the case of Cleveland. While average income rose among blacks outside of the poorest neighborhoods between 1960 and 1965, the indicators of socio-economic status declined in the very poor neighborhoods, especially in the Hough area, scene of riots soon afterward.

Black School Children

It is not surprising that black children do less well in school than white children, on the average, when one considers the disadvantages under which the black working-class children live. In comparing black with white children on school performance, the groups differ in socio-economic status as well as in race. Seldom has a comparison been made where the socio-economic status of the two racial groups was the same. In a few studies where the socio-economic status was the same for the two racial groups, the results tend to indicate that white children achieve slightly higher than Negro children, after they have been in segregated schools for a period of time. Most of the comparisons are similar to those in Table A-14, and Table 3.3, where the socio-economic status is not kept constant.

The most comprehensive study of school achievement in relation to race was made by the U.S. Office of Education under the direction of James S. Coleman in 1965, with results shown in Table A-13. This table compares scores made on school achievement tests by white, Oriental, black, Puerto Rican, and American Indian pupils. All except the Indian data refer to pupils living in metropolitan areas. In general, the black pupils come below white and Oriental, and above the Puerto Ricans. It should be emphasized that the black and Puerto Rican pupils come from families on the average much lower in socio-economic status than that of the white and Oriental pupils.

To see how these data look in a particular city, we may consult Table 3.3 of Chapter 3. This shows how the elementary school children of Chicago ranked in IQ and school achievement at the sixth grade and in "readiness" for reading at the first grade. Chicago's twenty-one school districts are ranked by socio-economic status of the adults, and the average IQ, sixth-grade school achievement and reading readiness is given for each district, as well as the percentage of black pupils. It will be seen that the lowest seven districts in socio-economic status all contain from 61 to 100 percent Negro school pupils, and tend to be the lowest in school aptitude and achievement. Less than half of the first graders scored average or above on the Metropolitan Reading Readiness test given at the beginning of the first grade. A score of "below average" on this test indicates that a child will have difficulty in first-grade work, and will not learn to read during the year unless he is given a good deal of individualized help. The Table also shows the test data for two districts which are in the top third in socio-economic status and have 37 and 77 percent black pupils. Although slightly below the other districts of high socio-economic status in school aptitude and achievement, those districts with a large proportion of middle-class black pupils are clearly higher in achievement than the districts which are populated mainly by working-class black families.

Table A-14 is taken from the Survey of Philadelphia Public Schools made in 1964–65, and shows how the white and Negro pupils who entered school in 1949 compared in IQ. The whites are obviously higher, and they are also higher in socio-economic status.

SCHOOL FACTOR VERSUS FAMILY FACTOR

It became quite clear during the 1960s that a massive effort must be mounted to assist Negro children to do better in school. The question was not *whether* to make such an effort, but *how* to do it. The answers to this question were being hammered out on the anvil of controversy through the 1960s, and they were by no means clearly stated by the middle of the decade, when President Johnson called for action in his Commencement Address at Howard University on June 4, 1965.

> Our earth is the home of revolution. In every corner of every continent men charged with hope contend with ancient ways in the pursuit of justice. They reach for the newest of weapons to realize the oldest of dreams—that each may walk in freedom and pride, stretching his talents, enjoying the fruits of the earth. . . .
>
> But nothing in any country touches us more profoundly, nothing is more freighted with meaning for our own destiny than the revolution of the Negro American.
>
> In far too many ways American Negroes have been another nation, deprived of freedom, crippled by hatred, the doors of opportunity closed to hope.
>
> In our time change has come to this nation too. The Ameri-

> can Negro, acting with impressive restraint, has peacefully protested and marched, entered the courtroom and the seats of government, demanding a justice that has long been denied. . . .
>
> We seek not just freedom but opportunity—not just legal equity but human ability—not just equality as a right and a theory but equality as a fact and as a result.
>
> For the task is to give 20 million Negroes the same chance as every other American to learn and grow, to work and share in society, to develop their abilities—physical, mental and spiritual—and to pursue their individual happiness.
>
> To this end equal opportunity is essential, but not enough. Men and women of all races are born with the same range of abilities. But ability is not just the product of birth. Ability is stretched or stunted by the family you live with, and the neighborhood you live in, by the school you go to, and the poverty or the richness of your surroundings.

The answer to the question centered around the relative importance of the family and the school in the mental development of the child.

There are four factors which determine the level of achievement of a child in school. One of them is the inborn ability or disability of the child. Another is the kind of family life or family training he experiences. A third is the quality of the schooling he gets. The fourth is his self-concept or aspiration level. He has it in his power, after several years of school experience, to determine how hard he will work in school, and toward what goals.

There are inborn or biological differences of intelligence, but these are among individuals, not between large social or racial groups. No doubt there are inborn differences of potential intelligence among the children of a particular family; and every class of 30 children has 30 different levels of inborn intellectual potential.

The schools receive children with a wide variety of inborn intelligence and also with a variety of family experience which helps or hinders school learning. The schools provide a program of teaching and an environment in which pupils are learning. The pupil's self-concept grows out of his family and his school experience.

Thus the two factors about which society may be able to do something after a child is born are the school factor and the family factor. A very good family experience can make a child with only average inborn ability look good in school. A very good school can make a child with only average innate ability look good. A very good school may also compensate a child in whole or in part for a weak family factor, and a very strong family factor may compensate for a weak school factor.

Since about 1955, studies of the bearing of the family factor on mental development have led to a revision of earlier beliefs about the relative importance of the family and school factors, with greater emphasis being given to the family factor. Research on the cognitive development of children, summarized by Bloom (1964), points to the family as the major influence, and to the preschool years as the crucial ones for mental development. The child's mind grows upon the language he hears, and the family provides his language environment. If the language is barren, the child's mind is stunted. If the language is rich, and if the family includes the child as an active person, his mind is stimulated to grow.

Every child's mind must feed on the language provided in the home. If families differ systematically in the nature of the language they use, their children's mental development must differ systematically. There is now substantial evidence that families do differ in this respect, and that the better-educated parents, with higher socio-economic status, provide a more stimulating and more elaborate language environment. The sociologist Basil Bernstein (1960, 1964) has analyzed family language patterns in the several social classes, and has concluded that working-class and rural families, as a general rule, but with exceptions, restrict the mental development of their children because they use a restricted language in the home. A child who has learned a *restricted* language at home is likely to have difficulty in school, where an *elaborate* language is used and taught by the teacher; and the difficulty of this child is likely to increase as he goes further in school, unless he learns the elaborate language that is expected in the school. On the other hand, the child who has had experience with an elaborate language in the home from his earliest years has a relatively easy time in school, because he must simply go on developing the kind of language and related thinking which he has already started.

Several studies made since 1965 have shown it is not income or socio-economic status of family that causes rapid or slow cognitive development; rather it is certain family characteristics which are only statistically related to socio-economic status. By interviewing families concerning their practices of reading to children, carrying on dinner-table conversations, taking children to see museums, etc., these studies derived scores to measure family environment and found that these scores were much closer related to children's school achievement than were the scores of these families based on income and occupation.

These studies have led to a number of experiments with preschool and kindergarten classes for children of lower working-class families. Martin Deutsch in New York and Robert Hess in Chicago have worked with socially disadvantaged children (mainly black children) at ages three to five, attempting to supplement the family factor. Deutsch (1965) summarized the situation with the following comments:

> Strong evidence can be adduced to support the assumption that it is the active verbal engagement of people who surround him which is the operative influence in the child's language development. The structuring of these verbal engagements in terms of the family's conditions and style of life, and the further relationship between style of life and social class membership leads to the analysis of children's language skills and verbal behavior in terms of their families' socio-economic status. In the cognitive style of the lower-class family, Bernstein (1960) points out, language is used in a convergent or restrictive fashion rather than a divergent, elaborative fashion. An exclamation or an imperative or a partial sentence frequently replaces a complete sentence or an explanation: if a child asks for something, the response is too frequently "yes," "no," "go away," "later," or simply a nod. The feedback is not such that it gives the child the articulated verbal parameters that allow him to start and fully develop normative labeling and identification of the environment. Family interaction data which we have gathered in both lower-class socially deprived and middle-class groups indicate that, as compared with the middle-class homes, there is a paucity of organized family activities in a large number of lower-class homes. . . .

Deutsch says that socially disadvantaged children need compensatory education at the preschool level as well as a more effective school age education. He and others are proponents of Operation Head Start, which in 1965 commenced a massive prekindergarten program for disadvantaged children with financing under the Economic Opportunity Act. However, they feel that the schools must do a much better job than they now are doing with socially disadvantaged children.

The influence of the family factor may be seen within the black working-class group in a study made in New York City's Harlem, where high achieving and low achieving fifth graders were compared. (Davidson and Greenberg.) Eighty boys and 80 girls were selected from twelve elementary schools. They all met the following criteria:

> Parents were of low socio-economic status according to occupation, educational level, and type of dwelling unit.
>
> Parents were all born in this country.
>
> Child attended school in a northern city since Grade I.
>
> IQ between 75 and 125.
>
> Age between 9 years, 11 months and 11 years, 4 months.

The 40 boys and 40 girls who were high achievers in October of the fifth grade averaged at the 6.45 grade level in reading and the 5.4 level in arithmetic. The 40 boys and 40 girls who were low achievers averaged 2.85 in reading and 3.35 in arithmetic.

The two groups—the high achievers and the low achievers—were compared on a number of psychological and social characteristics. High achievers were superior to low achievers on a number of psychological characteristics, as would be expected. But the striking thing was the relationship of certain home or family characteristics within this working-class group to school achievement. An experienced interviewer visited in the homes and talked with the mother about the child and about the mother's behavior with respect to the child. He was not informed as to the achievement level of the children. Ratings were made that are similar to those made by Wolf in his comparison of family background of middle-class and working-class children. The families of high achievers were rated as substantially superior to that of low achievers in "Concern for the Child's Education," "Thinking and Planning for the Child as an Individual," "General Social-Civic Awareness and Concern of the Parent," "Structure and Orderliness of the Home." Thus, within the black lower-class group some children score above the national norms on educational achievement, and they tend to come from homes that prepare them well for school achievement. It was also noted that certain socio-economic differences within the working class differentiated the high from the low achievers. Parents of the high achievers had more education, higher status occupations, and took better care of their apartments than parents of low achievers.

The most interesting and challenging experimentation with

disadvantaged children took place in the preschool years during the 1960s. The work of Bereiter and Engelmann (1966) stimulated a number of preschool projects with emphasis on direct and concentrated teaching of vocabulary and complex sentences as well as simple arithmetic. A series of projects under the direction of Susan W. Gray (1966) at George Peabody College in Nashville provided evidence that mothers of disadvantaged children could be brought directly into the program, and this would change the mother's behavior in relation to later children in the family. But an evaluation of Head Start programs over the country made by the Westinghouse Learning Corporation (1969) showed that most of these programs brought only transitory and small gains in learning ability, probably due in part to their brevity (a few summer weeks only) and in part to their tendency to rely on traditional middle-class nursery school play procedures.

The question is yet to be answered as to what balance of effort should be put on preschool work and on work with school age children. If stress is laid on preschool work, this emphasizes the family factor and seems to say that the lower-working-class family, and especially the black lower-working-class family is inadequate for rearing children in a complex urban society. If stress is laid on work with school age children, this emphasizes the school factor and seems to say that society has fallen down on the job of educating lower-working-class children and should improve its schools so as to do a better job.

When the family factor is stressed, some people see an inference that blacks are to blame for the shortcomings of the black working-class family, though they also recognize that society, through slavery and discrimination, is responsible for the Negro working-class family. Emotions are aroused. Some blacks and some civil rights workers as well as some people who are emotionally identified with the working class tend to charge the schools with the responsibility for present defects in black children, while some educators and some social workers and some social scientists see the root of the difficulty in the Negro working-class family. The Black Revolution is operating in this situation of emotional tension among people who want to improve the situation for the Negro working class but see the basic cause and therefore the basic solution differently. The Black Revolution is working out its strategy in this situation.

THE BLACK REVOLUTION

The *Black Revolution* is anything but a revolution as people have understood that term in the past, although it is something like the Industrial Revolution in the peaceable yet drastic quality of the social change it carries with it. The Black Revolution was first taken seriously by many Americans on August 28, 1963, when two hundred thousand black and white Americans marched to the Lincoln Monument in Washington, to demonstrate the urgency of action for political and economic equality for the Negroes of North America.

Organizations to support the Black Revolution have grown in strength and in number since World War II. Principal prewar organizations were the National Association for the Advancement of Colored People (NAACP) and the Urban League. Later came CORE, the Congress of Racial Equality, and the Southern Christian Leadership Conference, organized by Martin Luther King. These are not aligned with any political party and do not have any political program beyond that of getting civic and economic and educational opportunity for blacks.

More militant organizations were formed during the 1960s to take a leading role in the Black Revolution. These were SNCC (Student Nonviolent Coordinating Committee), the Black Panthers, and a number of Associations of black teachers, black students, black psychologists, and other professional groups.

The Problem of the "Black Role"

The basic obstacle to the black man's full participation in the American way of life is his assignment to the black role. Just as other ethnic groups have had negative roles ascribed to them in the past, which they have learned to overcome, the role of the "lazy nigger" must be overcome. The Irish overcame the role of "shanty Irish"; the Swedish immigrants had to go through a period when they were called "dumb Swedes"; and the Poles more recently have overcome the connotations of the term "Polack."

When an ethnic group is in a subordinate position in a society, there generally exists a stereotyped role which members of the group are expected to fit. The role of a lazy, shiftless, and dull person has been assigned to the black and has turned into a reality for some blacks by racial segregation and by economic and political and social discrimination.

The Black Revolution is engaged in changing the black role to one which connotes success in urban industrial society. The new black role is one that encourages black children to work hard in school, to set high educational and vocational goals for themselves, and to become confident of their ability to do anything that those of another color can do.

There is one positive role for black boys and men, which attracts them—that of the athlete. Commencing with prize-fighting, and moving on to track athletics, baseball, basketball and football, black boys have embraced this role and worked hard and successfully to live up to it. Their latest conquest has come in the upper-middle-class sport of tennis, where Arthur Ashe, a Negro, made a place for himself on America's Davis Cup team.

The more widely universal role that is coming for black boys and girls requires integration in economic life, political life, and especially in the schools. Already large numbers of black children are successfully learning this role, as is proven by the growing numbers of black college graduates, of black businessmen and professional workers including school teachers.

The strategy of the Black Revolution varies from one part of the country to another, and from one time to another, though it always emphasizes one or another of the following: better schooling, employment opportunity, better housing, better family life, access to community services.

Since about 1966 one striking form of strategy has been that of black separatism, which stresses the need of the black man to discover his own *identity* through living with other blacks, studying African cultures and history, and thus gaining the self-esteem that will enable him to meet other racial groups on an even footing.

Since the schools to which most black children go are public schools, and since better education is an obvious and basic need for blacks, and since there has obviously been discrimination against black children in the matter of education in the past, the schools have been a continuing focus for the efforts of the Black Revolution. Therefore the story of progress toward integration in the public schools and toward better education for black youth will be summarized.

INTEGRATION IN CITY SCHOOLS: 1954–70

The sixteen years from 1954 to 1970 have seen the attention of educators forcibly focused on the place of black pupils in the public schools. The problem has been concentrated generally in the cities. Only in the South have there been enough blacks in rural communities and small cities to make segregation a problem in these schools. In 1960, 73 percent of all Negroes were living in places of 2,500 or more, and 50 percent were living in cities of 50 thousand or more.

The period since 1954 can be divided into four phases.

Phase 1. Response to the Supreme Court Decision: 1954–58

When the United States Supreme Court declared the maintenance by law of a separate public school for Negroes to be illegal, there were at first only mild reactions. These reactions varied with the region of the United States.

A. *The Deep South.* In the Deep South there was at first very little response of any kind. This was followed by a period of several years spent in trying out various schemes to get around the Court's decision. Virginia, for example, made it legal for the state to pay tuition of pupils in private schools where public schools did not exist, and Prince Edward County proceeded to close its public schools. Negro children were left to fend for themselves, and had no public schooling for several years. Not much happened in the southern cities until the Little Rock incident exploded.

B. *Border Cities.* In the larger border cities—Baltimore, Washington, Cincinnati, Louisville, St. Louis and Kansas City—there was immediate compliance with the law in formally desegregating the schools. However, the residential distribution of blacks was such that segregation continued, on a *de facto* basis, for the vast majority of black pupils. Since the 1954 decision coincided in time with the largest north and westward Negro migration that had ever happened, the incoming blacks quickly filled up whatever vacant houses were available in areas partly but not entirely Negro, and thus made it economically easy for whites who were living in school districts inhabited largely by blacks to sell or rent their homes and to move to suburbs or other sections of the city where there was no immediate prospect of integration.

However, there was a movement of small numbers of black pupils into previously all-white schools, partly in the suburbs where the number of black families was relatively small and they did not "threaten to overwhelm" the white families. Open attendance rules in a number of these cities facilitated the movement of small numbers of black pupils to previously all-white schools.

C. *Northern and Western Cities.* The northern and western cities were experiencing a major in-migration of blacks, without the decades of previous association between the races that had given people in the border cities a chance to work out forms of accommodation which allowed a certain amount of social integration without great tension. *De facto* school segregation grew up in these cities rapidly, supported by patterns of residential segregation that had been established earlier for the relatively small group of blacks then living in these cities.

There was, however, the beginning of conscious attacks on the segregation problem in a few cities. New York City took the lead. The Board of Education on December 23, 1954, unanimously approved a statement which included the following paragraphs:

> The Supreme Court of the United States reminds us that modern psychological knowledge indicates clearly that segregated, racially homogeneous schools damage the personality of minority group children. These schools decrease their motivation and thus impair their ability to learn. White children are also damaged. Public education in a racially homogeneous setting is socially unrealistic and blocks the attainment of the goals of democratic education, whether this segregation occurs by law or by fact.
>
> In seeking to provide effective democratic education for all of the children of this city, the members of the Board of Education of the City of New York are faced with many real obstacles in the form of complex social and community problems. Among these problems is the existence of residential segregation which leads to schools predominantly of one race on the elementary and junior high school levels. In addition, prevailing racial attitudes and misinformation of some white and Negro parents reflect out-worn patterns of segregation as well as limited educational and vocational horizons which make it difficult for them to accept school procedures contrary to their attitudes.

> In spite of these and other difficulties, the Board of Education of the City of New York is determined to accept the challenge implicit in the language and spirit of the decision of the United States Supreme Court. We will seek a solution to these problems and take action with dispatch implementing the recommendations resulting from a systematic and objective study of the problem here presented. (New York City Board of Education, 1954.)

In Detroit, the Board of Education in 1958 appointed a Citizens Advisory Committee on School Needs, under the chairmanship of George Romney, who was later to become Governor of the State. This Committee made a variety of recommendations, including the suggestion that a new Committee on Equal Educational Opportunities be set up to study the problem of racial segregation and make recommendations. This was done.

In most northern and western cities, however, the official policy of the school administration was that the schools should be "color blind." This meant that the school system was to take no formal notice of the color of pupils or teachers, to keep no records of color, and under these conditions to strive to do the best job possible of educating all children in accordance with their needs and abilities.

In this situation the forces of economics and population produced more and more segregated black schools, due to prevailing attitudes of the white population, who abandoned most residential areas as soon as it became evident that a sizable fraction of the school children were black.

Thus the year 1958 saw a much larger black population living in segregated residential areas and attending *de facto* segregated schools than had been true in 1954 in the North and West.

Phase 2. Rise of Concern and Controversy: 1958–63

When it became more and more evident to white and black people alike that residential and school segregation were increasing in the northern and western cities and were not decreasing in the South, there came about an increasing concern on the part of black groups as well as of white and mixed groups which were interested in the public schools and their relation to society's problems. This was accompanied and perhaps caused to some extent, by the worsening of the economic position of low-income blacks, which followed the temporary economic depression of 1958. For instance, as President

Johnson pointed out in his Commencement Address at Howard University on June 4, 1965, the unemployment rate of black teen-age boys in 1948 was actually less than that of white boys; but by 1964 the black male teen-aged unemployment rate was 23 percent against 13 percent for white males of the same age group. Between 1949 and 1959 the incomes of black men relative to white men declined in every section of the country. From 1952 to 1963 the median income of black families compared to whites dropped from 57 percent to 53 percent. In the years 1955 through 1957, 22 percent of experienced black workers were unemployed at some time during the year. In 1961 through 1963, this proportion was 29 percent. Thus the blacks at the bottom of the social economic ladder were losing rather than gaining ground.

In both the South and the North, blacks began to assert their impatience with the slowness and inadequacy of efforts at integration in the schools. At the same time the black protest against segregation in public facilities and in places of business began to make itself felt. Only a few years before, Mrs. Rosa Parks had quietly started a revolt in Montgomery, Alabama, against segregation on city buses. The rule in Montgomery had been that the first ten seats were always held for whites whether they were on the bus or not; the remainder of the seats could be occupied by blacks, but if more white people got on the bus after the first ten seats were full, the blacks must give up seat after seat, moving back toward the rear of the bus. Mrs. Parks was a middle-aged Negro woman. She describes what happened on that November day in 1955.

> Well, in the first place, I had been working all day on the job. I was quite tired after spending a full day working. I handle and work on clothing that white people wear. The section of the bus where I was sitting was what we call the colored section, especially in this neighborhood because the bus was filled more than two-thirds with Negro passengers and a number of them were standing. And just as soon as enough white passengers got on the bus to take what we consider their seats and then a few over, that meant that we would have to move back for them even though there was no room to move back. It was an imposition as far as I was concerned. . . . Just having paid for a seat and riding for only a couple of blocks and then having to stand, was too much. These other persons had got on the bus after I did—it meant that I didn't have a right to do anything but get on the bus, give them my fare, and then be pushed wherever they wanted me. (Highlander Folk School, 1956.)

Mrs. Parks refused to leave her seat. The bus driver called a policeman who took Mrs. Parks to jail. This started the Montgomery Bus Protest, a movement on the part of blacks to boycott the city bus line. The Protest won, and the buses of Montgomery were desegregated.

Martin Luther King rose to leadership during this period, and his methods of nonviolent resistance to southern segregation practices spread throughout the South.

A. *The Deep South.* Controversy flared in southern cities as the public schools slowly commenced to desegregate. In Little Rock, President Eisenhower called out the National Guard in 1957 to maintain order while a few black students enrolled and attended a white high school. In New Orleans, federal marshals walked with a handful of black children every day for months past a picket line of white adults who were keeping their own children out of the elementary school in protest against the introduction of these black pupils. In Atlanta, the process of token integration of high schools went more smoothly. By 1963 there was token integration in a few southern states.

B. *Border Cities.* In the border cities a number of school systems made ineffectual efforts to reduce the amount of *de facto* segregation. Washington saw the most determined action at this time, and some improvements were made in the public schools which probably produced better schooling, but did not stem the flight of white families to the suburbs. In St. Louis there was a good deal of unrest, which resulted in the appointment by the Board of Education of a Citizens Committee to look into problems of segregation and to propose remedies. The Baltimore Board of Education appointed a Citizens Committee with a similar mandate.

C. *Northern and Western Cities.* The greatest concern over *de facto* segregation was expressed during this period in the northern and western industrial centers. In New York, Detroit, and Cleveland the school systems explicitly worked to reduce segregation by relatively mild measures. Open attendance rules were extended. A small amount of transportation was provided to encourage black pupils to attend integrated schools. New York City went farthest with free transportation.

Court cases were brought increasingly on behalf of black pupils, to force school boards to reduce segregation. In 1961, a federal judge held that the New Rochelle, N.Y., Board of Education was defining school attendance areas so as to promote segregated education. The New Rochelle Board was ordered to abandon this practice.

Several cases were brought by black plaintiffs to force school boards to take active steps to reduce segregation or "racial imbalance" as it was called.

The response of most school administrators and boards of education in northern cities was to defend the "neighborhood school" policy as the best form of school attendance rule, even if it brought about segregation. And during this period, several court cases were decided in favor of school boards which followed the neighborhood school policy—that is, which set up attendance districts for specific schools regardless of the race of the children, but only to direct children to schools as close to their homes as possible. The courts generally held that school segregation resulting from residential patterns was legal, as long as the board of education did not deliberately draw attendance lines so as to segregate pupils by race.

Phase 3. The Black Revolution: 1963–66

The controversy came to a head, both in the South and the North, during the period from 1963 to 1966. This was the time of the rise to major influence of Dr. Martin Luther King, and the time when he was awarded the Nobel Peace Prize. In August, 1963, came the March on Washington, in which many white churchmen joined with black and white leaders of organized labor and of civic organizations to give recognition to the Negro movement and to dignify it. During this period came two major laws to support the Black Revolution. The Civil Rights Act of 1964, among other things, prohibited a number of types of discrimination that had been practiced against blacks. Specifically, it required all state and local agencies as well as private persons or agencies who receive federal government funds to give written assurance that "no person shall be excluded from participation, denied any benefits, or subjected to discrimination on the basis of race, color, or national origin." The U.S. Commission on Civil Rights (1965) had found that in some circumstances,

> Libraries receiving Federal aid either have not allowed Negroes to use the facilities or have subjected them to segregation or discrimination.
>
> Elementary schools built and operated with Federal aid have discriminated in the admission and treatment of students.
>
> Hospitals constructed with Federal funds either have refused to admit patients because of their race or have discriminated in their placement after admission; they also have refused to allow Negro physicians to practice there.
>
> Vocational training programs established with Federal funds have not been available to all students.
>
> Employment offices financed entirely by Federal funds have refused to refer all job applicants to available openings on a nondiscriminatory basis. Agricultural Extension Service offices operating with Federal funds have been established on a segregated basis and have provided unequal service to Negroes.
>
> Dormitories have been built with Federal grants in colleges that have discriminatory admission policies.
>
> Employers receiving business loans from the Federal Government, designed to increase employment opportunities, have discriminated in their hiring policies.

The requirement that school systems receiving any federal payments must submit "assurances of compliance" with the law had the effect of stimulating desegregation in the schools.

The Voting Rights Act of 1965 further strengthened the movement for Negro civil rights in the southern states.

A. *The Deep South.* The conflict over black rights broke into violence in some areas of the South, especially Mississippi and Alabama. Black civil rights groups were aided by student groups and others from the North who came to assist in the drive for registration of black voters, and to teach in the summer schools.

Still, the civil rights movement made substantial gains. Even in the embattled state of Alabama there was some resolution of the conflict. For instance, in the small city of Tuskegee, black voters found themselves in the majority. They proceeded to elect a biracial city council, and to get several Negroes appointed to the police force and to jobs in the City Hall. However, the majority of the council and of the city employees remained white. The formerly all-white high school was integrated, though the all-black high school was maintained, allowing for a viable racial balance in the integrated school.

During the summer of 1965 and the following school year a number of in-service teacher-training institutes were held in southern universities and southern counties, supported by the U.S. Office of Education under the Civil Rights Act. These were aimed at preparing teachers and school systems for the process of desegration. The amount of explicit attention to desegration varied, depending on the local sentiment, but there was always an emphasis on the ways of working with socially disadvantaged children, regardless of color, and there was always an unspoken assumption that desegregated schools were coming.

A number of county school systems maintained in-service training programs in 1965–66, in which for the first time, all the black and white teachers of the county took part in integrated study groups.

Most of the school systems of the South were started on the process of integration by 1966. *The New York Times* of September 4, 1965, reported, "Under the threat of a loss of Federal assistance, the South is admitting probably 7 per cent of its Negro children to classes with white children this fall—a percentage that compares reasonably well with the national average. And for the first time school desegregation has come to the Black Belt and to hundreds of rural southern towns, with virtually no violence or resistance."

Faculty desegregation also got under way in some southern cities. For example, Little Rock public schools in 1965 assigned four black teachers to teach in predominantly white schools, and four white teachers to teach in black schools. It was announced that there were 260 black pupils in schools which formerly were all white.

B. *Border Cities and Northern Cities.* The drive for integration in the border cities and northern and western industrial cities reached a peak in this period. Civil rights organizations joined together, and were aided by federated church groups acting through such agencies as a Council on Religion and Race. Civic organizations became involved, and the most prominent domestic issue during this period was the schools. The majority of big cities saw school boycotts aimed at inducing the Board of Education to take more active measures against segregation.

A number of state legislatures passed laws requiring the public schools to reduce segregation as much as possible. Several city school systems began to publish annual data on the numbers of black and white children in the various schools, and also the numbers of black and white teachers.

The pressures that were pushing local school boards toward positive action on integration mounted. Several state departments of education took action. The strongest of them was the action by the New York State Commissioner of Education, James E. Allen, who in June of 1963 requested all school districts in the state to report to him concerning racial imbalance, and if any school existed with 50 percent or more black pupils to report on plans for eliminating racial imbalance. On the other side of the country, the California State Department of Education set up a Commission on Equal Opportunities in Education, which actively promoted integration of schools in that state.

A number of the major city school systems issued formal statements about integration. Those by the Superintendents of the New York City and Detroit Schools are reported here:

New York City

Responsibility of the Schools in Integration (A Reaffirmation of Policy Originally Adopted in 1954). Statement by Calvin E. Gross, Superintendent of Schools, October, 1963.

It has been said, correctly, that the schools alone cannot eliminate prejudice, discrimination and segregation. It is equally true that this task will not be accomplished with less than an all out effort of the schools.

Our schools must not be neutral in the struggle of society to better itself. We must not overlook the harmful effects of discrimination on the education of all children. Moreover, within the limits of our control, we must not acquiesce in the undemocratic school patterns which are a concomitant of segregated housing. Furthermore, we must continue our policy of not tolerating racial or religious prejudice on the part of any member of our staffs. If education is to fulfill its responsibility, it must recognize that the school world has a significant influence on each child's attitudes and affects the future of democracy.

To further its integration policy, the school system has responsibilities to its pupils and personnel and to the communities.

1. For pupils—We must seek ways to give every child an optimum opportunity for fulfillment and success: . . . .
2. For school personnel—We must develop personnel practices which will maximize the success of the integration program: . . . .

3. With communities—We must work closely and cooperatively with communities: . . . .

Detroit

Special Report to the Board of Education by S. M. Brownell, Superintendent of Schools, May 5, 1964.

The Detroit Board of Education is on record with adopted policies and procedures intended to provide a racially integrated school system, to promote intergroup understanding, to eliminate racial discrimination from any school practices, and to attain equal educational opportunities for all children. These policies and procedures statements include, among others:

1. The Intercultural Policy of 1945.
2. Fair Employment Practices Acts in 1955 and 1956.
3. Endorsement of the goals of Equal Educational Opportunity in 1957.
4. Approval of recommendations made by the Citizens Advisory Committee in 1958.
5. Passage of the Non-discrimination By-laws in 1959.
6. A Policy on School Overcrowding and Relief Measures in 1961.
7. An Open Enrollment and Transfer Policy in 1961.
8. Approval of recommendations made by the Committee on Equal Educational Opportunities in 1962.
9. A "Statement Concerning Non-discrimination in Schools" in August 1962.
10. A statement on "The Treatment of Minorities" in textbooks in December 1962.

The opportunities to obtain public school education, employment, and public accommodations without discrimination because of race, religion, color, national origin or ancestry are civil rights in Michigan. Schools, as an arm of state government, have a responsibility to further the understanding and the fulfillment of these rights for all citizens. In these days there is fear and unrest in many parts of the United States as to whether these civil rights will be secured and maintained for all citizens. There is also recognition in Detroit that there is still much to accomplish to achieve fully the goal of the Board of Education for a school system with equal educational opportunity for all and with freedom from any racial bias.

Achieving and maintaining a school system which is racially integrated requires not only that there is no racial discrimination in the determination of the school which a child shall attend; it means also that the organization, administration, and operation of all facets of the school system are without discrimination as to race. The selection, promotion, and placement of personnel need to be without regard to race. Pupils, as they progress through school, should have opportunities to work together in bi-racial or multi-racial situations which contribute to improved understandings of the dignity and worth of persons who differ in race. . . .

The majority of school boards, while issuing statements saying that they favored integrated school experience for as many pupils as possible, added that there were limits beyond which the school system could not go in fostering integration, and that the major limiting factor was the "neighborhood school policy," which places a high priority upon the pupil's attending school near his home. Since the big cities have a great deal of residential segregation by race, the neighborhood school policy makes it very difficult to get integrated schools, especially at the elementary school level.

Thus the majority of school systems were adapting their school attendance patterns and policies to the residential patterns of the city, and the school boards and superintendents were arguing that the schools could not and should not attempt to alter the patterns of the city. They should educate the children who came to the schools in accordance with neighborhood school policy, and they should do as good a job as possible within this framework.

On the other hand, the civil rights organizations and a growing number of educators argued that the school system should take an active part in promoting the changes in the city known as "social urban renewal," which are aimed at creating or stabilizing areas of integrated residence in the city, attractive to middle income families. The school system would need to operate with flexible attendance rules and with a close relationship with local community organizations to accomplish this. Thus there was talk of an "urban-community school" philosophy, which was opposed to the conventional "four walls school" philosophy.

Two school procedures which came into use during this period to facilitate integrated school experience for children and to stabilize integrated residential areas were the Princeton Plan, and Transport Plans.

Princeton Plan

The Princeton Plan is the pairing of schools so that they share the same attendance district. The Plan takes its name from Princeton, New Jersey, where it has been operating successfully for some years. This plan has been adopted with success in a number of communities where the residential pattern is such that the districts served by two schools, one all or largely white and the other all or largely black, can be converted into a single larger district with all the children attending one school for the first three or four grades, and then attending the other school for the next three or four grades. When the socio-economic status of the black and white group is rather similar, the Princeton Plan seems to work fairly well.

However, it appears desirable that other forces operate to help stabilize the residential pattern when the Princeton Plan is used. For example, there is a Princeton Plan in operation in two New York City schools close to the Lincoln Center. The attractiveness of this residential area is an added incentive for middle-class parents to remain in the neighborhood.

Transport Plans

Transporting children to relieve overcrowding was tried in a number of cities where there were overcrowded segregated black schools and underfilled schools in other parts of the city. In many cities, children were permitted to attend underfilled schools on an "open attendance" plan, but relatively few took advantage of this opportunity when they had to provide their own transportation. In a few cities the Board of Education provided buses to transport pupils in groups from overcrowded schools to underfilled schools. One way was to transport entire class groups, such as a sixth-grade class, which then would simply occupy the classroom in the "receiving" school, but remain a part of the "sending" school for administrative purposes. Or, it might be done by transporting children from an entire block in an overcrowded area to a "receiving" school, where they would be distributed among the various grades a few in a room, and thus become a part of the receiving school.

For example, for several years between 1964 and 1969 the Kansas City, Missouri, Public Schools transported about 1,500 ghetto-dwelling pupils to schools with empty seats, at a rate of three or four transported pupils to a classroom. This procedure was generally approved in advance by parents of children from the ghetto, and when put into practice it was acceptable to parents of the children from the ghetto as well as to parents and teachers in the receiving schools. On the other hand, when Superintendent Redmond of the Chicago Public Schools announced a similar scheme for relieving overcrowding in ghetto schools in Chicago, in 1967, there was vociferous objection from some parents in the receiving schools, and the program was reduced in size.

Increasingly, during the latter half of the 1960s, the more positive forms of integrative procedure were being pushed forward and tried out. This was partly due to pressure by groups working for integration, and partly due to a mounting series of court decisions that required active integrative practices.

The Legal Aspects of Integrated Schools

Since 1962 there have been a number of lawsuits in states outside of the South which raise the following questions:

> Do school boards have an affirmative duty under the equal protection clause of the Fourteenth Amendment to eliminate or reduce racial imbalance not caused by deliberate action of local or state authorities?
>
> Are the constitutional rights of Negro pupils infringed by *de facto* segregation which results from good faith adherence to a neighborhood school policy?
>
> Are the constitutional rights of white pupils violated when school boards take racial factors into account in drawing or redrawing school boundary lines or in adopting other plans to reduce or eliminate racial imbalance in the schools? (National Education Association, 1965.)

There were a number of court cases concerning *de facto* segregation during the 1960s. Some of them were decided in favor of the school system which maintained some segregated schools because of residential segregation. Gary, Indiana, and Kansas City, Kansas were examples. On the other hand, by 1970 it appeared that the court decisions were leaning toward rulings against *de facto* segregation. In South Holland, a suburb of Chicago, the federal district court required the school board to adjust attendance rules so as to balance the racial composition in the various school buildings.

Another federal district court in New York supported a claim by black parents that the strict neighborhood school policy in Manhasset, a Long Island suburb, violated their constitutional rights. In this case, all black elementary school children, together with a few white children, were enrolled in one of the district's three elementary schools. The court held that the maintenance of neighborhood school attendance lines by which all black elementary school children were separated from 99.2 percent of white children, coupled with an inflexible no-transfer policy, was equivalent to state-imposed segregation in violation of the Fourteenth Amendment. The school board was ordered to discontinue its no-transfer policy with respect to the children in this school.

The California Supreme Court made a similar ruling in the Pasadena case in 1963. It held that where there was racial imbalance in the school owing to residential segregation, the right of children to equal opportunity for education and the harmful consequences of segregation required school boards to take steps, in so far as was reasonably feasible, to alleviate the racial imbalance in the schools regardless of the cause.

In New York and New Jersey, the courts have upheld the actions of school boards in fixing boundary lines of schools so as to produce an ethnic balance among students. The New York Court of Appeals distinguished between an obligation on the part of the school board to reduce *de facto* segregation and the *right* (not the duty) of the school board to correct racial imbalance. The court held that an otherwise reasonable and lawful zoning plan does not become unlawful because racial factors were taken into consideration. The U.S. Supreme Court declined to review the case, and other New York and New Jersey courts have held that the school board is not prohibited from taking race into account in changing school boundary lines, school pairing plans and open enrollment plans designed to correct racial imbalance and to reduce or eliminate *de facto* segregation in the public shools.

In 1965 the State of Massachusetts went further than any other had gone up to that time by passing a law "providing for the elimination of racial imbalance in the public schools." The law states,

> It is hereby declared to be the policy of the commonwealth to encourage all school committees to adopt as educational objectives the promotion of racial balance and the correction of existing racial imbalance in the public schools. The prevention or elimination of racial imbalance shall be an objective in all decisions involving the drawing or altering of school attendance lines and the selection of new school sites. . . .
>
> Whenever the state board of education finds that racial

> imbalance exists in a public school it shall notify in writing the school committee or regional school district committee having jurisdiction over such school that such finding has been made. The school committee shall thereupon prepare a plan to eliminate such racial imbalance and file a copy of such plan with the board. The term "racial imbalance" refers to a ratio between non-white and other students in public schools which is sharply out of balance with the racial composition of the society in which non-white children study, serve, and work. For the purpose of this section, racial imbalance shall be deemed to exist when the per cent of non-white students in any public school is in excess of fifty per cent of the total number of students in such school.
>
> Said plan shall detail the changes in existing school attendance districts, the location of proposed school sites, the proposed additions to existing school buildings, and other methods for the elimination of racial imbalance. Said plan shall also include projections of the expected racial composition of all public schools. Any plan to detail changes in existing school attendance districts, the locations of proposed new school sites and proposed additions to existing school sites and proposed additions to existing school buildings with the intention of reducing or eliminating racial imbalance, must take into consideration on an equal basis with the above-mentioned intention, the safety of the children involved in travelling from home to school and school to home. . . . Said plan may provide for voluntary cooperation by other cities and towns in rendering assistance and in making available facilities to effectuate said plan. . . . (Commonwealth of Massachusetts, 1965.)

Up to 1967, six states—California, Connecticut, Massachusetts, New Jersey, New York, and Wisconsin—had taken the position, in statements by the governor or the courts, that racial isolation in the schools has a damaging effect on educational opportunity of black pupils.

In the Civil Rights Act of 1964, Congress authorized the Attorney General to bring desegregation suits against local school districts in certain circumstances, and gave the Department of Health, Education, and Welfare the power to refuse federal funds to school districts which practiced racial discrimination.

Phase 4. Integration vs. Black Separatism: 1966–70

By 1966 there was substantial improvement in the situation of blacks as compared with 1954. The Civil Rights Act and the Voting Rights Act had given Negroes much more political power in the southern states and more economic opportunity throughout the country. There was a general movement toward providing greater job opportunities for blacks. Black clerks could be seen in department stores, young black men and women worked at the counters of airlines, and black air stewardesses appeared on airplanes. Blacks were working as bank tellers. The proportion of black teachers had increased substantially in northern school systems. On television the scenes showing people in everyday groupings such as business and club meetings, school and college classes, and cocktail parties had unobtrusive Negro members. Television commercials used black women and men as persuasive salespeople for toilet articles and kitchen products. Several Negroes became television stars and worked in mixed black and white and male and female programs. To the casual observer the American society showed a greater degree of racial integration than it had shown ten years earlier.

There was actually more economic opportunity available for blacks in minor white-collar and technical jobs than there were blacks with adequate training for those jobs.

As Tables 7.5 and A-15 show, black people were making substantial gains in employment in middle-class occupations, relative to whites. Blacks living in central cities of SMSAs increased their proportions employed in professional and managerial jobs 50 percent between 1960 and 1968 for men, and 40 percent for women. The increase in clerical and sales jobs for black women was 75 percent, while white women actually decreased slightly in this job category. The black gains in middle-class occupations meant a corresponding reduction in the "labor" and the "private household worker" categories.

Nevertheless, the unemployment rates among blacks were higher than among whites, as shown in Table 7.4, though some gain was made in employment by Negroes over 20 years old. For young people 16 to 19 years old, there was a considerable increase in the rate of unemployment between 1960 and 1968, reflecting the decreasing demand of the labor force for the work of young people.

Thus the proportion of black middle-class people was increasing among the young adults, but at the same time the lot of the less-skilled and less-educated blacks was growing worse. There was a higher rate of illegitimate births to black women. The working-class black family was not growing stronger. It was also evident that a higher rather than a lower proportion of Negro children were attending effectively segregated schools in the northern cities, and

TABLE 7.5
Occupational Distribution: White and Nonwhite, 1967 and Change, 1960–67

	Persons employed, Age 16 and over					
	Number (Thousands)		*Change 1960–67*			
	1967		*Number*		*Percent*	
Occupation Category	*Non-white*	*White*	*Non-white*	*White*	*Non-white*	*White*
Total	8,011	66,361	970	6,721	14	11
Professional and Technical	592	9,287	263	2,141	80	30
Managers and Officials	209	7,286	31	396	17	6
Clerical	899	11,434	391	2,158	77	23
Sales	138	4,387	25	99	22	2
Craftsmen and Foremen	617	9,228	203	1,083	49	13
Operators	1,882	12,002	465	1,434	33	14
Service, except Household	1,519	6,037	287	1,136	23	23
Private Household Workers	835	934	−169	−278	−17	−23
Nonfarm Laborers	899	2,634	− 70	− 61	− 7	− 2
Farmers or Farm Laborers	423	3,131	−453	−1,389	−52	−31

Source: *U.S. Census Current Population Reports,* Series P-23, No. 6. Bureau of Labor Statistics Report No. 347, July, 1968.

that the rates of educational retardation and of school dropouts among black youth were as great as they had been a decade earlier.

The public schools were more than ever seen as the crucial institutions for helping blacks improve themselves, and critics continued to blame the schools for much of the difficulty experienced by blacks. Two massive programs had been set up by the federal government aimed to assist Negro children and their families. The Elementary and Secondary Education Act promised to give school systems substantially more money to work with children of poor families, which in most big cities meant predominantly black children. The Economic Opportunity Act provided funds for preschool classes, and for work-training and education of youth who were not doing well in school.

At this time the controversy over the Family versus the School factors gave rise to two opposed schools of thought among people who were working for the betterment of blacks.

Those who emphasize the Family factor wish to expand preschool classes for socially disadvantaged children, educational work with their mothers and fathers, spread of birth control knowledge and devices among working-class people, and a variety of forms of assistance and support through social workers to the working-class family. For them the school system can go on with its present program for school-age children, with whatever improvements may be made, including smaller classes and remedial instruction for disadvantaged children.

This group of people pin their hopes for improved educational performance on a widespread program of public-supported preschooling for at least one full year before the child is five. Some would select the four-year-olds and some the three-year-olds for this program. The New York State Board of Education has gone on record as favoring a state-supported program of voluntary preschools for children aged three and four. A few special students of the problem of disadvantaged children argue for public-supported residential and boarding schools for young children starting as early as age two.

There is a growing body of evidence that a preschool program at age three or four lasting at least one year and concentrating on cognitive development will raise the learning ability (the IQ) of disadvantaged children about ten to fifteen points and that they will retain this gain for several years, into the elementary grades. The evidence is not quite conclusive, as yet, and waits upon more data on the school achievement of these children when they are about ten years old and the effects of the preschool curriculum on test-taking ability (which are temporary effects) have had time to disappear.

Those who emphasize the School factor are after new forms of education, not just more of the old forms. They recognize that the schools are not succeeding adequately with lower working-class children, and they call for new and radical changes in the schools. It is up to the schools to find ways of teaching these children successfully. For example, the *Washington Post* of December 19, 1965 carried an account of a statement written by Judge David L. Bazelon, Chairman of the Advisory Committee of the Model School Division, which had been proposed by Superintendent Carl F. Hansen in June, 1964, and had been adopted for the Cardozo High School and its eighteen feeder junior high schools and elementary schools. Money had been provided to support this model program for, as Superintendent Hansen described it, "an across-the-board experiment—curriculum development, utilization of teachers, the management of the system itself—with provision for rapid feedback of results and rapid exploitation of new opportunities." After a year and three months of the experiment, Judge Bazelon charged that "Entering a school in the Model School District today, one finds few activities, atmosphere, teaching methods, or equipment different from what one found before the model school notion was expressed. . . . The concept of a sub-system advised by a citizens' advisory committee appears to have been abandoned before it began." The most that was accomplished, it was charged, was an extension of "more of the same." More after-school reading periods, more remedial teaching, and smaller classes. Instead of changing the school system so that the children would learn better, it was claimed that the schools were trying to change the children to make them fit the school program.

The educators who use conventional methods and "more of the same" when working with disadvantaged children remain unconvinced that they should make radical changes, and ask just what changes are suggested and what evidence there is that these would work better than existing methods.

EQUALITY OF OPPORTUNITY OR EQUALITY OF ACHIEVEMENT?

Those who insist that the schools can and must produce better achievement on the part of lower working-class children, and who at the same time feel that the School factor is more important than the Family factor in the strategy for betterment have been aroused and angered over a comment that was made in the "Moynihan Report" of the U.S. Department of Labor. The report states that the fundamental problem posed by the Black Revolution is that it is a movement for *equality* as well as for liberty.

> The ideal of equality does not ordain that all persons end up, as well as start out equal. In traditional terms, as put by Faulkner, "there is no such thing as equality *per se,* but only equality *to:* equal right and opportunity to make the best one can of one's life within one's capability, without fear of injustice or oppression or threat of violence." But the evolution of American politics, with the distinct persistence of ethnic and religious groups, has added a profoundly significant new dimension to that egalitarian ideal. It is increasingly demanded that the distribution of success and failure within one group be roughly comparable to that

within other groups. It is not enough that all individuals start out on even terms, if the members of one group almost invariably end up well to the fore, and those of another far to the rear. This is what ethnic politics are all about in America, and in the main the Negro American demands are being put forth in this now traditional and established framework.

Here a point of semantics must be grasped. The demand for Equality of Opportunity has been generally perceived by white Americans as a demand for liberty, a demand not to be excluded from the competitions of life—at the polling place, in the scholarship examinations, at the personnel office, on the housing market. Liberty does, of course, demand that everyone be free to try his luck, or test his skill in such matters. But these opportunities do not necessarily produce equality: on the contrary, to the extent that winners imply losers, equality of opportunity almost insures inequality of results.

The point of semantics is that equality of opportunity now has a different meaning for Negroes than it has for whites. It is not (or at least no longer) a demand for liberty alone, but also for equality—in terms of group results. In Bayard Rustin's terms, "It is now concerned not merely with removing the barriers to full *opportunity* but with achieving the fact of *equality*." By equality Rustin means a distribution of achievements among Negroes roughly comparable to that among whites.

As Nathan Glazer has put it, "The demand for economic equality is now not the demand for equal opportunities for the equally qualified: it is now the demand for equality of economic results. . . . The demand for equality in education . . . has also become a demand for equality of results, of outcomes."

The principal challenge of the next phase of the Negro revolution is to make certain that equality of results will now follow. If we do not, there will be no social peace in the United States for generations. (U.S. Department of Labor, 1965, p. 3.)

Some of the proponents of basic school reform have in effect argued that the schools must keep on experimenting with better methods for lower working-class youth until these youth are equal in educational achievement to the youth of other social groups. This can and must be done, they say.

For example, the program of school improvement proposed by the Kansas City planning group under the Model Cities Act in 1969 set as a practical goal the reduction of the gap in achievement between middle class and ghetto schools to half of what it was formerly.

The proponents of the Family factor approach argue that equality of educational results can only be achieved by improving the lower working-class family as an institution for rearing children. They argue that a child whose cognitive development has been neglected in a typical lower working-class family until he is of school age can never catch up. And that one who has been only partially handicapped by an inadequate family environment during preschool years may be further handicapped by an inadequate family environment during his school and adolescent years.

The basic disagreement will be worked out and perhaps partially reduced during the next few years, as educators experiment with a variety of ways of helping the socially disadvantaged child, and as social scientists learn more through research about the mental development of children. Government and foundation funds are available for this experimentation and research.

Emergence of Black Separatism and Its Effects on Schools

The cause of integration in the schools had widespread and growing support in the mid-sixties. White school administrators generally favored the principle, even if they did not find it possible to move their own school systems very rapidly toward integration in practice. School boards in the northern and western cities generally adopted policy statements favoring integrated schools. Virtually all blacks were advocates of integration which in their minds was associated with freedom and equal civil and economic rights. Public opinion polls showed increasing proportions of white parents, in the South as well as the North, saying that they approved of their children attending school with black children. However, it was also clear that the vast majority of white parents who approved integration would not make any special positive efforts to place their children in integrated schools.

Then, in 1965 and 1966, there emerged the movement for Black Separatism. Though a minority movement among blacks, it split the solid black front for integration, and effectively slowed down the drive for integrated schools. Black, as well as white liberals, became divided among themselves over the desirability of integration as an immediate goal. Some blacks even argued against integration as an ultimate objective, and advocated instead a black nation within the United States, separate socially and economically.

The black separatists found it difficult to distinguish between the objection of some whites to integration across social class lines and the objection of other whites to integration across the color line. They attributed all anti-integration objections by whites to white racism. Therefore they could not come to agreement with white parents on a program of integration which would bring white and black children together if their parents belonged to the same social class or if the middle-class tone of the school were maintained.

Since the pressure of blacks for school integration provided the power that was moving school boards in that direction, when this pressure abated, the integration movement lost momentum. Only a few places where there was a strong liberal white and black combination, essentially middle class in composition, pushed ahead with practical plans for integration. Examples of these communities were Berkeley, California; Evanston, Illinois; Teaneck, New Jersey; and White Plains, New York.

There are three arguments advanced by the proponents of black separatism. First is the argument that whites will not really support social integration in any of its forms, and especially in the form of school integration. They will give promises with no real intention of keeping those promises. The small minority of whites who really believe in integration will be stifled by the mass of whites who do not want it.

Second is the argument that the moves for residential integration are a device to disperse the growing political power of the blacks in the ghetto sections of the central cities. Black political power is growing, so this argument runs, through the growth of a segregated Negro population, which elects black members to the city council, black congressmen, and even black mayors. Therefore, the black separatist says, the talk of breaking up the ghettoes, open housing in the suburbs, attracting whites back to the central cities—all this is part of a racist strategy to reduce black political power.

The third argument, more subtle and perhaps more powerful, holds that meaningful integration—with true equality of the races—can only come when the blacks have achieved a group identity, pride in the race, and bargaining power based on unified black communities. Consequently the blacks in America should stay to themselves, study African culture and history, learn that they come from African centers of civilization and high culture which flourished when much of western Europe was inhabited by savages. They should have black teachers for black schools, and they should demand separate black colleges within the universities.

The leaders of Black Separatism tend to be young people who mistrust the established civil rights organizations—the NAACP and the Urban League—and call their leaders "Uncle Toms." Black Separatism favors the use of the term "black" to describe people of African descent, and uses the term "Negro" as an epithet practically synonymous with "Uncle Tom."

The emotional appeal of the "black identity" argument is very great for young people. One of their major prophets is Frantz Fanon, born in Martinique in the French West Indies in 1925, educated in Paris, where he became a psychiatrist. Fanon died at the age of 36 from leukemia. His book, *The Wretched of the Earth*, states the proposition that the nonwhite peoples of the world can only come out from under white domination by discovering their own racial identity and then overthrowing the white-dominated world by violent revolution, leading to a world-wide classless society.

Therefore, according to this view, Martin Luther King was wrong, and the song "We Shall Overcome—black and white together" is romantic nonsense.

There is an equally strong and passionate integration argument, which is supported vigorously by most civil rights leaders and probably in a less forceful way by the majority of black citizens. Such black leaders as Bayard Rustin, Roy Wilkins, and Whitney Young have argued that Black Separatism is bad strategy for black people in the United States.

The case for integration is argued forcefully by the so-called Kerner Commission, or, the National Advisory Commission on Civil Disorders, appointed by President Johnson. This Commission was mixed racially. The 1968 Report of this Commission announced "Our nation is moving toward two societies, one black, one white—separate and unequal." This Commission reported that improvement of the black part of the society is effectively blocked by racial discrimination. Also, the black ghetto is a responsibility of the white society. "White institutions created it, white institutions maintain it, and white society condones it."

The Commission went on to argue that separatism can never produce equality for Negroes. It "could only relegate Negroes permanently to inferior incomes and economic status." The goal of America, the Commission said, "must be achieving freedom for every citizen to live and work according to his capacities and desires, not his color."

Morris Janowitz, a student of social institutions, has found the Black Separatist movement not altogether dangerous (1969). He believes that the situation in the big cities since 1965 makes it desirable as well as possible to accept the separatist movement to some extent while working for racial integration in those local areas where this is practicable in the immediate future. There is no single definition of desirable social change in such a situation, and a form of cultural pluralism is useful, working for improvement of black schools where the schools are almost sure to be black for a decade, as well as for development or maintenance of integrated schools where this is practicable.

Black Separatism was pushed most vigorously in 1968, and especially in the field of education. In the universities, there were demands by black students for separate dormitories, separate social clubs, and separate academic programs in black studies, taught by black professors.

In the public schools there were pressures for local community control of the schools in the ghetto, with black teachers and principals. A black teachers' association was formed, which at times opposed the actions of the local teachers' organizations.

Cases of Successful Integration

While the cause of integration in the schools of the big cities marked time or lost ground during the late 1960s, there were a few cases of successful school integration in suburbs. These suburbs had two significant characteristics. They had "small ghettoes" with less than about 6,000 school age black children and youth. Their populations had a higher proportion of middle-class people (both white and black) than are found in a cross-section of the American population.

Thus these suburbs did not have to contend with the combined problems of a large ghetto and a large proportion of black children from lower working-class families. The attitudes of the majority of citizens were favorable to integration, and the discrepancy between achievement of white middle-class pupils and black lower-class pupils was not a serious factor.

Two suburban cities may be mentioned as examples of such a community. Berkeley, California, adopted a major busing program for its elementary schools, transporting almost one-third of the pupils, black and white, to schools chosen so as to achieve a racial balance. Berkeley has about 40 percent black children in the school population. At the junior high school level it adopted a Princeton Plan, sending all junior high school pupils in a given grade to one school, using an entire school building for each one of the three grades. This plan was worked out by a citizens' commission with the aid of a dynamic superintendent—Neil Sullivan.

The other example is that of Evanston, Illinois, where a citizens' committee worked for two years preparing the plan and communicating thoroughly with the public about the plan. The committee had the full support of the superintendent. The one all-black elementary school was changed into an integrated "magnet school" which attracted pupils from all over the community. Negro children who had formerly attended this school were distributed among surrounding schools, with no more than 20 percent black pupils in any school. Again, the superintendent, Gregory Coffin, was the key person in putting the plan into operation.

It is too soon at this writing (1970) to say whether these plans will persist in their present forms. They indicate, however, that a middle-sized community with less than 20 percent black population can integrate its schools without waiting for residential integration.

Social Integration or Social Segregation? 1970–1975

Although there is disturbing evidence about the black working-class family, and although the extent of segregation of black children in the public schools has increased in the northern cities and decreased only slightly in the southern states during the past ten years, the situation at the close of the 1960s was definitely more promising for urban schools than it had been during the preceding fifteen years. First of all, there is a much better understanding of the nature of the problem of educating socially disadvantaged children than there has been, and therefore society will do a better job with families and also with children in school. Beyond this, there are two trends among blacks that are working to increase the status of blacks and to improve the educational situation for black children.

One trend is toward better jobs and higher incomes for black men and women. This has been going on since 1940, but the rate of improvement was much greater in the 1960s than it was in the 1950s. Tables 7.5 and A-16 demonstrate these gains. This means that many blacks are moving into the middle classes, and integration is easier for a middle-class Negro to achieve than for a working-class Negro. If we say that approximately 40 percent of whites are in the middle classes, as we use the term, then about 20 percent of blacks are in the middle classes, as of 1970, and this compares with about 5 percent in 1940.

Still, salaries and wages average lower for blacks than for whites for a given kind of work. Approximately 30 percent of black families were below the poverty level in 1967, making up about 35 percent of the poor people, with 11 percent of the total population.

The other trend is the movement of black families out of the inner-city ghetto to the outer sections of the central city and to the suburbs. This movement has increased very much since 1967, and it is not yet possible to say with assurance how great it will be during the 1970s. The Census Bureau reported a sharp change in black population movement in metropolitan areas around 1966. Between 1960 and 1966 the central cities of the metropolitan areas were gaining 370,000 Negroes a year, on the average, but this dropped to 100,000 a year in 1967 and 1968. On the other hand, the black movement to the suburbs was 20,000 a year from 1960–1966, and 220,000 a year in 1967 and 1968.

This kind of population movement means an increase of black pupils in integrated schools in the suburbs, and also a stop to the increase of black pupils in the central city schools. It now seems likely that the numbers of black pupils in central cities, which have grown rapidly between 1955 and 1968, will level off and probably decrease between 1970 and 1980. This is due to the migration to the suburbs just mentioned and also to the fact that since 1965 the number of black women of child-bearing age has been decreasing in the big cities because the rate of in-migration of young Negro women is smaller since 1965 than it was from about 1955 to 1960.

As the numbers of school-age black children cease growing in the central cities, and as the black population gradually spreads into the suburbs, it will be much easier to maintain stable integrated schools than it was between 1955 and 1970.

What will these trends mean for integration-separation of the races during the next two decades? How will these trends interact with the movement of Black Separatism? These questions were the subject of a major address by Professor Thomas F. Pettigrew of Harvard University to the members of the Society for the Study of Social Issues given September 1, 1968 and entitled *Racially Separate or Together?* His analysis of the situation in 1968 is summarized here.

The situation of blacks in the United States in the 1965–70 period is one of swiftly rising aspirations for socio-economic benefits which have been more available to whites than to blacks. Civil rights legislation, the School Desegregation Decision of the Supreme Court, and the real gains of blacks in the economic sphere have whetted the appetites of blacks for a greater measure of equality. At the same time, blacks are comparing their status more and more to the whites, no longer resigned to feeling fortunate if they make some gains while whites make greater gains.

At the same time, there is still some difficulty for a Negro with a high school diploma to get an "appropriate" job, even though the situation is vastly improved over what it was before 1960.

Furthermore, the Negro lower working class, having migrated largely to the big cities, live in wretched conditions, many of them without regular employment, and many living on welfare payments.

The speed of improvement in the status of blacks is not satisfactory to the majority of blacks, though it seems satisfactory to most whites and to some economically successful blacks.

In this situation, Pettigrew finds that many whites and some black people favor a policy of Separatism, for different but complementary reasons. The White Separatist believes:

1. That both racial groups are more comfortable when separated.
2. That blacks are inferior to whites, perhaps by heredity but in fact, in any case. Therefore integrated schooling and other forms of integrated interaction will lower the standards for whites.
3. Strife and unrest can be kept at a minimum by separation of the races.

The Black Separatist believes:

1. That both racial groups are more comfortable when separated.
2. The central problem is white racism. White liberals should fight against this, and black leaders should work in separate institutions (schools, businesses, churches, etc.) to improve the situation for blacks.
3. Equal and mutually beneficial relations with whites are only possible when blacks have gained personal and group autonomy,

self-respect, and power. Equality and interdependence are goals which cannot be achieved until blacks have a period of separation during which they can develop themselves.

Pettigrew disagrees with both sets of beliefs, and argues, as a social psychologist that:

1. Separatism is a cause, not a remedy, for dissatisfaction and discomfort in interracial situations.
2. The belief of whites in their racial superiority is decreasing, as shown by scientific studies during the past three decades. The recent confrontations between whites and blacks have resulted in further reduction among whites of a belief in racial superiority.
3. Studies of the results of desegregation in buses, jobs, restaurants, and hotels, and in churches and schools, show that increased contact reduces racial friction and strife.
4. Doing nothing about integration means leaving the present institutional arrangements (segregated schools, housing, and churches) to continue to cause discrimination and prejudice.

For these reasons Pettigrew argues against Black Separatism, and urges a strong program of social integration.

Alternative Strategies

The various possibilities for moving from the typical urban ghetto situation of today to a state of true social integration are shown in the following diagram.

A	*B*
True Integration	Hypothetical "Black Power" Ghetto
C	*D*
Mere Desegregation	Typical Urban Ghetto Today

The stated goal of all people working for social integration is to move from the present situation *D* to True Integration *A*. True integration exists when persons and groups can choose freely where to live, to send their children for schooling, to attend church, to look for employment, and to do ordinary business—all within the personal limits of ability and income that affect all people regardless of their race. There are three possible strategies for achieving integration.

The Black Separatist Strategy, D *to* B *to* A. The movement should be from the economically and socially disadvantaged ghetto of today to the hypothetical "black power" ghetto in which blacks have local control of schools, business, political office, parks. As the black power ghetto succeeds in giving black people a black identity and more self-confidence, they will be able to negotiate successfully with whites for true equality and for conditions of true integration.

This argument states that the way to bring two diverse groups together is to separate them until the conditions are just right for them to come together as equals. Arguments on the other side, from the point of view of social psychology are that isolation and separation of two geographically contiguous groups (according to Pettigrew) lead to:

1. Diverse value development.
2. Reduced intergroup communication.
3. Uncorrected perceptual distortions of each other.
4. Growth of vested interests within both groups for continued separation.

The "Mere Desegregation" Strategy, D *to* C *to* A. Black separatists regard the indirect route through C to A as an affront to their dignity. They believe that reliance upon white liberals to open a limited amount of integrated housing and of new jobs in integrated work places is a tacit confession of black weakness. It would lead to ability grouping in schools as a means of limiting the extent of integration. It would support the present limited desegregation of colleges and high schools in the South and in other parts of the country, and would leave the black people to wait, with hat in hand, while the dominant white power structure gradually learned to accept and to assimilate them. There might be a very long period of desegregation with no real push for true integration, since the black people would not be militant enough to demand true integration.

The Direct Integration Strategy, D *to* A. Pettigrew as well as many black and white integrationists believe that more satisfactory progress toward true social integration can be made by moving directly and immediately as rapidly as possible toward integrated schools, residential areas, and work and worship.

They take this position with full knowledge of the facts of population distribution in the metropolitan areas, and of the facts of white resistance to residential integration. They call for mixed integration—ghetto enrichment strategy which guards against diminishing the push for true integration through diversion of almost all resources into enrichment of the ghetto.

Such a mixed strategy would be generally approved by blacks, according to public opinion surveys. Thus, on the basis of a survey of Negro residents in fifteen major cities, Campbell and Schuman (1968) concluded:

> Separatism appeals to from five to eighteen percent of the Negro sample, depending on the question, with the largest appeal involving black ownership of stores and black administration of schools in Negro neighborhoods, and the smallest appeal the rejection of whites as friends or in other informal contacts. Even on the questions having the largest appeal, however, more than three-quarters of the Negro sample indicate a clear preference for integration. Moreover, the reasons given by respondents for their choices suggest that the desire for integration is not simply a practical wish for better material facilities, but represents a commitment to principles of nondiscrimination and racial harmony.

Pointing to examples of successful integration in some suburbs, as well as growing sentiment of whites in favor of integration, Campbell and Schuman argue that it is a reasonable goal to expect true integration in smaller towns and cities with small ghettoes, and a reversal of the trend toward separatism in the big central cities. This is the goal for the late 1970s.

True integration of the big central cities cannot come so soon, but it may be a practical goal in the 1980s if appropriate steps are taken in the 1970s. One major step is the development of concerted metropolitan area action by school systems and by local governments to encourage areawide cooperation on a variety of interacting aspects of social urban renewal.

SUGGESTED ACTIVITIES

1. What are the principal intergroup conflicts (economic, ethnic, religious, or racial) in your community? in your school or college? Interview a member of each of the groups in question and obtain their views regarding the ways in which conflict could be alleviated.
2. Work out a teaching unit for elementary or high school on *The Negro in American Life*. What books and pamphlets would you

assign students? What topics would you suggest for individual projects? How would you treat contemporary black protest movements?

3. Investigate a school which has had a successful program of racial integration. Talk with some of the teachers and parents as well as the principal. Analyze the reasons for success.
4. Investigate a school in which efforts at racial integration have been unsuccessful. What are the reasons for failure?
5. To what degree does the thinking of black separatist groups and extremely militant groups represent the attitudes of the black population as a whole? Is there evidence that these attitudes are changing very rapidly? Consult such sources as the *Newsweek* polls and special editions of *The American Behavioral Scientist* in preparing a report on this topic.
6. Read the special Winter 1968 issue of the *Harvard Educational Review* on "Equal Educational Opportunity" and organize or write a debate illustrating the major points of views presented in it.

SUGGESTIONS FOR FURTHER READING

1. For various points of view on the problems of the urban Negro, read Silberman's *Crisis in Black and White,* Whitney Young's *Beyond Racism,* Pettigrew's *Profile of the Negro-American,* or Schuchter's *White Power/Black Freedom.*
2. General information and a variety of points of view on socially disadvantaged children and the causes of their disadvantage can be found in: Frank Reissman, *The Culturally Deprived Child;* Benjamin S. Bloom, *Stability and Change in Human Characteristics;* Joan Roberts, *School Children in the Urban Slum;* Mario Fantini and Gerald Weinstein, *The Disadvantaged: Challenge to Education;* and A. Harry Passow, *Education of the Disadvantaged.*
3. For an analysis of the crisis in urban education as seen and analyzed by a school survey team studying a big city school system, read William R. Odell, *Educational Survey Report on the Philadelphia Schools;* Robert J. Havighurst, *The Public Schools of Chicago: A Survey Report;* A. H. Passow, *Toward Creating a Model School System: A Study of the Washington, D.C. Public Schools;* or University of Chicago Midwest Administration Center, *Cincinnati School Survey Report.*
4. For more information on the social and economic conditions of working-class blacks, read the famous "Moynihan Report" around which a major controversy developed in 1965 and 1966. See *The*

Negro Family: The Case for National Action, published by the U. S. Department of Labor. Extended discussions on the black family are provided in Jessie Bernard, *Marriage and Family Life Among Negroes* and Andrew Billingsley, *Black Families in White America.* Problems of the urban working-class black male are described in *Tally's Corner* by Eliott Liebow.

5. A stimulating set of essays on the position of the Negro has been published as a two-volume report on *The Negro American,* edited by Stephen R. Graubard, *Daedalus* Fall, 1965 and Winter, 1966.
6. Two of the best sources providing historical perspectives on the development and effects of racial prejudice in the United States are Gossett's *Race: The History of an Idea in America* and Van den Berghe's *Race and Racism: A Comparative Perspective.*
7. Charles Valentine's *Culture and Poverty* argues that too much stress is placed on the alleged distinctiveness to be found in the behaviors and attitudes of people who live in poverty. Read Oscar Lewis' works on the culture of poverty and Lee Rainwater's essays on the urban poor for contrasting views on this important question.

CHAPTER

8

Teachers in Metropolitan Schools

ALTHOUGH 65 PERCENT of school teachers work in metropolitan areas, they do not distribute themselves randomly over the various types of schools in the area. Parallel with the great diversity of schools in the metropolitan area is a diversity of its teachers in terms of experience, age, and other qualities.

For example, Table 8.1 shows the differences of experience among teachers in the various types of elementary schools in Chicago. (The types of school have been described in Chapter 4.) The striking thing about this table is the difference in experience between teachers of high-status schools and teachers of inner-city schools. Teachers of high-status schools have a median of nineteen years' experience, while those of inner-city schools have only four years of experience.

Similar information is given in Table 8.2 concerning high school teachers in Chicago. In this table, teachers were asked to describe the socio-economic character of their school. Of those who said they taught in an "upper- or middle-class school," 36 percent had sixteen years or more of experience, while 16 percent of those

TABLE 8.1

Characteristics of Teachers in Various Types of City Schools: Chicago, 1964

	Type of School				
	High-Status	*Conventional*	*Common-Man*	*Inner-City*	*Total*
Percent of total enrollment	8	18	21	53	100
Median years' experience of regularly assigned teachers	19	15	9	4	
Percent regularly assigned teachers	94	91	86	64	
Percent of full-time substitute teachers*	6	9	14	36	
Percent distribution of regularly assigned teachers	11	23	22	44	100
Percent distribution of substitute teachers*	1	6	11	82	100

* Full-time substitute teachers are those who have a teacher's license, who are teaching full time and assigned to a particular school, but have not passed the examination for a certificate in Chicago schools.

Source: Robert J. Havighurst, *The Public Schools of Chicago,* Chicago: Board of Education, 1964, p. 170.

who said they taught in a "lower-class or slum school" had sixteen or more years of experience. Age differences showed the same effect.

In some metropolitan areas there is still a shortage of elementary-school teachers, as well as certain specialized secondary-school teachers. But in most metropolitan areas regardless of whether there is or is not a shortage of teachers, there is still a problem in that the youngest and least experienced teachers tend to be assigned to the "difficult" schools.

Another characteristic on which inner-city teachers tend to differ slightly from teachers in other schools is verbal test performance. Based on data obtained from the national sample of teachers included in the U.S. Office of Education *Equality of Educational Opportunity* study, Coleman et al., found that teachers in predominantly "blue-collar" schools scored lower on a verbal abilities test than teachers in "white-collar" schools and schools serving a cross section of the student population. (Coleman, et al., 1966.)

TABLE 8.2
Characteristics of High School Teachers Related to Socio-economic Area of School: Chicago, 1964 (Percentage Distribution for Each Type of Area)

	Area Served by High School				
	Upper or Middle-class	*Mixed Middle- and Working-class*	*Stable Working-class*	*Lower-class or Slum*	*Total*
Sex					
Male	47	44	54	52	47
Female	53	56	46	48	53
Age					
20–25	14	16	17	23	18
26–30	18	15	22	21	18
31–40	23	22	23	28	24
41–50	12	17	14	12	15
51–65	31	26	21	15	23
66+	23	3	3	2	3
Experience					
1 year	5	7	11	11	9
2	5	8	11	14	10
3–5	19	20	23	29	22
6–15	35	31	28	31	31
16+	36	34	27	16	29
Number	242	1,187	391	504	2,328
Percent of total	10	51	17	22	100

Note: The data are taken from a 60 percent sample of questionnaires returned by 65 percent of Chicago high school teachers.

Source: Robert J. Havighurst, *The Public Schools of Chicago,* Chicago: Board of Education, 1964, p. 343.

Differences in experience, training, verbal ability, and other characteristics among teachers in differing types of schools are important inasmuch as there is some evidence to indicate that these characteristics are associated with pupil performance. Burkhead's study of Chicago schools, for example, found that next to socio-economic characteristics of the schools, teacher experience was the only "input" variable (including class size) clearly associated with the reading performance of eleventh-grade pupils. (Burkhead, 1967.)

Similarly, the analysis of factors affecting student achievement in the *Equality of Educational Opportunity* study indicated that teacher characteristics remained associated with pupil performance after account was taken of the social background of the students and the social class level of the schools they attended. Teachers' characteristics measured by this study were: average educational level of the teachers' families; average years of experience in teaching; average score on a self-administered vocabulary test; preference for teaching middle-class students; whether teachers had lived in and attended high school and college in the area in which they taught; average level of education of the teachers; and proportion of teachers in a school who were white. After pointing out that pupil performance was much more closely associated with social characteristics of pupils and their schools than with other variables, the researchers concluded that:

> . . . the effect of teachers' characteristics shows a sharp increase over the years of school. The variance in achievement explained by variation in average teacher characteristics is very small at lower grades and increases for higher grades.
>
> . . . The apparent effect of average teacher characteristics for children in a given group is directly related to the "sensitivity" of the group to the school environment. In particular, Southern Negroes appear to be more affected than Northern Negroes, and whites appear least affected of all groups.
>
> This result is an extremely important one, for it suggests that good teachers matter more for children from minority groups which have educationally deficient backgrounds. It suggests as well that for any groups whether minority or not, the effect of good teachers is greatest upon the children who suffer most educational disadvantage in their background, and that a given investment in upgrading teacher quality will have most effect on achievement in underprivileged areas. (Coleman, et al., p. 317.)

However, the importance of teacher characteristics such as age, experience, and degrees earned should not be exaggerated. On the one hand, research results such as those reported by Burkhead and Coleman suggest that it is difficult for a teacher to communicate information or understandings he does not himself possess and that, other things being equal, a veteran teacher has acquired more skill in teaching than an inexperienced teacher. But other things often are not equal. Teacher characteristics such as conscientiousness, creativity, and flexibility, which are difficult to measure and therefore to study certainly are as important and probably more important than age and experience. Verbal facility of the teacher may be related to vocabulary scores of students, but in many cases other cognitive and affective outcomes of education are more important than vocabulary and in many respects verbal test scores are not a fair measure of pupil performance. The teacher's most important task is to motivate pupils, and here originality and dedication may be the most salient teacher characteristics, even though relationships between these aspects of teacher quality and pupil output are difficult to isolate in research.

Particular caution is needed to avoid overgeneralizations concerning the types of teachers needed in inner-city schools. It is more important for teachers to find a "style" which they can use with authenticity than to look for one "best" approach for teaching the disadvantaged. Studies by Hunt indicate that teachers who are methodical and provide structure in the classroom succeeded better with educationally retarded inner-city students than did other teachers, but the situation is reversed with respect to students able to operate more independently in the classroom. (Hunt, 1966.) Many knowledgeable observers believe that teachers with roughly four to nine years of experience are most likely to succeed in the inner city; teachers with too little experience generally have not learned to cope with problems of the inner-city classroom, but older teachers sometimes no longer have the unusually high degree of physical stamina and resilience required in the inner-city school. For all these reasons, it is important to avoid preconceptions concerning the types of teachers who should be sought for inner-city schools, while aiming to attract teachers with as much experience, formal training, and academic competence as possible after personality characteristics and other subjective personal qualities are taken into account.

SOCIAL ORIGINS OF METROPOLITAN AREA TEACHERS

In the decades prior to 1920, teachers were recruited in large numbers from middle-class urban families, and from rural families of probably upper-middle and lower-middle class. Relative to the general population, persons who entered the teaching field had large amounts of formal schooling and probably were persons who regarded teaching as a calling. In those years, teaching was one of the few occupations available to respectable and educated women; as the schoolmaster made way for the schoolma'am, a sizable number of teachers were women from upper-middle-class and upper-class backgrounds. While teaching has always offered an avenue of opportunity for certain groups of young people, especially rural groups, the over-all proportion of teachers who came from lower-status levels was probably smaller some decades ago than at present.

As America became increasingly urban; as the educational system mushroomed, with greater need for teachers; as teacher training institutions grew, with an increasing proportion of young people obtaining college education; and as more occupations became available to women; the social composition of the teaching profession changed.

There have been a number of studies of various groups of teachers and of various groups of students preparing to be teachers. While these studies show that there is considerable variability according to the region of the country and according to the size and the type of college attended, they nevertheless indicate that a large group of teachers is still drawn from business and professional families, that significant proportions come from farm families, and that there has been an increase in the number from urban working-class homes.

Table 8.3 shows the distribution by age and family origin of a national sample of teachers drawn in 1960–61. (NEA, April, 1963.) Of the total group, about 27 percent came from farm families and another 30 percent from blue-collar families (i.e., their fathers were unskilled, semiskilled, or skilled workers). However, these proportions are quite different in different age groups. For example, of the oldest teachers, those aged 56 and over, almost 40 percent came from farm families; while of the youngest teachers, those under age 26, it was only 27 percent.

These figures are for the country at large. There are differences, however, when large school systems are compared with small. In the largest school systems, the proportion of teachers who come from farm families is much lower and the proportion from urban working-class families is much higher than the national averages. As

TABLE 8.3

Age of Teacher in Relation to Father's Occupation: National Sample

Occupation of Teacher's Father	*Percentage in Each Group*					
	56+	*46–55*	*36–45*	*26–35*	*Under 26*	*Total*
Unskilled worker	1.9	5.0	4.9	10.8	7.6	6.5
Semiskilled or skilled worker	14.4	22.8	24.0	27.9	23.6	23.4
Farmer	39.2	34.5	28.7	13.9	20.3	26.5
Clerical or sales worker	9.0	5.2	6.0	9.2	6.3	7.1
Managerial or self-employed	23.6	18.7	21.7	24.6	21.9	22.0
Professional or Semi-professional	11.8	13.8	14.7	13.6	20.3	14.5
Number reporting	263	464	387	509	237	1,860

Source: National Educational Association, Research Division. *The American Public-School Teacher.* Research Monograph 1963–M2.

can be seen from the detailed listing of fathers' occupations of teachers in the Chicago public schools in 1964, less than 5 percent came from farms, while almost half came from working-class homes (see Table 8.4).

TABLE 8.4

Father's Occupation of Chicago Public School Teachers, 1964

Occupation of Teacher's Father	*Percentage of Teachers*					
	Elementary School			*Secondary School*		
	Male	*Female*	*Total*	*Male*	*Female*	*Total*
Semiskilled and unskilled	26	15	17	20	9	14
Farm laborer or renter	1	1	1	1	1	1
Skilled worker, foreman or similar	33	31	31	30	24	27
Farm owner	3	3	3	4	4	4
Clerical and small business	17	23	22	20	26	23
Professional and Managerial	20	27	26	25	36	31
Number	720	4,430	5,150	1,123	1,250	2,373

Source: Adapted from Robert J. Havighurst, *The Public Schools of Chicago,* Chicago: Board of Education, 1964, pp. 417–18.

SOCIAL ORIGIN AS A FACTOR IN EDUCATIONAL PERFORMANCE

It is important to know something of the social origin of any given teacher if we are to understand his performance in the teaching role. In this connection, however, we must look at social origin in relation to personality. It has been said, for instance, that social origin is the single most important fact in predicting a teacher's behavior. This is a gross oversimplification. Although a given teacher's social origin may have had an important influence upon his or her personality, it is virtually impossible to cite generalized effects that would be true for all teachers of any single origin. For example, a teacher who comes from a middle-class family is not necessarily ineffective in dealing with lower-class children. Some middle-class teachers, coming from fairly relaxed home environments, may emerge as adaptive personalities, who readily take on the color of their social surroundings. For them, it would be relatively easy to get along sympathetically with children and parents quite different from themselves. In another group, whose rigid upbringing might give them a tendency to panic when faced with the strange or unusual, prejudices may be easily aroused. Some of these persons may cling to their own ways as the only right or proper ones. They could easily drift toward treating with disdain children or parents who are of different races, religions, nationalities, or economic circumstances.

Some teachers with middle-class backgrounds do a very good job of teaching working-class children. They have a broad and sympathetic understanding of children and of society, and they enjoy working with socially disadvantaged pupils if the school structure is reasonably stable. Another teacher from a middle-class home may be dissatisfied and frustrated by a working-class group. For example, one teacher said of her first teaching assignment.

> The impressions of my very first day of teaching are still vivid. I saw a girl from the eighth grade who was several months pregnant. At first I thought she was just a very young mother bringing her child to school, but I found out that she was a thirteen-year-old pupil. (When she appeared in this obvious condition she was immediately withdrawn from school.)
>
> My other experiences that first day included listening to a dialect that was unfamiliar and almost uncomprehensive to me

> and to language that was shocking (most terms I had never heard before), and watching one seven-year-old boy emerge from the dressing room without any clothes on. When I went back with him to see that he dressed, I found that his underwear was filthy and ragged. It was held together with a large rusty safety pin that the boy claimed had been sticking him.
>
> I tried—I really tried my best. I remembered how I had to be tolerant, and how these were just children who didn't know any better. I remembered how I wanted to be a teacher, and how I wanted to succeed on my first assignment. But I simply couldn't take it. I applied for a transfer after a few weeks, deciding that I had to get into a different school or withdraw from teaching altogether. I did stick it out for the rest of that year, but I never could overcome my feelings.
>
> I've been in a middle-class school since then, and I'm happy with teaching now. But I still feel guilty and somehow ashamed of myself. I wish I could have been different. But at the same time, a person has to be honest with herself, and has to be comfortable in what she's doing, or she can't do anything at all. . . .

It is, of course, not only middle-class teachers dealing with lower-class children who can provide us with varying examples of how social origin and personality interact in influencing teaching behavior. Some teachers have difficulty in working with children whose families are of higher social levels than their own. Thus, while many teachers from lower-status families prefer to teach middle-class children, others do not. Sometimes a middle-class teacher may find it difficult to adjust to an upper-class group of children.

Among teachers coming from lower-status families, we must also expect to see differing patterns. One, for example, tortured by inner feelings of inferiority, may regard his origin as a thing of shame to be lived down. Another, having a powerful identification with his father and older siblings, may so conduct himself as to retain and exemplify his family's social rank, and in so doing ally himself with pupils and parents of similar origin. A third, imbued with strong achievement drives, may seek to deny his origin by accepting middle-class standards and by being unusually strict, if not actually punitive, against the children and parents from whose ranks he sees himself as having risen. These illustrations, of course, do not by any means exhaust the possibilities, as shown by the example of one teacher who has moved a long way up the social ladder, and whose flexible personality has made him unusually successful:

> Jim Mallory was born in 1917 in the state of Washington. His family's income was derived mainly from fruit picking, and each member was responsible for some aspect of the family endeavor. It was often Jim's lot to do the cooking, family wash, mending, and the making of clothes for the entire family. Since the Mallorys lived in a tent much of the time, it was also his job to erect the tent at the fruit picking locations and to "keep house" in any and all aspects.
>
> When Jim was sixteen he joined the army, but was given a medical discharge a year later. He stayed with his family for about two weeks subsequent to his discharge, and then stowed away on a fruit truck and went to Texas. There he enrolled in a junior college. After two years, he entered a large university in a pre-law curriculum. World War II interrupted his college work, but he received his bachelor's degree shortly after the war. He then went into graduate work in psychology, where he specialized in counselling and guidance. He became an avid student of "nondirective" counselling "student-centered" teaching, finding this general approach in keeping with his implicit world-view.
>
> Jim has been a successful teacher in high school and is now one of the most popular and admired teachers on a college faculty. His unique teaching methods in the classroom, and his sympathy and permissiveness in the counselling situation—his ability to give the student a sense of worth—this combination is one that appeals strongly to almost all his students.

A recent study of the role orientations of high school teachers in Chicago indicated that social class background does not operate alone to influence teaching behavior but interacts with other variables, particularly urban-rural origins, to affect a teacher's style and goals. (Kornacker, 1969.) One conclusion substantiated by interview data obtained in the study was that teachers who grew up as members of lower-class ethnic groups (Jewish and Polish) tended to emphasize subject matter knowledge and cognitive goals in their teaching orientation, but teachers from middle-class backgrounds (primarily Negro, in this study) tended to have a nurturant, child-centered orientation which emphasized affective aspects of learning. Teachers who grew up in ethnic subcultures with recent rural origins (Italian and Southern Negro) tended to be nurturant, and teachers with early experience in ethnic backgrounds predominantly urban in nature (Irish and Jewish) tended to favor subject-centered goals. Although these findings cannot necessarily be extended to other grade levels and situations, they do underline the fallacy of simplistic assumptions such as the assertion that all teachers of middle-class background are less concerned with understanding the emotional difficulties disadvantaged students experience in school than are teachers with economic or ethnic backgrounds similar to the pupils.

ATTITUDES OF BIG CITY TEACHERS

The attitudes of teachers toward their jobs are positive, on the whole, although the foregoing examples indicate that there are some negative attitudes. It can be safely assumed that suburban teachers are somewhat more content than central city teachers with their present situations.

A general indication of the attitudes of elementary teachers toward their job in a central city is given in Table 8.5, which reports data from a survey of Chicago teachers. The teachers were asked, "What is your attitude, in general, about your present position?" They could indicate their attitudes by checking on a five-point scale as follows: very favorable, favorable, neutral, unfavorable, very unfavorable. Their answers were heavily "favorable" and "very favorable," with 72 percent giving these two responses.

However, there are some reliable differences between subgroups of teachers, as can be seen in Table 8.5. The older and more experienced teachers give more favorable answers than the younger and less experienced. Also, women are more favorable than men in their answers to this question.

The type of school area has the closest relation to teachers' attitudes toward their present position. Elementary school teachers in upper- and middle-class areas are 65 percent "very favorable" toward their present position, while those in lower-class or slum area schools are only 17 percent "very favorable," with 22 percent "unfavorable" or "very unfavorable."

Impact on teacher attitudes of the concentration of disadvantaged students in many big city school districts also can be inferred from a study of a representative sample of Washington, D.C. teachers conducted as part of the Washington School Survey. (Passow, 1967.) At that time students in the Washington schools were assigned within a highly structured track system which placed low

TABLE 8.5
Elementary Teachers' Attitude Toward Present Position Related to Experience, Sex, and Type of School Area: Chicago, 1964
(Percentages, Unless Otherwise Stated)

Years of Teaching Experience	*VF*	*F*	*N*	*U*	*VU*	*Number*
1–2	20	42	19	14	5	806
3–15	25	43	16	12	4	2,768
16+	46	36	9	6	2	1,592
Total group	31	41	14	11	4	5,166
Type of School Area						
Upper- and middle-class	65	25	6	4	0	264
Mixed middle- and working-class	41	41	11	5	2	1,537
Stable working-class	38	39	13	7	3	912
Lower-class and slum	17	43	18	16	6	2,409
Total group	314	41	14	11	4	5,122
Sex						
Male	9	14	19	20	21	720
Female	91	86	81	80	79	4,430
Number	1,576	2,083	731	541	185	5,150

Note: *VF* = very favorable; *F* = favorable; *N* = neutral; *U* = unfavorable; *VU* = very unfavorable.

Source: Robert J. Havighurst, *The Public Schools of Chicago,* Chicago: Board of Education, 1964, p. 344.

achieving pupils in "special academic" classes. Particularly at the junior high school level, just before many working-class students drop out of school, very high percentages of Washington teachers of low-achieving pupils perceived a variety of "factors" which they said "interfered with teaching and learning" in their classrooms. For example, 76 percent of the junior high special academic teachers felt that "Too much time has to be spent on discipline," and 82 percent felt that "parents don't take enough interest in their children's schoolwork." Reflecting the fact that black teachers tended to teach in schools with relatively high concentrations of special academic students, black teachers at the elementary and junior level expressed these criticisms even more often than did white teachers.

Presumably, teachers who perceive a great deal of interference with learning in their classrooms are less likely to be satisfied with their positions than are other big city teachers. Thus it was not surprising that teachers of special academic classes and general classes were much more likely to say their jobs were "not very satisfying" or "not satisfying" than were teachers of regular and honors classes.

The types of problems which are of most concern to teachers in a big city school district were examined in a 1968 attitude study of teachers in the Cincinnati Public Schools. As part of the survey of the Cincinnati school system commissioned by Cincinnatians United for Good Schools, 130-item questionnaires were sent to a representative 20 percent sample of the district's staff. Seventy-eight percent of the questionnaires were returned. After the 130 items were statistically classified into fifteen categories, it was found that dissatisfaction among teachers was greatest with respect to administrative practices, school-community relations, teachers' voice in the educational program, and financial incentives for teachers. These findings reflect the special severity of the difficulties encountered by teachers working in large, centralized school districts with heavy concentrations of economically disadvantaged students. For example, only 14 percent of the teachers felt that administrators were attentive to suggestions from staff, only 9 percent were more satisfied than dissatisfied with relations between teachers and the school board, 66 percent were dissatisfied with the educational orientation of the communities in which they taught, 79 percent felt that teachers had too small a role in selecting textbooks, and 91 percent felt that outstanding performance was inadequately rewarded financially. (Midwest Administration Center, 1968.) Although the researchers point out that precisely comparable data are not available on attitudes of teachers in other big cities or other types of school districts, it is likely that the conditions which Cincinnati teachers are most dissatisfied about also are cause for frequent dissatisfaction among teachers in many other big city school districts.

Issues involving the attitudes and dissatisfactions of inner-city teachers became topics of major controversy in 1968 and 1969. Most observers agree that a substantial proportion of inner-city teachers either possess or develop somewhat negative expectations concerning the likelihood that a group of disadvantaged students generally will achieve as well, on the average, as a group of economically privileged students. Most observers also agree that negative expectations on the part of teachers play a part in dampening the performance of many disadvantaged students by causing them to become anxious about their performance and reducing their motivation to learn. Teachers who doubt whether their students will do well in the classroom will tend to hold lower goals for their students and to give less encouragement and help when students are performing poorly.

Starting with this fairly obvious observation, a number of educators justifiably unhappy with the situation in inner-city schools have asserted that negative or low teacher expectations are almost the sole root cause of low achievement among disadvantaged students; if only teachers would expect as much from students in the inner-city school as from students elsewhere, appropriate learning methods and materials in the classroom would be enough to overcome the performance deficit typically found in these schools.

Explanations attributing the relatively low academic performance of disadvantaged students primarily to negative teacher expectations received a boost with the 1968 publication of *Pygmalion in the Classroom* by Robert Rosenthal and Lenore Jacobson. The two authors reported the results of an experiment in which first- through sixth-grade teachers at a West Coast elementary school were given information stating that a randomly-selected 20 percent of their students were "bloomers" likely to spurt in academic performance during the subsequent school year. According to the researchers, students whose teachers had been given this information actually did improve rapidly on several measures of intellectual and social performance and did make more gains than other students. They concluded the book by observing that:

> Nothing was done directly for the disadvantaged child at Oak School. There was no crash program to improve the reading ability, no special lesson plan, no extra time for tutoring, no trips to museums or art galleries. There was only the belief that the children bore watching, that they had intellectual competencies that would in due course be revealed.

Following the lead given by Rosenthal and Jacobson, a number of writers gave minimal emphasis to the serious learning handicaps which many disadvantaged students acquire during their preschool experience. One reviewer referred to the "hard facts" presented by Rosenthal and Jacobson in pointing out that the "implications of these results will upset many school people." (Kohl, 1968.)

However, other reviewers began to point out methodological difficulties in the data presented and interpreted in *Pygmalion in the Classroom.* Writing in the *American Educational Research Journal,* Robert L. Thorndike concluded that the study was "so defective technically that one can only regret it ever got beyond the eyes of the original investigators." Reviewing the book in "Contemporary Psychology," Richard E. Snow asserted that "the research would have been judged unacceptable if submitted to an APA [American Psychological Association] journal in its present form."

With the issue far from settled, it could prove harmful to suggest a strategy that places nearly the entire burden of improving inner-city education on reductions in the negative attitudes and expectations found among many inner-city teachers. Teachers need to realize that their attitudes strongly affect the self-concepts pupils have of themselves as learners and human beings, and that the pupil's self-concept, along with other factors, is an important determinant of learning in the classroom. But effective early childhood programs, recruitment and selection of outstanding administrators, development of more suitable instructional methods and materials, close involvement of parents in school decision-making, as well as other changes probably will prove equally indispensable in working to improve the quality of education in the inner city.

TRAINING OF INNER-CITY TEACHERS

Most young teachers in the big city will work for a time in an inner-city school. Some will master the job and get real satisfaction from doing difficult work well. Some will hate the job and will transfer to an easier school as soon as possible. Some will find a well-run inner-city school and deliberately stay there, knowing that they are doing an important thing by teaching disadvantaged children effectively. Others will move to another type of school, but will remember that they served creditably for a time, even though they eventually made a change.

Teachers assigned to inner-city schools are generally even more outspoken than teachers of middle-class students in believing that their college training did not prepare them well for teaching. Partly as a result of inadequate preparation, many inner-city teachers are not able to cope with the special problems of the inner-city school and either leave teaching or seek transfers to other schools. Other inner-city teachers manage to achieve control either by maintaining a punitive classroom or by reaching accommodations in which pupils and teacher make few demands on each other. Neither condition is conducive to learning on the part of disadvantaged children.

Some colleges and universities have begun to offer better training for teachers of disadvantaged students and are beginning to turn out teachers better qualified for assignment to inner-city schools. Those which sponsor Teacher Corps or other special training programs have made particular progress. In general, the most important elements in a successful program to train inner-city teachers seem to be: (1) early experience in inner-city classrooms, before a teacher takes his educational methods and theory courses; (2) college instructors and supervisors who have first-hand knowledge of and experience in inner-city schools; (3) full-time assignments in inner-city schools during one or more semesters in which professional studies in various disciplines such as psychology and curriculum are closely integrated with each other and with opportunities to practice teaching skills in the classroom; and (4) sufficiently intensive experience in inner-city communities and institutions to allow future teachers to overcome negative stereotypes about disadvantaged persons and simplistic expectations which see the disadvantaged student as incapable of learning on the one hand or needing only love and sympathy on the other.

Even though programs for training inner-city teachers tend to be improving, big city school districts and universities seldom have worked out arrangements to provide for successful induction of new teachers into inner-city schools. As a result, the new training programs have not begun to have much impact on conditions in inner-city schools. Before long, induction rather than initial preparation may be widely viewed as the biggest bottleneck in efforts to improve teacher training for the inner city.

Closely related to the need for better preservice training is the necessity of providing more and better in-service training for teachers in big city school districts in general and in the inner city in particular. Unless teachers already staffing inner-city schools become more effective, better trained teachers coming into a school will have little permanent impact on their students and will tend to leave the inner city or reduce their level of effort. Thus one of the major recommendations of the Washington School Survey of 1966–1967 was that, "A substantial fraction (15 to 20 percent) of the teacher's time, as well as that of all other professionals, should be devoted to continuing in-service work designed to upgrade knowledge." (Passow, 1967, p. 5.)

In training and retraining big city teachers, some of the most difficult things for trainees to learn are that inner-city residents are not homogeneous in their attitudes and behaviors, that inner-city communities are not all alike, and that each such community has a style of life the teacher must understand and respect. The need for these understandings is illustrated by the incident described below, which has been written up by a teacher training group at Hunter College of the University of the City of New York. This is a real incident, though the names of the people have been changed. (Fuchs, 1966.)

> The Samuel Slater School, in New York City, was located in an area where Negroes and Puerto Ricans lived. The principal, Mr. Fields, had worked in this school for a number of years. He prided himself on his understanding of the community and its children.
>
> At the beginning of the year Mr. Fields sent a letter to the fifteen new, inexperienced teachers who had been assigned to his school. He knew that most of the new teachers were from middle-class communities and had not been exposed to the kind of community in which they would be working. He thought he would help them to get over the "culture shock" which he knew they would feel.
>
> In his letter he referred to the following facts: The children came mostly from families that were disadvantaged financially, academically, and socially; many of the children had no father at home; the language used at home was the speech of illiterate parents or it was Spanish; thus many of the children would not be "ready" to learn the school subjects, nor would they understand the care of textbooks and notebooks.
>
> On the other hand, these children could learn. They had as much innate ability as other children. The teacher's responsibility was to train the children in listening, reading, speaking, and arithmetic and also cleanliness, punctuality, care of school property, keeping neat notebooks, and desire for academic achievement.
>
> Mr. Fields sent a copy of this letter to the president of the Parent Teachers Association, because he wanted the parents to know that the new teachers were receiving this kind of assistance.
>
> The board of the PTA was angry about this letter, which they thought cast reflections on them as parents. They sent a

committee to ask the principal for an apology. Mr. Fields was surprised, annoyed, and refused to apologize for what he intended as an effort to improve his school.

The parents then began to circulate a petition calling for the resignation of Mr. Fields. They quoted a number of phrases from his letter to the new teachers and asked: Do these statements accurately describe you and your family?

This actual incident can help us to understand the complex matter of differences between the school staff and the parents and children of a socially disadvantaged section of the big city. It is an oversimplification to say that the problem is due to differences in values. Low-income citizens in the United States generally share the same goals and ideals as middle-class Americans; that is, they want their children to go to college and get good-paying jobs. They hope their children will obtain enough material possessions to live comfortably and be economically secure, and they hope they will grow up to establish a close, nuclear family based on mutual help and respect. If conditions of poverty and lack of equal opportunities in housing, employment, and education are such that economically or socially disadvantaged citizens do not experience success in reaching these goals and acquire behavior patterns which reflect frustration and failure, it does not mean that their value patterns are totally different from other groups. It does mean that in certain respects there is a "value stretch" between aspirations and expectations of the wider culture (which middle-class citizens also fall far short of living up to) and the realities they experience in a particular social and economic subculture. (Rodman, 1959.)

The parents who objected to Mr. Fields' letter did so not because they had different values from Mr. Fields and his staff. They did so because they share values with Mr. Fields, and are angry because he is critical of their performance as parents. But it is also over-simple to say that the parents and Mr. Fields have the same values. There are some value differences, and these need to be understood by the teacher.

AN ACTIVIST ROLE FOR THE METROPOLITAN TEACHER

Until the 1930s or 1940s it was easy for teachers to take the point of view that their only concern as professionals was with what happened in the classroom and the school building. Public education in those days was more oriented toward an intellectual elite in the sense that the schools were not expected to provide much beyond an eighth-grade education for most students. The schools were not yet held directly responsible for the United States having failed to orbit an earth satellite before the Soviet Union. Before 1954, few educators gave even occasional thought to the fact that a high percentage of the nation's black youngsters attended legally segregated schools.

All this has changed abruptly during the course of the past fifteen years. Nearly everyone agrees that the schools have a major role to play in achieving priority national and local goals ranging from full development of the nation's manpower resources to helping young people cope with the stress of rapid social change.

It took time for teachers and administrators to adjust to this situation and recognize its implications for the role of the educator. Gradually, however, teachers have begun to realize that they have a direct interest in conditions which affect teaching and learning in the classroom.

Because the influence of external conditions and decisions is most obvious in big city classrooms, acceptance of new roles for the teacher has tended to come first and most rapidly in the big cities. For a while, big city teachers tended to react with frustration to changes and problems in their schools. Many complained about how difficult it was to educate children growing up in the inner city, and about overcentralization in the big city school district. Eventually, however, many teachers began to understand that if they were professionally responsible for helping pupils learn, perhaps they had an obligation to work more closely with parents, to insist on change and improvement in curriculum and instruction, to work toward better structural arrangements for decision-making in their school or school district, and otherwise help change conditions detrimental to teaching and learning.

This new activism among teachers can be documented with many illustrations. For example, the teachers' union in New York has been instrumental in initiating the More Effective Schools program and other innovative programs for educating disadvantaged students. Teachers in Nashville played a leading role in supporting efforts which ended in the establishment of a metropolitan school district there. Teachers in Evanston, Illinois, were prominent in rallying support for Superintendent Gregory Coffin and his integration plans when the board of education announced its plan to terminate his contract in 1970. Teacher organizations in Washington, D.C. have been a prominent force in supporting plans for achieving administrative decentralization and increasing citizen participation in educational decision-making in that city.

Not all teachers are ready to admit or act on the conclusion that educators cannot be unconcerned with social conditions that directly affect their professional effectiveness, but such awareness seems to be growing fairly rapidly. The example of Evanston given above also indicates that willingness to take a decisive position on controversial social issues affecting the schools is not confined to teachers in the largest cities. As suburban schools evolve further, suburban teachers may become as vigorous a force for educational and social change as many of their big city counterparts are becoming.

TEACHER'S ORGANIZATIONS

By 1968 the number of teachers in American public elementary and secondary schools was over 2,100,000. Of this total, probably at least 90 percent were members of state teachers' associations affiiliated with the NEA; and over 50 percent—more than one million teachers —held memberships directly in the national organization.

One of the major differences between central city and suburban teachers lies in the nature of their professional organizations. Suburban teachers tend to belong to the National Educational Association and its state and local affiliates, and so do teachers in the smaller SMSAs. The major strength of the American Federation of Teachers is in the large central cities. Of the AFT's reported membership of 163,338 in the spring of 1968, approximately 90,000 were members of Federation locals in fourteen large central city school districts. Four locals—New York, Chicago, Detroit, and Philadelphia—accounted for about 73,000.

The growing activism and militancy among teachers in the 1960s were reflected in the affairs of the NEA and AFT and the competition between them to gain support from teachers. This competition often took the form of direct appeals to increasingly dissatisfied teachers. In January of 1964 *The New York Times* had noted that "teachers are no longer content to rule only the classroom to which they are assigned. They want a hand in the assignment and a voice in the policy that controls their professional lives. They are not asking to run the schools, but they want their views heard and heeded."

By 1967, the rhetoric as well as the demands were more insistent and more strident. The president of a union local told the California Federation of Teachers convention that "We, the teachers, intend to start running the schools. We are going to have to rearrange the relationship of the teacher to the administration and the board of education. To date, all the power has been with the board and the administrators." The president of the AFT wrote that "A new kind of teacher is active in the land . . . If boards of education and/or superintendents stand in our way, we must 'roll right over them.' " Occasional phrases referring to teachers as "slaves" and "lackeys" of the board of education could be found in the statements of leaders of education associations as well as unions. One of the few points of agreement in side-by-side interviews conducted with President Cogen of the AFT and Associate Executive Secretary Allan M. West of the NEA came in response to the question, "What in your view is negotiable, and what is not negotiable?" West's response summarized the answer of both men: "We take the position that everything that affects the quality of education is negotiable." (Kettering Foundation, 1968.)

It would be hard to determine whether action followed more closely on rhetoric or rhetoric followed reality. In 1962 the Representative Assembly of the NEA had passed resolutions insisting "on the right of professional associations . . . to participate with boards of education in the determination of policies of common concern, including salary and other conditions of professional service." (NEA Handbook, 1962–63.)

These resolutions provided the basis for *professional sanctions* and *professional negotiations* to implement the goals of teacher organizations. Professional sanctions involve the withholding of certain teacher services, generally through refusal to sign contracts, from a school district identified as "unethical" or "arbitrary." In many situations the effects of sanctions are equivalent to those of a strike. Professional negotiations are a form of collective bargaining, although many educators disavow the term. Negotiations are carried on according to formalized procedures between the local teachers' association and the school board about matters of joint concern. The AFT had long been on record in favor of strikes and collective bargaining where these tactics were thought to be necessary to improve the welfare of teachers and students. As a compromise in terminology, the term "collective negotiations" has become widely used to describe the process of a formal role in decision-making now demanded by both the NEA and the AFT.

Until 1966 or 1967 the AFT, with its strength centered in the big cities, was somewhat more militant than the NEA. There are several reasons why teachers in the large central cities have tended to organize and act collectively more than have teachers in suburbs and smaller cities. In some cases teachers in the latter districts feel less isolated from administrators and board members, but in other cases teachers feel powerless to make a stir in smaller districts where they are more easily identified and isolated as individuals. (Moeller, 1962.) Strikes have occurred in many of the big cities, at first largely for higher salaries but later for other objectives as well. In 1968 a strike in New York City centered on the issue of "the disruptive child."

Prior to 1968 or 1969 the AFT seemed to be gaining strength relative to the NEA. AFT membership was growing in the strategically located central cities where the union claimed to be demonstrating greater effectiveness than the NEA. In Kansas City, Missouri, for example, teachers had been fairly evenly divided between the union, the association, and independent organizations. The union, however, made a more radical appeal when teachers won the right to elect a single bargaining agent, and was elected by a narrow margin in 1968. Following this victory, the union appeared to gain in membership by attracting "cross-overs," new teachers, and teachers who now paid dues to both organizations. Union teachers in North Kansas City and other suburban districts also became more active.

Similar developments occurred in other big cities. The AFT won an election in Washington, D.C., for example, and the Washington Teachers Association lost 1,111 members. In 1967 the NEA gained 53,000 members, but only about 10,000 were in the large cities.

At some point in the late 1960s, however, the competition between the NEA and the AFT began to be stalemated. An NEA statement on professional sanctions insisted that, "Teachers will no longer tolerate educational conditions which impair their ability to do the best job possible" and "Teachers will no longer stand placidly by as the urban ghettos of our nation deteriorate both educationally and socially." (Kleinmann, 1968.) Association affiliates in the central cities became more militant, and the associations won representation elections in Milwaukee, Denver, and other large cities—particularly in those where affiliates had acted to exclude administrators and supervisors from participation in the same units as teachers. (This had long been a general policy of the AFT.)

As the smoke cleared, it became evident that teachers had established their right to negotiate collectively with the school boards which employed them. Among 7,161 school districts surveyed in 1968–69, 2,264 had written teacher/school board negotiations agreements, and 1,043,565 of the 1,776,749 staff members in the 6,049 responding districts were in districts covered by agreements. Larger districts were much more likely to have written negotiations agreements than smaller ones: 69.5 percent of districts with 100,000 or more pupils but only 17.9 percent of districts with 1,000 to 1,199 pupils had such agreements in 1968. (Committee on Educational Finance, 1968; National Education Association, 1969.) Equally important, legal provisions for negotiations had been made in at least sixteen states by April of 1968, and nearly every major educational organization such as the National School Boards Association had recognized that negotiations agreements were likely to become very nearly universal in the future.

Furthermore, both the NEA and the UFT were succeeding in their efforts to broaden the range of issues to be negotiated between teachers and school boards. A survey of the 2,225 known written agreements in 1967–68, for example, showed that 603 were comprehensive contractual agreements covering such matters as inservice training, class size, supervisory practices, and community relationships (National Education Association, 1969.) In Boston, for example, the AFT has negotiated arrangements to provide more remedial teachers, and by 1964 teacher associations in at least 40 Massachusetts school districts had obtained funds for professional libraries and for released time to utilize these libraries. In 1967–68, 55 school districts had agreed to provide contractual protection for academic freedom, as compared with only thirteen in 1966–67. By 1967 there were 193 contracts in which explicit provisions dealing with student discipline had been negotiated.

One development that may prove important in determining how large an influence teachers in metropolitan areas will exert in improving education is the possibility that mergers will occur between NEA and AFT organizations at the local, state, and national levels. The first merger of local affiliates of the NEA and the AFT took place in October, 1969 in Flint, Michigan, and discussions concerning a possible state-wide merger in Massachusetts were held throughout the summer of 1969. Many educators both inside and outside the association and union movements believe that unity through merger would allow teachers to become a much more potent force affecting the quality of education in the metropolitan system of education.

The next few years may prove crucial in determining how important a force teachers will be in bringing about needed improvements in metropolitan education. At the present time the interests of teachers in different parts of the metropolitan area tend to coincide. Salary schedules, for example, generally do not vary a great deal across the metropolitan area, since school districts in an SMSA tend to constitute one large market for teacher supply and demand. Where suburban districts are able to raise more money per pupil than central city districts, this means that suburban teachers have more and better equipment, facilities, and services than central city teachers. In many other cases, however, the relatively small size of suburban districts definitely handicaps the effectiveness of their teaching staffs. For the time being, suburban and central city teachers tend to have a common interest in being part of a unified area-wide professional organization which could negotiate from a position of strength for better salaries and a more rational structure for metropolitan education.

This situation may change in the future, however. As the financial disparities between the central city and its suburban rings continue to grow greater, average suburban salaries may rise far above central city schedules. Alternatively, unrestricted federal aid to the cities might result in a significant differential in favor of the central city teacher. In either case, groups of teachers in one part of the area may develop more of a vested interest in the existing arrangements for metropolitan education. Also, the further development of racial segregation in the metropolitan area and its schools could result in difficult-to-bridge racial differentials and misunderstandings between teaching staffs in the suburbs and the central cities. Just as is true with respect to metropolitan society as a whole, metropolitan teachers may have only a few years left during which to face up personally to the implications of social stratification and racial segregation in the nation's SMSAs.

BLACK TEACHERS AND ADMINISTRATORS IN METROPOLITAN SCHOOLS

The various nationality groups that came to the United States during the nineteenth and twentieth centuries entered the teaching profession as a natural part of the process of joining the American culture and of moving up the socio-economic scale. Thus the Irish, Germans, and Swedes became teachers in large numbers before 1900. People with names suggesting these nationalities and Anglo-Saxons make up the bulk of the teaching profession in the smaller school systems today. Then Jews, Poles, and Italians came into the school systems and now have important roles, especially in the large central cities. Since World War II there has been a substantial flow of Japanese into teaching positions in western and midwestern cities, and teachers of Japanese ancestry abound in Hawaii. Teachers of Puerto Rican and Mexican ancestry are just beginning to enter the profession.

The position of the black teacher is somewhat different from teachers of most other ethnic groups in that there was a segregated school system in the South and some border states for decades before 1954, and therefore there was a substantial group of black teachers in all-black schools. The majority of black teachers in the United States probably still teach in de facto segregated schools in the South.

Outside the South, most black teachers are employed in central city districts. Although no official figures are available to show how many black teachers and administrators work in suburban school districts outside the South, it is certain that the number is relatively small. For example, a report given at an AFT convention estimated that there were fewer than 50 black teachers in all the suburban schools in the Cleveland SMSA as of 1968. (Jacoby, 1969.)

Black teachers and administrators have been relatively well-represented on the professional staffs in border state central cities such as Kansas City, Cincinnati, and Louisville, partly because these cities had legally segregated school systems until 1954. In 1965, for example, 28 percent of the teachers in the Kansas City, Missouri Public Schools were black, as compared with 40 percent of the pupils. In Washington, D.C., where 91 percent of the pupils in 1966 were black, 81 percent of the elementary teachers and 64 percent of the secondary teachers were black. These figures compared with national percentages of 9 percent black teachers in elementary schools and 7 percent in secondary schools, respectively. (Passow, 1967.)

Many big city school districts in the North and West have had a fairly rapid increase in the percentage of black teachers on their teaching staffs as the number and proportion of black students in these districts increased during the 1950s and 1960s. In Detroit, for example, black teachers constituted 23 percent of the teaching staff by 1962. The proportion of black teachers in Chicago was about 32 percent in 1969. In some other cities, however, only a small percentage of the teaching staff is black. Less than 10 percent of the teachers in New York in 1968 were black, even though black students constituted more than 30 percent of the pupil population.

Employment of black administrators has tended to lag considerably behind increases in the percentage of black teachers in the big cities. As a rule, requirements for administrative positions in most big cities include several years of teaching experience as well as passage of verbally-oriented written and oral tests on which black teachers, many of whom have working-class or southern backgrounds, tend to do less well as a group than candidates from other ethnic groups with longer middle-class, urban origins. It was not until less stress was placed on formal selection procedures based on academic proficiency, as a matter of fact, that significant numbers of black administrators began to appear in the administrative hierarchy in many big cities of the North and West. (Many central city school districts in the border states already had black principals some of whom were promoted to central office positions when *de jure* segregation ended in 1954, but these promotions often were to visible positions which had very little authority.)

Detroit, Philadelphia, and Newark were among the cities which had a substantial rise in the number of black administrators achieved partly through relaxation of formal selection procedures in the latter half of the 1960s. Thus, by 1969, there were black deputy superintendents in Chicago and Philadelphia, and black principals constituted a substantial and growing proportion of the administrative staff in many big cities. In New York City, on the other hand, existing civil service and "merit" examination procedures were strictly adhered to, and, with the exception of three experimental sub-districts, there was only one black principal in the district's 1,000 schools as of 1969. And although a few black administrators had been assigned to positions administering predominantly white schools, as in the case of a junior high principal in Minneapolis and a district superintendent in Chicago, the large majority of black administrators were in schools or neighborhoods in which a majority of the students were black.

The appointment of black professionals to administrative positions has great symbolic as well as practical significance for the educational program in big city school districts. Black administrators can serve as positive role models for black students,particularly young working-class male students who may come from families without a father permanently in the home. Even when they may be considerably disliked by some black parents or neighborhood groups, black administrators can take action to counteract the harmful image of the school as a colonial white-run island in a largely black community—provided they are given or can gain sufficient authority and autonomy to provide leadership for the teachers, students, and parents with whom they work. Equally important, since formal and verbally-oriented selection procedures have little or nothing to do with the qualities needed for the successful administration of big city schools in general or inner-city schools in particular (Doll, 1969), going outside the established procedures to search for talented administrators with a minority background signals recognition of the central role administrators play in determining the success of inner-city schools as well as a willingness to institute basic reforms in the operation of big city school districts.

Whether to stress appointment of black teachers in predominantly black schools is a much more complicated question than is the case with regard to the present imperative need for more black administrators. Many black teachers with middle-class background and aspirations, for one thing, tend to be insensitive to the problems and needs of disadvantaged students and families, just as is true with respect to many middle-class white teachers. Until recently a significant proportion of black teachers in big city districts had rural or southern backgrounds which did not particularly qualify them for working with urban disadvantaged youth. As the black population of the central cities continues to grow and mature, this situation has begun to change, and there are indications that substantial numbers of minority teachers with working-class, urban backgrounds have entered the profession. In Washington, D.C., for example, 35 percent of the black elementary teachers employed by the district in 1967 grew up in the city, and 66 percent of these teachers grew up in low status families as indicated by a measure of parental occupation, income, and education. (Passow, 1967.) On the one hand, it is probable that some teachers with socially and economically disadvantaged backgrounds may find it easier to function perceptively and effectively in an inner-city school, but others will lack the patience, motivation, and understanding needed for this task. Social and racial or ethnic background notwithstanding, very few teachers have received the special training required for success in working with disadvantaged urban students. As noted above, the most important qualifications for teachers in the inner-city school are not gauged as well in terms of a candidate's background experience as by his personal qualities and characteristics.

Recognizing these considerations, many citizens and parent groups in the black ghettoes of the big cities have been insisting that more black administrators receive appointments as principals of their local schools, but generally there has been little equivalent insistence on an all-black teaching staff. On the one hand, black parents in the inner city tend to feel that their schools should have good black teachers whom their children can identify with and emulate; on the other hand, they generally plead for and welcome outstanding teachers regardless of racial or social background—even in the midst of embattled communities undergoing racial confrontations such as have occurred in the Ocean Hill and Two Bridges sections of New York City. (Swanson, Cortin, and Main, 1969.)

It is important not to exaggerate the influence of a few extremely nationalist black leaders who demand an all-black professional staff for ghetto schools; such leaders do not as yet represent the views of very many black Americans in the big cities. Even in the highly emotional atmosphere of the New York decentralization crisis of 1968–69, which was marked by charges and countercharges of white racism, planned genocide, and black anti-semitism, two-thirds of the new teachers hired by the experimental Ocean Hill-Brownsville district in which the controversy centered were white. In general, outstanding trainees and graduates from Teacher Corps or other special programs for preparing inner-city teachers have been well received by most parents in the inner city, provided that enough of their members are from black or other minority groups to show that a real effort has been made to open more opportunities for the disadvantaged population of the cities. With the possible exception of a few neighborhoods in the very largest ghettoes, there is still a place in predominantly-black inner-city schools for white candidates who demonstrate high potential as inner-city teachers.

Demands for black administrators also are easy to misinterpret. Black parents in the inner city are insisting that black principals and administrative personnel should be in charge of most predominantly black schools, but usually not to the complete exclusion of outstanding white administrators. For example, in 1968 one white principal was ousted from a ghetto school on Chicago's west side after so-called Black Power militants in the community insisted that he be removed; however, many of the same vocally militant people in the community then demanded—and won—approval of a white district superintendent with a well-earned reputation for vigorous leadership in working with local teachers and parents. In a situation such as this, some black militants will say that what they really mean in demanding "black" personnel are persons of whatever color who are willing to stand up and fight for the interests of people in the inner city. "The tendency to rely on doing things as they have been done in the past," the black president of the Washington, D.C. Teachers Union has been quoted as saying, "is a characteristic that has nothing to do with the color of one's skin. If all it took were black teachers and administrators to change a school system, we would obviously have the best school system in the world here in Washington. Which of course is not the case." (Jacoby, 1969.)

Another development involving black educators which can be easily misinterpreted or exaggerated is the increasing trend for black personnel to work more closely together, often with militant whites, to bring about improvements in big city schools and communities as well as to accomplish specific group goals. For example, the black teachers association in New York City has been growing more militant in recent years, and an active teachers division has been formed as part of the Operation Breadbasket Project which Reverend Martin Luther King started in Chicago. National meetings of Negro school board members were held for the first time in 1968, a national conference of black educators was convened in Chicago in the summer of 1968, and separate caucuses of black participants have become a relatively common occurrence at local, state, and national professional conventions and conferences. These developments in education are part of a much larger movement toward solidarity among black professionals which has included the first National Conference of Black Lawyers and Law Students held in June of 1969 and the establishment of closer working relationships among many black ministers and their congregations.

Solidarity among black educators has tended to focus on the issue of community control of schools in big city districts. Thus the New Caucus of militant black and white teachers which was formed within the AFT in 1967–68 coalesced around the demand that the AFT support "the right of democratic community control of schools in local communities," and the highly publicized position paper which black educators in the Five-State Organizing Committee for Community Control issued at the Harvard Conference on Educational Subsystems on January 25, 1968, proclaimed that, "We will do whatever is necessary to gain control of our schools. We view movements toward incorporation of the concept of community control into school systems whose basic control remains with the white establishment as destructive to the movement for self-determination among black people." (Phi Delta Kappa, 1968.)

Some of the reasons why black educators' organizations have tended to focus their efforts on the objective of decentralized community control have been described by *Washington Post* education reporter Susan Jacoby as follows:

> Many black teachers are just as fearful of what they regard as "parent interference" in the classroom as the average white teacher, although younger teachers of both races tend to be less rigid on this issue. Nevertheless, the evidence from cities with large numbers of Negro teachers indicates that if black teachers are not wholeheartedly in favor of more community control, they are at least less hostile toward it than their white counterparts. Says Keith Baird, a curriculum consultant to the embattled Ocean Hill-Brownsville school district in New York: "Community control simply means that blacks and Puerto Ricans will have the same say in running their schools that whites have always had. Naturally, that prospect doesn't frighten black teachers." (Jacoby, 1969.)

Obviously, black teachers who help organize or participate in all-black organizations will have many motivations for being active in these groups. That one should not automatically assume such organizations are basically separatist or divisive in their aims and actions was underlined by an angry letter to a Chicago newspaper which included the following statements by a co-chairman of Operation Breadbasket's Teachers Division:

> Once more the mass media has further compounded its errors—falsely labeling our movement to form a union of black teachers and educators as "back to racial segregation . . . reseparation . . . counter-revolution in the civil rights movement."
>
> Your definitions illustrate an ignorance of the meanings of segregation and separation, for you do not differ between the forced racial division for the benefits of one group and the separation of two consenting parties in order to develop individual concepts and decisions.
>
> No one cried "segregation" when the UAW left the AFL–CIO—or when the Irish policemen formed their group—or when the Jewish veterans established their organization.
>
> If our movement was for black resegregation, then we would be talking about putting black principals in every white school and black policemen on every white street to harass and intimidate.
>
> Your time could be more profitably spent in a study of the segregation that exists in all the operations and facilities of the Board of Education . . .
>
> Find out why there are only a few black students enrolled at Washburne Trade School even though this is a clear violation of board-union agreements.
>
> Question why no black contractor has ever put up a school in Chicago. Find out why black children are often without books, while $1,500,000 remains unspent in the textbook fund. . . .
>
> Only after you've done this can you sit down with black teachers and discuss separation and segregation and know that our movement is in harmony with a growing awareness within the black community that the Chicago Teachers Union will never address itself to the problems of the black community and of black teachers until they respect us. And they won't respect us until we collectively develop power. (David Harrison, 1969.)

On the other hand, the potential estrangement which may occur in the big cities between black and white teachers and particularly between black teachers and white teacher association officials should not be minimized. The community control issue is likely to become one on which teachers split by race in many cities, and black teachers in general are becoming much more activist on other issues involving the improvement of inner-city education. Thus when the Chicago Teachers Union struck the Board of Education in the spring of 1969, teacher attendance rates ranged as low as 6 percent in some predominantly white areas but as high as 95 percent in some inner-city areas where black teachers argued that the strike would damage the education of their students. Although a number of controversies involving such matters as teacher certification regulations and substitute teacher policies helped account for this pattern, probably the most fundamental difference was that many black teachers had lost faith in the Teachers Union. Unless teacher organizations become much more vigorous and effective in fighting for inner-city school improvements in addition to salary increases, similar racial divisions may well become apparent in other big cities.

THE CAREER LINE OF THE METROPOLITAN EDUCATOR

The career of the metropolitan educator is now undergoing a considerable alteration, as would be inferred from the fact that the population structure of the country and also the social backgrounds of teachers have both changed so much during the past few decades.

The Traditional Career Line

The traditional career for a school teacher began by teaching in a rural school, with one or two years of post high school preparation. After a few years the teacher went back to college and completed a four-year course; then he or she went to work in the schools of a small town or city. Often the line of progress was from grade school to high school, as well as from small town to larger town. Peterson (1956) studied the careers of women school teachers in the Kansas City school system. In the early 1950s the Kansas City system had been stable in numbers for a decade, as had other cities, as a result of the low birth-rates of the 1930s. Kansas City and other central cities adopted a policy of employing only experienced teachers. Thus the teachers were likely to be over 30 years old. In 1953, 78 percent of the Kansas City women high school teachers were over 40 years of age.

Unmarried rural-reared and small-town teachers typically began teaching in a school near their home at the age of seventeen or eighteen; moved to a larger school after about two years of experience and some additional education in summer school; secured a B.S. in education at about the age of 24; made two additional moves to large schools in larger towns; entered the Kansas City system at about age 31; moved twice within the Kansas City system; secured their current placement within the city system at the age of 35; and, in the course of continued summer school education, received an M.A. degree at about age 38.

The early career phases of unmarried urban-reared teachers are noticeably different from the others. As a rule, urban-born teachers completed their degrees before beginning to teach, taught in small town schools for a much shorter period, and entered the urban system when younger. They were not, however, much younger than teachers from small towns and farms when they moved to their present positions within the city system, perhaps because "settling" within the city system is more closely affiliated with age.

An alternative career line existed in a few large cities, mainly in the East. Here the teachers were more likely to come from working-class and lower middle-class families living in the central city. They went from the local high school to a municipal teachers' college or university, and then commenced teaching in the city schools. After a two- or three-year probationary period they secured tenure, and began looking for a school that was conveniently located near the area in which they wished to live. They would transfer once or twice until they found a school where they liked the principal, the pupils, and the neighborhood. A sub-group, of course, worked for promotion to an administrative position.

The Contemporary Line

Since 1950 a new career line has developed for teachers who come from the central city and attend a local teachers' college. Upon securing a bachelor's degree and a teaching certificate, they start teaching in the central city system. The central city has actively recruited new teachers since about 1955, when the post-war birth rate increase swelled school enrollment. Many teachers secure a master's degree through part-time study. Then those who want to be administrators start preparing for examinations and getting a variety of teaching experience. The others look for the kind of school assignment that will be best for them. The beginning teacher more likely than not will be assigned to inner-city schools which tend to have many vacancies because few teachers request to transfer to the difficult teaching situations which exist there.

There are, of course, a variety of reasons why teachers request transfers. Havighurst (1964) found only 16 percent of elementary and 12 percent of high school teachers were willing to admit having requested transfer because of dissatisfaction with pupils or with the local community. The most frequent reason given was personal convenience—distance from home, for instance. A teacher may also transfer for reasons of professional advancement, for example, to gain experience in another type of school, or a better position. Or a teacher may be dissatisfied with his principal, or with certain aspects of his assignment that he feels mitigate against professional service. Nevertheless, in Chicago more teachers request transfers from slum schools than from other schools.

Increasingly, this career line leads to a suburban school position. Since the suburbs have been growing rapidly, they cannot recruit entirely among teachers who were born in suburbs. They recruit from the central city or from the towns and cities outside the metropolitan area.

Thus there has developed a metropolitan teacher career line which remains entirely within a metropolitan area. More and more teachers are following their entire professional lines within a particular metropolitan area, teaching in a wide variety of schools.

The career line of the metropolitan administrator is beginning to differ from that of the teacher in that opportunities for mobility are beginning to flow in a variety of directions. Until recently, most big cities recruited administrative personnel almost entirely from within the ranks of their own teachers. As a spur to educational reform, some cities such as Philadelphia and Detroit have begun to recruit potentially talented administrators wherever they can be found—sometimes from outside the field of education. Central city teachers who want to go into administration but have no experience in the inner city tend more than before to apply for positions in the suburbs or in rural districts. At the level of the superintendent, on the other hand, the flow from suburb or small city to big city has begun to diminish. Traditionally, many big cities draw their superintendents from candidates with successful experience in that position in smaller districts. Increasingly, however, big city boards of education are asking whether superintendency candidates have shown leadership in solving educational problems involving integration and the disadvantaged while serving in smaller districts. Since many small districts do not have such problems and since superintendents in these districts often try to "keep the lid" on these problems where they do exist, many prominent superintendents in smaller cities and the suburbs are now finding that they have closed themselves off to advancement and have "nowhere to go."

These types of career lines are socially desirable if they do two things: (1) provide most educators with opportunities to grow in experience and skill and salary in a set of situations where their particular personality fits in well, and (2) distribute educators so that the teachers who are most competent in each of the several types of schools are able to find places in such schools. Except in the case of inner-city schools, where the need for more effective teachers and administrators is obvious and urgent, these purposes probably are being accomplished fairly well by existing career lines in the metropolitan educational system.

No discussion of the changing career patterns of educators in metropolitan school districts would be complete without at least briefly mentioning development of the role of teacher aide. Some school districts have been utilizing paid or volunteer lay persons to provide assistance to teachers for many years, but the number of teacher aides working in metropolitan schools now is increasing very rapidly. By 1969, more than 40,000 teacher aides were reported working in a sample of school districts enrolling 6,000 or more pupils, in contrast to only 29,938 reported one year earlier. (*NEA Research Bulletin*, May 1969.) Estimates of the number of aides employed by 1967 in programs funded through Title I of the Elementary and Secondary Act and in Headstart programs were 40,000 and 25,000, respectively. (Roby, 1968.)

Although several studies indicate that the majority of teacher aides in the nation's schools are persons with middle-class backgrounds, big city school districts have been making a concerted effort to train and employ aides from low-income neighborhoods to work in schools serving large numbers of disadvantaged students. Often referred to as "paraprofessionals," teacher aides are making an important contribution to education in inner-city schools. At first many teachers tended to resist having another adult in their classrooms and to be skeptical whether persons with disadvantaged backgrounds would prove helpful and competent in working with their students. Increasingly, however, teachers in the big cities have been expressing gratitude for the services rendered by these aides and even have started to demand that more aides be employed.

In addition, much work is now being done to develop a "new career" pattern which will make the position of teacher aide an entry into the professions for citizens with disadvantaged backgrounds. As an aide acquires more skills and competence working with and teaching children, she could advance to such positions as teacher assistant and auxiliary teacher, and some might acquire sufficient professional training and skills to become fully certified teachers. The New Career movement in education is exciting not just because it offers important employment opportunities to low-income citizens in the cities and towns of the metropolitan area but also because it aims to develop new kinds of differentiated teaching teams which, working under the supervision of a master teacher, may significantly improve educational programs for disadvantaged students. (Riessman and Gartner, 1969.)

It is too early to determine how large a part teacher aides may play in improving metropolitan education in general or inner-city schools in particular, or whether New Careers patterns for disadvantaged citizens may come to constitute a major career line among metropolitan teachers, but a great deal of attention and effort will be devoted to testing and evaluating these possibilities during the early 1970s.

SUGGESTED ACTIVITIES

1. If you have friends or colleagues who are black teachers, describe their attitudes toward teaching socially disadvantaged children. Can you relate differences among these people to differences in their personalities?
2. If you are teaching in a suburban school system, get career information from ten or twelve of your colleagues who have been teaching ten years or more. What has been a typical career line for them?
3. A number of studies and surveys of big city school districts have been conducted during the past five years. Most of these surveys have chapters dealing with the characteristics and attitudes of teachers. If such studies are available in your college library, compare the questions which were asked and the recommendations which were offered in two or more such studies.

4. Write out an imaginary debate between an inner-city teacher who is having trouble teaching disadvantaged students in her class and a parent who feels the teacher is not doing her job. What do you think might be done to reduce the misunderstandings and bad feeling on each side?
5. Is there a special program for training inner-city teachers somewhere in your region? Find out whether there is information to show if the program has been successful and how it differs from other teacher training programs in the region.

SUGGESTIONS FOR FURTHER READING

1. For a keen analytical and critical treatment of the American school teaching profession, read Myron Lieberman, *Education as a Profession.*
2. For questionnaire studies of school teachers see *The American Public School Teacher, 1960–61,* published by the Research Division of the National Education Association, and Chapter 16 and Appendix A of *The Public Schools of Chicago,* by Robert J. Havighurst.
3. Recent books describing teachers' reactions to inner-city schools are generally rather grim portrayals, though some of them present descriptions of positive learning behavior by children under creative and sympathetic teachers. Among these books are: *Up the Down Staircase,* by Bel Kaufman; *Thirty-Six Children,* by Herbert Kohl; *Death at an Early Age,* by Jonathan Kozol; *Our Children are Dying,* by Nat Hentoff; *The School Children* by Greene and Ryan; and *Teachers Talk* by Fuchs. Possibly the best of the books describing the experience of an inner-city teacher is *The Way It Spozed to Be* by Herndon.
4. *The Schools and the Urban Crisis* edited by Kerber and Bommarito includes several selections dealing specifically with the situation of teachers in the metropolis as well as with related topics brought up in other chapters of this book.
5. Studies by Wilbur Brookover and the chapter by John Glidewell in the *Review of Child Development Research* provide evidence and citations regarding the importance of self-concept in learning and the influence of teachers in forming pupil self-concepts.

CHAPTER

9

School Systems and Other Social Systems in the Metropolitan Area

THE PURPOSE of the human enterprise as a social venture is to make life more satisfying for all of those who live brief lives on the face of this ancient earth. This chapter asks and attempts to answer the question: how should the schools be related to other social systems in our urban industrial society so as to maximize human satisfaction and happiness?

To answer this question education needs to be looked at in a social setting; and for this a social setting of a certain magnitude needs to be chosen. Should it be the whole nation, for example? That would be useful, but too broad and distant a view for the kinds of interests developed in this book. Should it be the state? That would be better, but the metropolitan area is best from our point of view. It would not be useful to limit ourselves to the city or the municipality as the unit, for it cannot give us a cross-section of American life with its economic, social, and political problems to which education must be applied.

Having selected the metropolitan area as the unit of population and area upon which to focus, the major social changes which are now taking place, and which affect education and are affected by it should be singled out. Education should be developed to take account of these social changes and to give a degree of rational control and direction over them.

The principal social changes are:

1. The labor force is increasingly composed of people with technical and professional training at a post high school level. Industrial production workers are not a growing component of the working force and may decrease in relative numbers as have agricultural workers.
2. Services rather than production of goods are the principal elements of growth in the economy.
3. The basic problem of the American economy is no longer production of goods, but the widespread and equitable distribution and consumption of goods and services.
4. The redistribution of population and of jobs between central cities and suburbs is making the metropolitan area into the rational unit for economic and political organization.
5. Government is increasingly involved in the financing and location of housing, in the provision of social security, health services, and other forms of support for the material standard of living of a large segment of the population.
6. With the help of government subsidies, the metropolitan area is becoming a unit for a program of cultural development through the expansion of theater, concert music, graphic arts, adult education programs, libraries, and educational television.
7. A set of economic and political problems is arising out of the concentration of population in metropolitan areas—problems of water pollution, air pollution, urban sprawl and blight, transit, and economic and racial segregation.

GOALS OF METROPOLITAN DEVELOPMENT

A Great Society, as conceived by American leaders, is to be achieved through working toward the following goals in the metropolitan area:

1. A high material standard of living
2. Assistance to the disadvantaged through education and through specific forms of material aid
3. Equality of opportunity for high quality education
4. Freedom of choice in residence, occupation, politics, and religion
5. Growing appreciation of expressive culture, with support for creative work in the arts

6. Widespread participation by the common people in the making of social and political decisions about the metropolitan area

To achieve these goals, educational systems must cooperate with other *social systems* which carry on the business of a society. Where there is social change, there is change in these social systems. When there is rapid social change, as there is today, the various social systems change rapidly, and they change in their relations with each other.

The educational system should change and develop its functions in relation to other social systems—this is the basic proposition of this chapter.

SOCIAL SYSTEM DEFINED

The sociologist, as a scientist studying society, has invented several concepts as tools for his understanding of social structure and organization. One of the most useful of these concepts is that of a *social system.*

A social system is a system of the actions of individuals, the principal units of which are roles and constellations of roles. (Parsons and Shils, 1952.) A social system has one or more functions it does usefully. It performs these functions through its roles or constellations of roles. A *role* is a set of behaviors that is appropriate to a particular status in a society.

An educational system is a set of roles and role constellations devised to teach children and adults some things they are not likely to learn efficiently in the family or at work. For another example, a police system is a set of roles and role constellations designed to protect order and enforce the law. Thus a social system is a systematic organization of the efforts of people to achieve some purpose of a society.

It is possible and useful to study a social system as a set of roles and role constellations, without looking closely at the individuals who fill the roles. This will be done at first in this chapter; later, the personalities and individual characteristics of people who fill key roles in the educational system will be studied.

In keeping with the functional specialization characteristic of a modern society, the residents of the metropolitan community conduct their affairs through a variety of institutional systems organized to make specialized contributions to the society as a whole.

The following social systems and their subsystems are among the major ones which provide indispensable services in the metropolitan area.

Educational system, which includes public school districts, Roman Catholic schools, private schools, higher education institutions, teachers' organizations, adult education councils, and civic organizations interested in the schools

Local government system, which includes city and country governments as well as special districts and the court system

Welfare agency system, which includes welfare councils, community chests, public assistance bureaus, employment services, religious charities, settlement houses, youth-serving agencies, and family service organizations

Economic system, which includes banks, department stores, industrial corporations, labor unions, business associations, retail and wholesale business units, employment services, and real estate boards

Culture agency system, which includes libraries, museums, radio and television stations, park districts, booksellers, and recreation agencies

Transportation system, which includes rapid transit, airports, street departments, expressways, railroad terminals, and automobile service stations

Church system, which includes churches and church federations, intra-church systems, and denominational bodies

Health maintenance system, which includes boards of health, medical societies, hospitals, nursing homes, and health care associations

Public service system, which includes water departments, police departments, fire departments, sewage disposal departments, and weather bureaus

INTER-SYSTEM COOPERATION

Certain social systems can operate most effectively as a rule when they operate alone. The water supply system is an example. It performs a technical and mechanical function, one which is clearly necessary and is clearly defined. It is seldom called upon to cooperate with other systems. Recently, the water system has been asked to cooperate with the health maintenance system to supply fluoride in drinking water as a protection against tooth decay. Generally this new function has been taken on with little or no strain, but it involves an expansion of the functions of the water system which has caused conflict in some communities.

Other social systems must cooperate to a considerable degree because their functions are very similar and generally very complex. The educational system is an example of one that must cooperate with other systems.

For example, the school and the library systems have overlapping functions which are worked out differently in various situations. The story of school and library cooperation in the City of Chicago is a good example. Much of the early part of the story is told by John A. Vieg (1939, pp. 57–67) who studied the schools of metropolitan Chicago in the 1930s.

In 1910 there were no school libraries in Chicago. At that time the Chicago Public Library provided a large number of fifty-book collections on long-term loan to classrooms in the schools. During 1916–17 the Library set up branches in six high schools and maintained them for a short time, then closed them. A formal cooperative agreement was made in 1923 by which the Chicago Public Library provided books, magazines, and supplies; selected librarians and supervised them; and the Chicago School Board paid the salaries of the librarians. This agreement continued until 1937, when 38 high schools and two junior college branches had libraries under this plan. There were no elementary school libraries during this period, but the classroom loan collections were continued. Although the cooperative agreement ran over a period of more than a decade, there was some dissatisfaction. For example, the 1935 annual report of the Chicago Public Library says that the services of the librarians were not fully appreciated by the schools. After 1937, the Board of Education assumed the cost of books and magazines and later took over the selection and supervision of librarians. A complete library system was established in the Chicago Schools during subsequent years, including almost all of the elementary schools. Thus the school libraries became integral parts of the school system, though the long-term loan collections from the Public Library continued in the elementary schools on a declining basis, with 32,000 books out on loan in 1962.

In this case the new function (school libraries) was introduced into the school system through inter-system cooperation, and then the cooperation was gradually discontinued as it became less useful.

Other social systems with which the educational system has been deeply involved in the past are the cultural system and the recreational system. A significant example of the intensifying of cooperation between the educational and cultural systems can be seen in the cities where the National Arts and Humanities Foundation has joined with the United States Office of Education to establish repertory theater groups which perform before school-age audiences as well as adults.

Cooperation with the recreation system has also been a tradition in some school districts, going back at least as far as the heyday of the Progressive movement, when "outdoor learning" constituted a major tenet in the philosophy of many prominent educators. An authority on playground and recreational facilities, for example, has described how "cooperative school-park programs in outdoor education" can serve the needs of students as well as society by taking students out of doors, not only for nature study but to engage in "erosion control, providing food and cover for wildlife, growing horticultural stock, . . . the planting of school forests or arboretums, . . . [and] camping," and by bringing the outdoors "into the classroom to motivate . . . [and] stimulate students. . . ." (Wilson, 1966.) But the educational system and the recreational system are now moving beyond these more obvious opportunities for cooperation toward joint long-range planning aimed at improving the utilization and distribution of the scarce recreational resources of the metropolitan area. An example of such cooperation and the benefits it can bring was described by a planning official who explained that:

> . . . In working on park and recreation matters, you must keep in mind that the open space grants from the federal government can go to any local government agency. As a result, we were able to work out the following arrangement: Whenever the city school district built a new elementary school, the planning agency prepared applications for federal funds to help finance fifteen-acre parks next door to the school. The district might already have eight acres next to the school, and we'd get the additional money to bring the acreage up to the desirable number of fifteen. The arrangements benefited everyone. The park system was enhanced with more parks, the schools had more adequate park space adjoining them, and we in the planning commission had the satisfaction of knowing that the parks were in the right place—next to a school where they could be used most effectively. (Quoted in Levine, 1967.)

There are several current examples of inter-system cooperation in which the public schools are cooperating with welfare systems to develop a new function. One of them is the use of social workers by the school system. Although some big city systems have had school social workers or "visiting teachers" for years, others have not used social workers but have counted on social service agencies to help families who have maladjusted children in school. The proportion of such children in an inner-city school has grown so large that school administrators feel some kind of home-school coordinator is essential. Currently there is a good deal of experimentation with the position of home-school coordinators—This position can be filled by teachers who have additional social work training or have special knowledge of the resources of social agencies.

In some instances the problems faced by a social system are so difficult to solve and so interrelated with the activities of several other social systems that coordination between only two or three differing institutions is insufficient to accomplish any of their goals. This has been found to be the case, for example, with respect to providing a good environment for children who grow up in the inner city. Young children in the inner city need many kinds of assistance if they are to have anything resembling an equal chance to get ahead in life. Obviously, they need good education, but it is difficult for a child to learn much in school if he does not have enough to eat; if the physical and social environments in which he lives cause him to doubt his own worth as a human being; or if the only models of "successful" people around him are engaged in antisocial or illegal activities. Schools, mental health agencies, family service agencies, social welfare agencies, and other institutions all have a necessary contribution to make in helping him overcome these conditions.

The impact of these institutions is appreciably lessened, however, if coordination is not provided so that all suitable help can be given at the time it is most needed, as when a family crisis destroys the morale of its members or a major illness prevents a family or an individual from functioning effectively.

Methods for coordinating multi-agency family services including education are being tried out in a number of inner-city neighborhoods in the big cities. In most cases such projects involve the establishment of a local neighborhood service center where individuals or entire families can receive assistance without having to travel from agency to agency seeking fragmented assistance. One of the most promising of these demonstrations is a project to coordinate medical, mental health, and other services with preschool and primary education programs for young children in the Woodlawn community in Chicago. Studies conducted in response to requests from parents for help in providing a better life for their children established the following rationale for the project:

> Two systematic first-grade family studies have been done . . . which indicate that varieties of factors are related to the children's adaptation to first grade. Such issues as child rearing practices, whether both parents are present in the family, the social status of the family in the community, the physical and mental well-being of the mother, and many other features of family life are all related to the adaptation of children to first grade. Such diverse factors as whether the child was premature at birth or whether the mother rates herself as depressed or not are correlated with the child's adaptation to the classroom . . .
>
> . . . the obvious indication is that the problem of adapting to first grade, or for that matter to any life crisis period, is not purely a mental health problem. The solution lies in a synthesis of agency services . . . directed at a common assessment system which is carried out at strategic points beginning early in the school career of each student in the community. The family data support the idea that the future of independent agencies should be severely limited and that . . . the various independent agencies need to be synthesized. (Kellam and Schiff, 1968.)

Although families with serious problems elsewhere in the metropolitan area frequently need the same types and range of assistance in order to help their children succeed in the school, it may not be feasible to establish comprehensive neighborhood service centers in communities where such families are more spread out geographically than they are in the inner city. Rather than working as an integral part of a team including mental health counselors, nutrition experts, employment advisers, and other specialists, educators in a middle-class community may need to take much more initiative in diagnosing students' problems and referring students and their families to existing community agencies.

A variety of other kinds of efforts also are being made in several cities to coordinate educational services with other forms of assistance for families of very young disadvantaged children. In some projects, for example, mothers are taught home-making skills while receiving instruction in how to provide better language and cognitive environments for their children. In others instruction designed to develop conceptual skills is being given at day care centers for the children of working mothers. If evaluation of these programs continues to be positive, it is possible that federal, state, and local governments will join with the schools to make both kinds of service available in disadvantaged neighborhoods throughout the nation.

In addition to coordination with public service agencies, schools also must cooperate with other units of government in the city and the metropolitan area. Local city government is responsible for several social systems which might cooperate with a school system, but such city government agencies as the police department, public housing authority, department of human relations, and park department are often seen by the school administrator as sources of trouble for him. He feels that cooperation with them will involve him in "local politics." Yet city government is increasingly responsible for a program of *positive welfare of the city* which brings it very close to the activities of the school system. For this reason, mayors and city managers increasingly are seeking ways to cooperate with the superintendent of schools, as shown by a recent survey of the attitudes of big city mayors in which Richard W. Saxe (1969) concluded that:

> . . . powerful social forces seem to have caused a majority of the mayors cooperating in this survey . . . to reconsider their "hands off" attitude. We cannot improve on the words of the . . . [mayor who said] "The traditional concept of a separate government for the city and the school district ignores the mutuality of interest of the two."

Striving for cooperation between city government and school government has become more pronounced since about 1950, with the advent of urban renewal legislation and funds. Civic improvement, under the conditions of the 1950s and 1960s, was obviously tied up with improvement in the city schools, which were suffering generally from the inadequacies of aging buildings, were crowded by the post-war population boom, and were losing many of their best pupils and teachers to the growing suburbs.

Then, early in the 1960s, the federal government stepped in with substantial funds aimed at improving the quality of the city's population as workers, parents, and citizens. There was the Manpower Development and Training Act, the Vocational Education Act of 1963, the Economic Opportunity Act, and the Elementary and Secondary Education Act of 1965—all of which pumped money from Washington into the school systems, and all aimed at improving the quality of city life. These funds stretched the functions of the school system into forms of more direct service to the city. Increasingly, civic leaders were seeing education as serving to improve the city, not only through its effects on the mind and character of the pupil, but also through its effects on the economic system and the social structure of the city. The school system became a potential instrument for attracting and holding desirable population elements in the central city, for stabilizing racially integrated neighborhoods, and for solving or holding in check the problems of an alienated and economically marginal minority of slum dwellers.

However, cooperation between the schools and other social systems to improve the social environment of the metropolitan area can be blocked by either side. During the early 1960s in Chicago, for example, school officials ignored opportunities to work with public and private developers who needed assurances that good educational facilities would be located in urban renewal areas near the central business district. But in Englewood, New Jersey, it was the city administration that was reluctant to help the school board carry out a plan for eliminating the pattern of segregation and stratification that existed in the district's schools (Spengler, 1967.) In New Haven, Connecticut, by way of contrast, the schools received substantial funds for site acquisition costs by tieing school planning closely to the city's urban renewal program; the city, in turn, is estimated to have saved seven million dollars by becoming eligible for outside assistance to carry out part of its twenty-million dollar renewal plan.

Still another type of cooperative program involving the educational system which currently is being widely explored is the establishment of formal relationships between schools and industry. In Detroit, for example, partnerships are being set up in which industries such as the Chrysler Corporation "adopt" a high school and work with school officials to improve instruction, provide students with part-time job opportunities, make industry and community resources more available to teachers, and establish vocational training programs leading directly to skilled jobs in the cooperating industry. Somewhat similar projects are being started in Hartford, Philadelphia, and other school districts. According to the director of research of the American Vocational Association, "This trend towards more school-industry cooperation is just beginning. We believe it's education's sleeping giant." (National School Public Relations Association, 1968.)

It has long been a basic principle among school administrators that the school system should be protected from invasion by other social systems. Professor Strayer of Columbia University, the most influential leader among school administrators during the period from 1920 to about 1945, said frequently what he wrote in his report on the Chicago School Survey in 1932, "It is always a mistake for the schools to be organized so that agencies other than a board of education are responsible for the administration of vital and indispensable services in the schools." (Strayer, 1932, Vol. 3, p. 145.)

This principle of school administration may be interpreted broadly to mean that the schools should control the administration of all services they perform—even the new and marginal ones such as the school lunch program, recreation services in city parks, job placement of students taking part in work-experience programs, delinquency prevention programs, and transportation of pupils. As proponents of this principle see it, other social systems have an interest in these and other programs, and may not cooperate if the school system is too aggressive or too uncooperative. Thus in the present decade there are problems of cooperation between school systems and social welfare agencies, recreation agencies, police and youth serving agencies, and transportation systems. It is difficult for educators to change a role orientation which has been part of their professional ideology for a good many years, but the urgent need for inter-system cooperation in the metropolitan area is beginning to force them to make this adjustment.

While it provides services which other social systems must draw on, the educational system is itself dependent upon the contributions made by other social systems. Thus it must work with other systems far more closely than it has been accustomed or disposed to do in the past. The American Association of School Administrators and the International City Managers' Association have recognized the positive gains which can be made when city governments and school districts work together in such activities as planning the location of school and other public buildings and facilities, electronic data processing, provision and use of recreation facilities, maintenance of buildings and grounds, school crossing guards, library services, centralized purchasing, maintenance of automotive equipment, [and] adult education. (Alkin, 1965, p. 41.) There are problems involved in establishing formal and informal arrangements for cooperation among social systems, but there are also great opportunities for improving the quality of education at all levels of the educational system.

Cooperation Among Educational Systems in the Metropolitan Area

The educational sub-systems of a metropolitan area consist of the various public school districts in the area; the system of Roman Catholic schools, the system of Lutheran schools, other church-related school systems such as the Christian Schools, the Seventh-Day Adventist Schools; and the independent private schools.

These sub-systems have a tradition of working separately, and no doubt will continue to do so in large part. However, there are many possibilities and needs for cooperation, among the public school districts, on the one hand, and between public and private schools on the other hand.

Among public school districts there are a variety of shared educational projects, including television, special schools for handicapped children, junior colleges, and in-service teacher training programs. A good example is the program of the New York Board of Cooperative Educational Services which was described in Chapter 6.

Cooperation between the public school and some church school systems has been talked about a great deal and tried out to a small degree. Since there are laws against public support of church-operated schools in this country, the several church school systems have tended to operate in isolation from the public schools as well as from each other. However, the trend of social forces is pushing the public and church school systems closer together. Some "shared-time" or "dual enrollment" arrangements have been working, apparently with general satisfaction. The federal Elementary and Secondary Education Act of 1965 provides funds for "Supplementary Educational Centers" to serve children regardless of their school affiliations. This will require cooperation between public and church school systems.

INTRA-SYSTEM FUNCTIONING

The school system performs its functions through roles and constellations of roles filled by people. The roles which make up a school system are the following: administrator, teacher, nonprofessional personnel, student, board of education member, parents organization member, civic organization member.

Each of these names stands for a pattern of behavior which in the case of a successful school system is fitted into the other roles with the result that the school system performs its functions and the people filling the roles feel satisfaction.

These roles are now undergoing considerable change in metropolitan school districts. The social changes which have disarranged the functions of the school system have changed the patterns of behavior which were defined in an earlier day as appropriate for the various roles. The teacher's role is different if she teaches socially disadvantaged children from what it is when she works with docile children who are ready learners. The principal of an inner-city school has a different role from that of a principal of a school in a middle-income area. The administrator who has overall charge of the program needs a different set of skills and attitudes than the administrator of a stable system which performs the traditional functions of the common school.

At the present time in a changing metropolitan area there are three roles that need to be worked out intelligently in relation to each other and in relation to the social situation. The roles are: superintendent, board of education member, and member of civic organization.

The Superintendent's Role

Traditionally, the superintendent's role has consisted of the following kinds of behavior:

1. He meets with the Board of Education and discusses matters of policy with them, generally as a mentor to them, though he is careful to yield to them in the making of decisions after he has helped them to understand the various alternatives of policy and their consequences in action.
2. He selects and organizes his assistant administrators and divides the work of administration among them.
3. He draws up the annual budget and presents it clearly to the public and to the Board.
4. He represents and speaks for the school system in relations with the public—explaining the policies of the system, hearing suggestions and complaints, and persuading the public that the system

is performing its functions well or is working wisely on the problems it is meeting.

In the contemporary situation in most big cities, the role of the superintendent has four other major patterns of behavior.

5. He represents the Board of Education in negotiations with teachers and nonprofessional personnel on their salaries and working conditions.
6. He understands the society in which he works—its social systems and sub-systems—and he strives to work out agreement with the other systems on allocation of functions and on cooperation.
7. He plans for development of the school system, encouraging innovation and the evaluation of innovation.
8. He analyzes the tensions in the community that affect the schools, and works effectively to reduce these tensions by assisting diverse groups to communicate with one another and to achieve a peaceful modus vivendi.

The Board Member's Role

The Board of Education does the following things, if it performs its functions effectively:

1. It represents the public interest and their concerns about the school system in a balanced and temperate way.
2. It determines and formulates general policy with respect to the curriculum and methods of teaching, organization of the system into sub-districts, placing and building of schools, employment and working conditions of personnel, discipline of students, etc.
3. It conducts an independent and continuing scrutiny of the performance of the school system.
4. It determines the financial needs of the school system and works with appropriate government agencies to secure the money needed.

In the big city the roles of board member and superintendent must be separated, but they overlap and they overlap necessarily. Therefore every combination of school board and superintendent works out its own arrangements. These arrangements may be recorded in a temporary set of "ground rules." They may be guided to some extent by state law. They are often affected by statements of principles such as the one adopted by the Illinois Association of School Boards and the Illinois Association of School Administrators in 1955, entitled, *Statement of Principles and Procedures for Effec-*

tive Cooperation Between a Board of Education and its Chief Administrator.

The members of the school board are generally sensitive to the feelings and the moods of the public or of certain sections of the public to which they are especially tuned. They are likely to seek ways of meeting the desires of the public through adjusting the school program here and there and through compromise. Here they may find themselves dealing with a superintendent of flexible personality who works with them to make adaptations of policy. On the other hand, they may find themselves at odds with a superintendent who holds rigidly to time-hallowed precedents and principles.

When there is disagreement on matters of policy between the board and the superintendent, one of several things may happen.

1. The board may "give in" to the superintendent, on the ground that he has superior knowledge and experience.
2. The superintendent may yield to the board, and undertake to execute the policy determined by the board with all his energy and wisdom. At the same time he may warn the board that he believes the policy is unwise, and invite them to reconsider from time to time.
3. The superintendent may sabotage the board's policy by allowing or encouraging his subordinates to act on the policy stupidly or to ignore essential elements of it.
4. The superintendent may abdicate some of his executive responsibility to board members, asking or permitting them to draw up directives for putting policy into practice. He may then follow these directives to the best of his ability, or he may try to avoid following them.

Interaction of the Two Roles

There is a considerable amount of tension and conflict between the roles of superintendent and school board member in many big cities during the current decade. Several superintendents have resigned during such conflicts, and a number of school board members have been subjected to public criticism. An example of conflict which led to the resignation of the superintendent occurred in Cleveland.

In February, 1964, the superintendent of schools gave sudden notice that he would resign at the close of the school year. He declined to discuss the matter in public, saying "I will not engage in public debate. The most important thing is the welfare of the Cleveland school children." His predecessor had resigned rather suddenly in 1961.

The Cleveland Education Association, a teachers' organization affiliated with the National Education Association, called on the NEA through its Commission on Professional Rights and Responsibilities, to investigate the situation, and charged that members of the school board were "trying to administer the school system instead of merely setting policy." The National Education Association (1964) made an investigation and published the results under the title, "Cleveland, Ohio: When a Board of Education Fails to Fulfill its Proper Responsibilities."

We shall make no attempt to pass judgment on the Cleveland board or the superintendent, and we note that the report of the NEA Commission has not been balanced by a counter statement that is more friendly to the school board. It is clear, however, that the community and the schoolboard were split over issues of de facto segregation in the schools, and the superintendent was charged by the president of the board with inadequate and indecisive administration of policy with respect to racial integration.

Types of Superintendents

When an important role such as that of the superintendent is being considered, the candidate's own personality is of the utmost importance in determining the effectiveness with which the role is filled. And when cooperation among educational systems and between educational systems and other social systems is being studied, the personal characteristics of the principal actors in the directing roles need to be studied also.

To illustrate the significance of the personality which fills the role, consider the following two hypothetical profiles of suburban superintendents in a metropolitan area. If a given metropolitan area had these two men in the roles of superintendent, its chances of cooperation among social systems would be different from what they would be if two other men filled these roles.

Superintendent B. in a High-Status Suburb. Mr. B. is a relatively young man, just turned 40, who took his present job after a successful superintendency in a county seat of 30,000. He has a Ph.D. from a state university graduate school of education. He has written a number of joint articles on administrative problems that show a concern for efficiency, for good school facilities, and for the development of a first-class teaching staff.

With one of the highest per pupil expenditures in the state, and with a stable school population in his district, he aims to give his community the best there is in education. He says so repeatedly, and his board members are solidly behind him.

Superintendent B. has selected his school principals carefully for their ability to use the best of the new school methods effectively and to organize the teaching staff for this purpose.

Mr. B. attends meetings of the Metropolitan Area Superintendents' Study Council and was president for one term. He treats this largely as a social group. Whenever there are proposals for some cooperative project he asks for time to study it, and then goes along with it if he is sure it will not involve his district in taking on any responsibility beyond the bounds of the district. He has several times made it known that he does not favor cooperative activities which would in any way cost his district money.

Occasionally Mr. B. allows himself to think of what may come next in his career. The only superintendency that would be a promotion is a big city job, and he wonders whether it is worth the trouble it would be to him. Though ambitious, he congratulates himself when he reads in the papers about the conflicts and controversies that swirl around some of the big city superintendents. Alternatively, he might go on the faculty of a state college, teaching in the field of educational administration. This prospect interests him, because he enjoys scholarly work; but he would have to take a 50 percent reduction in salary if he made such a change.

Superintendent D. in an Employing Suburb. Mr. D. has been superintendent of schools in this suburban town of 20,000 for three years. The population is almost a cross-section of America, including a working-class black district on the edge of town and a number of middle-class black families. He came to this job directly after he obtained a Ph.D. from the state university and he then was 36 years old, having been a classroom teacher and a high school principal in the central city of this metropolitan area.

Superintendent D. has given this rather nondescript town a "shot in the arm," with a number of young teachers whom he has hand-picked from the central city school system and brought with him, even though they took a $500 cut in salary when they moved.

This year he succeeded in getting the town to vote the highest tax levy for schools in its history, and he has used some of the money to increase salaries.

Next year he will be president of the Metropolitan Area Superintendents' Study Council. He plans to start a cooperative special education program with two neighboring school districts, and has been chairman of the area-wide Educational Television Council which will receive state funds to inaugurate ETV as soon as the central city UHF transmitter is installed. His school district's plan for the use of federal funds for compensatory education of the socially disadvantaged was the first one to be submitted to the State Department of Public Instruction.

Since his is a relatively small district, he handles these details himself, with several of his younger teachers helping him on committees. One evening a week he attends a research seminar at Central City University on Metropolitan Problems in Education. Some of his colleagues have urged him to run for the county superintendency, an elective office with the potential for initiating area-wide cooperative programs.

Meanwhile the two new members of the Central City Board of Education and the Dean of the Central City University School of Education are hoping that he will stay where he is for the next five years and then be ready for the superintendency in Central City.

The Role of Civic Organization Member

Closely related to the roles of board member and of superintendent is the role of member of a civic organization who has an interest in the schools. The reason for this is that citizens are deeply concerned with the changing functions of the school system in a period of rapid social change, and they generally wish to deal actively with matters of educational policy, rather than to sit back and wait for the school board and the school administration to solve problems which they regard as *their* problems.

The civic organization, for the purposes of this discussion, consists of any organization of citizens with an explicit interest in the school system. Some organizations are city or areawide. Some represent a segment of the population, such as businessmen, or religious leaders. Some organizations come from local communities.

The Parent-Teacher Association may be considered as a civic organization, though its special interest in the schools and its relationship to local schools give it special importance.

The role of a member of a civic organization consists of the following kinds of behavior.

1. He studies the school system and attempts to understand its functions and its capabilities.
2. He formulates the educational needs of the particular group or section of the community which his organization represents—of the entire community if the organization represents the entire area.
3. He participates in communication with other organizations and attempts to arrive at a consensus.
4. He supports the board of education in its plans for financial support of the schools.

During a period of social change and its consequent social conflict, the tendency is for civic organizations to come into existence as pressure groups for one particular sub-group interest. Thus the past ten years has seen the rise of scores of pressure groups in every big city, which express their own needs as they see them, and take no responsibility for recognizing the needs and the attitudes of other groups in the city.

This is natural, and to some degree desirable, but it carries with it no method of making decisions. The pressure group separates itself from the decision-making function and feels no responsibility for a decision that balances the interests and the needs of the whole community. It assumes that some body, such as the board of education, makes the decisions. It strives to present its case persuasively to the decision-making body and naturally goes to extremes to push its own case.

The small number of community-wide civic organizations have a special responsibility to promote communication among the more narrowly-based groups and to help them take a more responsible part in decision-making. Probably a big city should have regional education councils to serve this purpose and to bring the various local civic associations and parent-teacher organizations into a regional group that has some common interests and problems which are different from those of other regions of the big city.

If a city consists of warring factions with respect to school policy and program, it is unlikely that the superintendent and the board of education can work together in full harmony. The board members will display varying degrees of sensitivity to the various pressure groups. The superintendent may ally himself more or less consciously with certain factions in the city.

To bring about some harmony in the city with respect to the schools, a city-wide organization of leaders of the moderate groups may assist the board of education to get decisions made which produce the maximum good for the maximum number.

Conclusions on Intra-system Functioning

For the next decade there is bound to be tension and conflict in the metropolitan area over school policies and practices. Social change will require new practices which must be worked out by people who have different interests and attitudes.

The board of education and the superintendent must adapt their roles to each other and to the changing situations. The cities which have the most success are those in which the board of education has worked out a relationship with the superintendent that allows the superintendent a maximum of freedom to administer and execute policies on which the board and the superintendent are fully agreed.

The superintendent is the key figure in the situation. He needs to understand the whole complex of social systems and sub-systems, and he needs to work out his own role as one who promotes communication and cooperation among the systems. This is difficult for the modern superintendent whose training has disposed him toward working for efficiency within his own sub-system of teachers, pupils, and administrators, and to guard jealously the isolation of these sub-systems from the other systems and sub-systems in the metropolitan area.

Civic organizations will learn to combine the function of special pleading for a special interest with that of seeking to communicate with other groups. They will learn to support a school system in which they have basic faith, even though they may be discontented with some specific programs.

The delicate art of operating a school system in a period of basic social change will contain action which

Maintains communication and sharing in decisions with other co-operating systems

Accepts new functions which are demanded by the social situation

Maintains flexibility within the system for new roles to emerge and for people to learn the new roles.

PATHS TO METROPOLITANISM

The purpose of this book has been to identify some of the characteristics of the metropolitan area which have important implications for public education. In addition to examining the implications for education and other social systems of complexity, fragmentation, and stratification in the metropolitan environment, emphasis was placed on evolutionary patterns which result in the appearance of such problems as educational inequality, pollution, physical ugliness, poverty, and overcrowding not just in the central city but in its suburban rings as well. These problems of industrialization and urbanism in the metropolitan area frequently are loosely associated together under such terms as "the urban crisis" or "the problem of the cities," signifying that they are intimately involved in the question of how to make the metropolitan area a place where human resources will be nurtured rather than crippled and human needs will be satisfied rather than frustrated.

Such problems should be a matter of great concern to every resident of the metropolitan area, partly because they directly or indirectly affect the quality of life throughout the area and partly because their solutions will continue to escape us without a substantial movement toward *metropolitanism*—that is, toward fresh approaches based on an areawide outlook and areawide planning and action. Many of these points and implications which were treated at some length in the preceding chapters have been briefly summarized in a message on "The Problems and Future of the Central City and Its Suburbs" which President Lyndon Johnson sent to the House of Representatives on March 2, 1965.

> Let us be clear about the core of this problem. The problem is people and the quality of lives they lead. We want to build not just housing units, but neighborhoods; not just to construct schools, but to educate children; not just to raise income, but to create beauty and end the poisoning of our environment. We must extend the range of choices available to all our people so that all, and not just the fortunate, can have access to decent homes and schools, to recreation, and to culture. We must work to overcome the forces which divide our people and erode the

vitality which comes from the partnership of those with diverse incomes and interests and backgrounds . . .

We begin with the awareness that the city,* possessed of its own inexorable vitality, has ignored the classic jurisdictions of municipalities and counties and states. That organic unit we call the city spreads across the countryside, enveloping towns, building vast new suburbs, destroying trees and streams. Access to suburbs has changed the character of the central city. The jobs and income of suburbanites may depend upon the opportunities for work and learning offered by the central city. Polluted air and water do not respect the jurisdictions of mayors and city councils, or even of Governors. Wealthy suburbs often form an enclave whereby the well-to-do and the talented can escape from the problems of their neighbors, thus impoverishing the ability of the city to deal with its problems.

The interests and needs of many of the communities which make up the modern city often seem to be in conflict. But they all have an overriding interest in improving the quality of life of their people. And they have an overriding interest in enriching the quality of American civilization. These interests will only be served by looking at the metropolitan area as a whole, and planning and working for its development.

As is true with respect to the preceding passages, education is not always explicitly mentioned in discussions advocating a metropolitan approach to the major problems of the central cities and the suburbs. Traffic congestion, air pollution, and other highly visible forms of blight have unmistakably metropolitan origins and obviously call for metropolitan solutions. Inadequacies in the metropolitan system of education or in other less visible metropolitan functions may not be as quickly recognized as requiring a metropolitan point of view.

Nevertheless, as education becomes increasingly more important in the lives of people in the metropolitan area, it becomes more difficult to ignore the need for cooperative and coordinated planning and action in the metropolitan system of education. Cooperation in metropolitan development tends to be minimal on matters involving the life styles which people in a community are most anxious to protect from outside influence, but metropolitanism is more likely to prevail in connection with services needed to main-

* In this message the word "city" is used to mean the entire urban area—the central city and its suburbs.

tain system-wide functions such as transportation and communications on which a network of interdependent local communities is dependent. Education undeniably is closely associated with the life style choices and preferred values of people in many communities within the metropolis, thus generating deep resistance to coordinated planning and action to improve the quality of education in the metropolitan area. At the same time, however, education has acquired a system-maintenance function in its own right. In a socially stratified society in which education is a principal developer of human resources and a primary determinant of individual success and social progress, unequal or inadequate educational opportunities in any substantial part of the metropolitan area diminish its capacity to sustain a democratic pluralistic social order. The effects of stratification and segregation in metropolitan society and its schools are such that education has become a primary mechanism for the accumulation of privileges which some social groups can pass on to their children and an institution which is unable to respond very well to the hope of less privileged groups that schooling will provide their children with anything resembling a truly equal chance in life.

As the function of education in either perpetuating or reducing blockages to human fulfillment and material progress has become unmistakably clear, educators have been challenged to take the initiative in moving toward greater metropolitanism in the structure and functioning of metropolitan area schools as well as in the operation of other major social systems in the metropolitan area. How, then, can the educator move to reduce fragmentation and lack of coordination within and among the major social systems of the metropolitan area? It need not be thought that there is only one well-lighted path to metropolitanism. As pointed out throughout this book, there are various steps that can be taken, and in some cases are being taken, to achieve a greater degree of coordination and unity in the operation of the metropolitan system of education. For example, public school officials can

1. Form and strengthen cooperative associations in which school districts work together to accomplish goals they cannot achieve alone
2. Support proposals to restructure and reorganize existing school district patterns so that area-wide educational functions are carried out by an areawide authority and local

educational functions are discharged by districts which are neither too large or small nor too homogeneous or financially-handicapped to allow for effective and equitable utilization of metropolitan resources for education

3. Initiate central city-suburban programs aimed at reducing stratification in metropolitan area schools
4. Establish exemplary experimental schools in which parents anywhere in the metropolitan area who recognize the value of pluralistic educational experiences can enroll their children
5. Establish formal mechanisms to ensure coordination between education and other major social systems at the regional level as well as the level of the local school district and the individual school.

Whether educators will give sufficient leadership—or will be forced by other institutions such as the federal governments or the courts—to progress toward the goals of metropolitanism before metropolitan society in its present form has lost the capacity to find constructive solutions to urban and metropolitan problems must be considered open questions at the present time. No one can doubt that educators who move to exert leadership in this direction will encounter enormous opposition from many quarters, or that substantial progress toward metropolitanism will nowhere be achieved overnight. In addition, it is obvious that other social institutions will play as large a role as education itself in determining whether proposals for a more rational structure and more coordinated area-wide planning and action in metropolitan education will succeed or fail. The mass media, for example, are a key element in creating support or opposition for significant educational change, and even more in developing perceptions of a community of interest on which metropolitanism inevitably must be based.

Perhaps the most important thing for the educator to keep in mind in contemplating the problem of the metropolitan area and its schools is that what he does—or does not do—today will have a profound effect on what happens years in the future. Inaction or lack of initiative today may be equivalent to assuring that there will be no choices left for action tomorrow. In this regard the conclusion reached by the National Commission on Urban Problems in its final report in 1968 to the President of the United States can be applied as well to education as to any other urban function. ("Excerpts from Summary of Urban Panel's Report," December 15, 1968.)

> Our crisis in urban growth springs from using 19th century controls and attitudes in an attempt to mold and contain 20th century cities faced with 21st century problems.
>
> Over the next 30 years, about 18 million acres of land will come into urban use for the first time, and in present urban areas the processes of rebuilding and rehabilitation will continue. Just as land-use decisions made many years ago have affected the quality of today's urban environment, so decisions which we make today and tomorrow will shape the quality of urban life for future generations. We cannot delay many of the most important decisions until those who will be most affected by them can make their own choices.

Teachers and administrators in the metropolitan area do not lack vision of what education might accomplish in improving the quality of living in metropolitan society. What *is* lacking is an educational structure to accomplish this high purpose and an understanding of how its accomplishment is dependent on movement toward metropolitanism in education and other major social systems. No more fitting commentary to help communicate this understanding can be found than the measured thoughts with which a President of the United States concluded his message to Congress on the problems of the metropolitan area. (Lyndon B. Johnson's "The Future Problems of the Central City and Its Suburbs," 1965.)

> There are a few whose affluence enables them to move through the city guarded and masked from the realities of the life around them. But they are few indeed. For the rest of us the quality and condition of our lives is inexorably fixed by the nature of the community in which we live. Slums and ugliness, crime and congestion, growth and decay inevitably touch the life of all. Those who would like to enjoy the lovely parks of some of our great cities soon realize that neither wealth nor position fully protects them against the failures of society. Even among strangers, we are neighbors.
>
> We are still only groping toward solution. The next decade should be a time of experimentation. Our cities will not settle into a drab uniformity directed from a single center. Each will choose its own course of development—whether it is to unite communities or build entirely new metropolitan areas . . . This is an effort which must command the most talented and trained of our people, and call upon administrators and officials to act with generosity of vision and spaciousness of imagination.

SUGGESTED ACTIVITIES

1. Make an analysis of your own school system as a social system. What are the new functions which are straining this system and forcing it to develop in new ways? What roles are best and what roles are least well-filled?
2. Study and report on the performance of two persons in important roles in a school system. How do their performances relate to the nature of the roles they fill? How do their personalities cause them to fill their roles in unique ways?
3. Study the relations between the school system and some other social system in your metropolitan area where there is or has been cooperation. What has happened in this connection?
4. How do the public and private educational systems in your area cooperate? What are some of the problems?
5. Study the relations between civic organizations and the superintendent and the board of education in your community. How well do you think the various roles are being filled?
6. Contact Office of Economic Opportunity officials in your community or region to find out how education is involved in local antipoverty programs and how well schools and other government agencies have been working together on this task.

SUGGESTIONS FOR FURTHER READING

1. For a study of the problems of a big city school board in working out its functions in relation to those of the superintendent, read the book by Joseph Pois entitled *The School Board Crisis: A Chicago Case Study.*
2. For a summary of examples of cooperation among systems in metropolitan areas, read Chapter 13, "The Cooperative Approach," in Bollens and Schmandt, *The Metropolis.*
3. For an analysis of the relations between personality factors and role structure in an educational system, read Jacob W. Getzels, "Conflict and Role Behavior in the Educational Setting," or *Education Administration as a Social Process* by Getzels, Lipham, and Cunningham.
4. Since about 1965, the *American Institute of Planners Journal* has been emphasizing articles on the need for cooperation between social and physical planners.

5. *Feasible Planning for Social Change* by Robert Morris and Robert Binstock and *Dilemmas of Social Reform* by Peter Marris and Martin Rein provide in-depth analyses of the problems which arise when various social institutions including the schools try to work more closely together to bring about social change and improvement in big cities.
6. "Social Systems of a Metropolitan Area" in *Metropolitanism: Its Challenge to Education* edited by Havighurst (1968) provides a number of examples of cooperation between social systems in Kansas City, Missouri and other metropolitan areas.

Appendix

TABLE A-1

Central Cities' Proportion of Manufacturing Production Workers in Metropolitan Areas, 1899–1954

	1899	*1929*	*1954*
Baltimore	91.8	85.5	62.9
Buffalo	74.7	59.8	43.1
Chicago	88.0	73.6	65.2
Detroit	83.6	75.2	53.5
Los Angeles	83.4	66.6	42.3
New York City, Jersey City, Newark	69.9	69.8	63.0
Philadelphia	78.4	65.7	56.0
Pittsburgh	53.1	27.1	22.6
St. Louis	80.6	69.9	63.9
San Francisco, Oakland	81.2	68.2	50.4

Source: Raymond Vernon, *The Changing Economic Function of the Central City*. New York: Committee for Economic Development, 1959, pp. 74–75.

TABLE A-2

School Age Population of Chicago and Suburban Area: 1950–80
(Percentages of Total Age-Group Populations As Shown
in Right-Hand Column)

	City of Chicago		*Suburban Ring*		*Grand*
Year	*White*	*Nonwhite*	*White*	*Nonwhite*	*Total*
1950					
5–14 years	55	11	33	1.0	697,000
15–19 years	58	10	31	1.0	300,000
1960					
5–14 years	36	15	47	1.5	1,133,000
5–19 years	42	13	44	1.4	405,000
1965					
5–14 years	32	17	49	2.0	1,250,000
15–19 years	34	16	48	1.9	523,000
1970					
5–14 years	26	21	51	2.4*	1,466,000
15–19 years	28	18	52	2.2*	637,000
1980					
5–14 years	22	22	52	4.4*	1,581,000
15–19 years	22	22	52	3.9*	751,000

* Estimates by the author.

Source: U.S. Census, and *Population Projections for the Chicago Standard Metropolitan Statistical Area and City of Chicago,* Population Research and Training Center, University of Chicago, 1964.

TABLE A-3

Educational Levels Completed by Males Age 25 to 54 Years

	Percentages					
	Metropolitan Areas		*Central Cities*		*Suburban Rings*	
	1968	*1960*	*1968*	*1960*	*1968*	*1960*
Elementary school						
8 years or less	15	26	19	29	13	23
High school						
1 to 3 years	18	22	20	23	16	22
4 years	36	26	24	25	37	28
College						
1 to 3 years	13	11	12	12	13	12
4 years or more	18	14	16	12	20	15
Completing high school	67	52	62	48	71	55

Source: U.S. Bureau of the Census. Series P–23, No. 27. February, 1969.

TABLE A-4

Proportion of Population in SMSAs that is Nonwhite, 1900–68

Year	*Percentage Living in SMSAs*	*Percent Living in Central City*	*Percent Living Outside Central City*
1900	7.8	6.8	9.4
1910	7.3	6.9	8.1
1920	7.2	7.3	7.0
1930	8.1	9.0	6.4
1940	8.6	10.1	6.0
1950	10.0	13.1	5.7
1960	11.7	17.8	5.2
1968	13.0	21.8	5.5

Source: U.S. Bureau of the Census. *U.S. Census of Population: 1960. Selected Area Reports. Standard Metropolitan Statistical Areas.* Final Report, PC(3)–1D; Current Population Reports, Series P–20, No. 181. April, 1969.

TABLE A-5
City-Suburban Income, Educational, and Occupational Differentials in SMSAs, 1960, by Age of Area

Census Year in Which Central City First Reached 50,000	*Median Family Income*		*Percent Who Completed High School*		*Percent Employed in White-collar Occupations*	
	City Higher	*Suburban Fringe Higher*	*City Higher*	*Suburban Fringe Higher*	*City Higher*	*Suburban Fringe Higher*
1800–1860	0	14	0	14	0	14
1870–1880	0	17	0	17	0	17
1890–1900	5	31	9	27	15	21
1910–1920	12	36	12	36	22	26
1930–1940	9	23	14	18	22	10
1950–1960	26	27	28	25	40	13

Source: Adapted from Leo F. Schnore (1963).

TABLE A-6
Check List for School Type

A	*B*	*C*	*D*
	1. Curriculum and Teaching Material		
Curriculum is enriched with extra work. Texts one year or more above grade level can be used.	Curriculum is used as planned. Texts at grade level can be used.	Curriculum is altered downward. Difficulty in the use of grade level texts.	Curriculum does not fit students' needs. Texts one to two years below grade level must be used in many cases.
	2. Teaching Emphasis		
Almost all of teacher's emphasis on academics. Students willing and able to cooperate in this	Most of teacher's emphasis on academics. Some students unwilling or unable to cooperate in this	Teacher's time divided between teaching academics and controlling student behavior. Some	Majority of teacher's time devoted to controlling student behavior. Much disorder in class

regard.	regard.	disorder in hall and around building but can be controlled.	and around building which is difficult to control.
	3. "Cultural Experience"		
Wide and meaningful "cultural" experiences part of student's every-day life. School can enrich and support these "cultural" experiences.	Some exposure to "cultural" experiences. Student accepts and enjoys these "cultural" experiences when such experiences are encouraged by school.	Little exposure to "cultural" experiences and reluctance on the part of many students to accept these experiences when they are encouraged by school.	Almost no exposure to "cultural" experiences. Often a struggle for school to prepare students for these experiences. Resistance on the part of students toward these experiences.
	4. Respect for Teacher		
Little or no disrespect from students and parents. Strong positive attitudes by almost all students and parents toward teacher.	A few instances of disrespect from students and parents. Positive attitudes by majority of students and parents toward teacher.	Wide range in attitudes of respect from students and parents. Some ambiguity in students' and parents' attitudes toward teacher.	Flippant attitudes and some disrespect toward teacher from many students and parents. Apathy on part of many students. Some damage to teacher's personal belongings.
	5. Attitudes of Parents		
Majority of parents most helpful and even initiate helpful programs and carry them out. Teachers may even feel some parents are	Parents accept what the school feels is best for the children and are willing and able to follow teacher's suggestion.	Many parents want children to do well but equate being good in school with doing well in academics. Teacher accepted	Many parents apathetic and many unable to offer any help to students even if they want to. Some hostility toward teacher

TABLE A-6 (*cont.*)
Check List for School Type

A	*B*	*C*	*D*
too "pushy" with children and that some parents "look down on teachers."		as authority by majority of parents.	on the part of some parents.
	6. Student Hostility		
Few or no fights among students. Hostility is verbal. Some teasing among students.	Hostility sometimes expressed in "shoving matches." Hostility is still mostly verbal.	Hostility expressed in some rough fights of "wrestling-punching" type. Verbal hostility may contain some profanity.	Hostility expressed in many rough fights, started easily with some being hard to stop. Verbal hostility contains some profanity.
	7. Climate of School		
Climate of school set by academically oriented pupils. Children with discipline problems can be easily handled within framework of the school. Discipline problems are mild.	Children with discipline problems are seldom leaders of student behavior but can exert influence in some cases. Discipline problems can be handled within the framework of the school.	Children with discipline problems may be leaders for some students and sometimes upset academic classroom situations. Majority of discipline problems can be handled within framework of the school; a few cannot.	Children with discipline problems are influential in setting climate of the school. Many children with discipline problems require the help of outside agencies such as police or Family Service.

8. Sources of Student Values

Students receive their values through contact with stable and respected adults. Students will identify with peer group but also identify with future adult role.	Students influenced by a well-behaved peer group. Behavior somewhat patterned after models offered by movies or TV. Students still identify with future adult role.	Students strongly influenced by peer group. Behavior and dress patterned almost entirely on models offered by movies or TV. Many have no identification with future adult role.	Students heavily influenced by an alienated peer group. Many students influenced by delinquent adolescent and adult models. Many have hostility toward wider society and little identification with future adult role.

Source: Doll (1969).

TABLE A-7

College Expectations in Relation to Social Class and Type of High School

12th Grade Students in Kansas City Metropolitan Area. Percent Expecting to go to College												
	Socio-economic Status											*12th*
	I		*II*		*III*		*IV*		*V*		*Total*	*Grade*
Type of High School	*No.*	*%*	*No.*	*%*	*No.*	*%*	*No.*	*%*	*No.*	*%*	*No.*	*Percent*
Middle-class	464	87	479	87	410	80	69	70	–	–	1422	84
Comprehensive	543	80	764	68	1537	61	1121	40	145	22	4110	58
Working-class												
Negro schools*	34	47	87	54	221	58	330	56	108	40	780	54
White schools	19	74	78	58	201	55	347	33	96	25	741	42
Small	23	74	88	58	273	52	345	29	99	30	828	41
Catholic	66	80	138	74	254	69	300	53	46	46	804	63
Total	1149	81	1634	72	2896	63	2412	42	494	30	8685	59

* These schools were almost entirely Negro in composition. Other schools had small minorities of Negro students.

Source: Levine, Mitchell, and Havighurst, *Opportunities for Higher Education in a Metropolitan Area,* Bloomington, Indiana: Phi Delta Kappa, 1970.

Table A-8

Family Structure in Metropolitan Areas, 1960–68

	Percent of Total Families Headed by a Woman					
	Metropolitan Areas		*Central City*		*Suburban Rings*	
	1968	*1960*	*1968*	*1960*	*1968*	*1960*
White	10%	8%	12%	10%	8%	6%
Black	29	22	30	23	22	18

Source: U.S. Bureau of the Census. Series P-20, No. 191. October, 1969.

Table A-9

Children Under 18 Not Living with Both Parents

	Percent of All Children in Central Cities		
All children	*Total*	*White*	*Black*
1968	19	12	39
1960	13	9	29
By family income in 1967			
Under $4,000	64	49	76
$4,000 to $5,999	26	22	33
$6,000 to $7,999	11	9	20
$8,000 to $9,999	7	6	11
$10,000 and over	5	3	6

Source: U.S. Bureau of the Census. Series P–23, No. 27. Feburary, 1969.

Table A-10

Female Heads of Families, Related to Income

	Female Heads as Percent of all Family Heads in Central Cities by Family Income (1967 dollars)					
	Total		*White*		*Black*	
Family Income	*1967*	*1959*	*1967*	*1959*	*1967*	*1959*
All families	15	12	12	10	30	23
Under $2,000	44	38	36	31	61	51
$2,000–$3,999	33	23	23	20	54	29
$4,000–$5,999	22	11	20	11	27	14
$6,000–$7,999	14	7	12	7	21	7
$8,000–$9,999	8	7	8	7	12	6
$10,000 and over	5	5	5	5	6	9

Source: U.S. Bureau of the Census. Series P–23, No. 27. February, 1969.

Table A-11

Census Reports on Ratio of Males to Females, By Color, 1968

Age	Males Reported per 100 Females White	Black
All ages	97.0	93.5
Under 15	104.3	100.5
15–24	103.3	98.9
25–44	98.8	88.3
45–64	92.6	86.2
65 and over	74.4	77.7

Source: U.S. Bureau of the Census. Series P–23, No. 27. February, 1969.

Table A-12

Comparison of Numbers of Children of Women Aged 35 to 44 Who Married Men of Two Different Social Classes, 1960

	Children Per Woman* White	Nonwhite
Wives married at age 14–21 to husbands who are laborers and did not go to high school	3.8	4.7
Wives married at age 22 or over to husbands who are professional or technical workers and have completed 1 year or more of college	2.4	1.9

* Wives married only once, with husbands present.

Source: U.S. Bureau of the Census. 1960. PC(2)3A, Tables 39 and 40, pp. 199–238. *Women by Number of Children Ever Born.*

Table A-13

Educational Ability and Achievement Scores for Various Ethnic Groups (Mean Scores, from the *Study of Equality of Educational Opportunity*) Fall, 1965

Type of Test	*Grade Level*				
Non-Verbal Ability	*1*	*3*	*6*	*9*	*12*
White-Midwest	54	52	54	53	53
Oriental	55	50	51	52	52
Black-Midwest	46	48	47	47	45
Puerto Rican	45	43	40	43	43
Indian	50	48	46	47	47

Verbal Ability					
White	53	52	54	54	53
Oriental	51	48	49	50	50
Black	47	46	45	45	44
Puerto Rican	43	42	39	42	43
Indian	48	46	45	45	44
Reading					
White		52	53	53	52
Oriental		50	49	50	50
Black		46	46	46	46
Puerto Rican		42	40	42	43
Indian		47	45	45	44
Mathematics					
White		52	54	53	52
Oriental		50	49	52	51
Black		44	44	45	44
Puerto Rican		42	40	42	44
Indian		47	44	45	46

Note: All data from metropolitan groups except for the Indians. Scores are Standard Scores, National Mean = 50. S.D. = 10.

TABLE A-14

Intelligence Quotients of Black and White Pupils in Philadelphia Public Schools

	Percentage of Pupils in the Various Quartiles			
	White: N = 1065		*Black: N = 418*	
	Boys	*Girls*	*Boys*	*Girls*
High I 112 plus	35	39	9	8
II 103–111	24	31	14	24
III 91–103	26	20	20	27
Low IV less than 90	15	10	56	42

Sample of children who entered the first grade in the fall of 1949.

Source: William R. Odell, *Educational Survey Report*, Board of Public Education, Philadelphia, 1965. Table 1, p. 35.

TABLE A-15

Employment in Central Cities of SMSAs, By Color, 1960–68

	Percentage Employed in Various Non-agricultural Occupations							
	Male				*Female*			
	White		*Black*		*White*		*Black*	
Occupational Category	*1968*	*1960*	*1968*	*1960*	*1968*	*1960*	*1968*	*1960*
Professional and managerial	30	26	9	6	20	19	11	8
Clerical and sales	17	19	12	12	48	49	23	13
Craftsmen	21	21	13	11				
Operatives	19	21	32	31				
Laborers	5	5	17	22				
Private household workers					3	3	20	34
All other service workers	8	7	17	17	12	11	27	26
Craftsmen, operatives and laborers					16	18	19	18

Source: *U.S. Census Current Population Reports.* Series P–23, No. 27. February, 1969.

TABLE A-16

Median Earnings in 1967 of White and Black Year-round Workers in Central Cities

	Median Earnings in 1967		*Black Median Earnings as % of White*	
Male	*White*	*Black*	*1967*	*1959*
Professional and managerial	$9,542	$6,208	65	B
Clerical and sales	6,878	5,515	80	82
Craftsmen and foremen	7,545	5,962	79	75
Operatives	6,475	5,414	84	79
Nonfarm laborers	5,355	4,492	84	77
Service Workers, except private household	5,536	4,159	75	67
Female				
Professional and managerial	$5,910	$6,209	105	B
Clerical and sales	4,310	4,425	103	99

Operatives	3,590	3,296	92	85
Private household workers	880	1,410	160	100
All other service workers	3,061	2,905	95	85

B = Base less than 75,000.

Source: U.S. Bureau of the Census. Series P–23, No. 27. February, 1969.

TABLE A-17

Partial List of Criteria Used to Determine School District Boundaries Proposed for the St. Louis Metropolitan Area

1. Each district should have its own board of education elected by the voters in the district.
2. Each district should be of an optimum size to use financial resources in the most effective manner, to insure competent lay and professional leadership, and to permit a high level of citizen participation and communication.
3. Each district should include a diverse population, based on economic, racial, and ethnic characteristics.
4. Each district should include property with an equalized assessed valuation per student sufficient to support a reasonable proportion of the total cost of the educational program.
5. Travel time to school should not exceed 60 minutes each way for secondary and 40 minutes each way for elementary pupils.
6. In all urban and suburban areas, no district should have fewer than 5,000 elementary and secondary pupils; an enrollment of 10,000 to 30,000 would be more desirable.
7. The boundaries of no district should be established, even though it may meet all of the criteria, if, by so doing, it leaves an adjacent area without the possibility of an appropriate assignment to an acceptable district.

TABLE A-18

Responsibilities Allocated to Regional School Districts and Local Units Proposed for Missouri

Activity	*Regional School District*	*Local School Unit*
I. The Instructional Program		
A. *Instructional Staff*		
Salary schedule and fringe benefits	X	
Recruitment and selection of teachers and administrators, placement, tenure, dismissal, supervision of instruction		X
Payment of salaries, in-service education	X	X
B. *Instructional Supplies*		
Textbook, library book, classroom supplies		X
Equipment, audiovisual	X	X
C. *Curriculum and Course of Study*		
Teaching methods, extracurricular activities, graduation requirements, course of study beyond requirements		X
D. *Ancillary Instructional Services*		
Secretarial selection, libraries, teacher aides		X
Radio and television	X	X
E. *Pupil Personnel Services*		
Guidance, psychological, attendance, census, health service, food service		X
Transportation	X	X
F. *Compensatory and Vocational Education*		
Mental retardation, handicapped, emotionally disturbed, remedial reading, speech correction, educational deprivation, vocational-technical schools and programs, post-secondary education	X	

II. Administration		
Areawide policy, population research and projection, selection of regional superintendent, auditing, school construction, school bonding	X	
Setting local school attendance areas, selection of local superintendents, outside use of schools, custodial services		X
Planning, evaluation, school boundary adjustments, appointment of advisory groups, budget preparation and control, site selection and purchase, supplies and purchasing, accounting, building repair and maintenance, taxing*	X	X

* Local operating units allowed to collect taxes up to 10 percent in excess of the areawide levy set by the regional district.

Source: *School District Organization for Missouri.* Report of the School District Reorganization Commission, November, 1968 (adopted).

Bibliography

Abrams, Charles (1965), *The City Is the Frontier.* New York: Harper & Row.
Advisory Commission on Intergovernmental Relations (1963), *Performance of Urban Functions: Local and Areawide.* Washington, D.C.: U.S. Government Printing Office.
——— (1964), *1965 State Legislative Program.* Washington, D.C. U.S. Government Printing Office.
——— (1966), *Metropolitan America: Challenge to Federalism.* Washington, D.C.: U.S. Government Printing Office.
AIP Task Force on New Communities (1968), *New Communities: Challenge for Today.* New York: American Institute of Planners.
Alkin, Marvin (1965), *Challenges in Municipal-School Relations.* Washington, D.C.: American Association of School Administrators and International City Manager's Association.
Banovetz, James M. (1968), *Perspectives on the Future of Government in the Metropolitan Areas.* Chicago: Loyola University.
Barker, Roger Garlock and Paul V. Gump (1962), *Big School, Small School.* Lawrence: Department of Psychology, University of Kansas.
Bendiner, Robert (1969), *The Politics of Schools.* New York: Harper and Row.
Bereiter, Carl and Siegfried Engelmann (1966), *Teaching Disad-*

vantaged Children in the Preschool. Englewood Cliffs, N.J.: Prentice-Hall.

Bernard, Jessie (1966), *Marriage and Family Life Among Negroes.* Englewood Cliffs, N.J.: Prentice-Hall.

Bernstein, Basil (1960), "Language and Social Class," *British Journal of Sociology,* 11, 271–76.

——— (1964), "Elaborated and Restricted Codes: Their Social Origins and Some Consequences," *American Anthropologist,* 66, No. 6, Part 2, 55–69, Special Publication. December.

Berry, Edwin C. and Walter W. Stafford (1968), "Critique on the Comprehensive Plan of the City of Chicago," pp. 15–31 in *The Racial Aspects of Urban Planning,* Harold M. Baron, ed. Chicago: Chicago Urban League.

Berry, Brian J. L. (1968), *Metropolitan Area Definition: A Re-Evaluation of Concept and Statistical Practice* (Bureau of the Census Working Paper No. 28). Washington, D.C.: U.S.: Bureau of the Census.

Billingsley, Andrew (1968), *Black Families in White America.* Englewood Cliffs, N.J.: Prentice-Hall.

Bloom, Benjamin S. (1964), *Stability and Change in Human Characteristics.* New York: Wiley.

Bloomberg, Warner and Morris Sunshine (1963), *Suburban Power Structures and Public Education.* Syracuse: Syracuse University Press.

Bollens, John C. and Henry J. Schmandt (1965), *The Metropolis: Its People, Politics, and Economic Life.* New York: Harper & Row.

Bosselman, Fred P. (1968), *Alternatives to Urban Sprawl: Legal Guidelines for Governmental Action.* Research report 15 prepared for the National Commission on Urban Problems. Washington, D.C.: U.S. Government Printing Office.

Brown, Claude (1965), *Manchild in the Promised Land.* New York: Macmillan.

Buehring, Leo E. (1958), "New Pattern: Community Schools," *The Nation's Schools.* January.

Burkhead, Jesse (1967), *Input and Output in Large-City High Schools.* Syracuse, New York: Syracuse University Press.

Burns, Leland S. and Alvin J. Harman (1968), *The Complex Metropolis.* Los Angeles: The Reports of the University of California.

Campbell, A. and H. Schuman (1968), "Racial Attitudes in Fifteen American Cities," *Supplemental Studies. National Advisory Commission on Civil Disorders.* Washington, D.C.: U.S. Government Printing Office.

Campbell, Roald F. (1965), "School-Community Collaboration in Our Cities," *White House Conference on Education: Consultants Papers,* pp. 144–51. Washington, D.C.: Superintendent of Documents.

Cherington, Charles R. (1958), "Metropolitan Special Districts: The Boston Metropolitan Commission," pp. 127–42 in *Metropolitan Analysis: Important Elements of Study and Action,* Stephen B. Senceney, ed. Philadelphia: University of Pennsylvania Press.

Cicourel, Aaron V. and John I. Kitsuse (1963), *The Educational Decision-Makers.* Indianapolis: Bobbs-Merrill.

Clark, Kenneth (1965), *Dark Ghetto: Dilemmas of Social Power.* New York: Harper & Row.

Clark, S. D. (1966), *The Suburban Society.* Toronto: University of Toronto Press.

Coleman, James S. et al. (1967), *Equality of Educational Opportunity.* Washington, D.C.: U.S. Government Printing Office.

Coleman, Richard P. (1959), "Social Mobility in a Midwestern City," pp. 38–48 in *Society and Education: A Book of Readings* edited by Havighurst, Neugarten, and Falk. Boston: Allyn and Bacon.

Committee for Economic Development (1966), *Modernizing Local Government.* New York: Committee for Economic Development.

Committee on Educational Finance (1968), "Financial Status of the Public Schools," *Negotiation Research Digest,* June 1969. Washington, D.C.: National Education Association.

Conant, James B. (1959), *The American High School Today.* New York: McGraw-Hill.

——— (1961), *Slums and Suburbs.* New York: McGraw-Hill.

Cox, James L. (1967), "Federal Urban Development Policy and the Metropolitan Washington Council of Governments: A Reassessment," *Urban Affairs Quarterly,* Vol. 3, No. 1, pp. 75–94.

Cunningham, Luvern L. (1968), "Organization of Education in Metropolitan Areas," pp. 91–122 in *Metropolitanism: Its Challenge to Education,* Robert J. Havighurst, ed. Chicago: Sixty-Seventh Yearbook of the National Society for the Study of Education, Part 1.

Dahl, Robert A. (1967), "The City in the Future of Democracy," *The American Political Science Review,* Vol. 61, No. 4, pp. 953–70.

Davidson, Helen H. and Judith W. Greenberg (1967), *School Achievers from a Deprived Background.* New York: The City College of the City University of New York.

Davis, Kingsley (1955), "The Origin and Growth of Urbanization in the World," *American Journal of Sociology,* 60, 433–34.

Detroit Area Study (1960), "Family Income in Greater Detroit: 1951–1959." Ann Arbor, Michigan: Survey Research Center, University of Michigan.

Deutsch, Martin (1965), "The Role of Social Class in Language

Development and Cognition," *American Journal of Orthopsychiatry,* 33, 78–88.

Dewey, Richard (1948), "Peripheral Expansion in Milwaukee County," *American Journal of Sociology,* 54, 118–25.

Dobriner, William, ed. (1958), *The Suburban Community.* New York: G. P. Putnam's Sons.

Doll, Russell (1969), "Categories of Elementary Schools in a Big City." Research Paper, Department of Education, University of Chicago.

——— (1968), *Varieties of Inner City Schools: An Investigation into the Nature and Causes of Their Differences.* Kansas City, Missouri: Center for the Study of Metropolitan Problems in Education.

Doyle, Patricia Jensen (1969), "The Pittsburgh Public Schools," Appendix H, pp. 93–110 in *Social Planning in Pittsburgh: A Preliminary Appraisal.* Kansas City, Missouri: Institute for Community Studies, March.

Doxiadis, C. A. (1966), *Urban Renewal and the Future of the American City.* Chicago: Public Administration Service.

Eisenhardt, Charles A. (1967), "The Crisis in Ambulance Service," *Nation's Cities,* Vol. 5, No. 9, pp. 20–2.

Eldredge, Hanford Wentworth, ed. (1967), *Taming Megalopolis.* New York: Praeger.

Ewald, William R., ed. (1967), *Environment for Man.* Bloomington, Indiana: University Press.

"Excerpts from Summary of Urban Panel's Report," *The New York Times,* p. 70, December 15, 1968.

Faltermayer, Edmund K. (1968), *Redoing America.* New York: Harper & Row.

Fanon, Frantz (1967), *The Wretched of the Earth.* New York: Grove Press.

Fantini, Mario D. and Gerald Weinstein (1968), *The Disadvantaged: Challenge to Education.* New York: Harper & Row.

Ferrer, Terry (n.d.), *The Schools and Urban Renewal: A Case Study from New Haven.* New York: Educational Facilities Laboratory.

Finlayson, Judith (1967), "Councils of Governments: What and Why Are They," *American County Government,* Vol. 32, No. 4, pp. 20–25.

Fitch, Lyle C. (1967), "Social Planning in the Urban Cosmos," pp. 329–58 in *Urban Research and Policy Planning.* Urban Affairs Annual Reviews, Vol. 1. Leo F. Schnore and Henry Fagin, eds. Beverly Hills, California: Sage.

Fortune, Editors of (1957), *The Exploding Metropolis.* Garden City, N.Y.: Doubleday Anchor Books.

Frazier, E. Franklin (1939), *The Negro Family in the United States.* Chicago: University of Chicago Press.

Friedmann, John and John Miller (1965), "The Urban Field," *American Institute of Planners Journal,* pp. 312–20, November.

Fuchs, Estelle (1966), *Pickets at the Gates.* New York: Free Press of Glencoe.

——— (1969), *Teachers Talk.* Garden City, New York: Doubleday.

Gans, Herbert J. (1967), *The Levittowners.* New York: Pantheon, Random House.

Garvey, John Jr. (1969), "What Can Europe Teach Us About Urban Growth?" *Nation's Cities,* Vol. 7, No. 4, pp. 13–18, 31.

Getzels, Jacob W. (1963), "Conflict and Role Behavior in the Educational Setting," pp. 309–18 in *Readings in the Social Psychology of Education,* W. W. Charters, Jr. and N. L. Gage, eds. Boston: Allyn and Bacon.

———, James M. Lipham and Roald F. Campbell (1968), *Educational Administration as a Social Process.* New York: Harper & Row.

Gibbs, Jack (1961), "The Growth of Individual Metropolitan Areas: A Global View," *Annals of the Association of American Geographers,* p. 381.

Gist, Noel P. and Sylvia Fleis Fava (1964), *Urban Society.* 5th ed. New York: Thomas Y. Crowell.

Gitchoff, G. Thomas (1969), *Kids, Cops, and Kilos: A Study of Contemporary Suburban Youth.* San Diego: Malter-Westerfield.

Glidewell, John C. et al. (1966), "Socialization and Social Structure in the Classroom," pp. 221–56 in *Review of Child Development Research,* Martin Leon Hoffman and Lois Wladis Hoffman, eds. New York: Russell Sage Foundation.

Gordon, Edmund W. and Doxey A. Wilkerson (1966), *Compensatory Education for the Disadvantaged.* New York: College Entrance Examination Board.

Gossett, Thomas F. (1963), *Race: The History of an Idea in America.* Dallas: Southern Methodist University Press.

Gottmann, Jean (1961), *Megalopolis: The Urbanized Northeastern Seaboard of the United States.* New York: The Twentieth Century Fund.

Graubard, Stephen R., ed. (1966), *The Negro American. Daedalus.,* 2 vols. Fall, 1965 and Winter, 1966.

Gray, Susan W. et al. (1966), *Before First Grade: The Early Training Project for Culturally Disadvantaged Children.* New York: Teachers College of Columbia University.

Great Plains School District Organization Project (1968), *Guidelines for School District Organization: A Project Report.* Lincoln, Nebraska: The State Department of Education.

Greene, Mary Frances and Orletta Ryan (1965), *The School Children: Growing Up in the Slums.* New York: Pantheon, Random House.

Grodzins, Morton (1958), *The Metropolitan Area as a Racial Problem.* Pittsburgh: University of Pittsburgh Press.

Hall, Edward T. (1966), *The Hidden Dimension.* New York: Doubleday.

Handlin, Oscar (1959), *The Newcomers.* Cambridge, Mass.: Harvard University Press.

Hanson, Royce (1966), *Metropolitan Councils of Governments: An Information Report.* Washington, D.C.: Advisory Commission on Intergovernmental Relations.

Harris, Chauncey D. and Edward L. Ullman (1945), "The Nature of Cities," *The Annals,* Vol. 242, pp. 7–17, November.

Harris, John H., Robert C. Hemberger, and Frederick H. Goodnight (1968), "School Reorganization in a Metropolitan Area," pp. 352–83 in *Metropolitanism: Its Challenge to Education,* Robert J. Havighurst, ed. Chicago: Sixty-seventh Yearbook of the National Society for the Study of Education, Part 1.

Harrison, David (1969), "Black Teachers Don't Want Re-segregation," *Chicago Daily News,* June 24.

Hauser, Philip (1969), "The Chaotic Society: Product of the Social Morphological Revolution," *American Sociological Review,* Vol. 34, No. 1, pp. 1–19, February.

Havighurst, Robert J. (1964), *The Public Schools of Chicago: A Survey Report.* Chicago: Board of Education.

——— (1968), ed. *Metropolitanism: Its Challenge to Education.* Chicago, Illinois: The University of Chicago Press.

———, Paul H. Bowman, Gordon F. Liddle, Charles V. Matthews, and James V. Pierce (1962), *Growing Up in River City.* New York: Wiley.

——— and Bernice L. Neugarten (1967), *Society and Education.* 3rd ed. Boston: Allyn and Bacon.

Hawley, Amos H. (1950), *Human Ecology.* New York: Ronald Press.

Hentoff, Nat (1966), *Our Children Are Dying.* New York: Viking.

Herndon, James (1969), *The Way It Spozed To Be.* New York: Simon and Schuster.

Hess, Robert D. and Roberta Bear (1968), *Early Education: Current Theory, Research, and Practice.* Chicago: Aldine.

——— and Virginia Shipman (1965), "Early Experience and the Socialization of Cognitive Modes in Children," pp. 74–85 in *Society and Education: A Book of Readings.* Edited by Havighurst, Neugarten, and Falk. Boston: Allyn and Bacon.

Hickrod, G. Alan and Cesar M. Sabulao (1969), *Increasing Social and Economic Inequalities Among Suburban Schools.* Danville, Illinois: Interstate.

Highlander Folk School (1956), Recorded from a Planning Conference at the School, Monteagle, Tennessee. March 3–4.

Hill, Mozell C. and Bevode C. McCall (1950), "Social Stratification in a Georgia Town," *American Sociological Review,* 15, 721–29.

Hillson, Henry T. (1963), *The Demonstration Guidance Project.* New York: George Washington High School, Board of Education of New York City.

Hodge, Patricia Leavey and Philip M. Hauser (1968), *The Challenge of America's Metropolitan Population Outlook–1960 to 1985.* Research Report No. 3 Prepared for the Consideration of The National Commission on Urban Problems. Washington, D.C.: U.S. Government Printing Office.

Hodges, Harold Jr. (1964), *Peninsula People.* Revised. San Jose, California: Spartan Book Store, San Jose State College.

Hooker, Clifford P., Van D. Mueller, and Donald E. Davis (1968), "Co-operation Among School Districts in a Metropolitan Area: A Case Study," pp. 328–51, in *Metropolitanism: Its Challenge to Education,* Robert J. Havighurst, ed. Chicago: Sixty-seventh Yearbook of the National Society for the Study of Education, Part 1.

Hoyt, Homer (1939), *The Structure and Growth of Residential Neighborhoods in American Cities.* Washington, D.C.: Federal Housing Administration.

——— (1962), *World Urbanization.* Technical Bulletin No. 43. Washington, D.C.: Urban Land Institute.

Hunt, David E. (1966), "A Conceptual Systems Change Model and Its Application to Education," in *Flexibility, Adaptability, and Creativity.* O. J. Harvey, ed. New York: Springer.

Jacobs, Jane (1961), *The Death and Life of Great American Cities.* New York: Random House.

Jacoby, Susan (1969), "New Power in the Schools," *Saturday Review.* January 18, 1969. Vol. 52, No. 3, pp. 49–60, 70–72.

Janowitz, Morris (1969), *Institution Building in Urban Education.* New York: Russell Sage Foundation.

Johnson, Lyndon B. (1965, I), *Problems and Future of the Central City and Its Suburbs.* Message to Congress, March 2. 89th Congress, First Session, U.S. House of Representatives, Document No. 99.

——— (1965, II), *Commencement Address to Howard University Graduates.* June 4. Washington, D.C.: The White House.

Joint Study Commission (1969), *High School Racial Confrontation.* February 4. New York: White Plains Board of Education.

Kallenbach, Warren and Harold Hodges, eds. (1963), *Education and Society. A Book of Readings.* Columbus, Ohio: Charles E. Merrill Books.

Kaufman, Bel (1964), *Up the Down Staircase*. New York: Avon Book Div.

Keith, Nathaniel S. (1968), "Analysis: The 1968 Housing Law, Digested," *City*, Vol. 3, No. 2, pp. 35–37.

Kellam, Sheppard G. and Sheldon K. Schiff (1968), "A Mental Health View of the Community." Paper delivered at the University of Chicago Center for Urban Studies Conference on Community Organization, Chicago, Illinois, April 12, 1968.

Kerber, August and Barbara Bommarito, eds. (1965), *The Schools and the Urban Crisis*. New York: Holt, Rinehart, and Winston.

Kerner, Otto, ed. (1968), *Kerner Report. National Advisory Commission on Civil Disorders*. New York: Bantam Books.

Kettering Foundation (1968), *IDEA Reporter*. Summer quarter.

Kleinmann, Jack (1968), "Professional Sanctions; What, Why, When, Where, and How," *NEA Journal* (1968), Vol. 57, No. 1, pp. 42–4.

Kohl, Herbert (1967), *Thirty-six Children*. New York: New American Library.

——— (1968), "Review of *Pygmalion in the Classroom*," *The New York Review of Books*, September 12.

Kornacker, Mildred (1969), "The Ethnic Teacher in the Urban Classroom: Differential Orientations to the Teaching Role," *Education and Urban Society*, 1, 246–64.

Kozol, Jonathan (1967), *Death at an Early Age*. Boston: Houghton Mifflin.

Lerner, Max (1965), "Urban Lights and Shadows," pp. 3–20, *The Schools and the Urban Crisis*, August Kerber and Barbara Bommarito, eds. New York: Holt, Rinehart, and Winston.

Levine, Daniel U. (1967), "Cooperation in an Age of Interdependence," pp. 7–22 in *Partners for Educational Progress*, Frank W. Markus, ed. Kansas City: Metropolitan School Study Group and Mid-Continent Regional Educational Laboratory.

——— and Jerry B. Clavner (1967), *Multi-jurisdictional Metropolitan Agencies and Education*. Kansas City, Missouri: Center for the Study of Metropolitan Problems in Education.

———, Edna Mitchell, and Robert J. Havighurst (1970), *Opportunities for Higher Education in a Metropolitan Area. A Study of High School Seniors in Kansas City, 1967*. Bloomington, Indiana: Phi Delta Kappa.

Lieberman, Myron (1956), *Education as a Profession*. Englewood Cliffs, N.J.: Prentice-Hall.

——— (1968), "Implications of the Coming NEA-AFT Merger," *Phi Delta Kappan*, Vol. 50, pp. 139–44.

Liebow, Elliot (1967), *Tally's Corner*. Boston: Little, Brown.

Lyford, Joseph P. (1966), *The Airtight Cage.* New York: Harper & Row.

Lynch, Kevin (1961), "The Pattern of Metropolis," pp. 79–98 in *The Future Metropolis. Daedalus.* Journal of the American Academy of Arts and Sciences.

Madge, John (1962), "The New Towns Program in Britain," *Journal of the American Institute of Planners,* vol. 28, pp. 208–219.

Malcolm X (1965), *The Autobiography of Malcolm X.* New York: Grove Press.

Marando, Vincent L. (1968), "Inter-local Cooperation in a Metropolitan Area," *Urban Affairs Quarterly,* Vol. IV, No. 2, pp. 185–200.

Marris, Peter and Martin Rein (1967), *Dilemmas of Social Reform.* New York: Atherton Press.

Martindale, Don, and Gertrud Neuwirth (1958), editors and translators of *The City* by Max Weber. New York: Free Press of Glencoe.

Masotti, Louis H. (1967), *Education and Politics in Suburbia.* Cleveland: Western Reserve University.

Massachusetts, Commonwealth of (1965), "An Act Providing for the Elimination of Racial Imbalance in the Public Schools," Approved August 18.

Midwest Administration Center (1968), *Supplementary Papers. Cincinnati School Survey.* Chicago: Midwest Administration Center, University of Chicago.

Moeller, Gerald (1962), "Bureaucracy and Teachers' Sense of Power," *Administrator's Notebook,* Vol. 11, No. 3.

Morris, Robert and Robert Binstock (1966), *Feasible Planning for Social Change.* New York: Columbia University Press.

Morrison, J. Cayce (1958), *The Puerto Rican Study.* Brooklyn: Board of Education of the City of New York.

Mumford, Lewis (1961), *The City in History.* New York: Harcourt, Brace & World.

——— (1968), *The Urban Prospect.* New York: Harcourt, Brace & World.

Myers, Phyllis (1969), "The Courts Tell the Chicago Housing Authority—and the City Council—to Look Beyond the Ghetto for Sites," *City Chronicle.* March, 1969, pp. 2–3.

Nam, Charles B. and Mary G. Powers (1965), "Variations in Socioeconomic Structure by Race, Residence, and Life Cycle," *American Sociological Review,* 30, 97–103.

National Advisory Commission on the Education of Disadvantaged Children (1969), *Title I-ESEA. A Review and a Forward Look—1969,* p. 3. Washington, D.C.: U.S. Government Printing Office.

National Association of Secondary School Principals (1970), *A Study of Large City High Schools.* Working paper by Robert J. Havighurst,

Frank Smith, and David Wilder. To be published in a monograph.
National Education Association (1963), *The American Public School Teacher, 1960–61.* Research Monograph 1963–M2. Washington, D.C.
——— (1964), National Commission on Professional Rights and Responsibilities, Cleveland, Ohio. *When a Board of Education Fails to Fulfill Its Proper Responsibilities.* Washington, D.C.: National Education Association.
——— (1965), *Research Bulletin.* "De Facto Segregation." 43, 35–37, May. (See also, *The Pupil's Day in Court.* Research Division of the NEA. Washington, D.C. 1965.
——— (1968), *Financial Status of the Public Schools.* NEA Commission on Educational Finance. Washington, D.C., 1968, p. 51.
——— (1969), *NEA Research Bulletin,* March 1969, pp. 7–10.
National School Public Relations Association (1968), "Industry Steps Up School Role," *Education U.S.A.,* May 13.
Nation's Cities (1967), *Conference Report.* "What Kind of City Do We Want?" Vol. 5. April.
New York City Board of Education (1954), Minutes of the Board Meeting for December 23.
——— (1959), *Sixtieth Annual Report of the Superintendent of Schools, School Year 1957–58. Statistical Section.* Brooklyn: Board of Education of the City of New York.
Odell, William R. (1965), *Educational Survey Report on the Philadelphia Schools.* Philadelphia: Board of Education.
Park, Robert E. (1952), *Human Communities: The City and Human Ecology.* New York: Free Press of Glencoe.
Parsons, Talcott and Edward A. Shils, eds. (1952), *Toward a General Theory of Action.* Cambridge, Mass.: Harvard University Press.
Passow, A. Harry (1963), *Education in Depressed Areas.* New York: Bureau of Publications, Teachers College, Columbia University.
——— (1967), *Education of the Disadvantaged.* New York: Holt, Rinehart and Winston.
——— (1967), *Toward Creating a Model Urban School System: A Study of the Washington, D.C. Public Schools.* New York: Teachers College, Columbia University.
Paul, Peter (1969), "Fort Lincoln's House of Cards," *City,* Vol. 3, No. 1, pp. 5–7.
Pell, Clairborne (1966), *Megalopolis Unbound.* New York: Praeger.
Peterson, Warren A. (1956), "Career Phases and Inter-Age Relationships: The Female High School Teacher in Kansas City." Unpublished Ph.D. dissertation, Department of Sociology, University of Chicago.

Pettigrew, Thomas F. (1964), *Profile of the Negro-American*. Princeton, N.J.: D. Van Nostrand.

——— (1969), "Racially Separate or Together?" *Journal of Social Issues,* Vol. 25, No. 1.

Phi Delta Kappa (1968), "Black Power 1968," *Phi Delta Kappan,* Vol. 49, pp. 447–52.

Pois, Joseph (1964), *The School Board Crisis: A Chicago Case Study*. Chicago: Aldine.

Prentice, Justus A. (1967), "A Cooperative Board Provides Regional Service," *Educational Leadership,* Vol. 24, No. 6, pp. 553–59.

Riessman, Frank (1962), *The Culturally Deprived Child*. New York: Harper & Row.

——— and Alan Gartner (1969), "The Instructional Aide: New Developments," *Integrated Education,* Vol. 11, No. 5, pp. 55–59.

Roberts Joan, ed. (1967), *School Children in the Urban Slum*. New York: Free Press.

Rockefeller Brothers Fund (1955), *The Performing Arts: Problems and Prospects*. New York: McGraw-Hill.

Rodman, Hyman (1959), "On Understanding Lower-Class Behavior," *Social and Economic Studies,* 7, 441–50.

Rosenthal, Robert, and Lenore Jacobson (1968), *Pygmalion in the Classroom*. New York: Holt, Rinehart, and Winston.

Saltzman, Henry (1963), "The Community School in the Urban Setting," pp. 322–31 in *Education in Depressed Areas,* ed. by A. Harry Passow. New York: Bureau of Publications, Teachers College of Columbia University.

Sargent, Cyril G., John B. Ward, and Allan R. Talbot (1968), "The Concept of the Educational Park," pp. 186–199 of *The Schoolhouse in the City,* edited by Alvin Toffler. New York: Praeger.

Saxe, Richard W. (1969), *A Report of a Survey of the Mayors of the Fifty Largest Cities Concerning Their Role in Educational Issues*. Toledo, Ohio: Department of Educational Administration and Supervision, The University of Toledo.

Schlivek, Louis (1957), "Man in Metropolis," in *The Exploding Metropolis,* eds. of *Fortune*. Garden City, N.Y.: Doubleday Anchor Books.

Schmid, Calvin F. and Charles E. Nobbe (1965), "Socioeconomic Differentials Among Non-white Races," *American Sociological Review,* 30, 909–22.

Schnore, Leo F. (1963), "The Socio-economic Status of Cities and Suburbs." *American Sociological Review,* 28, 76–85.

Schuchter, Arnold (1968), *White Power/Black Freedom*. Boston: Beacon.

Sears, Roebuck and Company (1962), *ABCs of Community Planning*. pp. 4–5. Chicago.

Sexton, Patricia (1961), *Education and Income*. New York: The Viking Press.

Silberman, Charles E. (1964), *Crisis in Black and White*. New York: Random House.

Spectorsky, Auguste C. (1955), *The Exurbanites*. Philadelphia: J. B. Lippincott.

Spengler, David (1967), "The Englewood-Teaneck, New Jersey Experience," pp. 202–48 in *School Desegregation in the North*. T. Bentley Edwards and Frederick M. Wirt, eds. San Francisco: Chandler.

Starr, Rodger (1966), *The Living End*. New York: Coward-McCann.

Strayer, George D. (1932), *Report of the Survey of the Schools of Chicago, Illinois*. New York: Bureau of Publications, Teachers College, Columbia University.

Strong, Josiah (1898), *The Twentieth Century City*. New York: Baker and Taylor.

Suttles, Gerald D. (1968), *The Social Order of the Slums*. Chicago: University of Chicago Press.

Swanson, Austin D. (1966), *The Effect of School District Size Upon School Costs*. Buffalo, New York: Western New York School Study Council.

——— (1969), "The Governance of Education in Metropolitan Areas," pp. 177–196 in *Urban School Administration*, Troy V. McKelvey and Austin D. Swanson, eds. Beverly Hills, California: Sage.

Swanson, Bert E., Edith Cortin, and Eleanor Main (1969), "Parents in Search of Community Influence in the Schools," *Education and Urban Society*, 1, 383–403.

Taeuber, Karl M. and Alma F. Taeuber (1964), "Migration and City-Suburb Differences," *American Sociological Review*, 29, 718–29.

Thomas, Piri (1967), *Down These Mean Streets*. New York: Knopf.

Toffler, Alvin, ed. (1968), *Schoolhouse in the City*. New York: Praeger.

United Nations Statistical Office, Department of Economic and Social Affairs, *Demographic Yearbook, 1960*. New York: 1960.

United States Commission on Civil Rights (1965), *Civil Rights under Federal Programs:* An Analysis of Title VI. CCR Special Publication No. 1. Washington, D.C.: U.S. Government Printing Office.

United States Commission on Civil Rights (1967), *Racial Isolation in the Public Schools*, Vol. I. Washington, D.C.: U.S. Government Printing Office.

United States Department of Commerce, Bureau of the Census (April 21, 1969), "Population of the United States by Metropolitan-Nonmetropolitan Residence: 1968 and 1969," *Current Population Reports*, Series P–20, No. 181. Washington, D.C.: U.S. Government Printing Office.

United States Department of Labor (1965), *The Negro Family: The Case for National Action.* Washington, D.C.: U.S. Government Printing Office.

U.S. Office of Education (1969), *Successful Compensatory Education Programs.* Washington, D.C.: U.S. Government Printing Office.

Valentine, Charles (1968), *Culture and Poverty.* Chicago: University of Chicago Press.

Van der Berghe, Pierre L. (1967), *Race and Racism: A Comparative Perspective.* New York: Wiley.

Vernon, Raymond (1959), *The Changing Economic Function of the Central City.* pp. 74–75. New York: Committee for Economic Development.

——— (1960), *Metropolis 1985.* Cambridge, Mass.: The Harvard University Press.

——— (1965), "The Myth and Reality of Our Urban Problems," *City and Suburb,* Benjamin Chinitz, ed. Englewood Cliffs, N.J.: Prentice-Hall.

Warner, W. Lloyd, Marchia Meeker, and Kenneth Eells (1960), *Social Class in America.* New York: Harper Torchbooks.

Warren, Roland L., ed. (1966), *Perspectives on the American Community.* Chicago: Rand McNally & Co.

Weaver, Robert C. (1964), "The City and Its Suburbs," *New City,* 2, pp. 4–6, March.

Weissbourd, Bernard and Herbert Channik (1968), "An Urban Strategy," *The Center Magazine,* Vol. 1, No. 6, pp. 3–13.

Westinghouse Learning Corporation/Ohio University (1969), *Evaluation of Head Start Programs.* Pittsburgh: Westinghouse Learning Corporation.

Williams, Oliver P. (1967), "Life Style Values and Political Decentralization in Metropolitan Areas," *The Southwestern Social Science Quarterly,* Vol. 48, No. 3, pp. 299–309.

Wilson, Alan B. (1959), "Residential Segregation of Social Classes and Aspirations of High School Boys," *American Sociological Review,* 24, 836–45.

——— (1963), "Social Stratification and Academic Achievement," pp. 217–35 in A. Harry Passow, ed., *Education in Depressed Areas.* New York: Teachers College Bureau of Publications, Columbia University.

Wilson, Andrew (1969), "The Grim Plight of Wellston's Schools," *St. Louis Globe-Democrat,* January 25–26.

Wilson, George T. (1966), "Joint School-Park Facilities Offer Advantages—Naturally," *American School Board Journal,* Vol. 153, No. 2, August.

Wilson, James Q. (1968), "The Urban Unease: Community Versus City," *The Public Interest,* No. 12, 25–29, Summer.

Wolf, R. (1965), "The Measurement of Environments," in *Proceedings of the 1964 Invitational Conference on Testing Problems,* pp. 93–106. Princeton, N.J.: Educational Testing Service.

Wood, Robert C. (1968), "The Challenge of Metropolitan Growth," *Metropolitan Viewpoints,* Vol. 3, No. 2, pp. 1–4.

Wurster, Stanley R. (1968), "The Intermediate Administrative Unit," *ERIC/CRESS Newsletter,* Vol. 3, No. 2, pp. 1–4.

Young, Whitney (1969), *Beyond Racism.* New York: McGraw-Hill.

Index

Advisory Commission on Intergovernmental Relations, 184–185, 189, 195
American Institute of Planners, 181, 195
American Association of School Administrators, 184, 189, 300
American Federation of Teachers, 272–276, 282
Arts and Humanities Foundation, 122, 133

Black
 man in the social structure, 13–17
 middle class, 16–17
 revolution, 204, 219–220
 role, 219–220
 school children, 212–214
 separatism, 235
 social class among, 15–16
 teachers and administrators, 277–284
 urbanization of, 206–212
 working-class family, 208–212
Boston, 135

Caste and caste-like groups, 14–15
Chicago
 black teachers, 278
 comprehensive plan, 198
 Housing Authority, 197–198
 library system, 294
 metropolitan area planning, 178
 Operation Wingspread, 156
 population trends, 59–60
 school achievement, 62, 212
 school finance inequity, 139
 socio-economic stratification, 56–57
 stratification in the school system, 59–62
 teachers, 253–256, 259, 262–263, 278, 283–284
 urban renewal, 162–164
 Woodlawn, 296–297
Children
 alienated, 108–111
 handicapped, 117
 maladjusted, 117
 socially disadvantaged, 123
Cincinnati study of teachers' attitudes, 265
Cities
 American, 34–38
 big, around the world, 29
 development of, 25–28
 in industrial society, 27–28
 planning (*see* Metropolitan planning)
Civic organizations, 307–309
Civil Rights Act of 1964, 226
Cleveland, 212, 305
Compensatory education, 122–126
Cooperation, among social systems, 149, 151–152, 181–185, 190, 301–314
 between schools and other social systems, 294–301
Cultural pluralism, 204
Culture shock and the teacher, 13

Decentralization
 general, 171–172, 191–193
 school system, 187–188, 282–284
Desegregation, 222–235
Detroit, 47, 139, 223, 230, 278
Disadvantaged children, 123, 215–218

Economic Opportunity Act, 124
Educational Opportunity Study, 212, 326–327
Educational parks, 131–132
Educational programs, 86–90
Elementary and Secondary Education Act, 123–125, 183, 190, 287
Evanston, Illinois, 154–155

Family factor
defined, 214–215
versus school factor, 213–218, 237–238
Federal government
Department of Housing and Urban Development, 159, 164–165, 179, 194
educational support, 88, 298–299
and urban renewal, 159
Flint, Michigan, schools, 128

Great Plains Project, 142, 203

Handicapped children, 117
Hartford, 156
Head Start, 125–126, 218
High schools
comprehensive, 119
of a metropolitan area, 112–116
socio-economic characteristics, 94–99
specialized, 120
Housing and Urban Development, 159, 164–165, 179, 194

Indianapolis, 174
Industry and education, 299–300
Inner-city schools, 108–111
expectations for students, 265–267
teacher-aides, 287–288
teachers, 253–257, 260–270
Integration
versus black separatism, 235–250
in city schools, 221–237
legal aspects, 226–233
and metropolitan development, 196–199
in northern cities, 222, 229
social, 121, 170, 245–247
in southern cities, 225, 227
of staff in city school systems, 276–284
in suburban schools, 151–156
transport plans, 232
and urban renewal, 299

Jacksonville, 175

Kansas City
metropolitan area, 14
regional schools proposal, 188
school districts, 138
teachers, 274, 277, 284–285

Language in the home, 215
Louisville-Jefferson County regional schools proposal, 188

Megalopolis, 47
Metropolitan area
cooperation, 168–170, 174–185, 301–314
defined, 9, 48
Education Authority, 186–189
educational planning, 197–202
evolution, 33–44
fragmentation, 172–174, 310–314
government, 174–175
planning, 176
problems, 42–43
school organization, 174–175, 183–190, 200
teachers, 270–272
the world's largest, 29
Metropolitan development
around the world, 51
goals, 291–292
Metropolitan Educational Authority, 185–190
new cities, 190–191
regional planning, 166–182
suburban areas, 133–137
in the U.S.A., 31–33
Metropolitan planning
description, 167–172, 176–178
history, 178–181, 195–196
physical planning, 176–177
planning agencies, 178–180, 194, 197–198
Metropolitanism, 310–314
Milwaukee, 70
Minority groups, 61
Model cities, 164–165, 194
Motivation ratio, 99
Moynihan Report, 239

Nashville, 174, 189
National Advisory Commission on Civil Disorders, 243
National Advisory Council on the Education of Disadvantaged Children, 124
National Education Association, 272–276, 305
Negroes (*see* Blacks)
in metropolitan areas, 61, 66
in suburbs, 140–142, 151–153
in the United States, 208

Neighborhood school, 130
New York State Board of Cooperative Educational Services, 182
New York City and metropolitan area, 57–58, 123, 129, 222, 229, 269, 278, 280–282

Operation Head Start, 125–126
Opportunity, equality of, 17, 239–250
Orientals, their socio-economic status, 206

Peer group, influence on student achievement, 80–82
Philadelphia, 213, 327
Planning
  city planning, 164–166
  cooperative planning in metropolitan areas, 176
  for metropolitan development, 50–51
Population
  in metropolitan areas, 29–32, 46
  racial aspects, 59, 66, 207
Poverty
  inner city, 162–164
  in suburbs, 153–154
  and values, 270
Pre-school education, 216–218, 238
Princeton Plan, 231–232
Public housing, 162–164

Racial stratification, 52–84
Recreation system and the schools, 295
Rochester, 155–156
Roles in social systems, 292, 302–304
Roman Catholic schools, 75

Saint Louis
  regional schools proposal, 188
  size of school districts, 142–143, 200
  suburbs, 140–142
Schools
  atmosphere, 99–111
  community school, 127–131
  comprehensive high school, 119
  cooperation among school districts, 149, 151–152, 181–185, 190, 301–314
  cooperation with other social systems, 294–301
  educational parks, 131–132
  ethos, 96
  finances, 83–85, 139
  four-walls school, 126
  functional types of schools, 117–121
  middle schools, 118
  mixed schools, 89
  private schools, 116–117
  response to segregation, 78–83
  school factor versus family factor, 213–218
  school system functions, 121–126
  segregation and the schools, 79–82
  social functions, 121
  specialized high school, 120
  suburban school systems, 134–156
  types of schools, 1–9, 100–112
  urban community school, 126–131
School board
  Detroit, 223
  and integration, 226–231
  member's role, 303–305
  New York City, 222
  and superintendent, 304
Segregation
  court cases, 226
  in northern cities, 57–60
  pathology of, 75–78
  in schools, 60, 79–80
  Supreme Court decision of 1954, 221
Social changes which affect education, 290–291
Social class
  defined, 10
  index of socio-economic characteristics, 10
  and life-style, 11
  and school achievement, 216–218
  as a sub-culture, 11
  usefulness of the concept, 12
Social mobility
  causes, 18–23
  defined, 17
  examples, 19–23
Social structure
  in the black group, 15–16
  of a metropolitan area, 9–12
  studies of, 14–16
Social stratification
  effects on schools, 61–65, 79–86
  measurement of, 55–57

Social stratification (*Cont.*)
in metropolitan areas, 36–43, 54–85, 196–199, 310–314
polarization between central city and suburbs, 65–69
Social systems
cooperation among, 292–300
defined, 292–293
optimal relations among educational systems, 300–301
schools related to other social systems, 294–301
social welfare system and education, 295–297
Socio-economic ratio
the "critical point," 96
defined, 55–56
in various schools, 94–95
Socio-educational motivation, 99
Student unrest, 149–150
Suburbs
development of, 34–43, 133–137
educational diversity, 143–144
and metropolitanism, 310–314
school conflicts, 143–150
school districts, 151–156
stratification, 70–72
teachers, 272
types of, 72–74, 134–136
Superintendents
interaction with board members, 304–305
role, 302–323
types, 305–307

Teachers
activism, 270–272
attitudes, 263–267
in big cities, 263–268, 272–275
black teachers, 277–284
career of metropolitan teacher, 284–286
inner city, 253–257, 260–270
organizations, 271–276
role orientations, 262
social origins, 259
style, 262
teacher-aides, 287–288
training, 267–270
Toronto, 175

Union, teachers, 273, 283–284
United States Commission on Civil Rights, 226
Urban-community school, 126–129
Urban development, 25–53
Urban population in the U.S.A., 30
Urban renewal
aims, 43, 50, 89, 160
effects on suburbs, 74
new directions, 164–166
related to schools, 161–166, 298–299
slum clearance, 159
and urban-community school, 129–131
Urbanization
of black population, 206–212
growth of cities, 26–31
sporadic, 28–29
systematic, 30

Washington, D.C.
model schools project, 238
Negroes in public housing, 77
school survey, 263–264, 268
teachers, 274, 277–280
Work-study programs, 88

VESTMAR COLLEGE LIBRARY